Texturing and Modeling
Second Edition

Texturing and Modeling
Second Edition

David S. Ebert
F. Kenton Musgrave
Darwyn Peachey
Ken Perlin
Steven Worley

AP Professional is a division of Academic Press

San Diego   London   Boston
New York   Sydney   Tokyo   Toronto

AP PROFESSIONAL
An Imprint of ACADEMIC PRESS
A Division of HARCOURT BRACE & COMPANY

ACADEMIC PRESS
525 B Street, Suite 1900, San Diego, CA 92101-4495, USA
1300 Boylston Street, Chestnut Hill, MA 02167, USA
http://www.apnet.com

ACADEMIC PRESS
24-28 Oval Road, London NW1 7DX, UK
http://www.hbuk.co.uk/ap/

Library of Congress Cataloging-in-Publication Data

Texturing and modeling: a procedural approach / David S. Ebert,
    editor ... et al. —2nd. ed.
    p. cm.
    Includes bibliographical references (p.) and index.
  ISBN 0-12-228730-4 (hardcover : alk.paper)
   1. Electronic digital computers—Programming. 2. Computer graphics
    I. Ebert, David S., 1964-   .
QA76.6.T44297   1998
006.6'6—dc21   96-25792
                                     CIP

Printed in the United States of America
98 99 00 01 02 IP 9 8 7 6 5 4 3 2 1

Table of Contents

PREFACE   **XI**

I   INTRODUCTION   **I**

Procedural Techniques and Computer Graphics   1
Procedural Techniques and Advanced Geometric Modeling   1
Aim of This Book   4
Organization   4

2   BUILDING PROCEDURAL TEXTURES   **7**

Introduction   7
Procedural Pattern Generation   16
Aliasing and How to Prevent It   48
Making Noises   64
Generating Irregular Patterns   81
RenderMan Esoterica   91

3   PRACTICAL METHODS FOR TEXTURE DESIGN   **97**

Introduction   97
Toolbox Functions   97

The User Interface   105
Efficiency   112
Parameter Preprocessing   113
Caching   114
C Coding Trick   114
Tricks, Perversions, and Other Fun Texture Abuses   116
2D Mapping Methods   119
Where We're Going   120

4   PROCEDURAL TEXTURE EXAMPLES   **123**

Introduction   123
LED Texture   123
2D Mapping   127
Planetary Rings   131

5   ADVANCED ALIASING   **135**

Advanced Aliasing   135
Spot Sizes   135
Supersampling   140
Index Aliasing   140
Optimization and Verification   146
Emergency Alternatives   148

6   PROCEDURAL MODELING OF GASES   **149**

Introduction   149
The Rendering System   151
A Procedural Framework: Solid Spaces   154
Geometry of the Gases   156
Single Column of Smoke   164

7   ANIMATING SOLID SPACES   **169**

Animating Solid Textures   171
Animation of Gaseous Volumes   176
Animating Hypertextures   194

8 VOLUMETRIC CLOUD MODELING WITH IMPLICIT FUNCTIONS 197

Volumetric Procedural Modeling with Implicit Functions   199
Volumetric Cloud Modeling   201
Animating Volumetric Procedural Clouds   206
Conclusion   208

9 NOISE, HYPERTEXTURE, ANTIALIASING, AND GESTURES 209

Introduction   209
Constructing the Noise Function   212
Raymarching   219
Interaction   222
Some Simple Shapes to Play With   223
Examples of Hypertexture   224
Architexture   230
Turbulence   240
Antialiased Rendering of Procedural Textures   241
Surflets   248
Textural Limb Animation   256
Examples   260
Texture for Facial Movements   261

10 A BRIEF INTRODUCTION TO FRACTALS 275

Fractals and Proceduralism   281
Procedural fBm   282
Multifractal Functions   284
Fractals and Ontogenetic Modeling   288
Conclusions   290

11 FRACTAL SOLID TEXTURES: SOME EXAMPLES 293

Clouds   294
Distortion of Cirrus Clouds and Global Circulation   298
Fire   304
Water   306
Earth   308
Random Coloring Methods   318

Random fBm Coloring   318
The GIT Texturing System   319
An Impressionistic Image Processing Filter   320
The "Multicolor" Texture   321

12   PROCEDURAL FRACTAL TERRAINS   **325**

Advantages of Point Evaluation   325
The Height Field   327
Homogeneous fBm Terrain Models   330
Heterogeneous Terrain Models   333

**13   QAEB RENDERING FOR PROCEDURAL MODELS WITH
        ADAPTIVE LEVEL OF DETAIL**   **341**

Introduction   341
QAEB Tracing   342
Problem Statement   343
Prior Art   344
The QAEB Algorithm   344
Near and Far Clipping Planes   346
Calculating the Intersection Point and Surface Normal   347
Antialiasing   347
A Speedup Scheme for Height Fields   348
Shadows, Reflections, and Refraction   348
Performance   349
QAEB-Traced Hypertextures   352
Billowing Clouds, Pyroclastic Flows, and Fireballs   353
Conclusions   357

14   ATMOSPHERIC MODELS   **346**

Introduction   361
Beer's Law and Homogeneous Fog   363
A Minimal Rayleigh Scattering Approximation   365
Trapezoidal Quadrature of $\sigma = e^{-r}$ GADD and RenderMan Implementation   367
Simplified RenderMan Atmosphere Shader   368
Numerical Quadrature with Bounded Error for General Radical GADDs   369
Conclusions   371

15 GENETIC TEXURES 373

Introduction: The Problem of Parameter Proliferation 373
A Useful Model: Aesthetic N-Spaces 374
Control Versus Automaticity 375
A Model from Biology: Genetics and Evolution 376
Interpretation of the Root Node 381
The Library of Genetic Bases 382
A Final Distinction: Genetic Programming Versus Genetic Algorithms 384
Conclusions 384

BIBLIOGRAPHY 387
INDEX 407

Preface

This book imparts a working knowledge of procedural approaches in texturing, modeling, shading, and animation. These include two-dimensional and solid texturing, hypertextures, volume density functions, and fractals. Readers are provided with the details often omitted from technical papers, enabling them to explore how the procedures are designed to produce realistic imagery. This book also contains many useful procedures and the description of how these procedures were developed. The reader will gain not only a powerful toolbox of procedures upon which to build a library of procedural textures and objects, but also a better understanding of how these functions work and how to design them. With procedures like *noise* and *turbulence* and an understanding of procedural design techniques, the reader will be able to design more complex procedures to produce realistic textures, gases, hypertextures, landscapes, and planets. The procedural techniques are explained not by people who have read some technical papers and tried to decipher them, but by the people who developed them, wrote the seminal papers in the area, and have worked with procedural design for many years.

Procedural Techniques in Computer Graphics

Procedural modeling, texturing, and shading is an area of active research and growing importance in computer graphics and animation. Procedural techniques have been used for many years to produce textures for objects. With the introduction of three-dimensional texturing techniques (solid texturing) by Ken Perlin, Darwyn Peachey, and Geoffrey Gardner in 1985, the use of procedural techniques exploded. Realistic images containing marble, wood, stone, and clouds were now possible. Procedural techniques became an area of active research in computer graphics. Many programmers and researchers started developing developed their own procedures to simulate natural materials and natural phenomena. What was lacking, however, was a clear understanding of the design of procedural techniques and of the primitive stochastic functions that were used to produce these amazing images. Since the mid-1980s, the use of procedural techniques has grown rapidly, and they can now be used to actually define the geometry of objects such as water, fire, gases, planets, and tribbles.

The use of procedural techniques is not limited to still images; they have been used successfully for animation and recently for the simulation and animation of natural phenomena such as fog, fire, water, and atmospheric patterns. The animation of procedural models requires knowledge of both animation principles and the characteristics of the procedural model. Procedural animation is a powerful technique for producing complex, realistic motion.

Our Objective

The objective of this book is to provide the reader with an understanding and working knowledge of several uses of procedural techniques in texturing, modeling, and animation. This book describes the current state of procedural techniques and provides the reader with the challenge and information necessary to extend the state of the art. The reader will gain the following from the book:

- A thorough understanding of procedural techniques for solid texturing.

- An insight into different design approaches used by the authors in designing procedures.

- A toolbox of procedures and basic primitive functions (noise, turbulence, etc.) to produce realistic images.

- An understanding of several advanced procedural approaches for modeling object geometry (hypertextures, gases, fractals).

- An introduction to animating these procedural objects and textures.

Development of This Book

The first edition of this book was an expansion of the courses on *Procedural Modeling and Rendering Techniques* that we have taught at SIGGRAPH '92 and

SIGGRAPH '93. At SIGGRAPH '91, Darwyn Peachey and David Ebert first discussed the need for a course to explain how texture and modeling procedures are designed to create impressive images of wood and marble objects, gases, landscapes, and planets. There were some classic papers on these topics, but they were lacking in several respects. First of all, not enough detail was given to enable the reader to reproduce the results in most of the papers. Second, if an image could be reproduced, the reader still didn't know how to modify the procedure to get a different effect. Finally, the reason why a procedure produced a given image was unclear. There seemed to be some "magic" behind the development of these procedures. From this discussion, our course at SIGGRAPH '92 arose. There was great demand for the course at both SIGGRAPH '92 and SIGGRAPH '93. We have received useful feedback, thanks, and requests for more material on this topic from the attendees of these courses.

With the success of these courses, we decided to produce the first edition of this book. It was similar in nature to our course notes, but greatly expanded and revised. The second edition is greatly expanded and contains new chapters discussing the work that we have done since 1994. It describes the procedural approaches of five researchers in the field of computer graphics. The authors slightly overlap their discussion to provide different viewpoints on important concepts such as the fractal noise function.

Source Code

All of the source code for the examples in this book are contained in the CD-ROM supplied with this book. The source code is also available for anonymous ftp on the Internet. The ftp site name is "`archive.cs.umbc.edu`" and the directory name is "`texture`."

Acknowledgements

First, we wish to thank Eric Haines and Rick Parent for reviewing drafts of this book. We also wish to thank the attendees of our SIGGRAPH courses for feedback and suggestions that led to the development of this book. Susan Wrights, Judy Peachey, Rick Sayre, and Julie Ebert have been of immeasurable help in reviewing parts of this book. Holly Rushmeier has helped with figure creation, Larry Gritz has provided RenderMan translations for Ken Musgrave's code and co-authored Chapter 15, Tom Deering has helped Darwyn Peachey with his Illustrator figures, Richard Chang has helped with file transfers, and Benjamin

Zhu, Xue Dong Wong, Rajesh Raichoudhury, and Ron Espiritu have helped Ken Perlin in the preparation of his chapter. We also wish to thank our families, friends, and co-workers for support during the development of this book. Finally, we wish to thank the staff at AP PROFESSIONAL for help in producing this second edition.

David S. Ebert

Author Addresses

Our current physical and e-mail addresses are given below.

Dr. David S. Ebert

> Computer Science and Electrical Engineering Department
> University of Maryland Baltimore County
> 1000 Hilltop Circle
> Baltimore, MD 21250
> ebert@umbc.edu

Dr. F. Kenton Musgrave

> MetaCreations
> 5550 Scotts Valley Dr.
> Scotts Valley, CA 95066
> musgrave@aiggraph.org

Darwyn Peachey

> Pixar
> 1001 West Cutting
> Richmond, CA 94804
> peachey@pixar.com

Dr. Ken Perlin

> NYU Media Research Lab
> 715 Broadway, Rm 1224
> NY, NY 10003
> perlin@nyu.edu

Steven Worley

> Worley Laboratories
> 405 El Camino Real Suite 121
> Menlo Park, CA 94025
> spworley@worley.com

Introduction

David S. Ebert

Procedural Techniques and Computer Graphics

Procedural techniques have been used throughout the history of computer graphics. Many early modeling and texturing techniques included procedural definitions of geometry and surface color. From these early beginnings, procedural techniques have exploded into an important, powerful modeling, texturing, and animation paradigm. During the mid- to late 1980s, procedural techniques for creating realistic textures, such as marble, wood, stone, and other natural material gained widespread use. These techniques were extended to procedural modeling, including models of water, smoke, steam, fire, planets, and even tribbles. The development of the RenderMan[1] shading language (Pixar 1989) in 1989 greatly expanded the use of procedural techniques. Currently, most commercial rendering and animation systems even provide a procedural interface. Procedural techniques have become an exciting, vital aspect of creating realistic computer-generated images and animations. As the field continues to evolve, the importance and significance of procedural techniques will continue to grow.

What Is a Procedural Technique?

We consider procedural techniques to be code segments or algorithms that specify some characteristic of a computer-generated model or effect. For example, a procedural texture for a marble surface does not use a scanned-in image to define

---

[1] RenderMan is a registered trademark of Pixar.

the color values. Instead, it uses algorithms and mathematical functions to determine the color.

The Power of Procedural Techniques

One of the most important features of procedural techniques is *abstraction.* In a procedural approach, rather than explicitly specifying and storing all the complex details of a scene or sequence, we *abstract* them into a function or an algorithm (i.e., a *procedure*) and evaluate that procedure when and where needed. We gain a storage savings, as the details are no longer explicitly specified but implicit in the procedure, and the time requirements for specification of details are shifted from the programmer to the computer. This allows us to have create inherent multi-resolution models and textures that we can evaluate to the resolution needed.

We also gain the power of *parametric control,* allowing us to assign to a parameter a meaningful concept (e.g., a number that makes mountains rougher or smoother). Parametric control also provides amplification of the modeler/animator's efforts: A few parameters yield large amounts of detail (Smith (Smith 1984) referred to this as *database amplification*). This parametric control unburdens the user from the low-level control and specification of detail. We also gain the serendipity inherent in procedural techniques: We are often pleasantly surprised by the unexpected behaviors of procedures, particularly stochastic procedures.

Procedural models also offer *flexibility.* The designer of the procedures can capture the *essence* of the object, phenomenon, or motion without being constrained by the complex laws of physics. Procedural techniques allow the inclusion of any amount of physical accuracy into the model that is desired. The designer may produce a wide range of effects, from accurately simulating natural laws to purely artistic effects.

Procedural Techniques and Advanced Geometric Modeling

Geometric modeling techniques in computer graphics have evolved significantly as the field matures and attempts to portray increasingly complex models and the complexities of nature. Earlier geometric models, such as polygonal models, patches, points, and lines, are insufficient to represent this increased complexity in a manageable and controllable fashion. Higher-level modeling techniques have been developed to provide an *abstraction* of the model, encode classes of objects, and allow high-level control and specification of the models. Many of these advanced geometric modeling techniques are inherently procedural. Grammar-based models [(Smith 1984), (Prusinkiewicz and Lindenmayer 1990)], including graftals and L-systems, allow the specification of a few parameters to simulate complex models of trees, plants, and other natural objects. These models use formal languages to specify complex growth rules for the natural objects.

Implicit surface models—also called blobby molecules (Blinn 1982b), meta-balls (Nishimura *et al.* 1985), and soft objects (Wyvill *et al.* 1986b)—are used in modeling organic shapes, complex manmade shapes, and "soft" objects that are difficult to animate and describe using more traditional techniques. Implicit surfaces were first introduced into computer graphics by Blinn (Blinn 1982b) to produce images of electron density clouds. They are surfaces of constant value, **isosurfaces**, created from blending primitives (functions or skeletal elements) represented by implicit equations of the form $F(x, y, z) = 0$. Implicit surfaces are a more concise representation than parametric surfaces and provide greater flexibility in modeling and animating soft objects. For modeling complex shapes, several basic implicit surface primitives are smoothly blended to produce the final shape. The detailed geometric shape of the implicit surface is not specified by the modeler/animator; instead, it is procedurally determined through the evaluation of the implicit functions, providing higher-level specification and animation control of complex models.

Particle systems (Reeves 1983) are procedural in their abstraction of specification of the object and control of its animation. A particle system object is represented by a large collection (cloud) of very simple geometric particles that change stochastically over time. Therefore, particle systems do use a large database of geometric primitives to represent natural objects ("fuzzy objects"), but the animation, location, birth, and death of the particles representing the object are controlled algorithmically. As with other procedural modeling techniques, particle systems have the advantage of database amplification, allowing the modeler/animator to specify and control this extremely large cloud of geometric particles with only a few parameters.

These advanced geometric modeling techniques are not the focus of this book. However, they may be combined with the techniques described in this book to exploit their procedural characteristics and evolve better modeling and animation techniques.

Additionally, some aspects of image synthesis are by nature procedural, that is, they can't practically be evaluated in advance (e.g., view-dependent specular shading and atmospheric effects). Our primary focus is *procedural textures, procedural modeling,* and *procedural animation.*

Aim of This Book

This book gives the reader a working knowledge of several procedural texturing, modeling, and animation techniques, including two-dimensional texturing, solid texturing, hypertextures, volumetric procedural models, fractal and genetic algorithms, and virtual procedural actors. We provide the reader with the details of these techniques, which are often omitted from technical papers, including useful and practical guidelines for selecting parameter values.

We provide a toolbox of specific procedures and basic primitive functions (noise, turbulence, etc.) to produce realistic images. An in-depth description of noise functions is presented, accompanied by several implementations, and a spectral comparison of these functions. Some of the procedures presented can be used to create realistic images of marble, brick, fire, steam, smoke, water, clouds, stone, and planets.

Organization

This book follows a progression in the use of procedural techniques from procedural texturing to volumetric procedural objects, and finally to fractals. In each chapter, the concepts are illustrated with a large number of example procedures. These procedures are presented in C code segments or in the RenderMan shading language.

The details of the design of these procedures are also explained to aid the reader in gaining insights into the different procedural design approaches taken by the authors. The reader should, therefore, be able to reproduce the images presented in this book and extend the procedures presented to produce a myriad of effects.

Darwyn Peachey describes how to build procedural textures in Chapter 2. This discussion includes two-dimensional texturing and solid texturing. Two important procedures that are used throughout the book are described in this chapter: *noise* and *turbulence*. Aliasing problems of procedural techniques are described, and several antialiasing techniques suitable for procedural approaches are presented and compared.

The design of procedural textures is also the subject of Chapters 3, 4, and 5 by Steve Worley. Chapter 3 contains useful guidelines and tricks to produce interesting textures efficiently. Chapter 4 describes some additional approaches to antialiasing. In Chapter 5 Steve describes some detailed example procedural textures.

The next three chapters by David Ebert describe how turbulence and solid texturing can be extended to produce images and animations of three-dimensional gases (particulate volumes). Chapter 6 concentrates on techniques to produce still images of volumetric "gases" (steam, fog, smoke). Chapter 7 discusses how to animate these three-dimensional volumes, as well as solid textures and hypertextures. Chapter 8 describes how to extend these volumetric procedural models to model and animate realistic clouds.

Chapter 9 by Ken Perlin discusses other types of volumetric procedural objects, such as hypertextures and surflets. Ken also gives a detailed explanation of his famous *noise* function and its implementation, as well as rendering of procedural objects and antialiasing. Ken also describes the use of high-level, nondeterministic "texture" to create gestural motions and facial animation for synthetic actors. By blending textural controls, the apparent emotional state of a synthetic actor can be created.

Finally, Chapters 10, 11, 12, 13, and 14, and 15[2] by Ken Musgrave describe fractals and their use in creating realistic landscapes, planets, and atmospherics. Ken begins by giving a brief introduction to fractals, and then discusses fractal textures, landscapes, and planets. The discussion proceeds to procedural rendering techniques, genetic procedural textures, and finally, atmospheric models.

[2] Chapter 15 is also co-authored by Larry Gritz and Steve Worley.

Building Procedural Textures 2

Darwyn Peachey

This chapter describes how to construct procedural texture functions in a variety of ways, starting from very simple textures and eventually moving on to quite elaborate ones. The discussion is intended to give the reader a thorough understanding of the major building blocks of procedural textures and the ways in which they can be combined.

Geometric calculations are fundamental to procedural texturing, as they are to most of 3D computer graphics. You should be familiar with 2D and 3D points, vectors, Cartesian coordinate systems, dot products, cross products, and homogeneous transformation matrices. You should also be familiar with the RGB (red, green, blue) representation of colors and with simple diffuse and specular shading models. Consult a graphics textbook such as (Foley *et al.* 1990) or (Hearn and Baker 1986) if any of this sounds new or unfamiliar.

Introduction

Throughout the short history of computer graphics, researchers have sought to improve the realism of their synthetic images by finding better ways to render the appearance of surfaces. This work can be divided into *shading* and *texturing*. Shading is the process of calculating the color of a pixel or shading sample from user-specified surface properties and the shading model. Texturing is a method of varying the surface properties from point to point in order to give the appearance of surface detail that is not actually present in the geometry of the surface.

Shading models (sometimes called illumination models, lighting models, or reflection models) simulate the interaction of light with surface materials. Shading models are usually based on physics, but they always make a great number of simplifying assumptions. Fully detailed physical models would be overkill for most computer graphics purposes, and would involve intractable calculations.

The simplest realistic shading model, and the one that was used first in computer graphics, is the diffuse model, sometimes called the Lambertian model. A diffuse surface has a dull or matte appearance. The diffuse model was followed by a variety of more realistic shading models that simulate specular simulate specular (mirror-like) reflection [(Phong 1975), (Blinn 1977), (Cook and Torrance 1981), (He *et al.* 1991)]. (Kajiya 1985) introduced anisotropic shading models in which specular reflection properties are different in different directions. (Cabral *et al.* 1987), (Miller 1988a), and (Poulin and Fournier1990) have done further research on anisotropic shading models.

All of the shading models I have described are so-called *local* models, which only deal with light arriving directly from light sources. In the early 1980s, most research on shading models turned to the problem of simulating *global* illumination effects, which result from indirect lighting due to reflection, refraction, and scattering of light from other surfaces or participating media in the scene. Ray tracing and radiosity techniques typically are used to simulate global illumination effects.

Texture

At about the same time as the early specular reflection models were being formulated, (Catmull 1974) generated the first textured computer graphics images. Catmull's surfaces were represented as parametric patches. A parametric patch is a function of two parameters (*u, v*) so there is a unique two-dimensional point associated with each 3D point on the surface. It is straightforward to set up a mapping from the pixels of a digital texture image to corresponding points in the (*u, v*) parameter space of a patch. The digital texture image can be *texture mapped* onto the patch. Although very simple in principle, texture mapping of image textures involves some tricky image filtering to avoid aliasing artifacts. A pixel of the rendered image could contain hundreds of pixels of the texture image, or conversely, could contain only a fraction of a pixel.

These first efforts proved that texture provided an interesting and detailed surface appearance, instead of a simple and boring surface of a single uniform color. It was clear that texture gave a quantum leap in realism at very low cost in human effort and computer time. Variations and improvements on the notion of texture mapping quickly followed.

(Blinn and Newell 1976) introduced *reflection mapping* (also called *environment mapping*) to simulate reflections from mirror-like surfaces. Reflection mapping is a simplified form of ray tracing. The reflection mapping procedure calculates the reflection direction R of a ray from the camera or viewer to the point being shaded.

$$R = 2(N \cdot V)N - V$$

where N is the surface normal and V points toward the viewer (both must be normalized). The texture image can be accessed using the "latitude" and "longitude" angles of the normalized vector $R = (x, y, z)$.

$$\theta = \tan^{-1}(y / x)$$
$$\phi = \sin^{-1} z$$

suitably scaled and translated to fit the range of texture image pixel coordinates. If the reflection texture is chosen carefully, the texture mapped surface appears to be reflecting an image of its surroundings. The illusion is enhanced if both the position of the shaded point and the reflection direction are used to calculate a ray intersection with an imaginary environment sphere surrounding the scene. The latitude and longitude of the intersection can be used to access the reflection texture.

(Blinn 1978) introduced *bump mapping*, which made it possible to simulate the appearance of surface bumps without actually modifying the geometry. Bump mapping uses a texture pattern to modify the direction of surface normal vectors. When the resulting normals are used in the shading calculation, the rendered surface appears to have bumps and indentations. Such bumps aren't visible at the silhouette edges of the surface, since they consist only of shading variations, not geometry.

(Cook 1984) described an extension of bump mapping called *displacement mapping* in which textures are used actually to move the surface, not just change the normals. Moving the surface does change the normals as well, so displacement mapping often looks just like bump mapping except that the bumps created by displacement are even visible on the silhouettes of objects.

(Reeves *et al.* 1987) presented an algorithm for producing antialiased shadows using an image texture based on a depth image of a scene rendered from the position of the light source. A stochastic sampling technique called "percentage closer filtering" was applied to reduce the effects of aliasing in the depth image.

(Peachey 1985) and (Perlin 1985) described space filling textures called *solid textures* as an alternative to the 2D texture images that had traditionally been used. Gardner used solid textures generated by sums of sinusoidal functions to add texture to models of trees, terrains, and clouds [(Gardner 1984), (Gardner 1985)]. Solid textures are evaluated based on the three-dimensional coordinates of the point being textured, rather than the 2D surface parameters of the point. Consequently, solid textures are unaffected by distortions of the surface parameter space, such as one might see near the poles of a sphere. Continuity between the surface parameterization of adjacent patches isn't a concern either. The solid texture will remain consistent and have features of constant size regardless of distortions in the surface coordinate systems.

For example, objects machined from solid wood exhibit different grain textures depending on the orientation of the surface with respect to the longitudinal growth axis of the original tree. Ordinary 2D techniques of applying wood grain textures typically result in a veneer or "plastic wood" effect. Although each surface of a block may resemble solid wood, the unrealistic relationship between the textures on the adjacent surfaces destroys the illusion. A solid texture that simulates wood gives consistent textures on all surfaces of an object (Figure 1).

Procedural Texture

From the earliest days of texture mapping, a variety of researchers used synthetic texture models to generate texture images instead of scanning or painting them. (Blinn and Newell 1976) used Fourier synthesis. (Fu and Lu 1978) proposed a syntactic grammar-based texture generation technique. (Schacter and Ahuja 1979) and (Schacter 1980) used Fourier synthesis and stochastic models of various

Figure 1.   A wood-grain solid texture.

kinds to generate texture imagery for flight simulators. (Fournier *et al.* 1982) and (Haruyama and Barsky 1984) proposed using stochastic subdivision ("fractal") methods to generate textures. Other researchers developed statistical texture models that analyzed the properties of natural textures and then reproduced the textures from the statistical data [(Gagalowicz and Ma 1985), (Garber 1981)].

(Cook 1984) described the "shade trees" system, which was one of the first systems in which it was convenient to generate procedural textures during rendering. Shade trees enable the use of a different shading model for each surface as well as for light sources and for attenuation through the atmosphere. Because the inputs to the shading model can be manipulated procedurally, shade trees make it possible to use texture to control any part of the shading calculation. Color and transparency textures, reflection mapping, bump mapping, displacement mapping and solid texturing can all be implemented using shade trees.

(Perlin 1985) described a complete procedural texture generation language and laid the foundation for the most popular class of procedural textures in use today, namely those based on *Noise*, a stochastic texture generation primitive.

(Turk 1991) and (Witkin and Kass 1991) described synthetic texture models inspired by the biochemical processes that produce (among other effects) pigmentation patterns in the skins of animals.

(Sims 1991) described a very novel texture synthesis system in which procedural textures represented as LISP expressions are automatically modified and combined by a genetic programming system. By interactively selecting among the resulting textures, the user of the system can direct the simulated evolution of a texture in some desired direction.

All of the texture synthesis methods mentioned in this section might be called "procedural." But just what *is* a procedural texture?

Procedural versus Nonprocedural

The definition of procedural texture is surprisingly slippery. The adjective *procedural* is used in computer science to distinguish entities that are described by program code rather than by data structures. For instance, in artificial intelligence there is a distinction between procedural representations of knowledge and declarative ones (see, for example, section 7.3 in (Rich 1983)). But anything we do with computers has a procedural aspect at some level, and almost every procedure takes some parameters or inputs that can be viewed as the declarative part of the description. In the mapping of a texture image onto a surface, the procedural component is the renderer's texture mapping module, and the declarative component is the texture image.

It is tempting to define a procedural texture as one that is changed primarily by modifying the algorithm rather than by changing its parameters or inputs. However, a procedural texture in a black box is still a procedural texture, even though you might be prevented from changing its code. This is true of procedural textures that are provided to you in a non-source-code form as part of a proprietary commercial renderer or texture package. Some rendering systems allow the user to create new procedural textures and modify existing procedural textures, but many others do not.

One major defining characteristic of a procedural texture is that it is *synthetic*, generated from a program or model, rather than just a digitized or painted image. But image textures can be included among procedural textures in a procedural texture language that incorporates image-based texture mapping as one of its primitive operations. Some very nice procedural textures can be based on the procedural combination, modification, or distortion of image textures. The question "How procedural are such textures?" is difficult to answer and hinges on the apparent amount of difference between the source images and the resulting texture.

Implicit and Explicit Procedures

We can distinguish two major types of procedural texturing or modeling methods: *explicit* and *implicit* methods. In explicit methods, the procedure directly generates the points that make up a shape. In implicit methods, the procedure answers a query about a particular point. The most common form of implicit method is the *isocurve* (in 2D) or *isosurface* (in 3D) method. A texture pattern is defined as a function F of points P in the texture space, and the pattern consists of a level set of F, that is, the set of all points at which the function has a particular value C: $\{P \mid F(P) = C\}$. For example, a simple definition of a unit circle is the isocurve model $\{P \in R^2 \mid P_x^2 + P_y^2 = 1\}$. Note that F must be reasonably well behaved if the function is to form a sensible pattern: we want F to be continuous and perhaps differentiable depending on the application.

Implicit geometric models traditionally have been popular in ray tracers, because the problem of intersecting a ray with the model can be expressed elegantly for implicit models: Given a model $F(P) = 0$ and a ray $R(t) = O + t D$ with origin O and direction D, the intersection point is simply $R(t_{hit})$ where t_{hit} is the smallest positive root of $F(R(t)) = 0$. On the other hand, explicit models are convenient for depth buffer renderers (Z buffers and A buffers), because the explicit model can directly place points into the depth buffer in arbitrary order as the model is evaluated.

In the texturing domain, implicit procedural methods seem to be best for textures that are evaluated during rendering. In both ray tracers and depth buffer renderers, texture samples usually must be evaluated in an order that is determined by the renderer, not by the texture procedure. An implicit procedure fits perfectly in such an environment, because it is designed to answer a query about any point in the texture at any time. An explicit procedure wants to generate its texture pattern in some fixed order which probably doesn't match the needs of the rendering algorithm. In most renderers, using an explicit texture routine would require running the texture procedure as a pre-pass and having it generate the texture image into an image buffer, where it could be looked up as necessary for texture application during rendering. Many of the advantages of procedural textures are lost if the texture must be evaluated in a pre-pass.

In principle the explicit and implicit methods can be used to produce the same class of texture patterns or geometric models (virtually anything), but in practice each approach has its own class of models that are convenient or feasible. Explicit models are convenient for polygons and parametric curves and patches. Implicit models are convenient for quadrics and for patterns that result from potential or force fields. Since implicit models tend to be continuous throughout a region of the modeling space, they are appropriate for continuous density and flow phenomena such as natural stone textures, clouds, and fog.

The remainder of this chapter focuses on building procedural textures that are evaluated during rendering, and therefore, on implicit procedural textures. Some of the texture synthesis methods mentioned earlier, for example, reaction-diffusion textures or syntactically generated textures, can be very difficult to generate implicitly during rendering. Other methods, such as Fourier spectral synthesis, fit well into an implicit procedural system.

Advantages of Procedural Texture

The advantages of a procedural texture over an image texture are as follows:

- A procedural representation is extremely compact. The size of a procedural texture is usually measured in kilobytes, while the size of a texture image is usually measured in megabytes. This is especially true for solid textures, since 3D texture "images" are extremely large. Nonetheless, some people have used tomographic X-ray scanners to obtain digitized volume images for use as solid textures.

- A procedural representation has no fixed resolution. In most cases it can provide a fully detailed texture no matter how closely you look at it (no matter how high the resolution).

- A procedural representation covers no fixed area. In other words, it is unlimited in extent and can cover an arbitrarily large area without seams and without unwanted repetition of the texture pattern.

- A procedural texture can be parameterized, so it can generate a class of related textures rather than being limited to one fixed texture image.

Many of these advantages are only *potential* advantages; procedural texturing gives you the tools to gain these advantages, but you must make an effort to use them. A badly written procedural texture could sacrifice any of these potential advantages. A procedural texture evaluated before rendering has only one of these advantages, namely, that it can be parameterized to generate a variety of related textures.

Disadvantages of Procedural Texture

The disadvantages of a procedural texture as compared to an image texure are as follows:

- A procedural texture can be difficult to build and debug. Programming is often hard, and programming an implicit pattern description is especially hard in non-trivial cases.

- A procedural texture can be a surprise. It is often easier to predict the outcome when you scan or paint a texture image. Some people choose to like this property of procedural textures and call it *serendipity*. Some people hate it and say that procedural textures are hard to control.

- Evaluating a procedural texture can be slower than accessing a stored texture image. This is the classic time vs. space tradeoff.

- Aliasing can be a problem in procedural textures. Antialiasing can be tricky and is less likely to be taken care of automatically that it is in image-based texturing.

The RenderMan Shading Language

Some renderers provide special-purpose shading languages in which program code for shading models and procedural textures can be written. The RenderMan[1] shading language [(Pixar 1989), (Hanrahan and Lawson 1990)] is perhaps the best known and most widely used of such languages. It is a descendant of the shade trees system described by (Cook 1984). The syntax of the language is C-like, but

---

[1] RenderMan is a registered trademark of Pixar.

the shading language contains built-in data types and operations that are convenient for computer graphics calculations, for example, data types for points and colors, and operators for common vector operations. The shading language lets us program any aspect of the shading calculations performed by the RenderMan renderer: surface shading, light source description, atmospheric effects, and surface displacement. Shading parameters can be made to vary across the surface to generate procedural texture effects. These could consist of variations in color, transparency, surface position, surface normal, shininess, shading model, or just about anything else you can think of.

The shading language is based on an implicit programming model, in which shading procedures called "shaders" are asked to supply the color, opacity, and other properties of specified points on a surface. As discussed in the previous section, this shading paradigm is used in most renderers, both depth buffers and ray tracers. I refer to the surface point being shaded as the "shading sample point" or simply as the "sample point." The color and opacity information that is computed by the shader for the sample point sometimes is called the "shading sample."

In the remainder of this chapter, I use the RenderMan shading language for my examples. Most of the images in the chapter were produced with Pixar's PhotoRealistic RenderMan[2] renderer, using the shading language code shown in the text. You should be able to understand the examples without RenderMan experience, but if you plan to write RenderMan shaders yourself, I encourage you to read (Upstill 1990).

Color Plates 2.1 through 2.6 are examples of images produced at Pixar for television commercials and films. All of the textures and lighting effects in these images were generated in the RenderMan shading language. Scanned texture images were used occasionally for product packaging materials and other graphic designs that contain text, since the shapes of letters are rather tedious to produce in an implicit procedural texture. Most of the textures are purely procedural. These examples demonstrate that the class of textures that can be generated procedurally is very large indeed.

What If You Don't Use RenderMan?

I want this chapter to be useful to a wide audience of people interested in procedural textures, not just to those who write RenderMan shaders. The RenderMan shading language is a convenient way to express procedural shaders and it allows

---

[2] PhotoRealistic RenderMan is a trademark of Pixar.

me to easily render high-quality images of my textures, so I use the shading language in my examples. However, I also provide a C language implementation of many of the procedural texture building-block functions that are built into the shading language. This should allow you to translate my shading language examples into C code that calls these building blocks, and to use the resulting C language shader in another rendering system. The RenderMan shading language is superficially so much like the C language that you might have to look closely to see whether a given fragment of code is in C or in the shading language.

The RenderMan shading language provides functions that access image textures. It is not practical to include an implementation of those functions in this chapter. Efficient image texture mapping with proper filtering is a complex task and the program code consists of several thousand of lines of C. Most other renderers have a similar scheme for accessing texture images, and you should be able to translate the RenderMan examples into the appropriate incantations for those renderers.

The last section of this chapter, entitled *RenderMan Esoterica*, discusses a number of idiosyncrasies of the RenderMan shading language that are unlikely to be of interest to people who don't use it. For those who *do* use RenderMan, this section might be among the most useful parts of our book.

Procedural Pattern Generation

Sitting down to build a procedural texture can be a daunting experience, at least the first few times. This section gives some hints, guidelines and examples that will help you stave off the anxiety of facing an empty text editor screen with no idea how to begin. It is usually much easier to start by copying an example and modifying it to do what you want than it is to start from scratch. Most of the time, it is better to borrow code than to invent it.

Much of my experience in building procedural textures has involved the writing of RenderMan shaders that generate textures on surfaces. Such shaders can be split into two components called *pattern generation* and *shading model*. Pattern generation defines the texture pattern and sets the values of surface properties that are used by the shading model. The shading model simulates the behavior of the surface material with respect to diffuse and specular reflection.

Shading Models

Most surface shaders use one of a small number of shading models. The most common model includes diffuse and specular reflection and is called the "plastic" shading model. It is expressed in the RenderMan shading language as follows:

```
surface
plastic(float Ka = 1, Kd = 0.5, Ks = 0.5;
        float roughness = 0.1;
        color specularcolor = color (1,1,1))
{
    point Nf = faceforward(normalize(N), I);
    point V = normalize(-I);
Oi = Os;
Ci = Os * (Cs * (Ka * ambient() + Kd * diffuse(Nf))
        + specularcolor * Ks * specular(Nf, V, roughness));
}
```

In the following paragraphs, I explain the workings of the `plastic` shader in detail, as a way of introducing the RenderMan shading language to readers who are not familiar with it.

The parameters of the `plastic` shader are the coefficients of ambient, diffuse, and specular reflectance, the roughness which controls the size of specular highlights, and the color of the specular highlights. Colors are represented by RGB triples, specifying the intensities of the red, green, and blue primary colors as numbers between 0 and 1. For example, in this notation, `color (1,1,1)` is white.

Any RenderMan surface shader can reference a large collection of built-in quantities such as `P`, the 3D coordinates of the point on the surface being shaded, and `N`, the surface normal at `P`. The normal vector is perpendicular to the tangent plane of the surface at `P` and points toward the outside of the surface. Because surfaces can be two-sided, it is possible to see the inside of a surface; in that case we want the normal vector to point toward the camera, not away from it. The built-in function `faceforward` simply compares the direction of the incident ray vector `I` with the direction of the normal vector `N`. `I` is the vector from the camera position to the point `P`. If the two vectors `I` and `N` point in the same direction (i.e., if their dot product is positive), `faceforward` returns − `N` instead of `N`.

The first statement in the body of the shader declares and initializes a surface normal vector `Nf`, which is normalized and faces toward the camera. The second statement declares and initializes a "viewer" vector `V` that is normalized and gives the direction to the camera. The third statement sets the output opacity `Oi` to be equal to the input surface opacity `Os`. If the surface is somewhat transparent, the opacity is less than one. Actually, `Os` is a color, an RGB triple that gives the opacity of the surface for each of the three primary colors. For an opaque surface, couis `color (1,1,1)`.

The final statement in the shader does the interesting work. The output color `Ci` is set to the product of the opacity and a color.[3] The color is the sum of an

---

[3] The color is multiplied by the opacity because RenderMan uses an "alpha blending" technique to combine the colors of partially transparent surfaces, similar to the method described by (Porter and Duff 1984).

ambient term and a diffuse term multiplied by the input surface color Cs, added to a specular term whose color is determined by the parameter specular-color. The built-in functions ambient, diffuse, and specular gather up all of the light from multiple light sources according to a particular reflection model. For instance, diffuse computes the sum of the intensity of each light source multiplied by the dot product of the direction to the light source and the surface normal Nf (which is passed as a parameter to diffuse).

The plastic shading model is flexible enough to include the other two most common RenderMan shading models, the "matte" model and the "metal" model, as special cases. The matte model is a perfectly diffuse reflector, which is equivalent to plastic with a Kd of 1 and a Ks of 0. The metal model is a perfectly specular reflector, which is equivalent to plastic with a Kd of 0, a Ks of 1, and a specularcolor the same as Cs. The specularcolor parameter is important because it has been observed that when illuminated by a white light source, plastics and other dielectric (insulating) materials have white highlights while metals and other conductive materials have colored highlights (Cook and Torrance 1981). For example, gold has a gold-colored highlight.

The plastic shader is the starting point for most of my procedural texture shaders. I replace the Cs in the last statement of the shader with a new color variable Ct, the texture color that is computed by the pattern generation part of the shader.

Pattern Generation

Pattern generation is usually the hard part of writing a RenderMan shader because it involves figuring out how to generate a particular texture pattern procedurally.

If the texture pattern is simply an image texture, the shader can call the built-in shading language function texture.

```
Ct = texture("name.tx", s, t);
```

The shading language texture function looks up pixel values from the specified image texture "name.tx" and performs filtering calculations as needed to prevent aliasing artifacts. The texture function has the usual 2D texture space with the texture image in the unit square. The built-in variables s and t are the standard RenderMan texture coordinates, which by default range over the unit interval [0, 1] for any type of surface. The shading language also provides an environment function whose 2D texture space is accessed using a 3D direction vector that is converted internally into 2D form to access a latitude -longitude or cube-face environment map (Greene 1986).

When the texture image is suitable there is no easier or more realistic way to generate texture patterns. Unfortunately it is difficult to get a texture image that is suitable for many texture applications. It would be nice if all desired textures could be implemented by finding a sample of the actual material, photographing it, and scanning the photograph to produce a beautiful texture image. But this approach is rarely adequate by itself. If a material is not completely flat and smooth, the photograph will capture information about the lighting direction and the light source. Each bump in the material will be shaded based on its slope, and in the worst case, the bumps will cast shadows. Even if the material is flat and smooth, the photograph often will record uneven lighting conditions, reflections of the environment surrounding the material, highlights from the light sources, and so on. This information generates incorrect visual cues when the photograph is texture mapped onto a surface in a scene with simulated lighting and environmental characteristics that differ from those in the photograph. A beautiful photograph often looks out of place when texture mapped onto a computer graphics model.

Another problem with photographic texture images is that they aren't infinitely large. When a large area must be covered, copies of the texture are placed side by side. A seam is usually visible because the texture pixels don't match from the top to the bottom or the left to the right. Sometimes retouching can be used to make the edges match up seamlessly. Even when this has been done, a large area textured with many copies of the image can look bad, because it is obvious that a small amount of texture data has been used to texture a large area. Prominent features in the texture map are replicated over and over in an obviously repetitive way. Such problems can be avoided by making sure that the texture photograph covers a large area of the texture, but this will result in visible pixel artifacts in a rendered image which magnifies a tiny part of the texture.

The right way to use image textures is to design the shader first and then go out and get a suitable texture photograph to scan. The lighting, the size of the area photographed, and the resolution of the scanning should all be selected based on the application of the shader. In many cases the required texture images will be bump altitude maps, monochrome images of prominent textural features, and so on. The texture images may be painted by hand, generated procedurally, or produced from scanned material after substantial image processing and retouching.

Procedural pattern generators are more difficult to write. In addition to the problems of creating a small piece of program code that produces a convincing simulation of some material, the procedural pattern generator must be antialiased to prevent fine details in the pattern from aliasing when seen from far away.

Procedural pattern generators are harder to write than texture image shaders, but they have several nice properties. It is usually easy to make the texture cover an arbitrarily large area without seams or objectionable repetition. It is easy to separate small-scale shape effects such as bumps and dimples from color variations; each can be generated separately in the procedural shader.

Writing procedural pattern generators is still an art form; I can't give a recipe that will work every time. This is a programming task in which the problem is to generate the appearance of some real-world material. The first step is to go out and examine the real material: its color and color variations, its reflection properties, and its surface characteristics (smooth or rough, bumpy or pitted). Photographs that you can take back to your desk are very valuable. Architectural and design magazines and books are a good source of pictures of materials.

Texture Spaces

The RenderMan shading language, which is used in my examples, provides many different built-in coordinate systems (also called *spaces*). A coordinate system is defined by the concatenated stack of transformation matrices that is in effect at a given point in the hierarchical structure of the RenderMan geometric model.

- The `current` space is the one in which shading calculations are normally done. In most renderers, `current` space will turn out to be either `camera` space or `world` space, but you shouldn't depend on this.

- The `world` space is the coordinate system in which the overall layout of your scene is defined. It is the starting point for all other spaces.

- The `object` space is the one in which the surface being shaded was defined. For instance, if the shader is shading a sphere, the `object` space of the sphere is the coordinate system that was in effect when the `RiSphere` call was made to create the sphere. Note that an object made up of several surfaces all using the same shader might have different object spaces for each of the surfaces if there are geometric transformations between the surfaces.

- The `shader` space is the coordinate system that existed when the shader was invoked (e.g., by an `RiSurface` call). This is a very useful space because it can be attached to a user-defined collection of surfaces at an appropriate point in the hierarchy of the geometric model so that all of the related surfaces share the same `shader` space.

In addition, user-defined coordinate systems can be created and given names using the `RiCoordinateSystem` call. These coordinate systems can be referenced by name in the shading language.

It is very important to choose the right texture space when defining your texture. Using the 2D surface texture coordinates *(s, t)* or the surface parameters *(u, v)* is fairly safe, but might cause problems due to nonuniformities in the scale of the parameter space (e.g., compression of the parameter space at the poles of a sphere). Solid textures avoid that problem because they are defined in terms of the 3D coordinates of the sample point. If a solid texture is based on the `camera` space coordinates of the point, the texture on a surface will change whenever the camera is moved. If the texture is based on `world` space coordinates, it will change whenever the object is moved. In most cases, solid textures should be based on the `shader` space coordinates of the shading samples, so that the texture will move properly with the object. The `shader` space is defined when the shader is invoked, and that can be done at a suitable place in the transformation hierarchy of the model so that everything works out.

It is a simplification to say that a texture is defined in terms of a single texture space. In general a texture is a combination of a number of separate "features," each of which might be defined in terms of its own *feature space*. If the various feature spaces that are used in creating the texture are not based on one underlying texture space, great care must be exercised to be sure that texture features don't shift with respect to one another. The feature spaces should have a fixed relationship that doesn't change when the camera or the object moves.

Layering and Composition

The best approach to writing a complex texture pattern generator is to build it up from simple parts. There are a number of ways to combine simple patterns to make complex patterns.

One technique is *layering*, in which simple patterns are placed on top of one another. For example, the colors of two texture layers could be added together. Usually it is better to have some texture function control how the layers are combined. The shading language `mix` function is a convenient way of doing this.

```
C = mix(C0, C1, f);
```

The number `f`, between 0 and 1, is used to select one of the colors `C0` and `C1`. If `f` is 0, the result of the `mix` is `C0`. If `f` is 1, the result is `C1`. If `f` is between 0 and 1, the result is a linearly interpolated mixture of `C0` and `C1`. The `mix` function is defined as:

```
color
mix(color C0, color C1, float f)
{
     return (1-f)*C0 + f*C1;
}
```

`C0` and `C1` can be fixed colors, or they can be two subtextures. In either case, they are combined under the control of the number `f`, which is itself the result of some procedural texture function.

When two colors are multiplied together in the shading language, the result is a color whose RGB components are the product of the corresponding components from the input colors. That is, the red result is the product of the red components of the two inputs. Color multiplication can simulate the filtering of one color by the other. If color `C0` represents the transparency of a filter to red, green, and blue light, then `C0 * C1` represents the color `C1` as viewed through the filter.

Be careful when using a four-channel image texture that was created from an RGBA image (an image with an opacity or "alpha" channel), because the colors in such an image are normally pre-multiplied by the value of the alpha channel. In this case, it is not correct simply to combine the RGB channels with another color under control of the alpha channel. The correct way to merge an RGBA texture over another texture color `Ct` is

```
color C;
float A;

C = color texture("mytexture", s, t);
A = texture("mytexture"[3], s, t);
result = C + (1-A) * Ct;
```

`C` is the image texture color and `A` is the alpha channel of the image texture (channel number 3). Since `C` has already been multiplied by `A`, the expression `C + (1 - A * Ct)` is the right way to "lerp"[4] between `C` and `Ct`.

Another way to combine simple functions to make complex functions is *functional composition*, using the outputs of one or more simple functions as the inputs of another function. For example, one function generates a number that varies between 0 and 1 in a particular way, and this number is used as the input to another function that generates different colors for different values of its numerical input. One function might take inputs that are points in one texture space and produce output points in another space that are the input to a second function; in this case, the first function transforms points into the feature space needed by the

---

[4] In computer graphics, linear interpolation is colloquially called *lerping*.

second function. Composition is very powerful, and is so fundamental to programming that you really can't avoid using it.

The computer science literature concerning *functional programming* is a good source of techniques for combining functions (Ghezzi and Jazayeri 1982). Functional languages such as LISP (Winston and Horn 1984) (also known as *applicative* languages) rely heavily on composition and related techniques.

The remainder of this section presents a series of primitive functions that are used as building blocks for procedural textures. The presentation includes several examples of the use of these primitives in procedural texture shaders.

Steps, Clamps, and Conditionals

From the earlier discussion on methods of combining primitive operations to make procedural patterns, it should be clear that functions taking parameters and returning values are the most convenient kind of primitive building blocks. Steps and clamps are conditional functions that give us much the same capabilities that if statements give us. But steps and clamps are often more convenient, simply because they are functions.

The RenderMan shading language function step(a, x) returns the value 0 when x is less than a and returns 1 otherwise. The step function can be written in C as follows:

```
float
step(float a, float x)
{
     return (float)(x >= a);
}
```

A graph of the step function is shown in Figure 2.

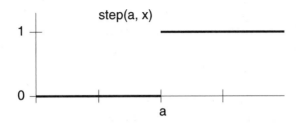

Figure 2.   The step function.

The main use of the `step` function is to replace an `if` statement or to produce a sharp transition between one type of texture and another type of texture. For example, an `if` statement such as

```
if (u < 0.5)
    Ci = color (1,1,.5);
else
    Ci = color (.5,.3,1);
```

can be rewritten to use the `step` function as follows:

```
Ci = mix(color (1,1,.5), color (.5,.3,1), step(0.5, u));
```

Later in this chapter when I discuss antialiasing, I'll explain how to convert the `step` function into an antialiased alternative. Writing your procedural texture with a lot of `if` statements instead of `step` functions can make antialiasing much harder.[5]

Two steps can be used to make a rectangular pulse as follows:

```
#define PULSE(a,b,x) (step((a),(x)) - step((b),(x)))
```

This preprocessor macro generates a pulse which begins at $x = a$ and ends at $x = b$. A graph of the pulse is shown in Figure 3.

The RenderMan shading language function `clamp(x, a, b)` returns the value a when x is less than a, the value of x when x is between a and b, and the value b when x is greater than b. The clamp function can be written in C as follows:

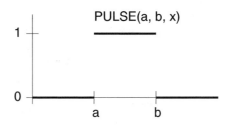

Figure 3.   **Two steps used to make a pulse.**

---

[5] Another reason for using `step` instead of `if` in RenderMan shaders is that it encourages you to compute the inputs of a conditional everywhere, not just in the fork of the conditional where they are used. This can avoid problems in applying image textures and other area operations. I discuss this further in the *RenderMan Esoterica* section at the end of this chapter.

```
float
clamp(float x, float a, float b)
{
     return (x < a ? a : (x > b ? b : x));
}
```

A graph of the `clamp` function is shown in Figure 4.

The well-known `min` and `max` functions are closely related to clamp. In fact,

$$\text{min(x, b)} \equiv \text{clamp(x, x, b)}$$

and

$$\text{max(x, a)} \equiv \text{clamp(x, a, x)}.$$

Alternatively,

$$\text{clamp(x, a, b)} \equiv \text{min(max(x, a), b)}.$$

In the name of completeness, here are the C implementations of `min` and `max`:

```
float
min(float a, float b)
{
     return (a < b ? a : b);
}
float
max(float a, float b)
{
     return (a < b ? b : a);
}
```

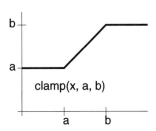

Figure 4.   The clamp function.

Another special conditional function is the `abs` function:

```
float
abs(float x)
{
    return (x < 0 ? -x : x);
}
```

A graph of the abs function is shown in Figure 5. The abs function can be viewed as a rectifier; it will convert a sine wave that oscillates between, say, -1 and 1 into a sequence of positive sinusoidal pulses that range from 0 to 1.

In addition to the "pure" or "sharp" conditionals step, clamp, min, max, and abs, the RenderMan shading language provides a "smooth" conditional function called smoothstep. This function is similar to step, but instead of a sharp transition from 0 to 1 at a specified threshold, smoothstep(a, b, x) makes a gradual transition from 0 to 1 beginning at threshold a and ending at threshold b. In order to do this, smoothstep contains a cubic function whose slope is 0 at a and b and whose value is 0 at a and 1 at b. There is only one cubic function that has these properties for a = 0 and b = 1, namely the function $3 x^2 - 2 x^3$.

Here is a C implementation of smoothstep, with the cubic function expressed according to Horner's rule: [6]

```
float
smoothstep(float a, float b, float x)
{
    if (x < a)
        return 0;
```

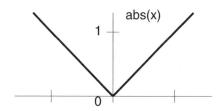

Figure 5.   The abs function.

---

[6] Horner's rule is a method of nested multiplication for efficiently evaluating polynomials.

```
    if (x >= b)
        return 1;
    x = (x - a)/(b - a); /* normalize to [0:1] */
    return (x*x * (3 - 2*x));
}
```

A graph of the `smoothstep` function is shown in Figure 6.

The `smoothstep` function is used instead of `step` in many procedural textures because sharp transitions often result in unsightly artifacts. Many of the artifacts are due to aliasing, which is discussed at length later in this chapter. Sharp transitions can be very unpleasant in animated sequences, because some features of the texture pattern appear suddenly as the camera or object moves (the features are said to "pop" on and off). Most of the motion in an animated sequence is carefully "eased" in and out to avoid sudden changes in speed or direction; the `smoothstep` function helps to keep the procedural textures in the scene from changing in equally unsettling ways.

Periodic Functions

The best-known periodic functions are `sin` and `cos`. They are important because of their close ties to the geometry of the circle, to angular measure, and to the representation of complex numbers. It can be shown that other functions can be built up from a sum of sinusoidal terms of different frequencies and phases (see the discussion on Spectral Synthesis on page 46. `sin` and `cos` are available as built-in functions in C and in the RenderMan shading language. Some ANSI C implementations provide single-precision versions of `sin` and `cos` called `sinf` and `cosf` which you might prefer to use to save computation time. A graph of the `sin` and `cos` functions is shown in Figure 7.

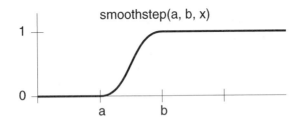

Figure 6.   The smoothstep function.

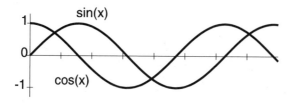

Figure 7.   The sin and cos functions.

Another important periodic function is the mod function. mod(a, b) gives the positive remainder obtained when dividing a by b. C users beware! Although C has a built-in integer remainder operator "%" and math library functions fmod and fmodf for double and float numbers, all of these are really remainder functions, not modulo functions, in that they will return a negative result if the first operand, a, is negative. Instead you might use the following C implementation of mod:

```
float
mod(float a, float b)
{
    int n = (int)(a/b);
    a -= n*b;
    if (a < 0)
        a += b;
    return a;
}
```

A graph of the periodic sawtooth function mod(x, a)/a is shown in Figure 8. This function has an amplitude of one and a period of a.

By applying mod to the inputs of some other function, we can make the other function periodic too. Take any function, say $f(x)$ defined on the interval from 0 to 1 (technically, on the half-open interval [0, 1]). Then f (mod $(x, a)/a$) is a periodic function. To make this work out nicely, it is best if $f(0) = f(1)$ and even better if the derivatives of f are also equal at 0 and 1. For example, the pulse function PULSE(0.4,0.6,x) can be combined with the mod function to get the periodic square wave function PULSE(0.4,0.6,mod(x, a)/a) with its period equal to a (see Figure 9).

I often prefer to use a different mod-like idiom instead of mod in my shaders. We can think of xf = mod(a, b)/b as the fractional part of the ratio a/b. In many cases it is useful to have the integer part of the ratio, xi, as well.

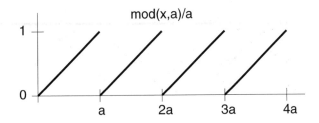

Figure 8.   The periodic function (x, a)/a.

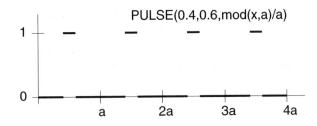

Figure 9.   How to make a function periodic.

```
float xf, xi;
xf = a/b;
xi = floor(xf);
xf -= xi;
```

The function `floor(x)` returns the largest integer that is less than or equal to x. Since the floor function is a built-in part of both the C math library and the RenderMan shading language, this piece of code will work equally well in either language. Some versions of ANSI C provide a `floorf` function whose argument and result are single-precision `float` numbers. In C, the following macro is an alternative to the built-in `floor` function:

```
#define FLOOR(x) ((int)(x) - ((x) < 0 && (x) != (int)(x)))
```

FLOOR isn't precisely the same as `floor`, because it returns a value of `int` type rather than `double` type. Be sure that the argument passed to FLOOR is the name of a variable, since the macro may evaluate its argument up to four times.

A closely related function is the ceiling function ceil(x) which returns the smallest integer that is greater than or equal to x. The function is built into the shading language and the C math library. ANSI C provides the single-precision version ceilf. The following macro is an alternative to the C library function:

```
#define CEIL(x) ((int)(x) + ((x) > 0 && (x) != (int)(x)))
```

Splines and Mappings

The RenderMan shading language has a built-in spline function, which is a one-dimensional Catmull-Rom interpolating spline through a set of so-called *knot* values. The parameter of the spline is a floating point number.

```
result = spline(parameter,
    knot1, knot2, ..., knotN-1, knotN);
```

In the shading language, the knots can be numbers, colors, or points (but all knots must be of the same type). The result has the same data type as the knots. If parameter is 0, the result is knot2. If parameter is 1, the result is knotN-1. For values of parameter between 0 and 1, the value of result interpolates smoothly between the values of the knots from knot2 to knotN-1. The knot1 and knotN values determine the derivatives of the spline at its endpoints. Because the spline is a cubic polynomial, there must be at least four knots.

Here is a C language implementation of spline in which the knots must be floating point numbers:

```
/* Coefficients of basis matrix. */
#define CR00    -0.5
#define CR01    1.5
#define CR02    -1.5
#define CR03    0.5
#define CR10    1.0
#define CR11    -2.5
#define CR12    2.0
#define CR13    -0.5
#define CR20    -0.5
#define CR21    0.0
#define CR22    0.5
#define CR23    0.0
#define CR30    0.0
#define CR31    1.0
#define CR32    0.0
#define CR33    0.0
```

```
float
spline(float x, int nknots, float *knot)
{
    int span;
    int nspans = nknots - 3;
    float c0, c1, c2, c3;    /* coefficients of the cubic.*/

    if (nspans < 1) { /* illegal */
        fprintf(stderr, "Spline has too few knots.\n");
        return 0;
    }

    /* Find the appropriate 4-point span of the spline. */
    x = clamp(x, 0, 1) * nspans;
    span = (int) x;
    if (span >= nknots - 3)
        span = nknots - 3;
    x -= span;
    knot += span;

    /* Evaluate the span cubic at x using Horner's rule. */
    c3 = CR00*knot[0] + CR01*knot[1]
        + CR02*knot[2] + CR03*knot[3];
    c2 = CR10*knot[0] + CR11*knot[1]
        + CR12*knot[2] + CR13*knot[3];
    c1 = CR20*knot[0] + CR21*knot[1]
        + CR22*knot[2] + CR23*knot[3];
    c0 = CR30*knot[0] + CR31*knot[1]
        + CR32*knot[2] + CR33*knot[3];

    return ((c3*x + c2)*x + c1)*x + c0;
}
```

A graph of a particular example of the `spline` function is shown in Figure 10.

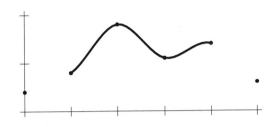

Figure 10.   An example of the spline function.

This code can easily be adapted to work with knots that are colors or points. Just do the same thing three times, once for each of the components of the knots. In other words,

```
spline(parameter, (x1,y1,z1), ..., (xN,yN,zN))
```

is exactly equivalent to

```
(spline(parameter, x1, ..., xN),
 spline(parameter, y1, ..., yN),
 spline(parameter, z1, ..., zN))
```

The `spline` function is used to map a number into another number or into a color. A spline can approximate any function on the [0, 1] interval by giving values of the function at equally spaced sample points as the knots of the spline. In other words, the spline can interpolate function values from a table of known values at equally spaced values of the input parameter. A spline with colors as knots is often called a *color map* or *color table*.

An example of this technique is a shader that simulates a shiny metallic surface by a procedural reflection map texture. The shader computes the reflection direction R of the viewer vector V. The vertical component of R in world space is used to look up a color value in a spline that goes from brown earth color below to pale bluish-white at the horizon and then to deeper shades of blue in the sky. Note that the shading language's built-in `vtransform` function properly converts a direction vector from the current rendering space to another coordinate system specified by name.

```
#define BROWN    color (0.1307,0.0609,0.0355)
#define BLUE0    color (0.4274,0.5880,0.9347)
#define BLUE1    color (0.1221,0.3794,0.9347)
#define BLUE2    color (0.1090,0.3386,0.8342)
#define BLUE3    color (0.0643,0.2571,0.6734)
#define BLUE4    color (0.0513,0.2053,0.5377)
#define BLUE5    color (0.0326,0.1591,0.4322)
#define BLACK    color (0,0,0)
surface
metallic()
{
    point Nf = normalize(faceforward(N, I));
    point V = normalize(-I);
    point R;       /* reflection direction */
    point Rworld; /* R in world space */
    color Ct;
    float altitude;
```

```
R = 2 * Nf * (Nf . V) - V;
Rworld = normalize(vtransform("world", R));
altitude = 0.5 * zcomp(Rworld) + 0.5;
Ct = spline(altitude,
    BROWN, BROWN, BROWN, BROWN, BROWN,
    BROWN, BLUE0, BLUE1, BLUE2, BLUE3,
    BLUE4, BLUE5, BLACK);
Oi = Os;
Ci = Os * Cs * Ct;
}
```

Figure 11 is an image shaded with the `metallic` reflection map shader.

Since `mix` functions and so many other selection functions are controlled by values that range over the [0, 1] interval, mappings from the unit interval to itself can be especially useful. Monotonically increasing functions on the unit interval can be used to change the distribution of values in the interval. The best-known example of such a function is the "gamma correction" function used to compensate for the nonlinearity of CRT display systems:

```
float
gammacorrect(float gamma, float x)
{
    return pow(x, 1/gamma);
}
```

Figure 12 shows the shape of the gamma correction function for `gamma` values of 0.4 and 2.3. If `x` varies over the [0, 1] interval, then the result is also in that interval. The zero and one endpoints of the interval are mapped to themselves. Other values are shifted upward toward one if `gamma` is greater than one, and shifted downward toward zero if `gamma` is between zero and one.

Figure 11.   A spline-based reflection texture.

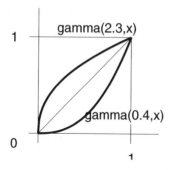

Figure 12.   The gamma correction function.

(Perlin and Hoffert 1989) use a version of the gamma correction function that they call the `bias` function. The `bias` function replaces the `gamma` parameter with a parameter b, defined such that `bias(b, 0.5) = b`.

```
float
bias(float b, float x)
{
     return pow(x, log(b)/log(0.5));
}
```

Figure 13 shows the shape of the `bias` function for different choices of b.

(Perlin and Hoffert 1989) present another function to remap the unit interval. This function is called `gain` and can be implemented as follows:

```
float
gain(float g, float x)
{
      if (x < 0.5)
          return bias(1-g, 2*x)/2;
      else
          return 1 - bias(1-g, 2 - 2*x)/2;
}
```

Regardless of the value of g, all `gain` functions return 0.5 when x is 0.5. Above and below 0.5, the `gain` function consists of two scaled-down `bias` curves forming an S-shaped curve. Figure 14 shows the shape of the `gain` function for different choices of g.

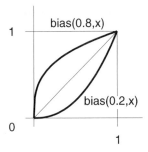

Figure 13.   The bias function.

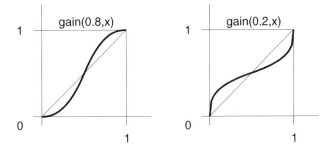

Figure 14.   The gain function.

(Schlick 1994) presents approximations to `bias` and `gain` that can be evaluated more quickly than the power functions given here.

Example: Brick Texture

One of the standard texture pattern clichés in computer graphics is the checkerboard pattern. This pattern was especially popular in a variety of early papers on antialiasing. Generating a checkerboard procedurally is quite easy. It is simply a matter of determining which square of the checkerboard contains the sample point and then testing the parity of the sum of the row and column to determine the color of that square.

This section presents a procedural texture generator for a simple brick pattern that is related to the checkerboard but is a bit more interesting. The pattern consists of rows of bricks in which alternate rows are offset by one-half the width of a brick. The bricks are separated by a mortar that has a different color than the bricks. Figure 15 is a diagram of the brick pattern.

The following is a listing of the shading language code for the brick shader, with explanatory remarks inserted here and there.

```
#define BRICKWIDTH          0.25
#define BRICKHEIGHT         0.08
#define MORTARTHICKNESS     0.01

#define BMWIDTH             (BRICKWIDTH+MORTARTHICKNESS)
#define BMHEIGHT            (BRICKHEIGHT+MORTARTHICKNESS)
#define MWF                 (MORTARTHICKNESS*0.5/BMWIDTH)
#define MHF                 (MORTARTHICKNESS*0.5/BMHEIGHT)

surface
brick(
    uniform float Ka = 1;
    uniform float Kd = 1;
    uniform color Cbrick = color (0.5, 0.15, 0.14);
    uniform color Cmortar = color (0.5, 0.5, 0.5);
```

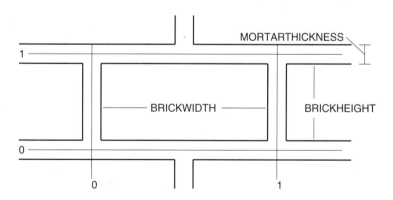

Figure 15. The geometry of a brick.

```
    )
{
    color Ct;
    point Nf;
    float ss, tt, sbrick, tbrick, w, h;
    float scoord = s;
    float tcoord = t;

    Nf = normalize(faceforward(N, I));

    ss = scoord / BMWIDTH;
    tt = tcoord / BMHEIGHT;

    if (mod(tt*0.5,1) > 0.5)
        ss += 0.5; /* shift alternate rows */
```

The texture coordinates scoord and tcoord begin with the values of the standard texture coordinates s and t, and then are divided by the dimensions of a brick (including one-half of the mortar around the brick) to obtain new coordinates ss and tt which vary from 0 to 1 within a single brick. scoord and tcoord become the coordinates of the upper-left corner of the brick containing the point being shaded. Alternate rows of bricks are offset by one-half brick width to simulate the usual way in which bricks are laid.

```
    sbrick = floor(ss); /* which brick? */
    tbrick = floor(tt); /* which brick? */
    ss -= sbrick;
    tt -= tbrick;
```

Having identified which brick contains the point being shaded, as well as the texture coordinates of the point within the brick, it remains to determine whether the point is in the brick proper or in the mortar between the bricks.

```
    w = step(MWF,ss) - step(1-MWF,ss);
    th = step(MHF,tt) - step(1-MHF,tt);

    Ct = mix(Cmortar, Cbrick, w*h);
    /* diffuse reflection model */

    tOi = Os;
    Ci = Os * Ct * (Ka * ambient() + Kd * diffuse(Nf));
}
```

The rectangular brick shape results from two pulses (see page 24), a horizontal pulse w and a vertical pulse h. w is zero when the point is horizontally within the mortar region and rises to one when the point is horizontally within the brick region. h does the same thing vertically. When the two values are multiplied together, the result is the logical AND of w and h. That is, w*h is nonzero only when the point is within the brick region both horizontally and vertically. In this case, the mix function switches from the mortar color Cmortar to the brick color Cbrick.

The shader ends by using the texture color Ct in a simple diffuse shading model to shade the surface. Figure 16 is an image rendered with the brick texture from this example.

Bump-Mapped Brick

Now let's try our hand at some procedural bump mapping. Recall that bump mapping involves modifying the surface normal vectors to give the appearance that the surface has bumps or indentations. How is this actually done? I will describe two methods.

(Blinn 1978), the paper that introduced bump mapping, describes how a bump of height $F(u, v)$ along the normal vector N can be simulated. The modified or "perturbed" normal vector is $N' = N + D$. The perturbation vector D lies in the tangent plane of the surface and is therefore perpendicular to N. D is based on the sum of two separate perturbation vectors U and V (Figure 17).

Figure 16. The brick texture.

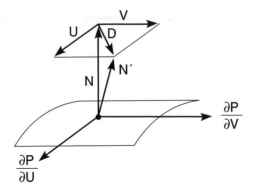

Figure 17.   The geometry of bump mapping.

$$U = \frac{\partial F}{\partial u}\left(N \times \frac{\partial P}{\partial v}\right)$$

$$V = -\left(\frac{\partial F}{\partial v}\left(N \times \frac{\partial P}{\partial u}\right)\right)$$

$$D = \frac{1}{|N|}(U + V)$$

Let's analyze the expression for U. Note that the cross product

$$N \times \frac{\partial P}{\partial v}$$

is perpendicular to N and therefore lies in the tangent plane of the surface. It is also perpendicular to the partial derivative of P, the surface position, with respect to v. This derivative lies in the tangent plane and indicates the direction in which P changes as the surface parameter v is increased. If the parametric directions are perpendicular (usually they are only approximately perpendicular), adding a perturbation to N along the direction of this cross product would tilt N as if there was an upward slope in the surface along the *u* direction. The partial derivative $\partial F / \partial u$ gives the slope of the bump function in the *u* direction.

This technique looks somewhat frightening, but is fairly easy to implement if you already have the normal vector and the parametric derivatives of P. In the RenderMan shading language, N, dPdu, and dPdv contain these values. The differencing operators *Du* and *Dv* allow you to approximate the parametric derivatives of any expression. So Blinn's method of bump mapping could be implemented using the following shading language code:

```
float F;
point U, V, D;

F = /* fill in some bump function here */

U = Du(F) * (N ^ dPdv);
V = -(Dv(F) * (N ^ dPdu));
D = 1/length(N) * (U + V);
Nf = N + D;
Nf = normalize(faceforward(Nf, I));
```

Then use Nf in the shading model just as you normally would. The resulting surface shading should give the appearance of a pattern of bumps determined by F.

Fortunately, the shading language provides a more easily remembered way to implement bump mapping, and even displacement mapping.

```
float F;
point PP;

F = /* fill in some bump function here */

PP = P + F * normalize(N);
Nf = calculatenormal(PP);
Nf = normalize(faceforward(Nf, I));
```

In this code fragment, a new position PP is computed by moving along the direction of the normal a distance determined by the bump height F. Then the built-in function calculatenormal is used to compute the normal vector of the modified surface PP. calculatenormal(PP) does nothing more than return the cross product of the parametric derivatives of the modified surface:

```
point
calculatenormal(point PP)
{
    return Du(PP) ^ Dv(PP);
}
```

To create actual geometric bumps by displacement mapping, you use very similar shading language code:

```
float F;

F = /* fill in some bump function here */

P = P + F * normalize(N);
N = calculatenormal(P);
```

Instead of creating a new variable PP that represents the bumped surface, this code assigns a new value to the original surface position P. In the shading language this means that the positions of points on the surface are actually moved by the shader to create bumps in the geometry. Similarly, the true normal vector N is recomputed so that it matches the displaced surface properly. I have omitted the last line that computes Nf, because displacement mapping should be done in a separate displacement shader, not in the surface shader.[7]

To get a better understanding of bump mapping, let's add bump-mapped mortar grooves to our brick texture. The first step is to design the shape of the groove profile, that is, the vertical cross section of the bump function. Figure 18 is a diagram of the profile of the bricks and mortar grooves.

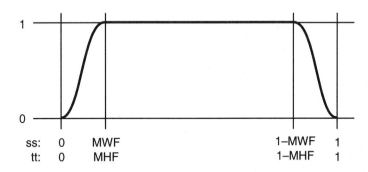

Figure 18.   Brick and groove profile.

---

[7] The PhotoRealistic RenderMan renderer requires you to specify a *displacement bound* that tells the renderer what the maximum value of the bump height or other displacement will be. This is fully explained in the user's manual for the renderer.

In order to realistically render the mortar groove between the bricks, we want the brick shader to compute a procedural bump-mapping function which will be used to adjust the normal vector before shading. To this end, we add the following code to the brick shader, immediately before the last statement (the one that computes `Ci` from the shading model).

```
/* compute bump-mapping function for mortar grooves */
sbump = smoothstep(0,MWF,ss) - smoothstep(1-MWF,1,ss);
tbump = smoothstep(0,MHF,tt) - smoothstep(1-MHF,1,tt);
stbump = sbump * tbump;
```

The first two statements define the bump profile along the *s* and *t* directions independently. The first `smoothstep` call in each statement provides the positive slope of the bump function at the start of the brick, and the last `smoothstep` call in each statement provides the negative slope at the end of the brick. The last statement combines the `sbump` vertical groove and `tbump` horizontal groove to make an overall bump value `stbump`.

```
/* compute shading normal */
Nf = calculatenormal(P + normalize(N) * stbump);
Nf = normalize(faceforward(Nf, I));
Oi = Os;
Ci = Os * Ct * (Ka * ambient() + Kd * diffuse(Nf));
```

Finally, the shading normal `Nf` is computed based on the bump height as described earlier in this section. The shader ends as before by using the texture color `Ct` and bump-mapped normal `Nf` in a diffuse shading model to shade the surface. Figure 19 is an image of the bump-mapped brick texture.

There is a subtle issue hidden in this example. Recall that the shader displaces the surface position by a bump height `stbump` along the normal vector. Since the built-in normal vector `N` was used without modification, the displacement is defined in the shader's `current` space, not in `shader` space. Even though the bump function itself is locked to the surface because it is defined in terms of the `s` and `t` surface texture coordinates, the *height* of the bumps could change if the object is scaled relative to the `world` space. To avoid this problem, I could have transformed the surface point and normal vector into `shader` space, done the displacement there, and transformed the new normal back to `current` space, as follows:

```
point Nsh, Psh;

Psh = transform("shader", P);
Nsh = normalize(ntransform("shader", N));
Nsh = calculatenormal(Psh + Nsh * stbump);
Nf = ntransform("shader", "current", Nsh);
Nf = normalize(faceforward(Nf, I));
```

Figure 19. The bump-mapped brick texture.

Note the use of `ntransform` rather than `transform` to transform normal vectors from one space to another. Normal vectors are transformed differently than points or direction vectors (see pages 216–217 of (Foley *et al.* 1990)). The second `ntransform` uses two space names to request a transformation from `shader` space to `current` space.

Example: Procedural Star Texture

Now let's try to generate a texture pattern that consists of a yellow five-pointed star on a background color `Cs`. The star pattern seems quite difficult until you think about it in polar coordinates. This is an example of how choosing the appropriate feature space makes it much easier to generate a tricky feature.

Figure 20 shows that each point of a five-pointed star is 72 degrees wide. Each half-point (36 degrees) is described by a single edge. The endpoints of the edge are a point at radius `rmin` from the center of the star and another point at radius `rmax` from the center of the star.

```
surface
star(
    uniform float Ka = 1;
    uniform float Kd = 1;
    uniform color starcolor = color (1.0000,0.5161,0.0000);
    uniform float npoints = 5;
    uniform float sctr = 0.5;
    uniform float tctr = 0.5;
    )
{
    point Nf = normalize(faceforward(N, I));
```

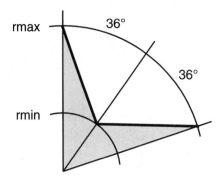

Figure 20.   The geometry of a star.

```
color Ct;
float ss, tt, angle, r, a, in_out;
uniform float rmin = 0.07, rmax = 0.2;
uniform float starangle = 2*PI/npoints;
uniform point p0 = rmax*(cos(0),sin(0),0);
uniform point p1 = rmin*
    (cos(starangle/2),sin(starangle/2),0);
uniform point d0 = p1 - p0;
point d1;

ss = s - sctr; tt = t - tctr;
angle = atan(ss, tt) + PI;
r = sqrt(ss*ss + tt*tt);
```

At this point, the shader has computed polar coordinates relative to the center of the star. These coordinates r and angle act as the feature space for the star.

```
a = mod(angle, starangle)/starangle;

if (a >= 0.5)
    a = 1 - a;
```

Now the shader has computed the coordinates of the sample point (r, a) in a new feature space: the space of one point of the star. a is first set to range from 0 to 1 over each star point. To avoid checking both of the edges that define the "V" shape of the star point, sample points in the upper half of the star point are reflected through the center line of the star point. The new sample point (r, a) is inside the star if and only if the original sample point was inside the star, due to the symmetry of the star point around its center line.

```
d1 = r*(cos(a), sin(a),0) - p0;
in_out = step(0, zcomp(d0^d1));
Ct = mix(Cs, starcolor, in_out);

/* diffuse ("matte") shading model */
Oi = Os;
Ci = Os * Ct * (Ka * ambient() + Kd * diffuse(Nf));
}
```

To test whether (r, a) is inside the star, the shader finds the vectors $d0$ from the tip of the star point to the $rmin$ vertex and $d1$ from the tip of the star point to the sample point. Now I apply a vector algebra trick. The cross product of two vectors is perpendicular to the plane containing the vectors, but there are two directions in which it could point. If the plane of the two vectors is the *(x, y)* plane, the cross product will point along the positive *z*-axis or along the negative *z*-axis. The direction in which it points is determined by whether the first vector is to the left or to the right of the second vector. So we can use the direction of the cross product to decide which side of the star edge $d0$ the sample point is on.

Since the vectors $d0$ and $d1$ have *z* components of zero, the cross product will have *x* and *y* components of zero. Therefore the shader can simply test the sign of zcomp($d0$^$d1$). I use step(0, zcomp($d0$^$d1$)) instead of sign(zcomp ($d0$^$d1$)), because the sign function returns − 1, 0, or 1. I want a binary (0 or 1) answer to the query "Is the sample point inside or outside the star?" This binary answer, in_out, is used to select the texture color Ct using the mix function, and the texture color is used to shade the sample point according to the diffuse shading model.

Figure 21 is an image rendered using the star shader.

Figure 21.   The star texture pattern.

Spectral Synthesis

(Gardner 1984) and (Gardner 1985) demonstrated that procedural methods could generate remarkably complex and natural-looking textures simply by using a combination of sinusoidal component functions of differing frequencies, amplitudes, and phases. The theory of Fourier analysis tells us that functions can be represented as a sum of sinusoidal terms. The Fourier transform takes a function from the temporal or spatial domain, where it is usually defined, into the *frequency domain,* where it is represented by the amplitude and phase of a series of sinusoidal waves [(Bracewell 1986), (Brigham 1988)]. When the series of sinusoidal waves is summed together, it reproduces the original function; this is called the *inverse Fourier transform.*

Spectral synthesis is a rather inefficient implementation of the *inverse* discrete Fourier transform, which takes a function from the frequency domain back to the spatial domain. Given the amplitude and phase for each sinusoidal component, we can sum up the waves to get the desired function. The efficient way to do this is the inverse fast Fourier transform (FFT) algorithm, but that method generates the inverse Fourier transform for a large set of points all at once. In an implicit procedural texture we have to generate the inverse Fourier transform for a single sample point, and the best way to do that seems to be a direct summation of the sine wave components.

In procedural texture generation, we usually don't have all of the frequency domain information needed to reconstruct some function exactly. Instead we want a function with some known characteristics, usually its power spectrum, and we don't care too much about the details of its behavior. It is possible to take a scanned image of a texture, compute its frequency domain representation using a fast Fourier transform, and use the results to determine coefficients for a spectral synthesis procedural texture, but in my experience that approach is rarely taken.

One of Gardner's simplest examples is a 2D texture that can be applied to a flat sky plane to simulate clouds. Here is a RenderMan shader that generates such a texture:

```
#define NTERMS 5

surface
cloudplane(
    color cloudcolor = color (1,1,1);
    )
{
    color Ct;
```

```
point Psh;
float i, amplitude, f;
float x, fx, xfreq, xphase;
float y, fy, yfreq, yphase;
uniform float offset = 0.5;
uniform float xoffset = 13;
uniform float yoffset = 96;

Psh = transform("shader", P);
x = xcomp(Psh) + xoffset;
y = ycomp(Psh) + yoffset;


xphase = 0.9; /* arbitrary */
yphase = 0.7; /* arbitrary */
xfreq = 2 * PI * 0.023;
yfreq = 2 * PI * 0.021;
amplitude = 0.3;
f = 0;
for (i = 0; i < NTERMS; i += 1) {
    fx = amplitude *
        (offset + cos(xfreq * (x + xphase)));
    fy = amplitude *
        (offset + cos(yfreq * (y + yphase)));
    f += fx * fy;
    xphase = PI/2 * 0.9 * cos(yfreq * y);
    yphase = PI/2 * 1.1 * cos(xfreq * x);

    xfreq *= 1.9 + i * 0.1; /* approximately 2 */
    yfreq *= 2.2 - i * 0.08; /* approximately 2 */
    amplitude *= 0.707;
}
f = clamp(f, 0, 1);

Ct = mix(Cs, cloudcolor, f);
Oi = Os;
Ci = Os * Ct;
}
```

This texture is a sum of five components, each of which is a cosine function with a different frequency, amplitude, and phase. The frequencies, amplitudes, and phases are chosen according to rules discovered by Gardner in his experiments. Gardner's technique is somewhat unusual for spectral synthesis in that the phase of each component is coupled to the value of the previous component in the other coordinate (for example, the *x* phase depends on the value of the preceding *y* component).

Making an acceptable cloud texture in this way is a battle to avoid regular patterns in the texture. Natural textures usually don't have periodic patterns that repeat exactly. Spectral synthesis relies on complexity to hide its underlying regularity and periodicity. There are several "magic numbers" strewn throughout this shader in an attempt to prevent regular patterns from appearing in the texture. Fourier spectral synthesis using a finite number of sine waves will always generate a periodic function, but the period can be made quite long so that the periodicity is not obvious to the observer. Figure 22 is an image rendered using the `cloudplane` shader with `Cs` set to a sky-blue color.

What Now?

You could go a long way using just the methods described so far. Some of these techniques can produce rich textures with a lot of varied detail, but even more variety is possible. I haven't yet introduced you to noise, the most popular of all procedural texture primitives. But that will have to wait until after I have revealed some of the seamy (or jaggy!) underside of procedural textures, namely the difficulties of aliasing and antialiasing.

Aliasing and How to Prevent It

Aliasing is a term from the field of signal processing. In computer graphics, aliasing refers to a variety of image flaws and unpleasant artifacts that result from improper use of sampling. The staircase-like "jaggies" that can appear on slanted lines and edges are the most obvious examples of aliasing. The next section pre-

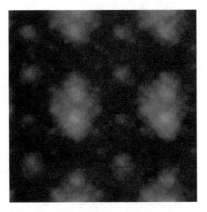

Figure 22.   The cloud plane texture pattern.

sents an informal discussion of basic signal processing concepts, including aliasing. For a more rigorous presentation, I refer you to (Oppenheim 1989), a standard signal processing textbook.

Signal Processing

As shown in Figure 23, a continuous signal can be converted into a discrete form by measuring its value at equally spaced sample points. This is called *sampling*. The original signal can be reconstructed later from the sample values by interpolation.

Sampling and reconstruction are fundamental to computer graphics.[8] Raster images are discrete digital representations of the continuous optical signals that nature delivers to our eyes and to our cameras. Synthetic images are made by sampling of geometric models that are mathematically continuous. Of course, our image signals are two-dimensional. Signal processing originally was developed to deal with the one-dimensional time-varying signals encountered in communications. The field of image processing is in essence the two-dimensional extension of signal processing techniques to deal with images.

Fortunately for computer graphics, the process of sampling and reconstruction is guaranteed to work under certain conditions, namely, when the amount of information in the original signal does not exceed the amount of information that

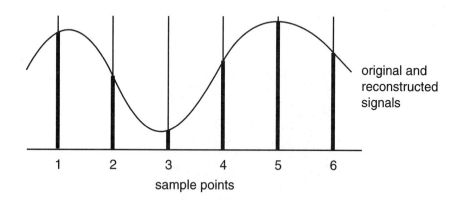

Figure 23.   Sampling and reconstruction.

---

[8] The paper by (Mitchell and Netravali 1988) includes an excellent discussion of the many places in which sampling and reconstruction arise in computer graphics.

can be captured by the samples. This is known as the *sampling theorem*. The amount of information in the original signal is called its *bandwidth*. The amount of information that can be captured by the samples is dependent upon the *sampling rate*, the number of sample points per unit distance.

Unfortunately for computer graphics, the conditions for correct sampling and reconstruction are not always easy to meet, and when they are not met, aliasing occurs.

The theory of Fourier analysis tells us that a function can be represented as a sum of sinusoidal components with various frequencies, phases, and amplitudes. The Fourier transform converts the function from its original form in the "spatial domain" into a set of sinusoidal components in the "frequency domain." A signal with limited bandwidth will have a maximum frequency in its frequency domain representation. If that frequency is less than or equal to one half of the sampling rate, the signal can be correctly sampled and reconstructed without aliasing. Aliasing will occur if the maximum frequency exceeds one half of the sampling rate (this is called the *Nyquist frequency*). The maximum frequency in the reconstructed signal cannot exceed the Nyquist frequency, but the energy contributed to the original signal by the excessively high frequency components does not simply disappear. Instead, it appears in the reconstructed signal as erroneous lower frequency energy, which is called an *alias* of the high frequency energy in the original signal. Figure 24 illustrates this situation. The original signal varies too often to be adequately captured by the samples. Note that the signal reconstructed from the samples is quite different from the original signal.The problem of aliasing can be addressed by changing the sample points to be closer together, or by modifying the original signal to eliminate the high frequencies. If it is possible to increase the sampling rate, that is always beneficial. With more samples, the original signal can be reconstructed more accurately. The Nyquist frequency threshold at which aliasing begins is increased, so the frequencies in the signal might now be below the Nyquist frequency.

Unfortunately, there is always some practical limit on the resolution of an image due to memory space or display limitations, and the sampling rate of an image is proportional to its resolution. It is impossible for an image to show details that are too small to be visible at the resolution of the image. Therefore it is vital to take excessively high frequencies out of the original signal so that they don't show up as aliases and detract from the part of the signal that *can* be seen given the available resolution.

There is another reason why increasing the sampling rate is never a complete solution to the problem of aliasing. Some signals have unlimited bandwidth, so there is no maximum frequency. Sharp changes in the signal, for example, a `step`

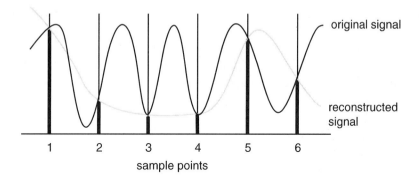

Figure 24.   Aliasing.

function, have frequency components of arbitrarily high frequency. No matter how great the image resolution, increasing the sampling rate to any finite value cannot eliminate aliasing when sampling such signals. This is why sloped lines are jaggy on even the highest resolution displays (unless they have been antialiased properly). Resolution increases alone can make the jaggies smaller, but never can eliminate them.

Since aliasing can't always be solved by increasing the sampling rate, we are forced to figure out how to remove high frequencies from the signal before sampling. The technique is called *low-pass filtering* because it passes low frequency information while eliminating higher frequency information.[9] The visual effect of low-pass filtering is to blur the image. The challenge is to blur the image as little as possible while adequately attenuating the unwanted high frequencies.

It is often difficult to low-pass filter the signal before sampling. A common strategy in computer graphics is to *supersample* or *oversample* the signal, that is, to sample it at a higher rate than the desired output sampling rate. For example, we might choose to sample the signal four times for every output sample. If the signal were reconstructed from these samples, its maximum possible frequency would be four times the Nyquist frequency of the output sampling rate. A discrete low-pass filter can be applied to the supersamples to attenuate frequencies that exceed the Nyquist frequency of the output sampling rate. This method alleviates

[9] In practice, effective antialiasing often requires a lower frequency filtering criterion than the Nyquist frequency because the filtering is imperfect and the reconstruction of the signal from its samples is also imperfect.

aliasing from frequencies between the output Nyquist frequency and the supersample Nyquist frequency. Unfortunately, frequencies higher than the supersample Nyquist frequency will still appear as aliases in the reconstructed signal.

An alternative approach to antialiasing is to supersample the signal at irregularly spaced points. This is called *stochastic sampling* [(Cook *et al.* 1984), (Cook 1986), (Lee *et al.* 1985), (Dippé and Wold 1985)]. The energy from frequencies above the supersample Nyquist frequency appears in the reconstructed signal as random noise rather than as a structured low frequency alias. People are far less likely to notice this noise in the rendered image than they are to notice a low frequency alias pattern. But it is preferable to low-pass filter the signal before sampling, because in that case no noise will be added to the reconstructed signal.

In summary, to produce an antialiased image with a specified resolution, the most effective strategy is to remove excessively high frequencies from the signal by low-pass filtering before sampling. If it isn't possible to filter the signal, the best strategy is to stochastically supersample it at as high a rate as is practical, and apply a discrete low-pass filter to the supersamples. The next section discusses ways to build low-pass filtering into procedural textures to eliminate aliasing artifacts.

You might wonder why aliasing is a problem in procedural textures. Doesn't the renderer do antialiasing? In fact, most renderers have some antialiasing scheme to prevent aliasing artifacts that result from sharp edges in the geometric model. Renderers that support image textures usually include some texture antialiasing in the texture mapping software. But these forms of antialiasing do not solve the aliasing problem for procedural textures.

The best case for "automatic" antialiasing of procedural textures is probably a stochastic ray tracer or, in fact, any renderer that stochastically supersamples the procedural texture. Rendering in this way is likely to be slow because of the many shading samples that are required by the supersampling process. And in the end, stochastic supersampling can only convert aliases into noise, not eliminate the unwanted high frequencies completely. If we can build a better form of antialiasing into the procedural texture, the result will look cleaner and the renderer can be freed of the need to compute expensive supersamples of the procedural texture.

PhotoRealistic RenderMan performs antialiasing by stochastically sampling the scene geometry and filtering the results of the sampling process (Cook *et al.* 1987). The geometry is converted into a mesh of tiny quadrilaterals and shading samples are computed at each vertex of the mesh before the stochastic sampling takes place. The vertices of the mesh are a set of samples of the location of the surface at equally spaced values of the surface parameters *(u, v)*. Many shaders can be viewed as signal-generating functions defined on *(u, v)*. A shader is evaluated at the mesh vertices and the resulting colors and other properties are assigned to the mesh. This is really a sampling of the shader function at a grid of *(u, v)* values and its reconstruction as a colored mesh of quadrilaterals. If the frequency content of the shader exceeds the Nyquist frequency of the mesh vertex *(u, v)* sampling rate, aliases will appear in the mesh colors. The reconstructed mesh color function is resampled by the stochastic sampling of the scene geometry. But once aliases have been introduced during the shader sampling process, they can never be removed by subsequent pixel sampling and filtering.

The separation of shader sampling from pixel sampling in PhotoRealistic RenderMan is advantageous because it permits a lower sampling rate for the shader samples than for the pixel samples. Shader samples are usually much more expensive to evaluate than pixel samples, so it makes sense to evaluate fewer of them. But this increases the need to perform some type of antialiasing in the shader itself; we can't rely on the stochastic supersampling of pixel samples to alleviate aliasing in procedural textures.

When image textures are used in the RenderMan shading language, the antialiasing is automatic. The texture system in the renderer filters the texture image pixels as necessary to attenuate frequencies higher than the Nyquist frequency of the *(u, v)* sampling rate in order to avoid aliasing.[10]

The brick texture from earlier in the chapter provides a concrete example of the aliasing problem. Figure 25 shows how the brick texture looks when the sampling rate is low. Notice that the width of the mortar grooves appears to vary in different parts of the image due to aliasing. This is the original version of the texture, without bump-mapped grooves. Later in the chapter I'll show how to add antialiasing to the brick texture to alleviate the aliases.

Methods of Antialiasing Procedural Textures

By now you should be convinced that some form of antialiasing is necessary in procedural texture functions. In the remainder of this section I will explain various ways to build low-pass filtering into procedural textures: clamping, analytic

---

[10] See [(Feibush *et al.*1980), (Williams 1983), (Crow 1984), (Heckbert 1986a), (Heckbert 1986b)] for detailed descriptions of methods for antialiasing image textures.

Figure 25.   Aliasing in the brick texture.

prefiltering, integrals, and alternative antialiasing methods. Clamping is a special-purpose filtering method that applies only to textures created by spectral synthesis. Analytic prefiltering techniques are ways to compute low-pass filtered values for some of the primitive functions that are used to build procedural textures. One class of analytic prefiltering methods is based on the ability to compute the integral of the texture function over a rectangular region. Finally, I will describe alternatives to low-pass filtering that can be used when proper filtering is not practical.

Some procedural texture primitives are inherently band-limited, that is, they contain only a limited, bounded set of frequencies. `sin` is an obvious example of such a function. The `texture` function and its relatives have built-in filtering, so they are also band-limited. Unfortunately, some common language constructs such as `if` and `step` create sharp changes in value that generate arbitrarily high frequencies. Sharp changes in the shading function must be avoided. `smooth-step` is a smoothed replacement for `step` that can reduce the tendency to alias. Can we simply replace `step` functions with `smoothstep` functions?

The `smoothstep` function has less high frequency energy than `step`, but using a particular `smoothstep` as a fixed replacement for `step` is not an adequate solution. If the shader is tuned for a particular view, the `smoothstep` will alias when the texture is viewed from further away, because the fixed-width `smoothstep` will be too sharp. On the other hand, when the texture is viewed from close up, the `smoothstep` edge is too blurry. A properly antialiased edge should look equally sharp and "non-jaggy" at all scales. The `smoothstep` width must be varied based on the sampling rate.

Determining the Sampling Rate

To do low-pass filtering properly, the procedural texture function must know the sampling rate at which the renderer is sampling the texture. The sampling rate is just the reciprocal of the spacing between adjacent samples in the relevant texture space or feature space. This is called the *sampling interval*. For simple box filtering, the sampling interval is also the usual choice for the width of the box filter.

Obviously, the sampling interval cannot be determined from a single sample in isolation. Earlier parts of this chapter have presented a model of procedural texture in which the implicit texture function simply answers queries about the surface properties at a single sample point. The procedural texture is invoked many times by the renderer to evaluate the texture at different sample points, but each invocation is independent of all of the others.

To determine the sampling rate or sampling interval without changing this model of procedural texture, the renderer must provide some extra information to each invocation of the procedural texture. In the RenderMan shading language, this information is in the form of built-in variables called `du` and `dv` and functions called `Du` and `Dv`. The `du` and `dv` variables give the sampling intervals for the surface parameters *(u, v)*. If the texture is written in terms of *(u, v)*, the filter widths can be taken directly from `du` and `dv`.

In most cases, procedural textures are written in terms of the standard texture coordinates *(s, t)*, which are scaled and translated versions of *(u, v)*, or in terms of texture coordinates computed from the 3D coordinates of the surface point *P* in some space. In these cases, it is harder to determine the sampling interval, and the functions `Du` and `Dv` must be used. `Du(a)` gives an approximation to the derivative of some computed quantity a with respect to the surface parameter *u*. Similarly, `Dv(a)` gives an approximation to the derivative of some computed quantity a with respect to the surface parameter *v*. By multiplying the derivatives by the *(u, v)* sampling intervals, the procedural texture can estimate the sampling interval for a particular computed texture coordinate a. In general, it is not safe to assume that the texture coordinate changes only when *u* changes or only when *v* changes. Changes along both parametric directions have to be considered and combined to get a good estimate, `awidth`, of the sampling interval for a.

```
awidth = abs(Du(a)*du) + abs(Dv(a)*dv);
```

The sum of the absolute values gives an upper bound on the sampling interval; if this estimate is in error, it tends to make the filter too wide so that the result is slightly too blurred. This is safer than making the filter too narrow, which would allow aliasing to occur.

It is desirable for the sampling interval estimate to remain constant or change smoothly. Sudden changes in the sampling interval result in sudden changes in the texture filtering and that can be a noticeable and annoying flaw in itself. Even if the derivatives Du and Dv are accurate and change smoothly, there is no guarantee that the renderer's sampling intervals in *(u, v)* will also behave themselves. Many renderers use some form of adaptive sampling or adaptive subdivision to vary the rate of sampling depending on the apparent amount of detail in the image. In PhotoRealistic RenderMan, adaptive subdivision changes the shader sampling intervals depending on the size of the surface in the image. A surface seen in perspective could have sudden changes in sampling intervals between the nearer and more distant parts of the surface. A renderer that uses adaptive sampling based on some estimate of apparent detail might end up using the values returned by the procedural texture itself to determine the appropriate sampling rates. That would be an interesting situation indeed—one that might make proper low-pass filtering in the texture a very difficult task.

The remedy for cases in which the renderer's sampling interval is varying in an undesirable way is to use some other estimate of the sampling interval, an estimate that is both less accurate and smoother than the one described above. One such trick is to use the distance between the camera and the surface position to control the low-pass filtering:

```
awidth = length(I) * k;
```

The filter width (sampling interval estimate) is proportional to the distance from the camera (length(I)), but some experimentation is needed to get the right scaling factor k.

It is especially tricky to find the right filter width to antialias a bump height function for a bump-mapping texture. Since the bump height affects the normal vector used in shading, specular highlights can appear on the edges of bumps. Specular reflection functions have quite sharp angular falloff, and this sharpness can add additional high frequencies to the color output of the shader that are not in the bump height function. It might not be sufficient to filter the bump height function using the same low-pass filter that would be used for an ordinary texture that changes only the color or opacity. A wider filter probably is needed, but determining just how much wider it should be is a black art.

Clamping

Clamping (Norton *et al.* 1982) is a very direct method of eliminating high frequencies from texture patterns that are generated by spectral synthesis. Since each frequency component is explicitly added to a spectral synthesis texture, it is fairly easy to omit every component whose frequency is greater than the Nyquist frequency.

Let's begin with the following simple spectral synthesis loop, with a texture coordinate s:

```
value = 0;
for (f = MINFREQ; f < MAXFREQ; f *= 2)
    value += sin(2*PI*f*s)/f;
```

The loop begins at a frequency of MINFREQ and ends at a frequency less than MAXFREQ, doubling the frequency on each successive iteration of the loop. The amplitude of each sinusoidal component is the reciprocal of its frequency.

The following version is antialiased using the simplest form of clamping. The sampling interval in s is swidth.

```
value = 0;
cutoff = clamp(0.5/swidth, 0, MAXFREQ);
for (f = MINFREQ; f < cutoff; f *= 2)
    value += sin(2*PI*f*s)/f;
```

In this version the loop stops at a frequency less than cutoff, which is the Nyquist frequency for the sampling rate 1/swidth. In order to avoid "pops," sudden changes in the texture as the sampling rate changes (e.g., as we zoom in toward the textured surface), it is important to fade out each component gradually as the Nyquist frequency approaches the component frequency. The following texture function incorporates this gradual fade-out strategy:

```
value = 0;
cutoff = clamp(0.5/swidth, 0, MAXFREQ);
for (f = MINFREQ; f < 0.5*cutoff; f *= 2)
    value += sin(2*PI*f*s)/f;
fade = clamp(2*(cutoff-f)/cutoff, 0, 1);
value += fade * sin(2*PI*f*s)/f;
```

The loop ends one component earlier than before, and that last component (whose frequency is between 0.5*cutoff and cutoff) is added in after the loop and is scaled by fade. The fade value gradually drops from 1 to 0 as the frequency of the component increases from 0.5*cutoff toward cutoff. This is really a result of changes in swidth and therefore in cutoff, rather than changes in the set of frequency components in the texture pattern.

Note that the time to generate the spectral synthesis texture pattern will increase as the sampling rate increases, that is, as we look more closely at the texture pattern. More and more iterations of the synthesis loop will be executed as the camera approaches the textured surface. The example code incorporates MAXFREQ as a safety measure, but if MAXFREQ is reached, the texture will begin to look ragged when viewed even more closely.

Clamping works very well for spectral synthesis textures created with sine waves. It is hard to imagine a clearer and more effective implementation of low-pass filtering! But when the spectral synthesis uses some primitive that has a richer frequency spectrum of its own, clamping doesn't work as well.

If the primitive contains frequencies higher than its nominal frequency, the low-pass filtering will be imperfect and some high frequency energy will leak into the texture. This can cause aliasing.

Even if the primitive is perfectly band-limited to frequencies lower than its nominal frequency, clamping is imperfect as a means of antialiasing. In this case, clamping will eliminate aliasing, but the character of the texture may change as high frequencies are removed, because each component contains low frequencies that are removed along with the high frequencies.

Analytic Prefiltering

A procedural texture can be filtered explicitly by computing the convolution of the texture function with a filter function. This is difficult in general, but if we choose a simple filter, the technique can be implemented successfully. The simplest filter of all is the box filter; the value of a box filter is simply the average of the input function value over the area of the box filter.

To compute the convolution of a function with a box filter the function must be integrated over the area under the filter. This sounds tough, but it's easy if the function is simple enough. Consider the step function shown in Figure 2. The

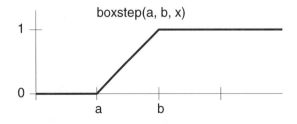

Figure 26.   Box-filtering the step function.

step function is rather ill-behaved because it is discontinuous at its threshold value. Let's apply a box filter extending from x to x+w to the function step(b, x). The result is the box-filtered step function, boxstep(a, b, x), where a = b-w (Figure 26). The value of boxstep is the area under the step function within the filter box. When the entire filter is left of b (that is, x+w ≤ b), the value is 0. When the entire filter is right of b (that is, x ≥ b), the value is 1. But boxstep is "smoother" than the step function; instead of being a sharp, discontinuous transition from 0 to 1 at b, boxstep is a linear ramp from 0 to 1 starting at a and ending at b. The slope of the ramp is 1/w.

The boxstep function can be written as a preprocessor macro in C or the shading language as follows:

```
#define boxstep(a,b,x) clamp(((x)-(a))/((b)-(a)),0,1)
```

Now the step(b, x) can be replaced with boxstep(b-w, b, x). If the filter width w is chosen correctly, the boxstep function should reduce aliasing compared to the step function.

Better Filters

We know how to generate a box-filtered version of the step function. The box filter is far from ideal for antialiasing. A better filter usually results in fewer artifacts or less unnecessary blurring. A better alternative to boxstep is the smooth-step function that was discussed earlier in this chapter. Filtering of the step with a first-order filter (box) gives a second-order function, namely the linear ramp. Filtering of the step with a third-order filter (quadratic) gives a fourth-order function, namely the cubic smoothstep. Using smoothstep to replace step is like filtering with a quadratic filter, which is a better approximation to the ideal *sinc* filter than the box filter is.

The boxstep macro is designed to be plug-compatible with smoothstep. The call boxstep(WHERE-swidth, WHERE, s) can be replaced with the call smoothstep(WHERE-swidth, WHERE, s). This is the filtered version of step(WHERE, s), given a filter extending from s to s+swidth.

Using the smoothstep cubic function as a filtered step is convenient and efficient because it is a standard part of the shading language. However, there are other filters and other filtered steps that are preferable in many applications. In particular, some filters such as the sinc and Catmull-Rom filters have so-called *negative lobes*, which means that the filter values dip below zero at some points. Such filters generally produce sharper texture patterns, although ringing artifacts are sometimes visible. A Catmull-Rom filter can be convolved with a step function (which is equivalent to integrating the filter function) to produce a `catstep` filtered step function that has been used with good results (Sayre 1992).

Integrals and Summed-Area Tables

(Crow 1984) introduced the "summed-area table" method of antialiasing image textures. A summed-area table is an image made from the texture image. As illustrated in Figure 27(a), the pixel value at coordinates (s,t) in the summed-area table is the sum of all of the pixels in the rectangular area $(0{:}s, 0{:}t)$ in the texture image. Of course, the summed-area table might need higher precision pixel values than those of the original texture to store the sums accurately.

   The summed-area table makes it easy to compute the sum of all of the texture image pixels in any axis-aligned rectangular region. Figure 27(b) shows how this is done. The pixel values at the corners of the region A, B, C, D are obtained from the summed-area table (four pixel accesses). The sum over the desired region is then simply $D + A - B - C$. This sum divided by the area of the region is the average value of the texture image over the region. If the region corresponds to the size and position of a box filter in the (s, t) space, the average value from the summed-area table calculation can be used as an antialiased texture value. The cost of the antialiasing is constant regardless of the size of the region covered by the filter, which is very desirable.

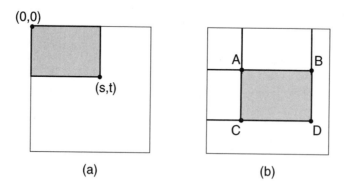

(a)   (b)

Figure 27.   The summed-area table.

The summed-area table is really a table of the integral of the original texture image over various regions of the *(s, t)* space. An analogous antialiasing method for procedural textures is to compute the definite integral of the procedural texture over some range of texture coordinate values, rather than computing the texture value itself. For example, a procedural texture function $f(x)$ on some texture coordinate x might have a known indefinite integral function $F(x)$. If the desired box filter width is w_x, the expression $(F(x) - F(x - w_x))/w_x$ might be used as a filtered alternative to the texture value $f(x)$. Integrals for many of the basic building blocks of procedural textures are easy to compute, but a few are tricky.[11]

Example: Antialiased Brick Texture

As an example of the application of these techniques let's build antialiasing into the brick texture described earlier in this chapter.

The first step is to add the code needed to determine the filter width. The width variables must be added to the list of local variable declarations:

```
float swidth, twidth;
```

To compute the filter widths, I add two lines of code just before the two lines that compute the brick numbers `sbrick` and `tbrick`:

```
swidth = abs(Du(ss)*du) + abs(Dv(ss)*dv);
twidth = abs(Du(tt)*du) + abs(Dv(tt)*dv);
sbrick = floor(ss);    /* which brick? */
tbrick = floor(tt);    /* which brick? */
```

The actual antialiasing is done by replacing the following two lines of the original shader that determine where to change from mortar color to brick color:

```
w = step(MWF,ss) - step(1-MWF,ss);
h = step(MHF,tt) - step(1-MHF,tt);
```

with an antialiased version of the code:

```
w = boxstep(MWF-swidth,MWF,ss)
  - boxstep(1-MWF-swidth,1-MWF,ss);
h = boxstep(MHF-twidth,MHF,tt)
  - boxstep(1-MHF-twidth,1-MHF,tt);
```

---

[11] The `noise` functions described in the section beginning on page 64 are among the tricky ones to integrate.

This is just the same code using `boxstep` instead of `step`. If the texture pattern consisted of a single brick in an infinite field of mortar, this would be sufficient. Unfortunately, more is required in order to handle a periodic pattern like the brick texture. The brick texture depends on a `mod`-like folding of the texture coordinates to convert a single pulse into a periodic sequence of pulses. But a wide filter positioned inside one brick can overlap another brick, a situation that is not properly accounted for in this periodic pulse scheme.

To solve the aliasing problem in a more general way, we can apply the integration technique described in the previous section. The integral of a sequence of square wave pulses is a function that consists of upward-sloping ramps and plateaus. The ramps correspond to the intervals where the pulses have a value of 1 and the plateaus correspond to the intervals where the pulses have a value of 0. In other words the slope of the integral is either 0 or 1, depending on the pulse value. The slope is the derivative of the integral, which is obviously the same as the original function.

The integrals of the periodic pulse functions in the `ss` and `tt` directions are given by the following preprocessor macros:

```
#define frac(x)            mod((x),1)
#define sintegral(ss)      (floor(ss)*(1-2*MWF) + \
                           max(0,frac(ss)-MWF))
#define tintegral(tt)      (floor(tt)*(1-2*MHF) + \
                           max(0,frac(tt)-MHF))
```

These are definite integrals from 0 to `ss` and 0 to `tt`. The `ss` integral consists of the integral of all of the preceding complete pulses (the term involving the `floor` function) plus the contribution of the current partial pulse (the term involving the fractional part of the coordinate).

To compute the antialiased value of the periodic pulse function, the shader must determine the value of the definite integral over the area of the filter. The value of the integral is divided by the area of the filter to get the average value of the periodic pulse function in the filtered region.

```
w = (sintegral(ss+swidth) - sintegral(ss))/swidth;
h = (tintegral(tt+twidth) - tintegral(tt))/twidth;
```

When using this method of antialiasing, you should remove the following lines of code from the shader:

```
ss -= sbrick;
tt -= tbrick;
```

because the `floor` and `mod` operations in the integrals provide the necessary periodicity for the pulse sequence. Forcing `ss` and `tt` to lie in the unit interval interferes with the calculation of the correct integral values.

Figure 28 shows the antialiased version of the brick texture, which should be compared with the original version shown in Figure 25. The widths of the mortar grooves are more consistent in the antialiased version of the texture.

Alternative Antialiasing Methods

Building low-pass filtering into a complicated procedural texture function can be far from easy. In some cases you might be forced to abandon the worthy goal of "proper" filtering and fall back on some alternative strategy that is more practical to implement.

One simple alternative to low-pass filtering is simply to blend between two or more versions of the texture based on some criterion related to sampling rate. For example, as the sampling rate indicates that the samples are getting close to the rate at which the texture begins to alias, you can fade your texture toward a color that is the average color of the texture. This is clearly a hack; the transition between the detailed texture and the average color might be quite obvious, although this is probably better than just letting the texture alias. The transition can be smoothed out by using more than two representations of the texture, and blending between adjacent pairs of textures at the appropriate sampling rates.

Figure 28.   Box-filtered version of the brick texture.

A more sophisticated antialiasing method is to supersample the texture pattern in the procedural texture itself. When the shader is asked to supply the color of a sample point, it will generate several more closely spaced texture samples and combine them in some weighted sum that implements a low-pass filter. As mentioned earlier, supersampling will at least decrease the sampling rate at which aliasing begins. If the positions of the supersamples are jittered stochastically, the aliases will tend to be broken up into noise that might not be objectionable.

Supersampling in the procedural texture can be complicated and expensive, but it might be more efficient than supersampling implemented by the renderer. The procedural texture can limit the amount of code that is executed for each texture sample and therefore do a more lightweight version of supersampling.

Making Noises

To generate irregular procedural textures, we need an irregular primitive function, usually called `noise`. This is a function that is apparently stochastic and will break up the monotony of patterns that would otherwise be too regular. When I use terms like "random" and "stochastic" in this discussion, I almost always mean to say "apparently random" or "pseudorandom." True randomness is unusual in computer science, and as you will see, it is actually undesirable in procedural textures.

I explained the importance of aliasing and antialiasing before discussing irregular patterns because issues related to antialiasing are of key importance in the design of stochastic texture primitives.

The obvious stochastic texture primitive is *white noise*, a source of random numbers, uniformly distributed with no correlation whatsoever between successive numbers. True white noise can be generated by a random physical process, such as thermal noise. Try tuning a television to a channel on which no station is currently broadcasting if you want to see a good approximation to white noise.

A pseudorandom number generator produces a fair approximation to white noise. But is white noise really what we need? Alas, a bit of thought reveals that it is not. White noise is never the same twice. If we generate a texture pattern on the surface of some object, let's say a marble pattern, we certainly will want the pattern to stay the same frame after frame in an animation, or when we look at the object from a variety of camera positions. In fact, we need a function that is apparently random but is a repeatable function of some inputs. Truly random functions don't have inputs. The desired stochastic texture primitive will take texture coordinates as its inputs and will always return the same value given the same texture coordinates.

Luckily it isn't hard to make such a function. Looking into the literature of hashing and pseudorandom number generation, we can find several ways to convert a set of coordinate numbers into some hashed value that can be treated as a pseudorandom number (PRN). Alternatively, the hashed value can be used as an index into a table of previously generated PRNs.

Even this repeatable sort of white noise isn't quite what is needed in a stochastic texture primitive. The repeatable pseudorandom function has an unlimited amount of detail, which is another way of saying that its values at adjacent points are completely independent of one another (uncorrelated). This sounds like what we want, but it proves to be troublesome because of the prevalence of point sampling in computer graphics. If we view an object from a new camera angle, the positions of the sample points at which the texture function is evaluated will change. A good PRN function will change its value markedly if the inputs change even slightly. Consequently the texture will change when the camera is moved, and we don't want that to happen.

Another way to look at this problem is in terms of aliasing. White noise has its energy spread equally over all frequencies, including frequencies much higher than the Nyquist frequency of the shading samples. The sampling rate can never be high enough to capture the details of the white noise.

To keep our procedural textures stable and to keep them from aliasing, we need a stochastic function that is smoother than white noise. The solution is to use a low-pass filtered version of white noise.[12] In the remainder of this chapter, I refer to these filtered noise functions simply as `noise` functions.

The properties of an ideal `noise` function are as follows:

- `noise` is a repeatable pseudorandom function of its inputs.

- `noise` has a known range, namely from –1 to 1.

- `noise` is band-limited, with a maximum frequency of about 1.

- `noise` doesn't exhibit obvious periodicities or regular patterns. Such pseudorandom functions are always periodic, but the period can be made very long and therefore the periodicity is not conspicuous.

- `noise` is *stationary*, that is, its statistical character should be translationally invariant.

- `noise` is *isotropic*, that is, its statistical character should be rotationally invariant.

---

[12] Low-pass filtered noise is sometimes called *pink noise*, but that term is more properly applied to a stochastic function with a $1/f$ power spectrum.

In the remainder of this section, I present a number of implementations of `noise` that meet these criteria to various extents.

Lattice Noises

Lattice noises are the most popular implementations of `noise` for procedural texture applications. They are simple and efficient and have been used with excellent results. Ken Perlin's *Noise* function (Perlin 1985), "the function that launched a thousand textures," is a lattice noise of the gradient variety; an implementation equivalent to Perlin's is described on page 69.[13]

The generation of a lattice noise begins with one or more uniformly distributed PRNs at every point in the texture space whose coordinates are integers. These points form the so-called *integer lattice*. The necessary low-pass filtering of the noise is accomplished by a smooth interpolation between the PRNs. To see why this works, recall that the correct reconstruction of a signal from a set of samples can never contain frequencies higher than the Nyquist frequency of the sample rate. Since the PRNs at the integer lattice points are equally spaced samples of white noise and since reconstruction from samples is a form of interpolation, it is reasonable to expect that the interpolated function will be approximately bandlimited below the Nyquist frequency of the lattice interval. The quality of the resulting `noise` function depends on the nature of the interpolation scheme.

All lattice noises need some way to generate one or more pseudorandom numbers at every lattice point. My `noise` functions use a table of PRNs that is generated the first time `noise` is called. To find the PRNs in the table that are to be used for a particular integer lattice point (`ix`, `iy`, `iz`), I use the following code:

```
#define TABSIZE         256
#define TABMASK         (TABSIZE-1)
#define PERM(x)         perm[(x)&TABMASK]
#define INDEX(ix,iy,iz) PERM((ix)+PERM((iy)+PERM(iz)))
```

The macro INDEX returns an index into an array with TABSIZE entries. The selected entry provides the PRNs needed for the lattice point. Note that TABSIZE must be a power of two so that performing `i&TABMASK` is equivalent to `i%TABSIZE`. As noted on page 28, using `i%TABSIZE` isn't safe, because it will yield a negative result if `i` is negative. Using the bitwise AND operation "&" avoids this problem.

The array perm contains a previously generated random permutation of the integers from zero to TABMASK onto themselves. Feeding sequential integers

---

[13] In case you wish to compare the implementations, note that Ken describes his *Noise* function in detail in Chapter 6.

through the permutation gives back a pseudorandom sequence. This hashing mechanism is used to break up the regular patterns that would result if ix, iy, and iz were simply added together to form an index into the noiseTab table. Here is the perm array that I use:

```
static unsigned char perm[TABSIZE] = {
    225, 155, 210, 108, 175, 199, 221, 144, 203, 116,  70, 213,  69, 158, 33, 252,
      5,  82, 173, 133, 222, 139, 174,  27,   9,  71,  90, 246,  75, 130, 91, 191,
    169, 138,   2, 151, 194, 235,  81,   7,  25, 113, 228, 159, 205, 253,134, 142,
    248,  65, 224, 217,  22, 121, 229,  63,  89, 103,  96, 104, 156,  17,201, 129,
     36,   8, 165, 110, 237, 117, 231,  56, 132, 211, 152,  20, 181, 111,239, 218,
    170, 163,  51, 172, 157,  47,  80, 212, 176, 250,  87,  49,  99, 242,136, 189,
    162, 115,  44,  43, 124,  94, 150,  16, 141, 247,  32,  10, 198, 223,255,  72,
     53, 131,  84,  57, 220, 197,  58,  50, 208,  11, 241,  28,   3, 192, 62, 202,
     18, 215, 153,  24,  76,  41,  15, 179,  39,  46,  55,   6, 128, 167, 23, 188,
    106,  34, 187, 140, 164,  73, 112, 182, 244, 195, 227,  13,  35,  77,196, 185,
     26, 200, 226, 119,  31, 123, 168, 125, 249,  68, 183, 230, 177, 135,160, 180,
     12,   1, 243, 148, 102, 166,  38, 238, 251,  37, 240, 126,  64,  74,161,  40,
    184, 149, 171, 178, 101,  66,  29,  59, 146,  61, 254, 107,  42,  86,154,   4,
    236, 232, 120,  21, 233, 209,  45,  98, 193, 114,  78,  19, 206,  14,118, 127,
     48,  79, 147,  85,  30, 207, 219,  54,  88, 234, 190, 122,  95,  67,143, 109,
    137, 214, 145,  93,  92, 100, 245,   0, 216, 186,  60,  83, 105,  97,204,  52
};
```

I borrowed this hashing technique from Ken Perlin, who uses a similar permutation scheme in his *Noise* function.

(Ward 1991) gives an implementation of a lattice noise in which the lattice PRNs are generated directly by a hashing function rather than by looking in a table of random values.

Value Noise

Given a PRN between –1 and 1 at each lattice point, a noise function can be computed by interpolating among these random values. This is called *value noise*.

I use the following routine to initialize a table of PRNs for value noise:

```
#define RANDMASK     0x7fffffff
#define RANDNBR ((random() & RANDMASK)/(double) RANDMASK)

float valueTab[TABSIZE];

void
valueTabInit(int seed)
{
    float *table = valueTab;
    int i;
```

```
    srandom(seed);
    for(i = 0; i < TABSIZE; i++)
        *table++ = 1. - 2.*RANDNBR;
}
```

Given this table, it is straightforward to generate the PRN for an integer lattice point with coordinates ix, iy, and iz:

```
float
vlattice(int ix, int iy, int iz)
{
    return valueTab[INDEX(ix,iy,iz)];
}
```

The key decision to be made in implementing value noise is how to interpolate among the lattice PRNs. Many different methods have been used, ranging from linear interpolation to a variety of cubic interpolation techniques. Linear interpolation is insufficient for a smooth-looking noise; value noise based on linear interpolation looks "boxy," with obvious lattice cell artifacts. The derivative of a linearly interpolated value is not continuous and the sharp changes are obvious to the eye. It is better to use a cubic interpolation method so both the derivative and the second derivative are continuous. Here is a simple implementation using the cubic Catmull-Rom spline interpolation function shown on page 30:

```
float
vnoise(float x, float y, float z)
{
    int ix, iy, iz;
    int i, j, k;
    float fx, fy, fz;
    float xknots[4], yknots[4], zknots[4];
    static int initialized = 0;

    if (!initialized) {
        valueTabInit(665);
        initialized = 1;
    }

    ix = FLOOR(x);
    fx = x - ix;

    iy = FLOOR(y);
    fy = y - iy;
    iz = FLOOR(z);

    fz = z - iz;
```

```
for (k = -1; k <= 2; k++) {
    for (j = -1; j <= 2; j++) {
        for (i = -1; i <= 2; i++)
            xknots[i+1] = vlattice(ix+i,iy+j,iz+k);
        yknots[j+1] = spline(fx, 4, xknots);
    }
    zknots[k+1] = spline(fy, 4, yknots);
}
return spline(fz, 4, zknots);
}
```

Since this is a cubic Catmull-Rom `spline` function in all three dimensions, the spline has 64 control points, which are the vertices of the 27 lattice cells surrounding the point in question. Obviously, this interpolation can be quite expensive. It might make sense to use a modified version of the `spline` function that is optimized for the special case of four knots and a parameter value that is known to be between 0 and 1.

A graph of a 1D sample of `vnoise` is shown in Figure 29(a) and an image of a 2D slice of the function is shown in Figure 30(a). Figure 31(a) shows its power spectrum. The noise obviously meets the criterion of being band-limited; it has no significant energy at frequencies above 1.

Many other interpolation schemes are possible for value noise. Quadratic and cubic B-splines are among the most popular. These splines don't actually interpolate the lattice PRN values; instead they approximate the values, which may lead to a narrower oscillation range (lower amplitude) for the B-spline noise. The lattice convolution noise discussed on page 74 can be considered a value noise in which the interpolation is done by convolving a filter kernel with the lattice PRN values.

(Lewis 1989) describes the use of *Wiener interpolation* to interpolate lattice PRNs. Lewis claims that Wiener interpolation is efficient and provides a limited amount of control of the `noise` power spectrum.

Gradient Noise

Value noise is the simplest way to generate a low-pass filtered stochastic function. A less obvious method is to generate a pseudorandom gradient vector at each lattice point and then use the gradients to generate the stochastic function. This is called *gradient noise*. The *Noise* function described by (Perlin 1985) and (Perlin and Hoffert 1989) was the first implementation of gradient noise. The RenderMan shading language `noise` function used in the irregular texture examples later in this chapter is a similar implementation of gradient noise.

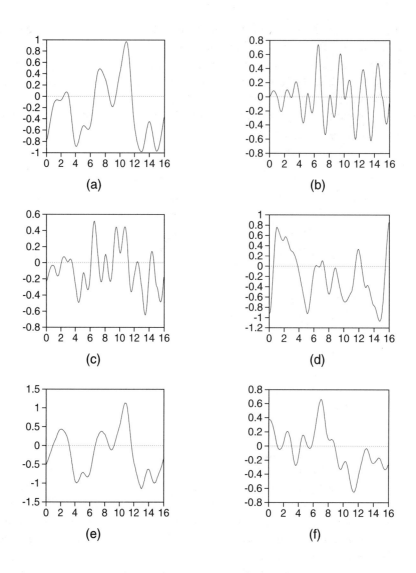

Figure 29.   Graphs of various noises.

The value of a gradient noise is 0 at all of the integer lattice points. The pseudo-random gradients determine its behavior between lattice points. The gradient method uses an interpolation based on the gradients at the eight corners of a single lattice cell, rather than the 64 vertex neighborhood used in the cubic interpolation method described in the previous section.

My implementation of gradient noise uses the following routine to initialize the table of pseudorandom gradient vectors:

```
#include <math.h>

float gradientTab[TABSIZE*3];

void
gradientTabInit(int seed)
{
    float *table = gradientTab;
    float z, r, theta;
    int i;
    srandom(seed);
    for(i = 0; i < TABSIZE; i++) {
        z = 1. - 2.*RANDNBR;
        /* r is radius of x,y circle */
        r = sqrtf(1 - z*z);
        /* theta is angle in (x,y) */
        theta = 2 * M_PI * RANDNBR;
        *table++ = r * cosf(theta);
        *table++ = r * sinf(theta);
        *table++ = z;
    }
}
```

This method of generating the gradient vectors attempts to produce unit vectors uniformly distributed over the unit sphere. It begins by generating a uniformly distributed z coordinate that is the sine of the latitude angle. The cosine of the same latitude angle is the radius r of the circle of constant latitude on the sphere. A second PRN is generated to give the longitude angle theta that determines the x and y components of the gradient.

Perlin's noise implementation uses a different scheme of generating uniformly distributed unit gradients. His method is to generate vectors with components between –1 and 1. Such vectors lie within the cube that bounds the unit sphere. Any vector whose length is greater than 1 lies outside the unit sphere and is discarded. Keeping such vectors would bias the distribution in favor of the directions toward the corners of the cube. These directions have the greatest volume within the cube per solid angle. The remaining vectors are normalized to unit length.

The following routine generates the value of gradient noise for a single integer lattice point with coordinates `ix`, `iy`, and `iz`. The value `glattice` of the gradient noise for an individual lattice point is the dot product of the lattice gradient and the fractional part of the input point relative to the lattice point, given by `fx`, `fy`, and `fz`.

```
float
glattice(int ix, int iy, int iz,
    float fx, float fy, float fz)
{
    float *g = &gradientTab[INDEX(ix,iy,iz)*3];
    return g[0]*fx + g[1]*fy + g[2]*fz;
}
```

Eight `glattice` values are combined using smoothed trilinear interpolation to get the gradient noise value. The linear interpolations are controlled by a `smoothstep`-like function of the fractional parts of the input coordinates.

```
#define LERP(t,x0,x1) ((x0) + (t)*((x1)-(x0)))
#define SMOOTHSTEP(x) ((x)*(x)*(3 - 2*(x)))

float
gnoise(float x, float y, float z)
{
    int ix, iy, iz;
    float fx0, fx1, fy0, fy1, fz0, fz1;
    float wx, wy, wz;
    float vx0, vx1, vy0, vy1, vz0, vz1;

    static int initialized = 0;
    if (!initialized) {
        gradientTabInit(665);
        initialized = 1;
    }
    ix = FLOOR(x);
    fx0 = x - ix;
    fx1 = fx0 - 1;
    wx = SMOOTHSTEP(fx0);
    iy = FLOOR(y);
    fy0 = y - iy;
    fy1 = fy0 - 1;
    wy = SMOOTHSTEP(fy0);

    iz = FLOOR(z);
    fz0 = z - iz;
    fz1 = fz0 - 1;
    wz = SMOOTHSTEP(fz0);

    vx0 = glattice(ix,iy,iz,fx0,fy0,fz0);
    vx1 = glattice(ix+1,iy,iz,fx1,fy0,fz0);
    vy0 = LERP(wx, vx0, vx1);
    vx0 = glattice(ix,iy+1,iz,fx0,fy1,fz0);
    vx1 = glattice(ix+1,iy+1,iz,fx1,fy1,fz0);
    vy1 = LERP(wx, vx0, vx1);
```

```
      vz0 = LERP(wy, vy0, vy1);
      vx0 = glattice(ix,iy,iz+1,fx0,fy0,fz1);
      vx1 = glattice(ix+1,iy,iz+1,fx1,fy0,fz1);
      vy0 = LERP(wx, vx0, vx1);
      vx0 = glattice(ix,iy+1,iz+1,fx0,fy1,fz1);
      vx1 = glattice(ix+1,iy+1,iz+1,fx1,fy1,fz1);
      vy1 = LERP(wx, vx0, vx1);
      vz1 = LERP(wy, vy0, vy1);

      return LERP(wz, vz0, vz1);
}
```

Figure 29(b) is a graph of a 1D sample of a gradient noise, and Figure 30(b) shows a 2D slice of the noise. Figure 31(b) shows its power spectrum. Most of the energy of gradient noise comes from frequencies between 0.3 and 0.7. There is more high-frequency energy in gradient noise than in value noise, and less low-frequency energy. These are consequences of the fact that gradient noise has zeros at each lattice point and therefore is forced to change direction at least once per lattice step.

Value-Gradient Noise

A gradient noise is zero at all of the integer lattice points. This regular pattern of zeros sometimes results in a noticeable grid pattern in the gradient noise. To avoid this problem without losing the spectral advantages of gradient noise, we might try to combine the value and gradient methods to produce a value-gradient noise function.

One implementation of value-gradient noise is simple: it is just a weighted sum of a value noise and a gradient noise. Some computation can be saved by combining the two functions and sharing common code such as the INDEX calculation from the integer coordinates, and the calculation of ix, fx0, and so on. Figure 29(c) shows a graph of a weighted sum of our Catmull-Rom vnoise and the gradient gnoise, and Figure 30(c) shows a 2D slice of it. Figure 31(c) shows the power spectrum of this function. The slice image looks a little less regular than the gradient noise slice, presumably because the regular pattern of zero crossings has been eliminated.

A more sophisticated form of value-gradient noise is based on cubic Hermite interpolation. The Hermite spline is specified by its value and tangent at each of its endpoints. For a value-gradient noise, the tangents of the spline can be taken from the gradients. (Ward 1991) gives the source code for just such a value-gradient noise. (Ward claims that this is Perlin's noise function, but don't be fooled— it is quite different.) Figure29(d) and Figure 30(d) show Ward's Hermite noise function, and Figure 31(d) shows its power spectrum.[14] The power spectrum is remarkably regular, rising quite smoothly from DC to a frequency of about 0.2

---

[14] In testing Ward's noise function, I actually used the source code that is provided on the diskette that accompanies *Graphics Gems IV*. This code is different from the code in Ward's article. It appears that the code on the diskette is a newer version with an improved interpolation method.

and then falling smoothly down to 0 at a frequency of 1. Since the power is spread quite widely over the spectrum and the dominant frequencies are quite low, this noise function could be difficult to use in spectral synthesis.

Lattice Convolution Noise

One objection to the lattice noises is that they often exhibit axis-aligned artifacts. Many of the artifacts can be traced to the anisotropic nature of the interpolation schemes used to blend the lattice PRN values. What I call *lattice convolution noise* is an attempt to avoid anisotropy by using a discrete convolution technique to do the interpolation. The PRNs at the lattice points are treated as the values of random impulses and are convolved with a radially symmetrical filter. In the implementation that follows, I use a Catmull-Rom filter with negative lobes and a radius of 2. This means that any lattice point within a distance of two units from the input point must be considered in doing the convolution. The convolution is simply the sum of the product of each lattice point PRN value times the value of the filter function based on the distance of the input point from the lattice point.

Here is an implementation of lattice convolution noise. It begins with the filter function `catrom2`, which takes a squared distance as input to avoid the need to compute square roots. The first time `catrom2` is called, it computes a table of Catmull-Rom filter values as a function of squared distances. Subsequent calls simply look up values from this table.

```
static float
catrom2(float d)
{
#define SAMPRATE 100 /* table entries per unit distance */
#define NENTRIES (4*SAMPRATE+1)
    float x;
    int i;
    static float table[NENTRIES];
    static int initialized = 0;

    if (d >= 4)
        return 0;

    if (!initialized) {
    for (i = 0; i < NENTRIES; i++) {
            x = i/(float) SAMPRATE;
            x = sqrtf(x);
            if (x < 1)
                table[i] = 0.5 * (2+x*x*(-5+x*3));
                else
                table[i] = 0.5 * (4+x*(-8+x*(5-x)));
```

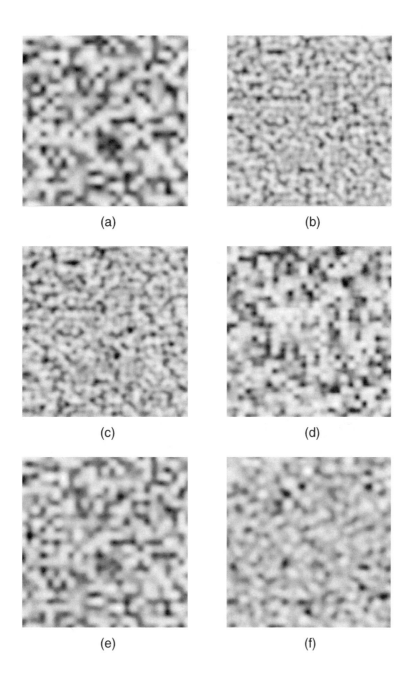

Figure 30.   Slices of various noises.

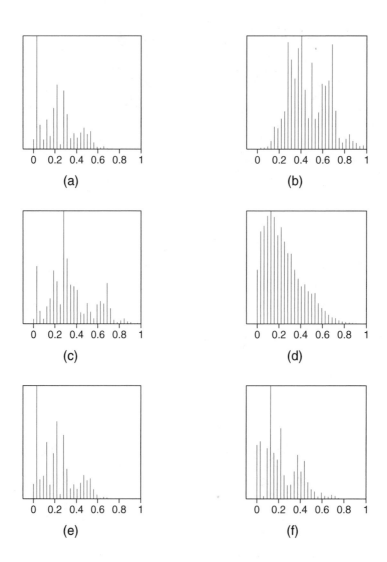

Figure 31.   The power spectra of various noises.

```
        }
        initialized = 1;
    }

    d = d*SAMPRATE + 0.5;
    i = FLOOR(d);
    if (i >= NENTRIES)
    return 0;
    return table[i];
}

float
vcnoise(float x, float y, float z)
{
    int ix, iy, iz;
    int i, j, k;
    float fx, fy, fz;
    float dx, dy, dz;
    float sum = 0;
    static int initialized = 0;

    if (!initialized) {
        valueTabInit(665);
        initialized = 1;
    }

    ix = FLOOR(x);
    fx = x - ix;

    iy = FLOOR(y);
    fy = y - iy;

    iz = FLOOR(z);
    fz = z - iz;

    for (k = -1; k <= 2; k++) {
        dz = k - fz;
        dz = dz*dz;
        for (j = -1; j <= 2; j++) {
            dy = j - fy;
            dy = dy*dy;
            for (i = -1; i <= 2; i++){
                dx = i - fx;
                dx = dx*dx;
                sum += vlattice(ix+i,iy+j,iz+k)
                    * catrom2(dx + dy + dz);
            }
        }
    }
    return sum;
}
```

Figure 29(e) shows a graph of lattice convolution noise, and 30(e) shows a 2D slice of it. Figure 31(e) shows its power spectrum. The spectrum is not unlike that of the other value noises. Perhaps this is not surprising since it is essentially a different value noise interpolation scheme. Some degree of spectral control should be possible by modifying the filter shape.

Sparse Convolution Noise

Various ways have been developed to generate noise functions that aren't based on a regular lattice of PRNs. One such method is called *sparse convolution* [(Lewis 1984), (Lewis 1989)]. A similar technique called *spot noise* is described by (van Wijk 1991).

Sparse convolution involves building up a noise function by convolving a filter function with a collection of randomly located random impulses (a Poisson process). The scattered random impulses are considered to be a "sparse" form of white noise, hence the term "sparse convolution." The low-pass filtering of the white noise is accomplished by the filter function. The power spectrum of the sparse convolution noise is derived from the power spectrum of the filter kernel, so some control of the noise spectrum is possible by modifying the filter.

Sparse convolution is essentially the same as the lattice convolution noise algorithm described in the previous section, except that the PRN impulse values are located at pseudorandom points in each lattice cell. Here is my implementation of sparse convolution noise, based on Lewis' description. The filter used is the Catmull-Rom filter described in the previous section. Three randomly placed impulses are generated in each lattice cell. A neighborhood of 125 lattice cells must be considered for each call to the noise function because a randomly placed impulse two cells away could have a non-zero filter value within the current cell. As a result this noise function is computationally expensive.

```
static float impulseTab[TABSIZE*4];

static void
impulseTabInit(int seed)
{
    int i;
    float *f = impulseTab;

    srandom(seed); /* Set random number generator seed. */
    for (i = 0; i < TABSIZE; i++) {
        *f++ = RANDNBR;
        *f++ = RANDNBR;
        *f++ = RANDNBR;
        *f++ = 1. - 2.*RANDNBR;
    }
}
```

```
#define NEXT(h) (((h)+1) & TABMASK)
#define NIMPULSES 3

float
scnoise(float x, float y, float z)
{
    static int initialized;
    float *fp;
    int i, j, k, h, n;
    int ix, iy, iz;

    float sum = 0;
    float fx, fy, fz, dx, dy, dz, distsq;

    /* Initialize the random impulse table if necessary. */
    if (!initialized) {
        impulseTabInit(665);
    initialized = 1;
    }

    ix = FLOOR(x); fx = x - ix;
    iy = FLOOR(y); fy = y - iy;
    iz = FLOOR(z); fz = z - iz;

    /* Perform the sparse convolution. */
    for (i = -2; i <= 2; i++) {
        for (j = -2; j <= 2; j++) {
            for (k = -2; k <= 2; k++) {
                /* Compute voxel hash code. */
                h = INDEX(ix+i,iy+j,iz+k);

                for (n = NIMPULSES; n > 0; n--, h = NEXT(h)) {
                    /* Convolve filter and impulse. */
                    fp = &impulseTab[h*4];
                    dx = fx - (i + *fp++);
                    dy = fy - (j + *fp++);
                    dz = fz - (k + *fp++);
                    distsq = dx*dx + dy*dy + dz*dz;
                    sum += catrom2(distsq) * *fp;
                }
            }
        }
    }

    return sum / NIMPULSES;
}
```

Figure 29(f) and Figure 30(f) show one- and two-dimensional sections of this sparse convolution noise. Figure 31(f) shows the power spectrum. The spectrum is similar to that of the other value noises, but the slice image appears to exhibit fewer grid-like patterns than the other noises.

Explicit Noise Algorithms

Some interesting methods of generating noises and random fractals aren't convenient for implicit procedural texture synthesis. These methods generate a large batch of noise values all at once in an explicit fashion. To use them in an implicit procedural texture during rendering, the noise values would have to be generated before rendering and stored in a table or texture image. A good example of such a technique is the midpoint displacement method (Fournier *et al.* 1982). A related method of random successive additions is described by (Saupe 1992). (Lewis 1987) and (Lewis 1986) describe a generalization of such methods to give greater spectral control. (Saupe 1989) shows that such methods can be more than an order of magnitude less expensive than implicit evaluation methods.

Fourier Spectral Synthesis

Another explicit method of noise generation is to generate a pseudorandom discrete frequency spectrum in which the power at a given frequency has a probability distribution that is correct for the desired noise. Then a discrete inverse Fourier transform (usually an inverse FFT) is performed on the frequency domain representation to get a spatial domain representation of the noise. (Saupe 1988) and (Voss 1988) describe this technique.

In the description of spectral synthesis textures on page 46, the example showed that many hand-picked "random" coefficients were used to generate the cloud texture. We could think of this as the generation of a random frequency domain representation and the evaluation of the corresponding spatial function using a spectral sum to implement the discrete inverse Fourier transform. This is far less efficient than an FFT algorithm, but has the advantage that it can be evaluated a point at a time for use in an implicit procedural texture. The complexity and apparent irregularity of Gardner's textures is less surprising when they are seen to be noise-like stochastic functions in disguise!

Direct Fourier synthesis of noise is much slower than the lattice noises described earlier, and is probably not practical for procedural texture synthesis. Lattice convolution and sparse convolution are other methods that offer the promise of detailed spectral control of the noise. There is a tradeoff between trying to generate all desired spectral characteristics in a single call to `noise` by using an expensive method such as Fourier synthesis or sparse convolution versus the strategy of building up spectral characteristics using a weighted sum of several cheaper gradient noise components.

Gradient noise seems to be a good primitive function to use for building up spectral sums of noise components, as demonstrated in the next section. When combining multiple `noise` calls to build up a more complex stochastic function, the gradient noise gives better control of the spectrum of the complex function because gradient noise has little low-frequency energy compared to the other noise functions; its dominant frequencies are near one-half.

Generating Irregular Patterns

Armed with the stochastic primitive functions from the preceding section, we can now begin to generate irregular texture patterns. Since most natural materials are somewhat irregular and nonuniform, irregular texture patterns are valuable in simulating these materials. Even man-made materials are usually irregular as a result of shipping damage, weathering, manufacturing errors, and so on. This section describes several ways to generate irregular patterns and gives examples in the form of RenderMan shaders.

The `noise` function in the RenderMan shading language is an implementation the lattice gradient noise described in the preceding section. The RenderMan function is unusual in that it has been scaled and offset to range from 0 to 1, instead of the more usual range of -1 to 1. This means that the RenderMan `noise` function has a value of 0.5 at the integer lattice points. Since the -1 to 1 range is sometimes more convenient, I often use the following signed noise macro in my RenderMan shaders:

```
#define snoise(x) (2*noise(x) - 1)
```

The RenderMan `noise` function can be called with a 1D, 2D, or 3D input point, and will return a 1D or 3D result (a number, a point, or a color).

Most textures need several calls to `noise` to independently determine a variety of stochastic properties of the material. Remember that repeated calls to `noise` with the same inputs will give the same results. Different results can be obtained by shifting to another position in the noise space. It is common to call

```
noise(Q * frequency + offset)
```

where `offset` is of the same type as the coordinate `Q` and has the effect of establishing a new noise space with a different origin point.

There are two approaches to generating time-dependent textures. Textures that move or flow can be produced by moving through the 3D noise space over time:

```
f = noise(P - time*D);
```

can be used to make the texture appear to move in the direction and rate given by the vector D as time advances. Textures that simply evolve without a clear flow direction are harder to create. A 4D noise function is the best approach. Unfortunately, RenderMan's noise function is limited to three dimensions.[15] In some cases the spatial part of the noise can be limited to one or two dimensions, so that the remaining dimension can be used to represent time.

The shading language function `pnoise` is a relative of `noise`. The noise space can be wrapped back on itself to achieve periodic effects. For example, if a period of 30 is specified, `pnoise` will give the same value for input $x + 30$ as for input x. The oscillation frequency of the noise value is unaffected. Here are some typical `pnoise` calls:

```
pnoise(f, 30);
pnoise(s, t, 30, 30)
pnoise(P, point (10, 15, 30))
```

It is easy to implement `pnoise` by making the choice of lattice PRNs periodic with the desired period. This technique is limited to integer periods.

When generating procedural textures using any of the `noise` functions described in this chapter, it is important to develop an understanding of the range and distribution of the noise values. It can be difficult to normalize a stochastic function so that the range is exactly -1 to 1. Furthermore, most of the noise values tend to lie close to 0 with only occasional excursions to the limits of the range. A histogram of the distribution of the noise values is a useful tool in designing functions based on `noise`.

Spectral Synthesis

The discussion on page 46 showed how complex regular functions with arbitrary spectral content can be built up from sine waves. As mentioned earlier, the many pseudo-random coefficients in Gardner's spectral synthesis textures might be viewed as a way of generating a noise function by the inverse Fourier transform method. Spectral synthesis using a noise function as the primitive gives an even richer stochastic content to the texture and reduces the need to use random coefficients for each component. When a stochastic function with a particular power spectrum is needed, spectral synthesis based on `noise` can be used to generate it.

---

[15] We use a 4D quadratic B-spline value noise in our in-house animation system with good results. It pays to keep the order of the interpolation fairly low for 4D noise to avoid having too many lattice point terms in the interpolation.

Several calls to `noise` can be combined to build up a stochastic spectral function with a particular frequency/power spectrum. A noise loop of the form

```
value = 0;
for (f = MINFREQ; f < MAXFREQ; f *= 2)
    value += amplitude * snoise(Q * f);
```

with amplitude varying as a function of frequency `f` will build up a value with a desired spectrum. `Q` is the sample point in some texture space.

Perlin's famous `turbulence` function is essentially a stochastic function of this type with a "fractal" power spectrum, that is, a power spectrum in which amplitude is proportional to $1/f$.

```
float
fractalsum(point Q)
{
    float value = 0;
    for (f = MINFREQ; f < MAXFREQ; f *= 2)
      value += snoise(Q * f)/f;
    return value;
}
```

This isn't quite the same as `turbulence`, however. Derivative discontinuities are added to the `turbulence` function by using the absolute value of the `snoise` function. Taking the absolute value folds the function at each zero crossing, making the function undifferentiable at these points. The number of peaks in the function is doubled, since the troughs become peaks.

```
float
turbulence(point Q)
{
    float value = 0;
    for (f = MINFREQ; f < MAXFREQ; f *= 2)
        value += abs(snoise(Q * f))/f;
        return value;
}
```

Figure 32 shows a slice of the `fractalsum` function on the left and a slice of the `turbulence` function on the right. The `fractalsum` is very cloud-like in appearance, while `turbulence` is apparently lumpier, with sharper changes in value. Figure 33(a) shows the power spectrum of the `fractalsum` function and Figure 33(b) shows the power spectrum of the `turbulence` function. As one might expect, the power spectra show a rapid decline in energy as the frequency increases; this is a direct result of the $1/f$ amplitude scaling in the spectral synthesis loops.

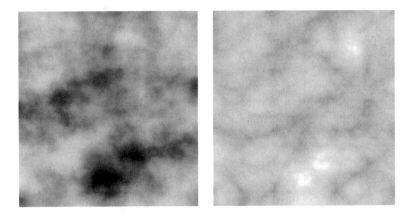

Figure 32.   Slices of fractalsum and turbulence functions.

Spectral synthesis loops should use clamping to prevent aliasing. Here is a version of `turbulence` with clamping included:

```
float
turbulence(point Q)
{
     float value = 0;
     float cutoff = clamp(0.5/Qwidth, 0, MAXFREQ);
     float fade;

     for (f = MINFREQ; f < 0.5*cutoff; f *= 2)
         value += abs(snoise(Q * f))/f;
     fade = clamp(2*(cutoff-f)/cutoff, 0, 1);
     value += fade * abs(snoise(Q * f))/f;
     return value;
}
```

Marble is a material that is typically simulated using an irregular texture based on spectral synthesis. The following marble shader uses a four-octave spectral synthesis based on `noise` to build up a stochastic value called marble that is similar to `fractalsum`. It is best to use a solid texture space for a `marble` texture, so that the texture can be used to shade curved surfaces as if they were carved out of a solid block of marble. This is accomplished by using the 3D surface point as the argument to the `noise` calls.

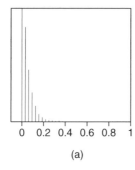
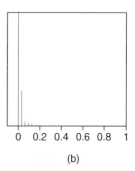

(a)   (b)

Figure 33.   Power spectra of fractalsum and turbulence functions.

```
#define PALE_BLUE           color (0.25, 0.25, 0.35)
#define MEDIUM_BLUE         color (0.10, 0.10, 0.30)
#define DARK_BLUE           color (0.05, 0.05, 0.26)
#define DARKER_BLUE         color (0.03, 0.03, 0.20)
#define NNOISE              4

color
marble_color(float m)
{
    return color spline(
        clamp(2*m + .75, 0, 1),
        PALE_BLUE, PALE_BLUE,
        MEDIUM_BLUE, MEDIUM_BLUE, MEDIUM_BLUE,
        PALE_BLUE, PALE_BLUE,
        DARK_BLUE, DARK_BLUE,
        DARKER_BLUE, DARKER_BLUE,
        PALE_BLUE, DARKER_BLUE);
}
surface
blue_marble(
    uniform float Ka = 1;
    uniform float Kd = 0.8;
    uniform float Ks = 0.2;
    uniform float texturescale = 2.5;
    uniform float roughness = 0.1;
```

```
    )
{
    color Ct;
    point NN;
    point PP;
    float i, f, marble;

    NN = normalize(faceforward(N, I));
    PP = transform("shader", P) * texturescale;

    marble = 0; f = 1;
    for (i = 0; i < NNOISE; i += 1) {
        marble += snoise(PP * f)/f;
        f *= 2.17;
    }
    Ct = marble_color(marble);

    Ci = Os * (Ct * (Ka * ambient() + Kd * diffuse(NN))
        + Ks * specular(NN, normalize(-I), roughness));
}
```

The function `marble_color` maps the floating-point number marble into a color using a color spline. Figure 34 shows an example of the marble texture.

The spectral synthesis loop in this shader has no clamping control to avoid aliasing. If the texture is viewed from far away, aliasing artifacts will appear.

Note that the frequency multiplier in the spectral synthesis loop is *2.17* instead of exactly *2*. This is usually better because it prevents the alignment of the lattice points of successive `snoise` components, and that tends to reduce lattice artifacts. In Chapter 3, Steve Worley describes another way to reduce lattice artifacts: randomly rotating the texture spaces of the different components.

Figure 34.   Blue marble texture.

Changing the frequency multiplier from *2* to some other value (like 2.17) affects the average size of gaps or *lacunae* in the texture pattern. In the fractal literature, this property of the texture is called *lacunarity* (Mandelbrot 1982). The scaling of the amplitude of successive components affects the *fractal dimension* of the texture. The $1/f$ amplitude scaling used here gives a $1/f^2$ scaling of the power spectrum, since power spectral density is proportional to amplitude squared. This results in an approximation to fractional Brownian motion (fBm) (Saupe 1992).

Perturbed Regular Patterns

Purely stochastic patterns tend to have an amorphous character. Often the goal is a more structured pattern with some appearance of regularity. The usual approach is to start with a regular pattern and add noise to it in order to make it look more interesting and more natural.

For example, the brick texture described on page 36 is unrealistically regular, as if the bricklayer were inhumanly precise. To add some variety to the texture, `noise` can be used to modify the relative positions of the bricks in the different rows. The following is the code from the original shader that calculates which brick contains the sample point.

```
sbrick = floor(ss); /* which brick? */
tbrick = floor(tt); /* which brick? */
ss -= sbrick;
tt -= tbrick;
```

To perturb the ss location of the bricks, I rewrite this code as follows:

```
tbrick = floor(tt); /* which brick? */
ss += 0.1 * snoise(tbrick+0.5);
    sbrick = floor(ss); /* which brick? */
    ss -= sbrick;
    tt -= tbrick;
```

There are a few subtle points to note here. The call to `snoise` uses `tbrick` rather than `tt` so that the noise value is constant over the entire brick. Otherwise, the stochastic offset would vary over the height of the brick and make the vertical edges of the brick wavy. Of course, I had to reorder the calculation of `sbrick` and `tbrick` so that `sbrick` can depend on `tbrick`. The value of the perturbation will change *suddenly* as `tbrick` jumps from one integer to the next. That's okay in this case, because the perturbation affects only the horizontal position of a row of bricks, and changes only in the middle of the mortar groove between the rows.

Since `snoise` is a gradient noise that is zero at all integer points, the perturbation always would be zero if the shader used `snoise(tbrick)`. Instead, it uses `snoise(tbrick+0.5)` to sample the value of the noise halfway between the integer points, where it should have an interesting value.

The `0.1` multiplier on the `snoise` simply controls the size of the irregularity added to the texture. It can be adjusted as desired.

A more realistic version of this brick texture would incorporate some noise-based variations in the color of the bricks and mortar as well as a small stochastic bump-mapping of the normal to simulate roughness of the bricks. It is easy to keep layering more stochastic effects onto a texture pattern to increase its realism or visual appeal. But it is important to begin with a simple version of the basic pattern and get that texture working reliably before attempting to add details and irregularity.

Perturbed Image Textures

Another valuable trick is to use a stochastic function to modify the texture coordinates used to access an image texture. This is very easy to do. For example, the simple texture access

```
Ct = texture("example.tx", s, t);
```

using the built-in texture coordinates `s` and `t` can be replaced with the following:

```
point Psh;
float ss, tt;

Psh = transform("shader", P);
ss = s + 0.2 * snoise(Psh);
tt = t + 0.2 * snoise(Psh+(1.5,6.7,3.4));
Ct = texture("example.tx", ss, tt);
```

In this example, `snoise` based on the 3D surface position in "shader" space is used to modify the texture coordinates slightly. In Figure 35 the image on the left shows the original image texture and the image on the right is a texture produced by perturbing the image texture with the code above.

Random Placement Patterns

A random placement pattern is a texture pattern that consists of a number of regular or irregular subpatterns or "bombs" that are dropped in random positions and

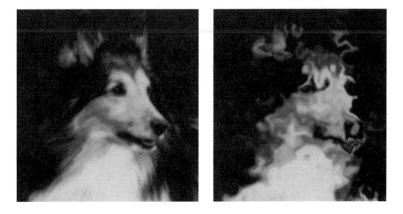

Figure 35.   Perturbing an image texture.

orientations to form the texture. This bombing technique (Schacter and Ahuja 1979) was originally used in an explicit form to generate image textures before rendering. With some difficulty, it can be used in an implicit texture function during rendering.

The most obvious implementation is to store the positions of bombs in a table and to search the table for each sample point. This is rather inefficient and is especially hard to implement in the RenderMan shading language since the language has no tables or arrays. With a little ingenuity, we can devise a method of bombing that uses only `noise` to determine the bomb positions relevant to a sample point. The texture space is divided up into a grid of square cells, with a bomb located at a random position within each cell.

In the following example shader, the bomb is the star pattern created by the procedural texture on page 43.

```
#define NCELLS 10
#define CELLSIZE (1/NCELLS)
#define snoise(s,t)    (2*noise((s),(t))-1)

surface
wallpaper(
    uniform float Ka = 1;
    uniform float Kd = 1;
    uniform color starcolor = color (1.0000,0.5161,0.0000);
    uniform float npoints = 5;
    )
{
    color Ct;
    point Nf;
```

```
float ss, tt, angle, r, a, in_out;
float sctr, tctr, scell, tcell;
uniform float rmin = 0.01, rmax = 0.03;
uniform float starangle = 2*PI/npoints;
uniform point p0 = rmax*(cos(0),sin(0),0);
uniform point p1 = rmin*
    (cos(starangle/2),sin(starangle/2),0);
uniform point d0 = p1 - p0;
point d1;

scell = floor(s*NCELLS);
tcell = floor(t*NCELLS);
sctr = CELLSIZE * (scell + 0.5
     + 0.6 * snoise(scell+0.5, tcell+0.5));
tctr = CELLSIZE * (tcell + 0.5
     + 0.6 * snoise(scell+3.5, tcell+8.5));
ss = s - sctr;
tt = t - tctr;

angle = atan(ss, tt) + PI;
r = sqrt(ss*ss + tt*tt);
a = mod(angle, starangle)/starangle;

if (a >= 0.5)
    a = 1 - a;
d1 = r*(cos(a), sin(a),0) - p0;
in_out = step(0, zcomp(d0^d1));
Ct = mix(Cs, starcolor, in_out);

/* "matte" reflection model */
Nf = normalize(faceforward(N, I));
Oi = Os;
Ci = Os * Ct * (Ka * ambient() + Kd * diffuse(Nf));
}
```

A couple of improvements can be made to this procedural texture. The requirement to have exactly one star in each cell makes the pattern quite regular. A separate noise value for each cell could be tested to see whether the cell should contain a star.

If a star is so far from the center of a cell that it protrudes outside the cell, this shader will clip off the part of the star that is outside the cell. This is a consequence of the fact that a given star is "noticed" only by sample points that lie inside the star's cell. The shader can be modified to perform the same shading tests for the eight cells that surround the cell containing the sample point. Stars that crossed over the cell edge will then be rendered correctly. The tests can be done by a pair of nested for loops that iterate over − 1, 0, and 1. The nested loops generate nine different values for the cell coordinate pair (scell, tcell). The star in each cell is tested against the sample point.

```
scellctr = floor(s*NCELLS);
tcellctr = floor(t*NCELLS);
in_out = 0;

for (i = -1; i <= 1; i += 1) {
    for (j = -1; j <= 1; j += 1) {
        scell = scellctr + i;
        tcell = tcellctr + j;
        if (noise(3*scell-9.5,7*tcell+7.5) < 0.55) {
            sctr = CELLSIZE * (scell + 0.5
                   + 0.6 * snoise(scell+0.5, tcell+0.5));
            tctr = CELLSIZE * (tcell + 0.5
                   + 0.6 * snoise(scell+3.5, tcell+8.5));
            ss = s - sctr;
            tt = t - tctr;

            angle = atan(ss, tt) + PI;
            r = sqrt(ss*ss + tt*tt);
            a = mod(angle, starangle)/starangle;

            if (a >= 0.5)
                a = 1 - a;
            d1 = r*(cos(a), sin(a),0) - p0;
            in_out += step(0, zcomp(d0^d1));
        }
    }
}
Ct = mix(Cs, starcolor, step(0.5, in_out));
```

The first `noise` call is used to decide whether or not to put a star in the cell. Note that the value of `in_out` can now be as high as 9. The additional `step` call in the last line converts it back to a 0 to 1 range so that the `mix` will work properly. Of course, the `step` functions in the wallpaper shader should be `smoothstep` calls with appropriate filter widths to prevent jaggy edges on the stars. Figure 36 shows the star wallpaper pattern generated by the shader.

The wallpaper texture in Pixar's film *Knickknack* (Color Plate 2.1) is a more elaborate example of a procedural texture based on bombing.

Note that the bomb subpattern used for a random placement texture doesn't have to be a procedural texture like the star. An image texture can be used instead, so that you can bomb with faces rather than stars.

RenderMan Esoterica

I have chosen to talk about several items of arcane RenderMan lore here at the end of the chapter where it won't disturb the main discussion. Those of you who

Figure 36. Random-placement wallpaper texture.

have no interest in using the PhotoRealistic RenderMan renderer can comfortably move on to the next chapter without fear of missing anything. Those of you who write RenderMan shaders should find it rewarding to read the next few pages carefully.

Point and Area Operators

Most RenderMan shading language operators are *point* operations in the sense that they look at a single point sample of the shading process. They can be evaluated at a single point in isolation. A few operations are *area* operations; in Photorealistic RenderMan, they are implemented by looking at adjacent point samples of the shading process.

This is a subtle and important aspect of the computational model embodied in the shading language. If you think in terms of writing a C subroutine that is called once for every shading sample, you will be puzzled by various bugs and artifacts that appear in your shaders.

The `texture` function and its siblings `environment`, `shadow`, and `bump` are area operations because they look at the differences between the texture coordinates of adjacent shading samples to determine the sampling rate for filtering.

When using these operations in conjunction with conditional statements, be careful to compute the texture coordinates used in the `texture` calls at all sample points, not just at the ones where texture is used. For example, the following code won't work reliably:

```
if (u+v < 0.5) {
    ss = u;
    tt = v;
    Ct = texture("example.tx", ss, tt);
} else
    Ct = color (1,0,0);
```

This looks perfectly reasonable, but it will fail along the seam between the textured area and the red area. It will fail because the `texture` call will look at the values of `ss` and `tt` at adjacent sample points, some of which are in the red zone and have undefined rubbish values in `ss` and `tt`. A safer version of this shader is:

```
ss = u;
tt = v;
if (u+v < 0.5)
    Ct = texture("example.tx", ss, tt);
else
    Ct = color (1,0,0);
```

Notice that it is fine to put the `texture` call inside the conditional, as long as the texture coordinate values are computed everywhere.

Another class of puzzling bugs stems from the fact that PhotoRealistic RenderMan is working with a small group of shading samples at any given time. The samples are organized into a rectangular grid of quadrilaterals in (u, v) parameter space. The quadrilaterals are called *micropolygons*. The strategy of looking at adjacent shading samples to evaluate area operations begins to break down for samples at the edges of the grid. A lot of cleverness was applied to figure out what to do in such cases, so everything usually works just fine. But it is possible to write shaders that will exhibit bugs on the shading samples at the edges of the sample grid. One way to create problems is to use higher-order derivatives. For example, `Du(Du(ss))` is likely to behave oddly at the edge of a grid. The normal vectors that are computed by `calculatenormal` are also suspect along the edges of the grid.

Filter Position

Each shading sample in PhotoRealistic RenderMan can be used to determine the color of an entire micropolygon. Alternatively, the micropolygons can be Gouraud shaded using the colors of all four corners (if the smooth shading interpolation option is turned on). In the case where the micropolygons are entirely one color, that color is taken from the shading sample at the corner with the lowest (u, v) coordinates. It is important to know this when positioning the antialiasing filter. If a box filter is used, it should cover the micropolygon. That means that a shading sample at (u_0, v_0) should filter over the micropolygon defined by $(u_0 : u_0+du, v_0 : v_0+dv)$. You already might have noticed that in my shaders I position the filters so that they extend from the texture coordinate value s to the value $s + swidth$ instead of the more obvious positioning from $s - swidth / 2$ to $s + swidth / 2$ with s at the center. This is appropriate for the constant shading interpolation mode.

The built-in image texture functions shift their filter positions based on the shading interpolation mode. Unfortunately, there is no way to test the interpolation mode in the shading language, so procedural texture patterns can't shift their filters in the same way. This makes it hard to do the "right" thing, and, moreover, it creates the possibility of odd discrepancies between image textures and procedural textures if the shading interpolation mode is changed. Using only smooth shading interpolation isn't ideal, because it is inefficient and it tends to make textures somewhat blurrier. The best advice seems to be to keep micropolygons small and use the constant shading interpolation mode.

Micropolygon Tiling Direction

Two adjacent surface patches can share a common edge that is precisely the same curve but has different parameter directions in the two patches. This happens when the control points of the curves are the same but are listed in the opposite order in the two patches. When this happens, procedural textures on the two patches can have a discontinuity at the seam between the patches. This can happen even with a solid texture defined on 3D points rather than surface parameters!

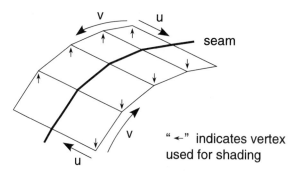

Figure 37. **Tiling direction discrepancy in a texture.**

The culprit here is the use of a shading sample from one corner of a micropolygon to determine the shading of the micropolygon. If the two surfaces are parameterized oppositely to one another, micropolygons along the seam will be shaded using the samples at opposite corners in the two surfaces. This can create a noticeable shift in the texture pattern along the seam. Figure 37 illustrates this situation.

This bug won't affect image textures since they are filtered properly over the area of the micropolygon. Antialiased procedural textures with properly positioned filters should enjoy the same protection. But the bug can appear even in shaders without textures, because the shading normals come from different surface points along the seam. There is an obvious sudden jump in the normals from one side of the seam to the other. Doing a "null bump-mapping" operation `N = calculatenormal(P)` tends to eliminate this problem because it recomputes the normals to be those of the micropolygons themselves instead of the normals of the original surfaces. If the surfaces were smooth across the seam, these micropolygons are aligned with one another and have similar normals.

The best solution is to make sure that abutting surfaces have the same parameter directions whenever possible.

Seams in Cylindrical Projections

When a periodic texture pattern is wrapped around a cylinder using the surface parameters (u,v) or the standard texture coordinates (s, t), everything works out because micropolygons never cross the seam of the cylinder where $u = 0$ is adjacent to $u = 1$. Sometimes a shader computes texture coordinates using a cylindrical or spherical projection of 3D points. In this case, a micropolygon can certainly span the seam in the cylindrical or spherical projection where the longitude angles wrap from 360 degrees back to zero degrees. The danger is that antialiasing filter width calculations will be based on the computed texture coordinates. If the coordinate at one shading sample is 0.99 and the coordinate at the next shading sample has wrapped back to 0.01, the filter width estimate might be 0.98 (`abs(0.01- 0.99)`) instead of the correct value of *0.02*. This will certainly cause problems for the built-in `texture` operation and probably for an antialiased procedural texture too.

The solution to the problem is to watch for filter width estimates that seem unreasonable. If the texture coordinate is supposed to go from 0 to 1 in one circuit around the object, then a filter width estimate greater than one-half is suspect, because that would mean that the micropolygon extends from one side of the object to the other. This could actually happen if the micropolygon is right at the center of the projection, but in that case the shader is likely to break down anyway because the projection has a singularity at its center. If the filter width seems to be too large, the smaller texture coordinate should be incremented by 1, so that the sample at 0.99 is followed by a sample at 1.01. The width will then be correctly estimated as 0.02. If the image texture or procedural texture is periodic, it should yield the same value for 1.01 as it would for 0.01, so the texture itself will not change, just the filter width estimate.

Bear in mind that there is no guarantee that the computed texture coordinate increases when u or v increases. Therefore, it is usually incorrect to assume that a decrease in the texture coordinate indicates that the micropolygon crosses the projection seam.

Conclusion

As with any complex and sophisticated tool, PhotoRealistic RenderMan has quirks and subtleties that can yield unexpected results when you push the envelope. Most of these idiosyncrasies can be avoided if you are aware of them. That will leave you free to tap the enormous potential of procedural textures implemented as RenderMan shaders.

Practical Methods for Texture Design 3

Steven Worley

Introduction

This entire book is primarily about texturing: different ways to use a mathematical formula to decide how to color the surface of an object. This chapter talks about aspects of texturing from a practical point of view, especially in dealing with texture controls (parameters) users manipulate. This chapter shares many topics with the previous one by Darwyn Peachey, but from a different point of view.

I have written over 150 algorithmic surface textures (mostly for commercial use by other animators), and after a while you definitely get a feel for the design of the algorithms, as well as a toolbox full of utilities and ideas which make writing the textures easier and the final surface quality higher. Several recurring themes and tricks occur over and over (such as mapping a computed value into a color lookup table, or adding a bump-mapping effect to a color texture), and these topics form the basis of this chapter.

Toolbox Functions

After building a large library of textures, it has become clear that many new textures are just variants of each other—new ways to organize a set of stock routines together. Building blocks such as fractal noise functions, color mapping methods, and bump mapping definitions occur in nearly every texture! This section discusses these common elements since their ubiquitous use immediately makes them important.

The Art of Noise

Fractal noise is, without question, the most important element currently used in procedural texturing. I won't discuss the basic implementation of the fractal noise function here, since each of the other four sections of this book discusses it in some detail (this alone is evidence to its importance in procedural texturing). Instead I'll discuss some enhancements and modifications to the basic noise algorithm, mostly to produce higher quality and easier to use noise.

The biggest problem with the "plain" fractal noise algorithm is artifacts. The basic routine interpolates over a cubic lattice, and you'll be able to *see* that lattice on your surface especially if you are using a small number of summed scales. Purists will also note that the basic Perlin noise isn't very isotropic, since diagonal directions have a longer distance gap between sample points than the points along the coordinate directions.

A good way to hide this artifacting is to rotate each summed scale to a random orientation. Since the lattices of the different scales won't line up, the artifacts will at least be uncorrelated and a lot less noticeable. I do this by rotating each scale with a random, precomputed rotation matrix. If you want to return derivatives for each scale (for bump mapping), you'll have to post-multiply the vector result from each scale with the appropriate inverse rotation matrix (which is the transpose of the original rotation matrix) before you add them.

I made these matrices by generating random rotation matrices and taking only those that point inside a single octant of a sphere. Since a 90-degree rotation (or 180 or 270) will still let the lattices match up, a single octant is the most rotation that is necessary.[1] Keeping the rotations confined within one octant also helps you check that there are not two similar rotations for different scales. (Remember this is a one-time precompute: you can manually sort through about 10 of these to make sure the matrices are all reasonably different.) To test what octant a rotation matrix maps to, just pump the vector (1 0 0) through the matrix and look for a vector with all positive components. You can generate the rotation matrices using the algorithm(s) in *Graphics Gems III* by Ken Shoemake and Jim Arvo. Figure 1 shows two examples of matrices that might be used.

This rotation trick is most useful when bump mapping, since the differentiation of the noise value clearly exposes the lattice artifacts: there are sharp discontinuities of the second derivatives along the lattice lines. When you differentiate for bump mapping, these second derivatives become discontinuous *first* derivatives and are easily visible.

---

[1] Note that these are full 3D rotations, not 2D, but you know what I mean.

Rotation Matrix   Inverse

$$\begin{pmatrix} 0.98860 & -0.07651 & -0.12967 \\ 0.07958 & 0.99665 & 0.01871 \\ 0.12780 & -0.02881 & 0.99138 \end{pmatrix} \quad \begin{pmatrix} 0.98860 & 0.07958 & 0.12780 \\ -0.07651 & 0.99665 & -0.02881 \\ -0.12967 & 0.01871 & 0.99138 \end{pmatrix}$$

$$\begin{pmatrix} 0.85450 & 0.46227 & -0.23691 \\ 0.48691 & -0.55396 & 0.67530 \\ 0.18093 & -0.69240 & -0.69845 \end{pmatrix} \quad \begin{pmatrix} 0.85450 & 0.48691 & 0.18093 \\ 0.46227 & -0.55396 & -0.69240 \\ -0.23691 & 0.67530 & -0.69845 \end{pmatrix}$$

Figure 1.   Two random rotation matrices (and inverses).

Another strategy to help hide noise artifacts is to choose the lacunarity (the ratio between the sizes of successive scales) intelligently. A natural lacunarity to use is 0.5, but *don't use this.* It's better to use a value with a lot of digits (like 0.485743 or 0.527473), which will give you the same effective ratio. A ratio of exactly 0.5 will make the different scales "register" closely (the next smaller scale repeats exactly twice on top of the larger scale), so artifacts can appear periodically. This periodicity is broken by using a number that's not a simple ratio.

Don't overlook enhancements or variants on the fractal noise algorithm. Extending the noise interpolation to four-dimensional space is particularly useful, as this allows you to make time-animated fractal noise. Another interesting variation I've used is to replace the random gradient and values of each noise "cell" with a lookup table of a function such as a sine wave. This lets you use your fractal noise machinery (and all the textures that have been designed to use it) with different patterns. Fractal noise is not sacred; its usefulness should actually *encourage* you to experiment with its definition.

Color Mappings

Looking in our toolbox of common routines, the continual use of mappings makes this topic very important to discuss. Most textures use a paradigm that computes a value such as fractal noise and then uses this value to decide what color to apply to your object. In simpler textures this added color is always of a single shade, and the noise value is used to determine some "strength" from 0 to 1, which is used to determine how much to crossfade the original surface color with the applied texture color.

This mapping allows the user quite a bit of control over the applied color, and its simplicity makes it both easy to implement and easy for the user to control even with raw numeric values as inputs. One mapping method I have used with great success defines four "transition" values. These transition values control the position and shape of a certain mapping function that turns the fractal noise (or other function) value into an output value from 0 to 1. Figure 2 shows the shape of this function. Two transitions, labeled T1 and T2, are each defined by a beginning value and and ending value. By setting the different levels where these transitions occur, a large variety of mappings can be made from gradients to step functions to more complex "bandpass" shapes.

The implementation of such a mapping is trivial. The mapping is worth discussing mostly because this method is so useful in practice, since it is easy for users to manipulate even numerically. A more sophisticated mapping method is much more general: color splines.

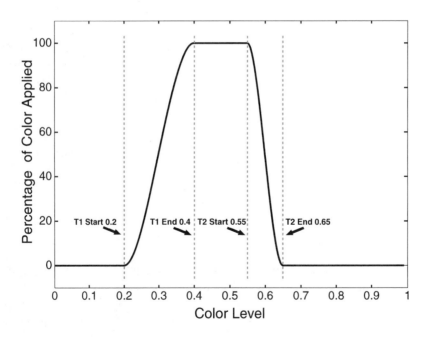

Figure 2. A mapping defined by four user values.

A color spline is simply an arbitrary mapping of an input value to an output color.[2] Often this mapping consists of a piecewise continuous interpolation between color values using a spline. Any number of spline knots (and node colors) can be defined, so the method is truly arbitrary. In practice, color splines are very effective and produce excellent color mappings, but they require more sophistication to compute. Even worse, it becomes very difficult for a user to control or manipulate an arbitrary spline mapping method without a good graphical interface; columns of color values and knot positions aren't easily visualizable.

Bump Mapping Methods

The most important element of *impressive* textures is the use of coordinated bump mapping. Changing the surface normal can result in the most useful textures since the object's surface *structure* appears changed. Instead of just painting some colors onto the object, you can actually add gouged-out depressions, ridges, or bumps. I've found that nearly any texture can have bump mapping added to it! Feedback from users shows that the added bump mapping is perhaps the most useful "extra" ability that a texture can have.

It's usually not even hard to figure out how to add the bump mapping. If you have a function that maps a scalar field to a value (like a color mapped fractal noise value, or a perturbed sine for marble veins), you can take the derivative of the scalar function in all three directions $(x, y, z,)$ add these values to the surface normal, then renormalize it. You should also add a parameter for users to control the apparent height of the bump. This is just multiplied to the derivative before the addition so the user can turn off the bump mapping by using a zero value, or make the bump "go the other way" by using a negative value.

In the case of geometric figures (say a hexagon mesh, or even plain checkerboard), there's not really a function to take the derivative of. In this case, I like making a "ridge," which is basically a line that follows along the exterior boundary of the figure at a fixed (user-defined) distance inside the boundary. This ridge basically makes a bevel around the outside rim of the figure, allowing the user to make the figure look raised or depressed into the surface. Figure 3 shows an example of how a simple bevel makes a flat pattern appear three dimensional.

---

[2] You might recognize that the word "color" throughout this chapter (and book) is always used loosely. Most object surface attributes can be controlled through textures, and while the object's diffuse reflection color is the most often modified value, any of the other surface attributes are controllable using the exact same methods. It's just a lot easier to say "color" than "surface attributes specified by some vector that you can modify with your texture interface."

Figure 3.   A ridged hexagon mesh.

But a simple triangular bevel is awfully plain. It would be great to give the user more control over the shape of this outer rim to make a variety of shapes, from a boxy groove to a circular caulk bead. In the case of a checkerboard, a user might make a concave rounded depression, which would make the squares look like they were surrounded by mortared joints.

I tried several ideas to give the user control over the shapes of these ridges, but one has turned out to be the most useful. You don't want to have too many parameters for the user to juggle, but you still want to give them enough control to make a variety of joints. I've found that a combination of just four parameters works very well in defining a variety of bevel shapes.

The first parameter is the ridge width. What is the total width of the seam or bevel? In many (most!) cases this bevel is going to be butted up against another seam, so you might want to halve the number internally. (An example of this is a checkerboard: every tile is next to its neighbor. It's easier for the user to think about the total width of the joint instead of the width of the part of the joint in just one square.)

The second parameter is what I call the "plateau width." This is a distance along the outside of the ridge that isn't affected. This allows users to make joints that have a flat part in the middle of a seam, sort of a valley between the cliff walls that are formed by the bevel. This plateau obviously must be less than the total width of the bevel.

The last two parameters control the *shape* of the bevel. If you think of the ridge as being a fancy step function (it starts low, ends high, and does something in between), you want to be able to define that transition by a straight line, a smooth S curve, or anything in between. I've found that using a smooth cubic curve over the transition allows the users to define most useful shapes by setting just two numbers, the slopes of the curve at the start and end of the transition. Slopes of 0.0 would make a smooth blending with the rest of the surface, and if both slopes were 1.0 the transition would be a classic straight line bevel. This is best shown in the following figure, which also shows how the plateau is used.

The ridges shown are just examples, since there's really a continuum of curves that can be made. The slopes could even be continuously changed over time to animate the bevel morphing its shape.

These slope controls are obviously useful for making different ridge profiles, but how do you actually convert the parameters into numbers that can be used for bump mapping? The best way is to use the simple Hermite blending curves. Hermite curves are a simple type of spline, defined by a cubic polynomial over a range from 0 to 1. A cubic polynomial is very convenient since it's cheap to compute and has four degrees of freedom to control its shape. We can completely define this cubic curve by setting the starting and ending values and slopes.

Bottom Slope	Top Slope	Plateau?	Ridge Shape
1.0	1.0	Yes	
0.0	0.0	Yes	
0.0	1.0	Yes	
-1.0	-1.0	Yes	
0.0	0.0	No	

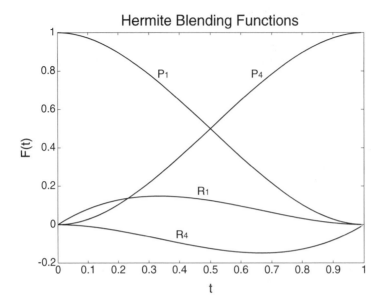

This is perfect for us, since our ridge is basically a smooth curve that starts at a low height (0) and ends up high (1). We have the user specify the starting and ending slopes, defining the curve's last two degrees of freedom. The slope of this curve controls the amount of bump added to the surface normal. We'll parameterize the width of the bevel from 0 to 1 to make using the Hermite spline easy.

Computer Graphics: Principles and Practice by Foley has a good general chapter on splines, and Hermite curves are discussed on pages 483–488. Basically, if we have these four values (start and end heights, start and end slopes) we can construct the cubic polynomial by adding together weighted copies of the four Hermite "blending functions." The sum, *F(t)*, is the unique cubic polynomial that satisfies the four constraints.

These blending functions are called P_1, P_4, R_1, and R_4, and represent the values of *F (0)*, *F (1)*, *F'(0)*, and *F'(1)*, respectively.

$$
\begin{aligned}
P_1 &= 2t^3 - 3t^2 + 1 \\
P_4 &= -2t^3 + 3t^2 \\
R_1 &= t^3 - 2t^2 + t \\
R_4 &= t^3 - t^2 \\
P'_1 &= 6t^2 - 6t \\
P'_4 &= -6t^2 + 6t \\
R'_1 &= 3t^2 - 4t + 1 \\
R'_4 &= 3t^2 - 2t
\end{aligned}
$$

In the case of the ridge, the start and end values will always be fixed to 0 and 1 respectively. The user supplies the two slopes (call them s_b and s_t). The curve that represents our ridge shape is therefore $P_1 + s_b R_1 + s_t R_4$. The derivative of the curve at the hit point is $P'_1(t) + s_b R'_1(t) + s_t R'_4(t)$. This tells us the slope of our ridge at the hit point: the weight we use when adding to the surface normal.

So, explicitly, the "Ridge" algorithm is

1. Decide if the hit point lies within the bevel width. You'll need to come up with a measure of how close a hit point is to the "edge" of the figure.

2. If the hit is outside the bevel width or inside the plateau width, exit. The surface is flat at this location.

3. Set N_{add} equal to the normal vector perpendicular to the bevel. (This is the vector that points from the hit point toward the closest edge). For example, on a checkerboard, if the hit point is on a bevel on the right (+ X) side of a square, the normal would be (1,0,0), and the bevel on the bottom (−Y) of the square would have a normal of (0,− 1,0).

4. Set t to the normalized (dimensionless) distance along the slope. (If the hit point was d units from the edge, $t = 1.0—(d—$Plateau Width) /(Ridge Width–Plateau Width.)

5. Compute s, the slope of the cubic curve at the hit point. This is $P'_1(t) + s_b R'_1(t) + s_t R'_4(t)$, where s_b and s_t are user parameters.

6. Weight N_{add} by sA and add it to the hit point's surface normal. A is yet another user parameter, controlling the amplitude of the bump effect.

7. Renormalize the surface normal.

This is actually pretty easy to implement. The hardest part is probably determining the distance to the edge of a figure like a hexagon.

Note that this kind of bump mapping doesn't have to be restricted to geometric figures! It's easy to add to 3D scalar field functions, too. This lets you use something like fractal noise to make weird squiggly canyons, or raise marble veins out of the surface of a stone. In this case the t variable is usually set by a high and low value defined by the user. The derivative of the field provides the N_{add} vector.

The User Interface

Writing an algorithm that makes an interesting surface is only half the battle! One of the overlooked aspects of texture design is defining the user-accessible parameters. Even when an environment has a fancy GUI for manipulating the texture, the user is usually faced with setting a whole bunch of parameters with vague labels. The usability of your textures can be dramatically increased by using some thought and planning during your implementation. This is especially true when designing the interface that you or users will use to control the texture. This interface often is not a fancy previewer, but simply a set of parameter values. Even then careful parameter design can make the texture significantly easier to use.

Parameter Ranges

It might seem obvious, but the user should be provided with suggestions for acceptable ranges for each parameter. Some ranges are easy enough to define, like colors or a percentage level. But, since all interesting textures seem to use adhoc code that even the programmer doesn't quite understand, there are always going to be mystery constants that the user has to play with to get different effects. It's awfully inelegant to have a parameter named "Squiggliness" which only makes useful patterns when it is between 55 and 107.[3]

One way to help the user control vague parameters like this is to *remap* a parameter's range. If "Squiggliness" is just a mystery constant (which happens to be interesting over that 55–107 range), it's silly to expect users to enter these weird values. If you find that a parameter like this has one particular range of usability, you can use a linear transformation to remap the range: the user would enter a number from 0 to 1 for "squiggliness," not a value in the nonintuitive internal range. The new range of values provide the exact same amount of control as before, but at least the user knows that values like 0.3 or 0.9 might be interesting to try. (They can also experiment and try –0.2 or 1.1, of course, but they'll understand if the result isn't useful.) The remapped range then serves as an indirect guide to selecting *useful* parameter settings.

Remapping linear ranges like this is easy, especially when you're remapping from 0 to 1. Since the transformation is linear, it's just a multiply and an addition. If x is between 0 and 1, you can map to the values from L and H by the simple formula $L + x(H-L)$.

This does *not* mean that you should make all parameters map to a 0–1 range! RGB colors are often easiest to enter as three 0–255 values. The width of a check in a checkerboard texture should be measured in the coordinate system's units. Common sense should be your guide.

---

[3] This may seem like a contrived example, but veteran texture authors know it's not. Mystery constants seem to be an integral, recurring aspect of texture design.

Color Table Equalization

Color splines were discussed on page 101. Fractal noise textures in particular work well with this mapping method. However, while it is very easy to say "just feed the fractal noise value into a lookup table," how is this table designed? Obviously it depends on whether you're making a texture that will be manipulated with a fancy GUI or one that is a subroutine the user has specified with raw parameter values. In practice, it usually boils down to the latter, since the GUI is just a front end for setting numeric parameters.

The biggest problem *users* find with setting color splines or levels is the fact that it is hard to know how much effect their color choices will have. This is critically true for renderers that can't quickly preview textures interactively. I've found that the biggest obstacle to users in setting color levels is that they do not know how much impact their choices will have on the rendered surface. Say that the users can define a color scheme where fractal noise below the value of − 0.5 is black, a value above 0.5 is white, and in between values are a smooth gray transition. The problem is that the users have no idea how much of their object is going to be colored! Is the surface going to be dominated by huge patches of black and white, with narrow gray transitions in between? Or will it be gray values everywhere which never quite get to solid black or white?

Of course, the user can experiment and try to find the right levels to start and end color applications, but it is frustrating to have such an arbitrary, nonlinear scale! It is even worse, since if you change the number of noise octaves added onto the fractal sum, the scale changes again! If you think about it, it would be *much* easier if the users could deal with constant *percentage* levels and not weird, unknown ranges. Thus, a user could set the "lower" 20% of the noise to map to black, the "upper" 20% to white, and the remaining 60% to a gray gradient. This way the user has some idea how large each color range will be on the surface.

Thus there are two steps to making the noise levels "behave." First, they need to be normalized so that the amplitude ratio between scales and the total number of scales don't make the noise ranges change too much. The second part consists of making a table to map these values to percentages. The second step is really just a histogram equalization or a cumulative probability function.

The normalization step is pretty easy. Ideally, you want the fractal noise, no matter how many scales or what scale size or ratio you use, to return a value over the same range. You can do this adequately well by dividing the final sum by the square root of the sum of the squares of all the amplitudes of the scales. For those who don't want to parse that last sentence:

$$F(x) = \frac{\sum_{i=0}^{n-1} a^i N\left(\dfrac{x}{Ls^i}\right)}{\sqrt{\sum_{i=0}^{n-1} \left(a^i\right)^2}}$$

where

F Normalized fractal noise value
L Largest scale size
s Size ratio between successive scales (usually around 0.5)
a Amplitude ratio between successive scales (usually around 0.5)
n Number of scales added (usually between 3 and 10)
x Hit location (a vector)

This normalization makes it a lot nicer when you are tweaking textures: the relative amounts of colors or size of the bumps won't be affected when you change the scale or amplitude ratio or number of summed scales.

The equalization step is a little more involved. The values of fractal noise will fall into a range, probably within -2 to 2, with most values around 0. It looks a lot like a normal distribution except the tails die out quickly. The histogram shown in Figure 4 shows the distribution of 10,000 sample values of fractal noise. In practice, more samples should be used, but with this number the slight random errors are visible to remind you this is an empirical measurement, not an analytic one.

The histogram is very interesting, but we're really looking for a way to map the user's percentage level to a noise value. If, for example, 10% of all noise values fell below -0.9, we'd know to map 10% to that -0.9 value. Zero percent would map to the very lowest noise value, and 100% would map to the very highest. This is a *cumulative* function and is used in probability and statistics quite often. Luckily the way to explicitly measure this relation empirically is straightforward.

First, store many random values of fractal noise in an array. Computing 25,000 samples is probably sufficient, but more is even better. (This is a one-time computation, so speed doesn't matter.) Sort the values into an ascending array. If you plotted the sorted array, you'd get a curve similar to the normalization plot shown in Figure 5. This is now a lookup table! For example, if you used 100,000 samples, the 50,000th number in the sorted array would correspond to the 50% level: half of the noise values would be less than the value stored in this location in the sorted array. (It's the median!) The 10,000th number corresponds to the 10% level, since 10% of the 100,000 values are less than this value.

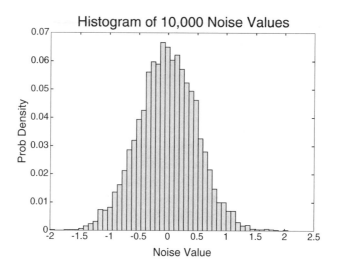

Figure 4.

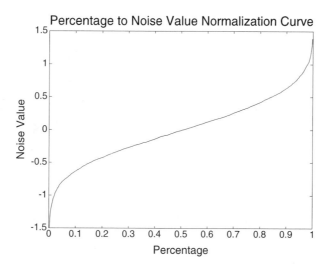

Figure 5.

You obviously don't need to store 100,000 lookup values in your texture code! You can store perhaps just eleven equally spaced samples and linearly interpolate between them: a 15% level would be computed by averaging the 10% and 20% levels. If you don't care about a little extra RAM usage, using 1000 values is probably a fine enough "grain" that you don't even need to bother interpolating.

Adding the translation from user parameter values (probably expressed in a 0 to 1 fractional value) to a noise value is easy enough, probably done as a first step and stored in a static variable. If you have a fancy GUI it can even be done as a preprocess as soon as the user has set the levels.

I cannot stress how useful this equalization is to users. They can actually plan out the coverage of different colors fairly accurately the first time. If they want a sky 20% covered with clouds, they immediately know the settings to use. This convenience is no real computational load, but for the user it makes using the texture a *lot* more intuitive.

Exploring the Parameter Domain

Even as author of a texture algorithm, determining appropriate parameter values to use can be very difficult. A mere texture *user* should have some strategies for manipulating a set of parameters.

The easiest method of setting a texture's parameters is to simply use previously interesting values! It may seem silly, but if you don't keep track of settings you have already produced, you'll always be starting from scratch whenever you wish to produce a new surface appearance. Keeping track of previous successful settings will give you a starting point for surfaces with the absolute minimum amount of future effort.

The library of settings is obviously not practical until you *build* that library first, and even then the library won't always have an example of the surface you desire. Other strategies for modifying the parameters give you significantly more control.

The most obvious but most demanding method is simply to understand the texture well and use your intelligence to choose the proper settings. When you are familiar with what each parameter does, you can predict what the modified surface will look like and just set the values appropriately. A trivial example is when you wish to change the colors applied by the texture, so you simply edit the color parameters. However, knowledge of the texture's controls still isn't enough; if you want a surface that has a more "blobby" behavior, but there's no convenient parameter named "Blobbiness," you'll be forced to determine what parameters (or set of parameters!) will produce the effect you want.

While in theory you can simply use your experience and judgment to set the parameters, in practice this can be difficult. Oddly, often the most effective editing method is just to vary different parameters wildly! Blindly adjust them! Don't be conservative! When the dust settles, look at the surface produced; it may be something you like and can use. If it's not, it only takes a few seconds to try again.

This random method is arguably just as powerful as the "forethought" editing method. Even when I feel I understand the texture well (because I wrote it!) random settings will sometimes make interesting appearances I didn't expect and couldn't even plan for. It's a great starting point, since from here you can use the "intellectual," planned editing steps. Note also that the random method will give you a wide variety of surfaces which, even if they are not immediately useful, you can still save in an attribute library; it's likely you might be able to use it sometime in the future.

The final editing strategy is what I call the "polish" step. When you have a setting you are happy with, you can use a methodical last pass to optimize your settings. The idea is that if the surface looks as good to you as possible, then changing any of the parameters must make a less perfect surface. (If it didn't, you'd have an even better surface than you started with, right?) With this in mind, you can go through each parameter sequentially. Perturb the value by a small amount, but enough to make a visible change. If you like the new pattern better, then congratulations, you've just refined your surface and improved it! If not, try adjusting the parameter a small amount the *other* way. If neither adjustment improves your surface, reset the value to what it was initially, then proceed to the next parameter. After you've gone through all the parameters, your surface is optimized; any parameter changes will make it less attractive.

While there are many strategies for editing parameters, the best strategy of all has got to be the long term accumulation of a library of example parameter settings for each texture. You'll find new surfaces all the time when exploring (especially using the random flailing method), and if your attribute library is large, the next time you need a specific surface, you'll be that much more likely to have a good starting surface; otherwise you'd be forced to start from scratch.

Previews

Especially when you are initially developing textures, it is painful to run test after test to see how the texture is behaving. Obviously, the faster your development platform is, the better, but even then the design cycle time can be painfully slow.

Ken Perlin gave advice on this problem which which I now heartily agree. Generate *low* resolution tests! Most problems are glaring errors, and even 100 by

100 pixel test images are often enough detail to judge the gross behavior of a texture very quickly. If you're in a compile–render–recode–compile loop, you might be surprised how much time is wasted just waiting for the next render.

If you can't speed up your computer, the best way to help cut the design cycle time is to have the renderer display the image as it is rendering (if it can!) This way you can abort the render as soon as you know there is a problem, as opposed to waiting for the whole thing to finish before discovering there's a problem.

Even better is to design a previewer specifically for editing texture parameters. Place each parameter on a slider, and implement a progressive refinement display. This is a rendered image (perhaps just a simple plane or image of a sphere) that is rendered at a very coarse resolution. After the image has been computed, the image should be recomputed at a resolution which is twice as fine, updating the display appropriately. (Note that one fourth of the pixels have already been computed!) This refinement continues until you've computed the texture down to the individual pixel level.

If this preview can be interrupted and restarted by changing a parameter (ideally by just grabbing and changing a slider) the design cycle for setting parameters becomes *enormously* faster. Even with a very slow computer, the update is interactive (due to the progressive display scheme). An editor like this increased the utility of my entire set of textures by a (conservatively estimated!) factor of five. *The utility of a texture to a user (especially a nontechnical one) is inversely proportional to the time for a complete design cycle.*

Efficiency

As important and useful as they are, procedural texturing has one glaring flaw that still limits their potential. That flaw is simply efficiency. A complex surface tends to require complex computations to define it.[4] In particular, the most used building block of texturing (Perlin's fractal noise) is, unfortunately, exceptionally slow.

When a new texture is designed, efficiency is usually not a major design issue; the look and behavior of the surface is. But when textures are developed for a large user base, the efficiency problem becomes *very* important; in a scene where even a simple fractal noise texture is used, often the texturing computations out-

---

[4] The notable exceptions to this rule are patterns such as the fractal Mandelbrot set, but these have an *uncontrollable* complexity; you can't easily use the Mandelbrot set to make an image of granite paving stones.

weigh the rendering and shading! Especially for animation, this often makes procedural texturing nonviable simply because of its expense. As the author of commercial texture modules, users *demand* the textures I produce to be of a reasonable speed. Thus, I often spend as much time optimizing textures as I do designing them.

With the breadth of textures that are possible, it is nearly impossible simply to come up with any universal cures to increase texture speed. There are two main strategies that will help most. The first is to identify any general methods that can be used universally. This may be careful C coding techniques; the use of lookup tables; or simplifications of every texture. The second strategy is a brute-force, explicit hand optimization of routines, like fractal noise, which are called by many textures.

Parameter Preprocessing

One of the easiest optimizations to perform on textures is an examination of the input parameters of a texture. These parameters can frequently be preprocessed to increase the texture's speed. Often values that need to be computed are only functions of the input parameters; if the parameters are constant, then these computations do not have to be performed during every texture evaluation.

A simple example might be a transformation of a value (like a fractal noise level) into the range from 0 to 1 by the use of two "transition" levels specified by the user. If the fractal noise value is less than the first user level, the output value should be zero. If the noise value is greater than the second user level, the output value should be one. Otherwise, we want the output to be a linear transition between 0 and 1 based on the noise's level.

This computation is performed by using two compares to determine the 0 and 1 limiting cases, and evaluating the expression $(N - L)/(H - L)$ for the gradient case, where N is the fractal noise value and H and L are the user's high and low transition levels respectively. Note that if we can precompute the quantity $1/(H - L)$ we can save a variable access, a subtraction, and we transform a slow division into a faster multiplication.

These sorts of savings are admittedly quite minor. But they are very easy to do and often a savings of up to 20% can be achieved. When writing textures where efficiency is paramount, this is one of the most viable means of immediately speeding up the textures without any real effort.

Caching

Some texture algorithms can greatly benefit by the use of *caches,* values that are stored from *previous* calls to the texture. This uses the assumptions that repeated calls to a texture will often have similar (or identical) arguments and that information computed on the first call might be usable in the next.

The best example of this savings is with fractal noise, since this routine is both common and slow. I have found that often users layer two or more textures, for example using one to produce a color pattern and the next to make a normal bumping displacement. Dramatic effects are possible when two textures use similar pattern basis functions, so often fractal noise is called with the same arguments twice in a row! When I rewrote my fractal noise routine to compare the input arguments to the previous call, I was able to immediately return the proper noise value when the call was repeated. Since the fractal noise evaluation dominated the computation, this sped up the layered textures by 90%! The overhead the check applied otherwise was insignificant compared to the computation the noise normally takes, and was not measurable (less than 1% slowdown).

This caching can be used not only for functions but for other computations as well. The precomputation of the input parameters discussed on page 113 could be modified to behave as a cached value instead. This allows you to vary the input parameters from call to call.

One type of "cache" is actually just an explicit lookup table that can be computed at need. The sine function is quite slow to evaluate, but if high accuracy is not needed, a table of 256 or 1024 entries can be produced and just indexed into. The color lookup tables discussed at length on page 107 could also be computed only at need; a precomputation like this can be viewed as a cache that is always valid after it is set up.

C Coding Tricks

There are many books dedicated to efficient C coding, but I'll digress to discuss one particular trick which is inspired by the following question: What is the most important C math function used in textures? It's not what you expect. It's the `floor()` function! This function returns the largest integer that is smaller than or equal to the input value. `floor(1.23)` is 1, `floor(1.0)` is 1, and `floor(-1.23)` is –2. `floor()` is important because it is the *most common function* used in texturing. It's used in fractal noise routines at least three times per scale of noise, which can easily add up to 20 invocations per sample! Many other textures, from simple checkerboards to fancy abstract patterns, use `floor()` as well. It therefore deserves special attention, especially when trying to build *efficient* textures.

Since `floor()` is a standard function in the ANSI C library, it seems like there's not much to optimize. But that's not true: on most systems (read, all three I've tried) the speed of the function can be dramatically improved by making a replacement macro version of the function, removing the overhead of a function call. This is an obvious and simple change, and it can *quadruple* the speed of the routine. In routines where `floor()` is often used, this adds up: in my implementation of fractal noise, the macro replacement speeds the entire routine about 15%, which is definitely significant.

A macro to replace `floor` is very simple, based on the fact that ANSI C defines how integer casts perform: they truncate any fractions. So 1.1 becomes 1.0, but −1.1 becomes −1. We can fix this up a bit with a simple conditional to subtract 1 if the argument is negative.

```
#define floor(a) ((double)((long)(a)-((a)<0.0)))
```

This macro works identically to the C math function: the extra cast to a double at the front is to ensure the same output type as the ANSI function. Most of the time this cast won't matter, but for robustness it is necessary. I live dangerously and leave the double cast out, since I am usually assigning the value to a long, but C purists will argue that doing this is a Bad Thing.

One important note: if you use the excellent *Graphics Gems* series of books, they provide two macros called `FLOOR()` and `CEILING()` in their C header code which are incorrect in the first three volumes. They assume a rounding toward or away from zero, not higher or lower. Do *not* use these! They're still good routines, it's just that they are misnamed. This problem is corrected in the errata of the books.

It might seem like this is all there is to speeding up `floor()`: it's impossible to get that macro any tighter. But this isn't quite true: the macro works perfectly, but a subtle effect can make the macro *orders of magnitude* slower than it should be. The problem is easy to miss: it's that the argument to the macro is expanded *twice*. If you have a call like `floor(log(x))`, then `log(x)` is computed two times, completely eliminating your carefully crafted speedup. The solution is to have a different macro that prevents this by expanding the argument only once. A global variable named `tempdoub` is used to hold the expanded value.

```
#define floor(a) ((tempdoub=(a))<0.0?((long)tempdoub)-1L:
(long)tempdoub)
```

This macro is still much faster than a function call, and it doesn't have any traps. Unfortunately the extra assignment to a dummy variable makes it slower than the previous macro. What I do is use *both* macros, name the original macro `simplefloor()`, and manually use whichever is appropriate. Thus, I would use `y=simplefloor(x)` but `y=floor(PHI*n)`.

Since speed is always an important issue, you might examine your own macros and functions to catch this kind of problem. In particular, macros like `MIN()`, `MAX()`, `ROUND()`, and `SQR()` are prey to this subtle but important double computation. You might also think about macro versions of functions like `fabs()`, `fmod()`, and `modf()` if you find you use them often.

Special Cases

Often textures are not used in the most generic way possible; in fact this is quite common. Users may not activate all of your texture options. The 3D texture might only be evaluated on a flat 2D plane. Your complex surface texture that adds both color and normal perturbation effects might only be used for one effect and not another.

Make a special case for these simpler cases. An excellent example is fractal noise. Half of the time when you use noise it is on a flat surface, like applying woodgrain on a table top. If you make a 2D version of fractal noise, it will be over *twice* as fast as a 3D version (which basically computes two "layers" of noise and interpolates). I have a test in my noise subroutine that checks for the Y (vertical) component of the surface to be 0 (this is measured in texture coordinate space), and branches off into a special case subroutine. If you're clever, you can even make the 2D special case be a perfect subset of the 3D case: that is, the *sides* of the tabletop will call the 3D noise routine, but they will mesh up with the fast 2D version that is called for the *top* of the table. There's even an easy way to be clever: take your original code and globally replace the variable "Y" with the constant value 0. You can then manually edit the routine, removing any terms that vanish. This guarantees that your special case will return the same value as your general 3D routine, but you won't have to think too hard about how to implement it.

Tricks, Perversions, and Other Fun Texture Abuses

Basic textures are often implemented in the same rough method. A function is passed an *XYZ* location in space, the current surface attributes, and perhaps some user parameters, and the texture modifies the attributes based on some internal function. This generic design is sufficient for more general surface texturing, but if you are creative you can actually produce some truly unique and interesting effects even with the limited information most textures usually have.

Volume Rendering with Surface Textures

One of the sneakiest tricks is to change a surface texture into a true volume texture. This has been done since the beginning of algorithmic texturing; Geoffrey Gardner, as early as 1985, was fabulously effective at turning simple ellipsoid surfaces into apparent cloud volumes (Gardner 1985). This wasn't a true volume integration, but it looked great!

You can actually do a *true* volume rendering with simple surface textures as long as you limit your surfaces to have a somewhat restricted geometry. The easiest method of doing this relies on the texture knowing which direction the incoming ray is arriving from and assuming the user is applying the texture only to one type of surface like a sphere. The trick is simple; since you know the hit point of the ray, the direction of the ray, and you're assuming you're hitting a sphere (so you know the geometry), you know exactly what path the ray would take if it passed through the sphere.

Now, if you perform a volume rendering with this information (which might be an analytic integration of a fog function, a numeric integration of a 3D volume density, or some other volume rendering technique[5]) you can just use the final output color as a *surface* color. In particular, this is the surface *emittance;* often renderers will let you define this emittance (which is sometimes called luminosity), or, just as useful in this case, allow you to specify the true RGB surface color the surface will be treated as (and no shading will be done). By setting this surface color to the volume density computed intensity, the illusion of a gas can be complete! The gas must be contained by the sphere that defines it, but it is a true 3D effect and as such can be viewed from any angle. The biggest caveat is that the camera cannot fly through the volume density.

Odd Texture Ideas

If you think about the abilities of textures, you might realize that textures might be useful for more than just applying a color onto the surface of an object. In particular, if your host renderer passes the current surface color to the texture, you can design routines that can manipulate that color. You might map a bitmap onto

---

[5] Chapter 4 by David Ebert discusses this topic extensively.

a surface, then use a "gamma correction" texture to brighten the image. This texture would just be called after the brushmap is applied and would correct the image "on demand."

In fact, I've found quite a few "utility" textures like this that don't really apply a pattern at all. One is a solid color texture that has just two arguments, an RGB surface color and a "fade" value. By applying a solid color to an object, you can *cover up* previous textures. The fade value allows you to make the surface any opacity you want. If you linearly change this opacity over time, you can "fade in" an image map or previous texture. Or you could use the texture at a small (10%) opacity to just tint a surface's color.

Another useful texture transforms the RGB surface color to HSV, then lets the user "rotate" the hue around the color wheel. This is a cheap form of color cycling, and is especially useful for animations.

You also shouldn't get stuck thinking that textures have to be fractal noise patterns or endlessly tiled figures. I've found that textures can be useful in adding fairly specific, structured features that you might think would be better implemented with an image map. One example is an LED display like a watch or calculator. The texture takes a decimal number as an argument and displays it on the simulated seven-segment digits! This might seem weird, but you can now make something like an animated countdown without having to make hundreds of image maps manually. In a similar vein, a "radar" texture can make a sweeping line rotate around a circle tirelessly, with radar "blips" that brighten and fade realistically. All sorts of items that need to be continually updated (clocks, blinking control panel lights, simulated computer displays) can often be implemented as a semi-specific surface texture.

A fun texture is the Mandelbrot set. Just map the hit point's *XY* position to the complex plane. As the camera approaches the surface of the object, the texture automatically zooms the detail of the set! This is an awfully fun way to waste valuable CPU time.

Don't get stuck in always layering an image onto the surface, either. One of my most often used textures uses fractal noise to *perturb* the brightness of the surface. A user might use a brushmap or another texture to provide surface detail, then use this "weathering" texture to add random variations to the surface. An example might be a texture which takes a fractal noise value F and scales the object surface color by a factor of $1 + aF$. Even for subtle values of α the perfect hue of the surface is given some variation. This is dramatically impressive when a regular grid of squares suddenly becomes the weathered hull of an ocean liner.

2D Mapping Methods

Fully 3D textures are more versatile than 2D textures for obvious reasons. Often, though, a renderer might require a 2D surface, in particular if the "procedural" texture must be precomputed and stored as an image map. This is unfortunately quite common with commercial renderers that do not have software hooks for users (or third parties) to add their own procedural surfaces.[6]

Even when textures must be precomputed as 2D images, quite a bit of versatility can be retained. In particular, the 3D basis of the textures can be exploited to make some types of image maps that cannot be manually produced in a paint program. These unique maps exploit the fact that certain image transformations are common during mapping, in particular a "spherical image map" option found in most renderers.

A spherical image map is sometimes called a "globe wrap" since it adds an image map to a surface using *spherical* coordinates. This allows you for example, to take an image of the Earth (showing continents, oceans, etc.) and apply it to a sphere, producing a final spherical planet with the proper appearance. This polar coordinate mapping method allows the renderer to use the surface's 3D *XYZ* point to find the 2D *UV* coordinates of the corresponding position on the image map. This mapping is an "equal-angular" mapping, not a Mercator mapping, so the transformation is particularly simple:

$$U = \frac{\tan^{-1}(X,Y)}{2\pi}$$

$$V = \frac{\sin^{-1}(Z/\sqrt{X^2+Y^2+Z^2})}{2\pi} + 0.5$$

Since we know this transformation explicitly, we might ask the inverse problem. If we have a 3D procedural texture (which allows us to evaluate the surface anywhere we like), how do we produce a 2D image map such that when wrapped by a renderer the image will be exactly reproduced on the surface of a sphere? We want to be able to loop through the U and V image coordinates of the image map we're building and determine the proper *XYZ* position to evaluate the texture.

---

[6] These hooks are surprisingly rare, partly because of difficulty in writing an interface that can load executable procedures at runtime and partly due to apathy. Note the success of 3D Studio IPAS plugin routines, however; this is a great advantage to technical users and artists alike.

Assuming we are evaluating the texture on the surface of a sphere of unit radius, this reverse transformation is not difficult. Simply,

$$X = \cos((V - 0.5) \cdot 2\pi) \sin(U \cdot 2\pi)$$
$$Y = \cos((V - 0.5) \cdot 2\pi) \cos(U \cdot 2\pi)$$
$$Z = \sin((V - 0.5) \cdot 2\pi)$$

Where We're Going

Procedural texturing (and modeling) is certainly still in the frontier of computer graphics. It's an open-ended niche that is well over a decade old, but has been growing in importance. This book is one of the first attempts at a comprehensive collection of texturing techniques and algorithms, and it certainly won't be the last. You can look at the growing power of computers to see that soon the rendering process will not be the dominating design factor and production bottleneck; it will enable production of *complex* material appearances and geometry. With past rendering limitations, artists have been able to design objects and surfaces manually, but this is now becoming difficult. Imagine the complexity present in a full model of a city; a single animator *cannot* be able to design each building and surface manually. The answer is of course procedural definition, which is why it is steadily becoming more and more important over time.[7]

But what topics will be at that frontier? There are obviously many, but I see several "holes" in classical texturing that will likely be important soon.[8] One of the largest gaps in even simple texturing is a strategy for more intelligent textures; ones that examine their environment (and particularly the object geometry) to change their appearance. The strategy used by Greg Turk in (Turk 1991) for reaction-diffusion textures is one of the only forays into this field, but the potential is enormous. Imagine designing a dragon, but having the dragon scales behave differently over the belly of the dragon than the wings. Individual scales might change size based on the curvature of the skin (where there is high curvature, the plates need to be smaller to keep the area flexible). What is a good method for doing

---

[7] To give an interesting benchmark, this chapter was written in early 1994. I see a new era of rendering and proceduralism occurring in the future, one where it might be possible to have a synthetic planet be produced. It would be able to be viewed from orbit, showing continents and weather systems, but could be descended upon all the way to arbitrary resolution. Perhaps this won't even be just landscapes, but cities and highways on the surface as well. I don't see this happening before the turn of the millenia at the soonest. Advances are needed in both texturing, object synthesis, and rendering methods.

[8] Hint, hint, SIGGRAPH paper topic ideas abound! If you're truly interested in these frontiers and have ideas, send me e-mail!

even this size scaling? What other effects could be modulated by object geometry? What about the geometry should the textures examine? The applications are obvious, but there has been no great developments in this area. Yet.

I see another topic becoming important soon. With the complexity of textures continually increasing (both in application methods and in internal design complexity), a "black box" texture starts to become unwieldy for users to control. The "black box" is a texture personified by many control parameters, almost always numbers. When textures grow, the number of controls grow. It is not unusual to have up to 30 or 40 of these parameters! Even when carefully chosen and labeled, this many levers and knobs become difficult for the user to handle! This can be minimized through a good user interface (see page 112), but even then it is easy for a user (especially a nontechnical artist) to become swamped.

The black box design is likely to be around for quite a while; it is a convenient way to design textures for the programmer. These parameters must therefore somehow be abstracted or hidden from users to avoid overwhelming them. This probably implies a user interface similar to the ones used by both Sims (Sims 1991) and Latham (Todd and Latham 1993). Essentially, the user is presented not with many parameters to adjust, but with a collection of images. Each image is computed using different parameters (which are hidden from the user), and the user empirically ranks or sorts the images to identify the ones that are most interesting. From an artist's point of view, this is obviously appealing; it is very easy to use. The abstraction can also hide "parameters" of arbitrary complexity; Sims' textures are actually giant LISP expressions, not a mere vector of numeric parameters.

The big question that remains is what sort of method is best for deciding how to choose the parameters to make the image to present to the user, and how to use the user's preferences to guide the production of new trial settings. Latham presents a rudimentary answer to this question, mainly involving parameter "momentum," but especially for complex models this can become inadequate. I feel that development of a robust method for "texture evolution" based on numeric parameter vectors will be one of the most important tools to making procedural textures more useful from a user's point of view. In particular two topics need to be studied: accounting for past explorations of the texture's parameter space, and compensating for parameter correlations (where connections between parameters will complicate a "gradient" optimum search method). The growing complexity of textures really demands a new style of interface design, and this looks like the most promising.

So, while texturing is now a decade old, it is more important than ever. In computer graphics during the 1970s, the surface visibility problem was the main frontier. In the 1980s, lighting and surface properties (including the development of radiosity and BRDF surface models) were probably the most important developments. It is too early to tell what this current decade will be dominated by, but my prediction, especially for the next ten years, will be procedural object and surface definition. We finally know how to render; now let's make the computer help us make models *to* render.

Practical Texture Examples 4

Steven Worley

Introduction

This chapter gives a few specific examples for several simple textures. The first two textures are written as most textures are, full of cryptic lines and variables that seem to typify most texture coding. They are included to show some interesting texture possibilities. The last example is a "modern" texture that carefully antialiases itself, yet still remains simple enough to understand and modify.

LED Texture

As an example of one of the "offbeat" textures described on page 118, I present the LED counter routine. This function will return an integer corresponding to the background or an on or off LED segment. The implementation of this texture is very straightforward, mostly just geometry acceptance and rejection tests. A more elaborate version—perhaps including outline fonts—might be worth writing to some.

```
#define BACKGROUND  0
#define LEDON       1
#define LEDOFF      2

int counter(double dispnumber, double exponent, double
            modulus, double digwidth, double digheight,
            double digspacing, double numdigits, double
            numdecimals)
```

```
double num;
double xp,yp;
int maxplace,digit,segment,led_on,negflag,i,inum,
    numdigits,numdecimals;
double xf,yf;

/* Strategy: first find what LED element we're nearest. Next
   find if we're in any LED segments. Finally, determine if
   that segment is lit. */

yp= Y+digheight*0.5;
yf=yp/digheight;
if (yf<0.0 || yf>1.0) return(BACKGROUND); /* way above or
                                             below LEDS */
xp=X+(digwidth+(numdigits-1)*digspacing)*0.5;
if (xp<0.0 || xp>(numdigits-1)*digspacing+digwidth*1.15)
    return(BACKGROUND);

digit=floor(xp/digspacing); /* closest digit! */
xf=(xp-digit*digspacing)/digwidth;
if (xf>1.15) return(BACKGROUND); /* beyond end of digit*/

    /*    1 33333 6
          1       6
          1       6
          1       6
           4444444
          2       7
          2       7
          2       7 88
          2 55555 7 88

          possible LED segments
          */

if (xf<0.16666666) /* left hand, 1 or 2 */
  {
    if (yf>0.525) segment=1;
    else if (yf<.475) segment=2;
    else return(BACKGROUND);
  }
else if (xf>0.83333333)
  {
    if (xf<1.0)
      {
        if (yf>0.525) segment=6;
        else if (yf<.475) segment=7;
        else return(BACKGROUND);
      }
    else
      {
```

```
            if (xf<1.05 || yf>0.10) return(BACKGROUND);
            segment=8;
         }
    }

else if (xf<.25 || xf>.75) return(BACKGROUND);
else if (yf<.1) segment=5;
else if (yf>0.90) segment=3;
else if (yf>.45&&yf<.55) segment=4;
else return(BACKGROUND);
if (segment<1) return(BACKGROUND);

/* we're in a segment, now tell us if it's lit! */

num=dispnumber;
while (exponent>0)
   {
     exponent--;
     num*=10.0;
   }

while (exponent<0)
   {
     exponent++;
     num*=.1;
   }
if (modulus>=0.001)
     num-=(modulus*floor(num/modulus));
if (num<0.0)
   {
     negflag=1;
     num= - num;
   }
else negflag=0;

inum=floor(num+0.5); /* now integer */
maxplace=1;

while (inum>=10.0)
   {
     inum=inum/10;
     maxplace++;
   }

for(i=0;i<numdecimals;i++) num*=10.0;
inum=floor(num+0.5); /* now integer */
for(i=numdigits;i>digit+1;i—) inum=inum/10;

led_on=0;

/* This table tells us what segments must be lit for
```

```
     each kind of digit. */
switch (inum%10){
case 0:
  if (segment!=4) led_on=1;
case 1:
  if (segment==6||segment==7) led_on=1;
  break;
case 2:
  if (segment!=1&&segment!=7) led_on=1;
  break;
case 3:
  if (segment!=1&&segment!=2) led_on=1;
  break;
case 4:
  if (segment!=2&&segment!=3&&segment!=5) led_on=1;
  break;
case 5:
  if (segment!=2&&segment!=6) led_on=1;
  break;
case 6:
  if (segment!=6) led_on=1;
  break;
case 7:
  if (segment==3||segment==6||segment==7) led_on=1;
  break;
case 8:
  led_on=1;
  break;
case 9:
  if (segment!=2) led_on=1;
  break;
default:
  break;
}

if (segment==8)
  {
    if (digit==(numdigits-numdecimals-1)
        && numdecimals!=0)
      led_on=1;
    else led_on=0;
  }

/* no leading zeros */
if (digit<numdigits-numdecimals-maxplace) led_on=0;

/* negative sign*/
if (negflag&&segment==4 && (digit==(numdigits-numdecimals
    -maxplace-1)))
  led_on=1;
```

```
    if (led_on) return(LEDON);

    return(LEDOFF);

}
/* Done! */
```

2D Mapping

The discussion on page 119–120 discusses how 2D maps can be made using distorted coordinates such that they remap back into 3D seamlessly. The 2D image produced by this transformation will look distorted when viewed directly. Color Plates 2.1 and 2.2 show an example of how this works in practice. A basketball was defined algorithmically by using a brute-force procedure to evaluate a function over the surface of a sphere. Simple rules were used to determine whether a point was in a stripe or not (this is a quick geometric decision). A large lookup table of points distributed over the surface of the sphere was examined to see if the sample point was within a "pip" on the surface.[1] The inverse spherical mapping transformation was used to loop over the pixels of a texture map, and depending on whether the corresponding 3D surface point is located within a line or a pip, the image map was set to a gray value. This texture map was then used directly in a renderer.

In practice this trick works extremely well, since the predistortion of the image map exactly compensates for the renderer's subsequent distortion when wrapping. No seams are visible, and the image is not stretched; both occur when naive maps (such as digitized imagery) are used.

Note that this exact same method can be used to evaluate a texture over a cylinder or other shapes as long as the transformation the renderer uses to map a 3D *XYZ* location to a *UV* image sample is known and an inverse transformation can be determined.

I'll close this subsection by giving the (admittedly inelegant) code for computing this basketball pattern. This is actually a program for producing an image map, though it could be converted to a procedural very quickly. The program requires an input file of points distributed over the surface of a sphere to make the "pips"; these might be random or, much better, generated using a "collision" detection to avoid pips from overlapping.

---

[1] No subtlety here, every element in the lookup table of a couple thousand points was examined. This example was not a procedural texture designed for rendering (it was to produce a one-shot image map), so efficiency was not a big concern.

```c
#include <stdio.h>
#include <math.h>

void main(void);
int inlines(double x,double y, double z, double w);

/* These are constants used to jimmy the
   basketball parameters. */

#define BBRADIUS      123.3

#define DOTRADIUS    (2.55/BBRADIUS)
#define DOTSPACING   (2.9/BBRADIUS)
#define NOSPOTWIDTH  (7.566666/BBRADIUS)
#define COLORWIDTH   (4.775/BBRADIUS)
#define CIRCPOS       66.5
#define CIRCRAD       47.0
#define PIPCLOSE      .99994652

#define OUTWIDTH 1024
#define OUTHEIGHT 512

void main(void)
{
 unsigned char g[OUTWIDTH*OUTHEIGHT];
 int t,i,p;
 double rad,x,y,z,phi,theta,r;
 double dotx[19000],doty[19000],dotz[19000];
      /* Ugly hardcoded arrays */
 int numspots;
 FILE *infile;

 infile=fopen("spherepoints","r");
         /* file of spherically distributed points */
 p=0;
 while (fscanf(infile,"%lg%lg%lg",&dotz[p],
              &doty[p],&dotx[p])!=EOF)
   {
     /* Normalize points to be at surface of the sphere */
     rad=1.0/sqrt(dotx[p]*dotx[p]+doty[p]*doty[p]+
                  dotz[p]*dotz[p]);
     dotx[p]*=rad;
     doty[p]*=rad;
     dotz[p]*=rad;
     /* If the points are not too close to one of the lines
        of the ball, add them to the list of pips. */
     if (!inlines(dotx[p],doty[p],dotz[p],
         NOSPOTWIDTH/2.0+DOTRADIUS)) p++;
   }
```

```
    fclose(infile);
numspots=p;
for (i=0;i<OUTHEIGHT;i++) /* loop over output rows */
   {
     phi=3.14159265*(i/(OUTHEIGHT-1.0)-0.5);
     z=sin(phi);
     printf("Rendering line %d\n",i);

     for (t=0;t<OUTWIDTH;t++) /* loop over output columns */
        {
          g[t+OUTWIDTH*i]=128;
          /* The default output color is gray=128 */
          theta=t*2*3.141592654/OUTWIDTH;
          r=cos(phi);
          x=r*cos(theta);
          y=r*sin(theta);
          /* The spherical coordinate transform! */

          /* if we're inside the lines of the ball,
             color this sample black. */
          if (inlines(x,y,z,COLORWIDTH/2.0))
            g[t+OUTWIDTH*i]=0;

          else for (p=0;p<numspots;p++)
             {
           /* Brute force, loop through the list of
              points. We use the dot product of the
              pip location and the surface to determine
              if the sample is "within" the pip. If it
              is, we'll color the surface  with the
              pip color. */

              if (x*dotx[p]+y*doty[p]+z*dotz[p]>PIPCLOSE)
                g[t+OUTWIDTH*i]=155;

             }
        }
   }

   /* A simple output function, writes the image to disk. */
   writeimage("bbout.raw",g,OUTWIDTH,OUTHEIGHT);
}


int inlines(double x,double y, double z, double w)
{

/* This routine decides whether an XYZ point on the surface
   of the sphere is within a certain distance of one of
   the lines on the basketball. */
   double r;
```

```
/* easy tests... Z=0, Y=0 equator and meridian lines */

if (fabs(z)<w) return(1);
if (fabs(y)<w) return(1);

/* 45 degree stripes outside of curve. Near the equator
   another case needs to be used, though   */

if (fabs(y)>35.0/BBRADIUS && fabs(z)>35.0/BBRADIUS)
   {
     if (fabs(z-y)<1.4142*w) return(1);
     if (fabs(y+z)<1.4142*w) return(1);
     return(0);
   }

/* Do a trivial rejection of areas far from the curved
   part of the lines */

if (fabs(x)<80.0/BBRADIUS) return(0);

/* curved bit. We assume the curve is in the shape of a
   circle defined by some (empirically determined)
   constants. We find the radius from this circle and
   see whether we are within w units of it. We use y and z
   symmetrically depending on which half (x positive or
   negative) of the ball we are on.   */

if (x>0.0)
   {
     if (y>0.0) r=sqrt(z*z+(y-CIRCPOS/BBRADIUS)
                         *(y-CIRCPOS/BBRADIUS));
     else r=sqrt(z*z+(y+CIRCPOS/BBRADIUS)
                         *(y+CIRCPOS/BBRADIUS));
     if (fabs(r-CIRCRAD/BBRADIUS)<w) return(1);
   }

else
   {
     if (z>0.0) r=sqrt(y*y+(z-CIRCPOS/BBRADIUS)
                         *(z-CIRCPOS/BBRADIUS));
     else r=sqrt(y*y+(z+CIRCPOS/BBRADIUS)
                         *(z+CIRCPOS/BBRADIUS));
     if (fabs(r-CIRCRAD/BBRADIUS)<w) return(1);
   }

return(0);
}
```

Planetary Rings

Planetary rings like the ones that surround Saturn are impressive. They lend them-selves well to a procedural texture, since their fine ring detail can be simulated with fractal noise. Unfortunately the real rings of Saturn have thousands of tiny concentric bands, and we're going to be sampling these bands. This immediately leads to aliasing, so we have to design the texture to avoid it.

The main design of the texture is the thought that the texture itself is just a simple radius value with a very detailed color map. We can precompute the radial distance function and use the index antialiasing methods as described on page 140.

Once we make this decision, the design is straightforward. This texture allows thousands of tiny radial rings and antialiases them automatically. The following code is heavily commented so you can follow along each step.

```
/* this is a 1D table, we can splurge for lots of entries and it still
   won't be too large to store. */

#define TABLESIZE 16384

int initialized=0;
float table[TABLESIZE];



static double RingTexture(double *pos, double spotsize,
                double inner, double outer, double transition,
                double varyscale, double ampratio,
                double low, double high)
{
   double R0, R1, weight;
   int I0, I1;

   /* We need a color table premade for us with the accumulated densities. */
   if (!initialized) MakeColorTable(inner, outer, transition,
                        varyscale, ampratio, low, high);

   /* OK, lets find our range of radii. The range of radii are centered
      at the point's radius from the origin, and we split the spot radius
      between the two.
      To tweak the antialiasing, we could scale the spotsize up or down
      here before we use it. */


   R0=sqrt(pos[0]*pos[0]+pos[1]*pos[1]+pos[2]*pos[2])-0.5*spotsize;
   R1=R0+spotsize;
```

```
/* R0 may be negative if we  have huge spot sizes, which is obviously
   wrong and awkward. Lets make sure it's at least 0.0. */

R0=MAX(R0, 0.0);

/* OK, we know what range we want to average over. Let's transform those
   into index numbers in our color table. We know that at radius = [outer],
   we want to be at index [TABLESIZE-1]. So we multiply by a
   constant.

   Note that we lose a little resolution because we quantize the
   index into an integer. If the table were smaller, we could
   compensate by using a linear interpolation, but with a really big
   table the effect is negligable, and it definately makes the code simpler.*/

I0=(int)(R0*(TABLESIZE-1)/outer);
I1=(int)(R1*(TABLESIZE-1)/outer);
/* we make a tiny change to make sure I0 and I1 are not coincident, which
   simplifies tests later. This case will rarely happen anyway. */
if (I0==I1) I1++;

/* These indexes may be out of range. If so, lets do the right thing. */
if (I0>=TABLESIZE) return 0.0; /* we're completely outside the rings,
                         no effect */
if (I1>=TABLESIZE)
  {
     /* our outer range has run "off" of the end of the result. We have to
        take this into account by figuring the ratio of what's fallen off
        to what remains, and make sure our final output is properly
        weighted */

     weight=((double)(TABLESIZE-I0))/(I1-I0);
     /* now we change I1 to start within the range. The weight parameter
        will compensate for the range change. */
     I1=TABLESIZE-1;
  }
else weight=1.0; /* we're fully within the rings, we'll use the full
                weight. */

/* we now want the average value between I0 and I1. This is the
   easy part!  */

return weight*(table[I1]-table[I0])/(I1-I0);
}


/* routine to build the summed color table itself. This includes the
   computation of the ring density tucked within a simple loop to
   build the sum table as it goes. This is a precomputation that only
   needs to be done once. */
```

```
static MakeColorTable(double inner, double outer, double transition,
               double varyscale, double ampratio,
               double low, double high)
{
  double R, A, F;
  int i;

  /* sweep the radii out to the outer radius. Accumulate samples in
     the summed color table. Point sample the ring density at each sample.
     A radius of 0 is index 0. A radius of [outer] is equal to the table
     size-1.    */

  table[0]=0.0;  /* start with a 0 table */

  for (i=0; i<TABLESIZE-1; i++)
    {
      R=outer*(i+0.5)/(TABLESIZE-1);  /* R varies between 0 and [outer] */

      /* compute the simple inner/outer transitions to form an alpha channel
         of a simple washer-like disk. This will be used to modulate the
         density of the fine rings and prevent any rings from being too
         close or too far from the center. */

      if (R<=inner) A=0.0;
      else /* in first transition zone */
       if (R<inner+transition)
         {
           A=(R-inner)/transition;  /* linear 0 to 1 ramp */
           A*=A*(3.0-2.0*A);         /* hermite curve smooth transition */
         }
       else /* in outer transition zone? */
         if (R>outer-transition)
            {
              A=(outer-R)/transition; /* linear 1 to 0 ramp */
              A*=A*(3.0-2.0*A);       /* hermite curve smooth transition */
            }
         else A=1.0; /* we're in the main body of the ring */

      /* now let's compute the ring density. We use a 1D version of
         fractal noise. We use a 3D noise routine but pass in (R, 0, 0)*/

      F=fractal3(R, 0.0, 0.0, varyscale, ampratio);

      /* F is now between -1 and 1. But we use the low and high values as
         a clipping range for the noise. */

      if (F<=low) F=0.0; /* F is too low, we set the ring density to 0.0 */
      else if (F>=high) F=1.0; /* full ring density */
      else /* we're in a transition zone */
       {
         F=(F-low)/(high-low); /* now a 0 to 1 range */
```

```
        F*=F*(3.0-2.0*F); /* Hermite it to make it smooth */
    }


    /* OK, our ring density is F and our shaping alpha value is A. The
       net density is the PRODUCT of these two. */

    table[i+1]=table[i]+R*F;
    }
    initialized=1;
    return;
}
```

Advanced Antialiasing 5

Steven Worley

Advanced Antialiasing

It's very tempting to ignore the problem of antialiasing when writing textures. Certainly the first textures anyone writes are very quick tools that make you happy to get any kind of pattern at all on your objects. But as you mature, you learn that even the simplest textures behave very poorly because of the problem of aliasing. This is why the topic of antialiasing is avidly discussed so frequently in this book.

Aliasing has different definitions depending on context, but it ultimately resolves to the problem that you want to show the *average* effect of a texture over an area, yet it's a lot easier to just return a *sample* of the texture at just one infinitely small point. If you ignore the problem of antialiasing, you'll start making imagery that simply looks bad. You'll find artifacts like stippling or stairstepping in your images. You'll have visible problems when you make animations, since the motion of objects tend to highlight any aliasing problem by causing buzzing in the image, or worse.

It's very tempting to try to ignore the problem anyway, especially since most renderers have options to perform supersampling of the image for you, which will automatically reduce the aliasing problems. But don't depend on this! Your users may not need the whole image supersampled if the only problem is *your* texture. Image supersampling is expensive. *Supersampling is not an answer to the problem of aliasing.* It's just a final brute-force attempt to hide the problem.

The obvious objection to adding antialiasing abilities to textures is efficiency. Textures tend to be slow, and adding any more baggage (such as built in integra-

135

tion for antialiasing) is bound to slow them even more. This seems to argue for shorter, dumber textures, but in practice this is not true; a texture that can antialias itself can do so with a single (albeit slower) evaluation. Supersampling might take half a dozen samples and still be less accurate. Correct antialiasing can therefore be an efficiency issue and an important one.

Antialiasing is unfortunately a lot of work for the texture designer, since it often requires careful thought. Many times a different design method is required to do proper texture area integration, and the new method is never easier than simple point sampling.

This chapter covers only some aspects of antialiasing and in particular does not discuss band limiting, which Darwyn Peachy covers in Chapter 2.

Spot Sizes

Your antialiasing goal is usually to find the *average* texture value over a small area. This area is known as the *spot size* and usually the renderer will tell you what this size is. Some renderers like RenderMan are very careful in computing these spot sizes, but others (especially ray tracers, it seems) are very careless and give no spot size or (perhaps worse) an incorrect spot size.

This spot size is easy to understand if you think about a very simple renderer that takes one sample per pixel and renders a simple plane with a texture on it. Since it's rendering with just one sample per pixel, the texture algorithm will ideally return the average color of the texture pattern over that pixel. But textures don't know or care about pixels; they almost always want to be given a *distance*, in texture coordinates. What you usually want is a texture center location, in X, Y, Z coordinates and a radius (the spot size) measured in that same coordinate system.

If you're lucky, the renderer will give you this radius at the same time as the sample location. There are different ways that this can be computed. The most accurate method is one used by RenderMan. Its rendering method chops objects into smaller and smaller parts until each bit is smaller than a pixel when it is projected onto the output image. During this slicing and dicing, it keeps track of the exact range of texture coordinates for each little bit, known as a micropolygon. It ultimately computes with a rectangular chunk of texture with exactly known texture coordinate ranges, which it passes to the texture to be evaluated. RenderMan is extremely texture-friendly because of this careful coordinate treatment.

More conventional renderers usually concern themselves with projecting the geometry onto the screen and then, grudingly, determining the texture coordinates to pass to the texture code. These tend to be point locations computed by starting with a world coordinate value and transforming first to object and then to texture coordinates. The spot size is then ideally computed by analyzing the transformation between texture space and image space and using this to approximate a texture spot size.

If the previous sentence sounds like vague hand-waving, that's because *very few renderers compute spot sizes very well*. They all use different techniques and approximations. I've had personal experience with three different renderers, and each had *inaccurate* spot sizes. There are several ways of dealing with this inaccuracy, even if you have no control over the renderer itself. One method is to find correction factors to "massage" the spot size back to be more accurate by using different correction factors. This method is discussed on page 136.

Another method is to compute the spot sizes yourself if you have enough information. The derivation is straightforward but involves several steps and simplifying assumptions. It can be frustrating to locate all the information needed to complete each step.

First, we must know what size the spot we are antialiasing is in *the output image*. This is often the size of one pixel, but in the case of image supersampling the size may be smaller.

To begin, we need a conversion to change a world coordinate into a image coordinate I. (This is the formula that takes any 3D location in world coordinates and predicts where the point will project onto your output image.) This relation is usually computed by two transformations. The first is a rotation and offset transformation to translate the camera to a coordinate system where it is at 0, 0, 0 and looking forward. The second transformation is the perspective transform, which projects the (transformed) 3D point onto the screen. They are often combined into a single operation, though I find it easier to think of them as two sequential operations.

We then need a transformation from world coordinates to texture coordinates. This is usually a simple linear matrix equation with an offset. It is often the concatenation of two transformations, the first from world to object space and the second from object to texture space.

By concatenating the effects of each transformation in the sequence together, we arrive at a nonlinear transformation function, $I(T)$, which relates texture coordinates to screen coordinates. Its exact representation depends on your camera model and coordinate system definitions, so even its form tends to be unique to every renderer. This is only the first half of determining spot sizes.

We make an assumption that the texture area we are averaging over is so small that it can be well approximated by a planar sample through the texture. This is not always true (think of a sphere that is so distant that it is a single pixel in size), but the assumption holds well in almost every case.

If the antialiasing spot we are averaging over is a flat 2D area, the direction perpendicular to this region must be the same direction as the surface normal (in texture coordinates). The surface normal in fact defines the plane's normal. We can pick two vectors (call them R and S) that are mutually perpendicular to each other and also to the surface normal N. These three vectors define a new coordinate system. We know that the texture spot is defined only in the plane of R and S.

We can choose which R and S to use by thinking about the geometry of the texture spot. If the surface normal N directly faces the camera, the spot will be a flat circle, and we can use any R and S that are perpendicular to N, since there's no preferred spot direction.

If the surface normal does not directly face the camera, the texture spot will be tilted slightly away from us. This will make the texture spot *elongated* in one direction. If the view direction toward the camera is V, the elongated texture direction will lie in the direction of V projected onto the surface.

We want to align our texture spot in this direction in order to simplify our antialiasing later. In practice, we often do this in world coordinates first. We start with V_w, the view direction from the texture location towards the camera, and N_w, the surface normal in world coordinates. We form S_w as the *nonelongated* direction by taking the cross product $V_w \times N_w$ and normalizing. R_w, the direction along the elongation, is computed by normalizing $S_w \times N_w$. We then transform S_w and R_w into texture coordinates by using the world to object and object to texture transformations.

If the texture sample position (which defines the center of the area we want to average over) is T, we can write the formula of the area we want to sum over parametrically as $T + rR + sS$ where r and s are scalars. We don't know what range of r and s will be used yet. To determine them, we can use the formula we computed earlier for transforming from texture coordinates to screen coordinates. If we substitute our parametric spot equation into the projected image formula, we have $I(T + rR + sS)$.

We can now differentiate I with respect to r and s. We do this twice, since I is really a coordinate pair (x, y). This gives us $\dfrac{dI_x}{dr}$, $\dfrac{dI_y}{dr}$, $\dfrac{dI_x}{ds}$, and $\dfrac{dI_y}{ds}$.

We can stop here and return an isotropic spot size that gives just a single radius to average over by noting that if we want to average over a pixel, we want to move a small delta of 0.5 to up, down, left, and right in the image. We can use something similar to

$$\left(\frac{dI_x}{dr}\right)r + \left(\frac{dI_x}{dr}\right)s = 0.5$$

$$\left(\frac{dI_y}{dr}\right)r + \left(\frac{dI_y}{ds}\right)s = 0.5$$

to get a kind of "average spot radius." This isn't bad, and most renderers stop here and give a value similar to this.

But we've nearly derived a much higher quality spot computation that accounts for stretched spots. We know how *I* changes with both *s* and *r*. We can set up two linear equations,

$$\left(\frac{dI_x}{dr}\right)r + \left(\frac{dI_x}{dr}\right)s = 0.5$$

$$\left(\frac{dI_y}{dr}\right)r + \left(\frac{dI_y}{ds}\right)s = 0.5$$

which states that we assume our image spot to vary half a pixel in both *x* and *y*, and we require our *r* and *s* values to allow the image spot to vary that much. The solution of these equations is

$$s = \frac{\dfrac{dI_x}{dr} - \dfrac{dI_y}{dr}}{2\left(\dfrac{dI_x}{dr}\dfrac{dI_y}{ds} - \dfrac{dI_x}{ds}\dfrac{dI_y}{dr}\right)}$$

and

$$r = \frac{\dfrac{dI_x}{ds} - \dfrac{dI_y}{ds}}{2\left(\dfrac{dI_x}{dr}\dfrac{dI_y}{ds} - \dfrac{dI_x}{ds}\dfrac{dI_y}{dr}\right)}$$

These give us the ranges (*–r, r*) and (*–s, s*) which multiply the *R* and *S* direction vectors to define the texture antialiasing geometry. You can view this as an ellipse or rectangle in texture space. This is a great spot geometry, because we can antialias over an elongated spot if we care to, and we can also change our spot size if we know more about the shape of the sample in image space.

This computation seems somewhat daunting, with multiple transformations to compute on the fly and terrible math equations to solve. In practice, it's not quite so bad because the transformation formula *I(T)* doesn't change from texture sample to sample. The work that must be done does involve several multiplications and divisions, but most of the overhead comes from the square roots used in normalizing the S and R vectors.

With a computation like this, it's easy to see how a renderer can give poor spot size estimates if it is careless.

Supersampling

Some textures can be analytically integrated, like step functions and thick lines. Other textures have certain behaviors that can give at least better approximations than point sampling, such as band-limiting fractal noise scales to match the sample size. However, really odd textures just aren't practical to modify, because of their custom design or complexity.

Supersampling is the final, last resort to reduce aliasing artifacts. It always works. It's usually inefficient and crude, but if we're forced to do this supersampling, we can at least do it intelligently.

We can benefit from having the *texture* perform its own antialiasing (even by supersampling) instead of the renderer. A short header at the beginning of the texture does its own supersampling of the surface area and returns the mean result. This is useful for several reasons. First, this means that all textures are treated the same by the renderer; a position and spot radius are passed, and the texture returns an integrated texture estimate. The renderer does not need to treat antialiasing textures differently than ones that can only be point sampled. Second, since the evaluation loop for the samples is within the texture, not the renderer, overhead (in particular, function calls) are reduced. This is a small savings in general, but for simple textures like checkerboards it can be significant in proportion to the texture's overall speed.

The supersampling header is not difficult to write. We merely need to take samples over the area by sampling points on the spot. Several strategies can be employed, from random sampling to "stratified" Monte Carlo sampling. The strategies for integrating over a region are commonly known and well documented; (Shirley 1993) offers a good summary.

Index Aliasing

It can be useful to look at the sources of aliasing in order to identify any components that we might be able to improve in behavior. In particular, nearly all textures can be summarized as being some formula or procedure (call it the "pattern" function) that returns a scalar defined over space. This value is transformed into a color using a second function. This final transformation function might be something as simple as a linear gradient, but it can be abstracted to be a general lookup table that can characterize any behavior at all.[1] This design paradigm is convenient because it's not difficult to implement, and it is very versatile for the user.[2]

If we have a texture that follows this design method, we can see that aliasing is not caused from a single source but from two. Imagine a point color sample being computed. The scalar pattern function is called, which returns a number. This number is used to index into the color transformation (lookup table), which identifies the color to return.

There is a source of aliasing in both steps of this process. Point sampling the scalar pattern function obviously cannot characterize the average behavior of the pattern over the area. Less obviously, aliasing is caused in the color transformation step. A single value is used to determine the output color. This causes aliasing too, though it's more difficult to identify.

As an example, imagine our pattern function is a single scale of Perlin-style noise, and it varies between roughly –1 and 1. We choose a color map that is green for all input values except a very narrow band of bright red centered at the value corresponding to 0. This would make a pattern that is primarily green everywhere except for tiny spots of red where the noise value happens to be right at 0.0. Now, if we try to antialias this texture, we run into a large problem if our integration spot size is very large compared to the variation scale of the noise function. The average value of the noise over the large integration spot will converge to 0. Yet if we feed this perfectly integrated value into our color lookup table, we get a solid red color even though the true average color is a mostly green shade! This is a worst-case demonstration of aliasing in the final color transformation stage, sometimes termed *index aliasing*.

This aliasing is caused by rapid changes of the function used to transform scalar pattern values into output colors. Another example can help show how this aliasing might occur. Figure 1 shows a nontrivial color map that might be used to

---

[1] A caveat here: Since a table has only a finite number of entries, of course it can't perfectly represent any transformation. Luckily in practice most of these transformations are simple enough that using just a few hundred entries does an excellent job of "summarizing" the transformation. Using a few thousand table entries is very likely to be adequate for any task. This is just a couple K of storage, so it's not a big overhead.

[2] Note that there is more discussion of this methodology on pages 101 and 107.

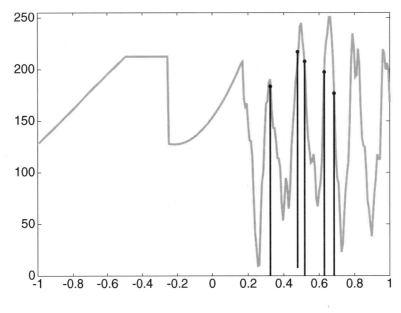

Figure 1.

transform a fractal noise value into one component of the surface color. If we evaluate the fractal noise function several times, we get several corresponding color point evaluations. It can be seen that in this example, the samples lie in one region of the color map; does the average of the point samples accurately reflect the average of the region? We can convince ourselves that other noise samples are likely to occur through the region from 0.3 to 0.7, and that the set of five current samples, by simple bad luck, probably show a color value that is higher than the true mean color over this region.

With some thought, we can design a strategy to reduce or eliminate this source of aliasing. To do this, we need to think about what the true output should be and how it is created. Then we can examine our approximations and see how we might modify our strategy. We'll consider the scalar "pattern" function as a black box function so the method will be applicable to any texture that uses a color map in this way.

The true output of an antialiased texture cannot be described by a single sample of our color spline. This is quickly seen by our red/green color example, since the average integrated color doesn't even appear in the color spline. If we consider what the average of an infinite number of point texture and color samples would converge to, we'll recognize the fact that the final average color is a weighted sum of the color spline. These weights are determined by the distribution of the pattern function's samples over the area in question. We can immediately see that since the *distribution* is what is important, a single sample value (like one evaluated at the mean of the distribution) is inadequate for determining the final average color.

What is the distribution defined by the pattern function over the integration area? *We don't know,* since we're treating the pattern function as a black box. We can make at least one assumption: The distribution is probably roughly continuous. We can make this assumption because most useful pattern functions (think of fractal noise, or a field that changes linearly with distance from a point or line, or a perturbed sine wave value) do not have discontinuities. Sharp changes tend to occur in the color transformation step, not the pattern function. If the pattern function is continuous, the samples taken over a local area will tend to cover a local range of values. This does not mean that all of these covered values will be equally likely, just that it's unlikely to have multiple separate peaks in the distribution with no samples in between.

Our only method of exploring the pattern function's distribution is to take point samples. We could implement naive supersampling by just indexing each of these samples into the color lookup table and averaging the output colors. But we can do better by thinking about the problem a bit more, perhaps with a simple example. Imagine we take just two samples of the pattern function. What is our best estimate for the final surface color?

Here we use our assumption of continuity. We can make an admittedly vague guess that the samples we took imply that future samples will occur *between* the two samples we have. Without any more information, a valid argument is that we can make a best guess of the distribution of the pattern value by simply assuming that all values between the two samples are equally likely.

If we have a guess like this for the distribution of the pattern values, how can we turn this into a best guess for the final color output? For a certain input distribution, we can compute the final color distribution and therefore the mean of this output. Since we're modeling our input distribution as a box of equally likely values between the samples we've taken, we can simply integrate the color lookup table between these values to find the mean. The trick to try to eliminate the index aliasing is to try to *model the input distribution as best we can,* since then we can integrate the (explicitly known) color map using that distribution as a weighting to get an as accurate estimate of the average color as possible.

Two important questions remain: how to best model that input distribution and how to compute the weighted integration of the color map efficiently. The first problem must be solved by sampling the black box pattern function. For two samples, an argument can be made for using a uniform distribution between the two sample values. How about for three samples? If values of 1.0, 1.1, and 1.5 are returned, what is our best guess for the distribution? With such limited information, we can somewhat visualize a range of values between 1.0 and 1.5, with a lopsided distribution toward the low values. Yes, this might not be what the true distribution looks like, but it is our best guess.

Such a vague definition of a distribution is inadequate, and especially when higher numbers of samples are known, we must have a general method of computing an approximation to the input distribution. The best method seems to be the following: If we take N samples, we make the assumption that if we sort the values in ascending order, new samples are equally likely to occur between each adjacent pair of samples. This models a piecewise flat distribution, much like a bar graph. Figure 2 shows a collection of point samples from some (unknown) distribution, as well as a best-guess reconstruction of the distribution function. Each "bar" that forms the distribution denotes an equal probability, and therefore each has the same area. Note that this transforms a high density of samples (which are spaced closely together) into tall, high probability regions.

This method for reconstructing a "best-guess" distribution has three advantages. First, it behaves as we would expect for small numbers of samples; one sample isn't enough to guess a distribution; two make a simple bar; and our example with three points does compensate for the lopsidedness of the sample points. Second, the reconstruction behaves better and better as more points are used. It will converge to the true distribution, even those with discontinuities or gaps. Third, we'll see that a piecewise constant distribution helps us perform the second required task for index antialiasing, which is to weight the color lookup table by the distribution and efficiently find the mean output color.

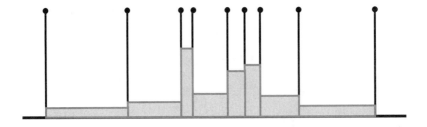

Figure 2.

To do this integration, we can first develop a method of integrating a lookup table quickly over a range of values with uniform weight. This is equivalent to finding the sum of the table entries over the range, then dividing by the number of entries summed. There is an easy method for performing sums like this called a *sum table*. These are in fact already used in computer graphics, primarily for 2D image map antialiasing. Here we wish to perform the sum on a mere 1D function, which is even easier.

A sum table is a simple concept. If we have an array of values and want to be able to sum those values over a certain interval, we can use a second, precomputed array called the sum table. Each entry of the sum table is equal to the sum of the entries of the original table up to that entry number. If our original table T were [1 3 4 2 3], our sum table S would be [1 4 8 10 13]. Now if we want to sum the values of entries a to b in T inclusively, we can simply evaluate $S(b)-S(a-1)$.[3]

Thus, by two simple table lookups and one subtraction, it is an easy matter to sum any number of entries in the original table. Looking at our reconstructed input distribution, the piecewise uniform weights lend themselves to this summed table evaluation perfectly. Each interval of the distribution is assigned a weight (inversely proportional to its width). The mean value of the color table over the interval is found through the difference of two sum table entries divided by the number of entries spanned. This mean is weighted by the region's weight, and the complete weighted color sum is divided by the sum of all the weights to determine the final output color estimate.

Since the end of one interval is shared by the start of the next, we can even combine the terms containing the same indexing into the sum table. When we have N samples of the pattern function, we only need N indexes into the sum table. This makes the evaluation extremely economical.

In some cases you can simplify the calculation further by calculating the mean and standard deviation of the samples. You can average the texture value over the color table range defined by the central mean value with total width equal to twice the standard deviation. This method simplifies the color map calculation to two lookups and also does not require sorting.

Index antialiasing is just one step of full texture antialiasing, but it's an extremely useful one. It's much more effective than blind supersampling, since (especially for low numbers of samples) at least a reasonable model of the variation of the texture is used to estimate the variation the color map undergoes.

---

[3] A bit of care has to be taken when $a=1$, where we assume $S(0)$ is 0.

Implementation of index antialiasing is very easy, though it does assume a lookup table for your color map. This table will need to be filled, taking some preprocessing time and extra memory. This overhead is very small, however, even for a very large table, since the tables are only one-dimensional.

There are several extensions and adaptations of this algorithm, especially if you know something more about your pattern function. Sometimes you might be able to make assumptions about the shape of the sample distribution, or be able to compute the true distribution analytically. For example, if the pattern function is defined by the distance of a point from a line, then the spot size defines a circle[4] of points. The true distribution of the sample values can also be determined algebraically or even geometrically. This can allow you to perform nearly perfect antialiasing! Obviously the more you know about your pattern function, the better you'll be able to model its sample distribution over an area, and the better your antialiasing will become.

Optimization and Verification

After you've added antialiasing support, it can be difficult to determine exactly how well it's working. The most common method is to render an image, zoom into the detail, see that it looks kind of blurry, and congratulate yourself.

This obviously isn't very scientific! In fact, it's hard to judge by eye whether your antialiasing is adequate or not. You can argue that if your eye can't tell, it doesn't matter, but in practice it's good to minimize it even below visible levels, since a different application (perhaps with more extreme conditions) may amplify even a small amount of aliasing artifacts into a real problem.

There's a surprisingly straightforward and useful method for tweaking antialiasing for optimum results. It is important to reduce your measure of antialiasing "goodness" into a measurable number that you can actually try to increase.

This can be done in nearly any situation by forming a controlled scientific experiment. It's usually very easy to adapt the following procedure to optimize antialiasing in every case.

First, you need to design a scene to render that exercises your texture. Strive to include situations that will typically cause problems. You want to have a single image that shows your texture at different scale sizes (infinite planes work well for this) as well as different viewing angles (spheres work well for this). I often

---

[4] An ellipse, actually

use four infinite planes forming a box, receding to infinity, with about ten spheres at different depths.

You need to generate a "reference" image of this scene, one that is as accurate as possible, including texture antialiasing. This can be done by rendering your scene at very high resolution, such as 2048 by 2048, then reducing the image down in size to something more manageable like 256 by 256. This "manual supersampling" is nearly foolproof in making a good antialiased image since so many samples are used per pixel. Be wary of letting your renderer do supersampling for you when building a reference image! Its own supersampling may be biased or have subtle errors of its own.

When you have a reference image prepared, it provides a measure that we can compare our antialiasing to. When we render an image with no image supersampling, we can detect errors due to aliasing by simply comparing the rendered image with the reference image, pixel by pixel. The match is rarely perfect because the reference image also includes *geometric* antialiasing, but this doesn't upset our texture antialiasing comparison.

The comparison between our test render image and the reference image should be done numerically. The most obvious error metric to use is a simple sum of the squared differences for each pixel. If the images are identical, this value will be 0. You can write a small application that takes the difference between two images and returns the *numeric* error value. It can also be interesting to output an image that highlights the pixels that have the most error.

With a tool for determining the antialiasing error, it becomes very easy (and surprisingly, a little fun if you're a math geek) to optimize your texture antialiasing to minimize it. In particular, the simplest yet most useful variation to explore is a "tweak" value that scales your texture spot size.

Even if you've been careful in determining spot size, it's very easy for the spot size to "drift" from its optimal value. It is not uncommon for the spot size to be off significantly! One renderer I deal with is returning a spot size that is at least four times larger than it should be, and I have to scale it down appropriately to reduce the error.

With an error metric in hand, you can vary any part of your antialiasing code to determine whether it has a positive effect. Are there strange constants in your antialiasing code for dealing with spot size or sample rates? How about estimates of texture variability for use with index antialiasing? Cutoff frequencies for fractal noise? You can tweak all of these to optimize your algorithm's output.

You can also use the reference comparison to investigate the efficiency and quality of different algorithms. You can test a supersampling method to determine its speed and error as compared to a more intelligent but slower band limiting method.

This method does not do well at catching *temporal* aliasing problems since it considers only a single image at a time. You could make a similar test that uses multiple images to determine the antialiasing error metric. Even this is not perfect, but it does help in characterizing the final error better.

Emergency Alternatives

Sometimes with deadlines looming, you may still be tearing out your hair due to aliasing problems. While you can always throw more supersampling onto the problem, this often still isn't acceptable because of time or CPU limits. The ideas that follow may be technically dubious and even repugnantly crude, but elegance tends not to matter when you have a shot deadline in three hours.

The most common and obvious texture "tweak" is to scale the texture spot size. Even without a reference image comparison as discussed in the previous section, you can usually reduce aliasing artifacts by using an exaggerated spot size. Often this may eliminate aliasing at the expense of a softened look to your surface.

If your texture is aliasing and it uses a color map, you can try applying a blur to the color map. This will soften the transition zones between colors, which can hide a lot of terrible artifacts. Since the blur only has to be done once to the simple 1D color map, the computational overhead is inconsequential and does not slow final rendering. I first used this method to solve an aliasing problem, but I later found that it was a handy control for users to use at their own discretion.

A painful alternative that should only be used in true emergencies is a simple image blur effect. Make a mask that isolates the pixels that show the texture, and apply a 2D image blur to the final rendered image using that mask. This mask may be an alpha channel that the renderer can output, or even a hand-painted one. By applying a small blur of just one or two pixels radius, aliasing artifacts in your texture are usually hidden very quickly. It has the unfortunate side effect of softening your surface features and even geometry details.

A final desperate alternative is effective with simple geometry. If you render your texture out as a 2D image you can use the rendered image as a map on your surface. Most renderers have decent image-map antialiasing using a MIP map or summed area table. 2D antialiasing with these methods tends to do especially well in high compression areas, where a large amount of detail gets crammed into just a few pixels.

Procedural Modeling of Gases $\mathbf{6}$

David S. Ebert

Introduction

This chapter presents a framework for procedural modeling and texturing using volumetric procedural models, a general class of procedural techniques for modeling natural phenomena. Volumetric procedural models use three-dimensional volume density functions ($vdf(x,y,z)$) that define the density of a continuous three-dimensional space. Volume density functions (vdf's) are the natural extension of solid texturing (Perlin 1985) to describe the actual geometry of objects. Volume density functions are used extensively in computer graphics for modeling and animating gases, fire, fur, liquids, and other "soft" objects. I have used them for modeling and animating gases such as steam, fog, and smoke (Ebert *et al.* 1994a, Ebert 1991, Ebert and Parent 1990, Ebert *et al.* 1990). Hypertextures (Perlin and Hoffert 1989), described by Ken Perlin in Chapter 9, and Inakage's flames (Inakage 1991) are other examples of the use of volume density functions. In this chapter, I will focus on the use of volumetric procedural models for creating realistic images of *gases*, specifically smoke, steam, and fog. I will use the term *gas* to encompass gas and particulate volumes, both of which are governed by light-scattering models for small particles. Atmospheric attenuation and lighting models are robust enough to encompass both types of volumes and produce visually correct results.

As in the preceding chapters, the procedures in this chapter will make use of the stochastic functions *noise()* and *turbulence()*. I will give a simple implementation of the *noise()* and *turbulence()* functions used in my system.

This chapter first summarizes previous approaches to modeling gases, then presents a brief description of my rendering system for gases and an explanation of solid spaces. Finally, it concludes with a detailed description of how to create still images of gases.

Previous Approaches

Attempts to model gases in computer graphics started in the late 1970s. Since that time, there have been many different approaches. These can be categorized as techniques for modeling the geometry of gases and techniques for rendering scenes with gases and atmospheric effects.

There have been several approaches to modeling the geometry of gases. Some authors use a constant density medium (Klassen 1987, Nishita *et al.* 1987) but do allow different layers of constant densities. Still, only very limited geometries for gases can be modeled. Voss and Musgrave uses fractals (Voss 1983, Musgrave 1990) to create realistic clouds and fog effects. Max uses height fields for simulating light diffusion effects (Max 1986), and Kajiya uses a physically-based model for modeling clouds (Kajiya and Von Herzen 1984). Gardner has produced the most realistic images of clouds (Gardner 1985, Gardner 1990) by using Fourier synthesis to control the transparency of hollow ellipsoids. The main disadvantage of this approach is that it is not a true three-dimensional geometric model for the clouds. I have developed several approaches for modeling gases based on volume density functions (Ebert 1991, Ebert and Parent 1990, Ebert *et al.* 1990, Ebert *et al.* 1989). These models are true three-dimensional models for the geometry of gases and provide more realistic results than previous techniques. Stam also uses a three-dimensional geometric model for gases (Stam and Fiume 1991, Stam and Fiume 1993, Stam and Fiume 1995). This model uses "fuzzy blobbies," which are similar to volumetric metaballs and particle systems, for the geometric model of the gases. Finally, Sakas uses spectral synthesis to define three-dimensional geometric models for gases (Sakas 1993).

The rendering of scenes containing clouds, fog, atmospheric dispersion effects, and other gaseous phenomena has also been an area of active research in computer graphics. Several papers describe atmospheric dispersion effects (Willis 1987, Nishita *et al.* 1987, Rushmeier and Torrance 1987, Musgrave 1990), while others cover the illumination of these gaseous phenomena in detail (Blinn 1982a, Kajiya and Von Herzen 1984, Max 1986, Klassen 1987, Ebert and Parent 1990). Most authors use a low-albedo reflection model, while a few, Blinn (Blinn 1982a), Kajiya (Kajiya and Von Herzen 1984), Rushmeier (Rushmeier and Torrance 1987), Max (Max 1994), and Nishita (Nishita *et al.* 1996), discuss the implementation of a high-albedo model. (A low-albedo reflectance model assumes that secondary scattering effects are negligible, while a high-albedo illumination model calculates the secondary and higher order scattering effects.)

The Rendering System

For true three-dimensional images and animations of gases, volume rendering must be performed. While any procedure-based volume rendering system can be used, such as the systems described in (Perlin 1985, Kajiya and Von Herzen 1984), I will discuss my system, which is described in detail in (Ebert and Parent 1990). This hybrid rendering system uses a fast scanline a-buffer rendering algorithm for the surface-defined objects in the scene, while volume modeled objects are volume rendered. The algorithm first creates the a-buffer for a scanline containing a list for each pixel of all the fragments that partially or fully cover the pixel. Then, if a volume is active for a pixel, the extent of volume rendering necessary is determined. The volume rendering is performed next, creating a-buffer fragments for the separate sections of the volumes. (It is necessary to break the volume objects into separate sections that lie in front of, in between, and behind the surface-based fragments in the scene to generate correct images.) Volume rendering ceases once full coverage of the pixel by volume or surfaced-defined elements is achieved. Finally, these volume a-buffer fragments are sorted into the a-buffer fragment list based on their average Z-depth values, and the a-buffer fragment list is rendered to produce the final color of the pixel.

Volume Rendering Algorithm

The volume rendering technique used for gases in this system is similar to the one discussed in (Perlin and Hoffert 1989). The ray from the eye through the pixel is traced through the defining geometry of the volume. For each increment through the volume sections, the volume density function is evaluated. The color, density, opacity, shadowing, and illumination of each sample is then calculated. The illumination and densities are accumulated based on a low-albedo illumination model for gases and atmospheric attenuation.

The basic gas volume rendering algorithm is the following:

```
for each section of gas
    for each increment along the ray
        get color, density, & opacity of this element
        if self_shadowing
```

```
       retrieve the shadowing of this element from the solid
          shadow table
color =calculate the illumination of the gas
          using opacity, density and the
          appropriate model
final_clr = final_clr + color;
sum_density =sum_density +density;
if( transparency < 0.01)
     stop tracing
increment sample_pt
create the a_buffer fragment
```

In sampling along the ray, a Monte Carlo method is used to choose the sample point to reduce aliasing artifacts. The opacity is the density obtained from evaluating the volume density function multiplied by the step size, because in the gaseous model, we are approximating an integral to calculate the opacity along the ray (Kajiya 1984). The approximation used is

$$\text{opacity} = 1 - e^{-\tau \times \sum_{t_{near}}^{t_{far}} \rho(x(t),y(t),z(t)) \times \Delta t}$$

where τ is the optical depth of the material, $\rho()$ is the density of the material, t_{near} is the starting point for the volume tracing, and t_{far} is the ending point. The final increment along the ray may be smaller, so its opacity is scaled proportionally (Kajiya and Kay 1989).

Illumination of Gaseous Phenomena

A low-albedo illumination model based on (Kajiya and Von Herzen 1984) is used for the gases. The phase-functions that are used are sums of Henyey-Greenstein functions as described in (Blinn 1982a). The illumination model is the following

$$B = \sum_{t_{near}}^{t_{far}} e^{-\tau * \sum_{t_{near}}^{t} \rho(x(u),y(u),z(u)) \times \Delta u} \times I \times$$

$$\rho(x(t), y(t), z(t)) \times \Delta t,$$

where I is

$$\sum_{i} I_i(x(t), y(t), z(t)) \times \text{phase}(\theta).$$

Phase(θ) is the phase function, the function characterizing the total brightness of a particle as a function of the angle between the light and the eye (Blinn 1982a). $_{Ii}(x(t),y(t),z(t))$ is the amount of light from light source i reflected from this element.

Self-shadowing of the gas is incorporated into I by attenuating the brightness of each light. An approximation for a high-albedo illumination model can also be incorporated by adding an ambient term based on the albedo of the material into I_i. This ambient term accounts for the percentage of light reflected from the element due to second and higher order scattering effects.

Volumetric Shadowing

Volumetric shadowing is important in obtaining accurate images. As mentioned above, self-shadowing can be incorporated into the illumination model by attenuating the brightness of each light. The simplest way to self-shadow the gas is to trace a ray from each of the volume elements to each of the lights, determining the opacity of the material along the ray using the preceding equation for opacity. This method is similar to shadowing calculations performed in ray tracing and can be very slow. My experiments have shown that ray-traced self-shadowing can account for as much as 75% to 95% of the total computation time.

To speed up shadowing calculations, a precalculated table can be used. Kajiya discusses this approach with the restriction that the light source be at infinity (Kajiya and Von Herzen 1984, Kajiya and Kay 1989). I have extended this approach to remove this restriction. Using my technique, the light source may even be inside the volume. This shadow-table-based technique can improve performance by a factor of 10 to 15 over the ray-traced shadowing technique. A complete description of this shadowing technique can be found in (Ebert 1991).

The shadow table is computed once per frame. To use the shadow table when volume tracing, the location of the sample point within the shadow table is determined. This point will lie within a parallelepiped formed by eight table entries. These eight entries are trilinearly interpolated to obtain the sum of the densities between this sample point and the light. To determine the amount of light attenuation, the following formula is used.

$$\text{light\_atten} = 1 - e^{-\tau \times \text{sum\_densities} \times \text{step\_size}}$$

As mentioned above, this shadow-table algorithm is much more efficient than the ray-tracing shadowing algorithm. Another benefit of this approach is the flexibility of detail on demand. If very accurate images are needed, the size of the shadow table can be increased. If the volume is very small in the image and very accurate shadows are not needed, a small resolution shadow table (e.g., 8^3) can be chosen. For most images, I use a shadow table size of 32^3 or 64^3.

A Procedural Framework: Solid Spaces

Development of Solid Spaces

My approach to modeling and animating gases started with work in solid texturing. Solid texturing can be viewed as creating a three-dimensional color space that surrounds the object. When the solid texture is applied to the object, it is as if the defining space is being carved away. A good example of this is using solid texturing to create objects made from wood and marble. The solid texture space defines a three-dimensional volume of wood or marble, in which the object lies.

Most of my solid texturing procedures were based on the noise and turbulence functions. This work extended to modeling gases when I was asked to produce an image of a butterfly emerging from fog or mist. Since gases are controlled by turbulent flow, it seemed natural to somehow incorporate the use of noise and turbulence functions into this modeling. My rendering system already supported solid texturing of multiple object characteristics, so the approach that I developed was to use solid textured transparency to produce layers of fog or clouds. The solid textured transparency function was, of course, based on turbulence. This approach is very similar to Gardner's approach (Gardner 1985) and has the same disadvantage of not being a true three-dimensional model even though the solid texture procedure is defined throughout three-space. In both cases, these three-dimensional procedures are evaluated only at the surfaces of objects. To remedy this shortcoming, my next extension was to use turbulence-based procedures to define the density of three-dimensional volumes, instead of controlling the transparency of hollow surfaces.

As you can see, the idea of using three-dimensional spaces to represent object attributes such as color, transparency, and even geometry is a common theme in this progression. My system for representing object attributes using this idea is termed *solid spaces*. The solid-space framework encompasses traditional solid texturing, hypertextures, and volume density functions within a unified framework.

Description of Solid Spaces

Solid spaces are three-dimensional spaces associated with an object that allow for control of an attribute of the object. For instance, in color solid texturing, described in Chapters 2 and 3, the texture space is a solid space associated with the object that defines the color of each point in the volume that the object occupies. This space can be considered to be associated with, or represent, the space of the material from which the object is created.

Solid spaces have many uses in describing object attributes. As mentioned above, solid spaces can be used to represent the color attributes of an object. This is very natural for objects whose color is determined from procedures defining a marble color space, as in Color Plate 6.1. Solid color spaces have been used by many authors for creating realistic images of natural objects (Perlin 1985, Peachey 1985, Musgrave and Mandelbrot 1989). Often in solid texturing (using solid color spaces) there are additional solid spaces which are combined to define the color space. For example, in most of my work in solid texturing, a noise and turbulence space is used in defining the color space. Other solid-space examples include geometry (hypertextures and volume density functions), roughness (solid bump mapping), reflectivity, transparency, illumination characteristics, and shadowing of objects. Solid spaces can even be used to control the animation of objects, as will be described in the next chapter.

Mathematical Description of Solid Spaces

Solid spaces can be described simply in mathematical terms. They can be considered to be a function from three-space to n-space, where n can be any nonzero positive integer. More formally, solid spaces can be defined as the following function:

$$S(x, y, z) = F, F \in R^n, n \in 1,2,3,\ldots.$$

Of course, the definition of the solid space can change over time; thus, time could be considered to be a fourth dimension to the solid-space function. For most uses of solid spaces, S is a continuous function throughout three-space. The exception is the use of solid spaces for representing object geometries. In this case, S normally has a discontinuity at the boundary of the object. For example, in the case of implicit surfaces, S is normally continuous throughout the surface of the object, but thresholding is used to change the density value abruptly to 0 for points whose density is not within a narrow range of values that defines the surface of the object. The choice of F determines the frequencies in the resulting solid spaces, and, therefore, the amount of aliasing artifacts that may appear in a final image.

Geometry of the Gases

Now that some background material has been discussed, this section will describe detailed procedures for modeling gases. As mentioned in the introduction, the geometry of the gases is modeled using turbulent-flow-based volume density functions. The volume density functions take the location of the point in world space, find its corresponding location in the turbulence space (a three-dimensional space), and apply the turbulence function. The value returned by the turbulence function is used as the basis for the gas density and is then "shaped" to simulate the type of gas desired by using simple mathematical functions. In the discussion that follows, I will first describe my noise and turbulence functions, and then describe the use of basic mathematical functions for shaping the gas. Finally, the development of several example procedures for modeling the geometry of the gases will be explored.

My Noise and Turbulence Functions

In earlier chapters of this book, detailed descriptions of noise and turbulence were discussed, including noise and turbulence functions with much better spectral characteristics. I am providing my implementations to enable the reader to reproduce the images of gases that I describe in this chapter. If other noise implementations are used, then the gas shaping needed will be slightly different. (I have experimented with this.) My noise implementation is trilinear interpolation of random numbers stored at the lattice points of a regular grid. I use a grid size of 64 x 64 x 64. The 3D array is actually 65 x 65 x 65 with the last column equalling the first column to make accessing entries easier (noise[64][64][64]= noise[0][0][0]).

The noise lattice is computed and written to a file using the following code:

```
*/
*****************************************************************
*                       WRITE_NOISE.C                          *
*  This program generates a noise function file for solid texturing  *
*                    by David S. Ebert                         *
*****************************************************************
*/
#include <math.h>
#include <stdio.h>
```

```
#define SIZE 64
double drand48();

main()
{
   float    tmp,u,v;
   long     i,j, k, ii,jj,kk;
   float    noise[SIZE+1][SIZE+1][SIZE+1];
   FILE     *noise_file;

  noise_file = fopen("noise.data","w");

  for (i=0; i<SIZE; i++)
    for (j=0; j<SIZE; j++)
      for (k=0; k<SIZE; k++)
         {
            noise[i][j][k] = (float)drand48();
         }
/* This is a hack, but it works. Remember this is only done once.
 */
  for (i=0; i<SIZE+1; i++)
    for (j=0; j<SIZE+1; j++)
      for (k=0; k<SIZE+1; k++)
         {
            ii = (i == SIZE)? 0:  i;
            jj = (j == SIZE)? 0:  j;
            kk = (k == SIZE)? 0:  k;
            noise[i][j][k] = noise[ii][jj][kk];
         }
  fwrite(noise,sizeof(float),(SIZE+1)*(SIZE+1)*(SIZE+1), noise_file);
  fclose(noise_file);
}
```

To compute the noise for a point in three-space, the *calc_noise()* function given below is called. This function replicates the noise lattice to fill the positive octant of three-space. To use this procedure, the points must be in this octant of space. I allow the user to input scale and translation factors for each object to position the object in the noise space.

The noise procedure given below, *calc_noise*, uses trilinear interpolation of the lattice point values to calculate the noise for the point. The *turbulence()* function given below is the standard Perlin turbulence function (Perlin 1985).

```
typedef struct xyz_td
  {
    float     x, y, z;
  } xyz_td;

float   calc_noise();
float   turbulence();
```

```
/*
**********************************************************************
*                            Calc_noise                            *
**********************************************************************
* This is basically how the trilinear interpolation works. I lerp   *
* down the left front edge of the cube, then the right front edge of *
* the cube(p_l, p_r). Then I lerp down the left back and right back  *
* edges of the  cube (p_l2, p_r2). Then I lerp across the front face *
* between p_l  and p_r (p_face1). Then I lerp across the back face   *
* between p_l2 and p_r2 (p_face2). Now I lerp along the line between *
* p_face1 and  p_face2.                                             *
**********************************************************************
 */

float
calc_noise(pnt)
     xyz_td   pnt;
{
  float   t1;
  float   p_l,p_l2,    /* value lerped down left side of face 1 & face 2 */
          p_r,p_r2,    /* value lerped down left side of face 1 & face 2 */
          p_face1,     /* value lerped across face 1 (x-y plane ceil of z) */
          p_face2,     /* value lerped across face 2 (x-y plane floor of z)*/
          p_final;     /* value lerped through cube (in z)               */
  extern float noise[SIZE_1][SIZE_1][SIZE_1];
  float     tnoise;
  register int      x, y,  z,px,py,pz;

  px = (int)pnt.x;
  py = (int)pnt.y;
  pz = (int)pnt.z;
  x = px &(SIZE-1); /* make sure the values are in the table        */
  y = py &(SIZE-1); /* Effectively, replicates the table thoughout space */
  z = pz &(SIZE-1);

  t1 = pnt.y - py;
  p_l  = noise[x][y][z+1]+t1*(noise[x][y+1][z+1]-noise[x][y][z+1]);
  p_r  = noise[x+1][y][z+1]+t1*(noise[x+1][y+1][z+1]-noise[x+1][y][z+1]);
  p_l2 = noise[x][y][z]+ t1*( noise[x][y+1][z] - noise[x][y][z]);
  p_r2 = noise[x+1][y][z]+ t1*(noise[x+1][y+1][z] - noise[x+1][y][z]);

  t1 = pnt.x - px;
  p_face1 = p_l + t1 * (p_r - p_l);
  p_face2 = p_l2 + t1 * (p_r2 -p_l2);

  t1 = pnt.z - pz;
  p_final =  p_face2 + t1*(p_face1 -p_face2);

  return(p_final);
}
```

```
/*
*******************************************************************
*                        TURBULENCE                              *
*******************************************************************
*/
float turbulence(pnt, pixel_size)
    xyz_td    pnt;
    float     pixel_size;
{
  float t, scale;
  t=0;
  for(scale=1.0; scale >pixel_size; scale/=2.0)
    {
      pnt.x = pnt.x/scale; pnt.y = pnt.y/scale; pnt.z = pnt.z/scale;
      t+= calc_noise(pnt)* scale;
    }
  return(t);
}
```

Neither of these routines is optimized. The access of the noise lattice can be optimized by using bit-shifting operations to index into the integer lattice. The turbulence function can be optimized by precalculating a table of scale-multipliers and using multiplication by reciprocals instead of division.

Basic Gas Shaping

Several basic mathematical functions are used to shape the geometry of the gas. The first of these is the power function. Let's look at a simple procedure for modeling a gas and see the effects of the power function, and other functions, on the resulting shape of the gas.

```
basic_gas(pnt,density,parms)
      xyz_td    pnt;
      float     *density,*parms;
{
  float turb;
  int   i;
  static float pow_table[POW_TABLE_SIZE];
  static int calcd=1;

  if(calcd)
    { calcd=0;
      for(i=POW_TABLE_SIZE-1; i>=0; i--)
        pow_table[i] = (float)pow(((double)(i))/(POW_TABLE_SIZE-1)*
                        parms[1]*2.0,(double)parms[2]);
    }
  turb =turbulence(pnt, pixel_size);
  *density = pow_table[(int)(turb*(.5*(POW_TABLE_SIZE-1)))];
}
```

This procedure takes as input the location of the point being rendered in the solid space, *pnt*, and a parameter array of floating point numbers, parms. The returned value is the density of the gas. *Parms[1]* is the maximum density value for the gas with a range of 0.0 to 1.0, and *parms[2]* is the exponent for the power function.

Figure 1 shows the effects of changing the power exponent, with *parms[1]=0.57*. Clearly, the greater the exponent, the greater the contrast and definition to the gas plume shape. With the exponent at 1 there is a continuous variation in the density of the gas; whereas, with the exponent at 2, it appears to be separate individual plumes of gas. Therefore, depending on the type of gas being modeled, the appropriate exponential value can be chosen. This procedure also shows how precalculated tables can increase the efficiency of the procedures. The *pow_table[]* array is calculated once per image and assumes that the maximum density value, *parms[1]*, is constant for each given image. A table size of 10,000 should be sufficient for producing accurate images. This table is used to limit the number of *pow* function calls. If the following straightforward implementation were used, a power function call would be needed per volume density function evaluation:

```
*density = (float) pow((double)turb*parms[1],(double)parms[2]);
```

Assuming an image size of 640 x 480, with 100 volume samples per pixel, the use of the precomputed table saves 30,710,000 *pow* function calls.

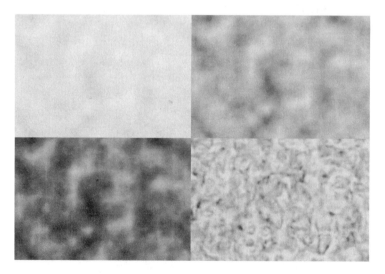

Figure 1.   **The effects of the power and sine function on the gas shape. (a) has a power exponent of 1, (b) has a power exponent of 2, (c) has a power exponent of 3, and (d) has the sine function applied to the gas.** © 1994 David S. Ebert.

Another useful mathematical function is the sine function. Perlin (Perlin 1985) uses the sine function in solid texturing to create marble, which will be described in a later section. This function can also be used in shaping gases, which can be accomplished by making the following change to the *basic_gas* function:

```
turb =(1.0 +sin(turbulence(pnt, pixel_size)*M_PI*5))*.5;
```

The above change creates "veins" in the shape of the gas, similar to the marble veins in solid texturing. As can be seen from these examples, it is very easy to shape the gas using simple mathematical functions. The remainder of this chapter will extend this *basic_gas* procedure to produce more complex shapes in the gas.

Patchy Fog

The first example of still gas is patchy fog. The above *basic_gas* function can be used to produce still images of patchy fog. For nice fog, *parms[1]=0.5, parms[2]=3.0*. The *parms[2]* value determines the "patchiness" of the fog, with lower values giving more continuous fog. *Parms[1]* controls the denseness of the fog that is in the resulting image.

Steam Rising from a Teacup

The goal of our second example is to create a realistic image of steam rising from a teacup. The first step is to place a "slab" (Kajiya 1986) of volume gas over the teacup. (Any ray-traceable solid can be used for defining the extent of the volume.) As steam is not a very thick gas, a maximum density value of 0.57 will be used with an exponent of 6.0 for the power function. The resulting image in Color Plate 6.2(a) was produced from the preceding *basic_gas* procedure.

The image created, however, does not look like steam rising from a teacup. First, the steam is not confined to be only above and over the cup. Second, the steam's density does not decrease as it rises. These problems can be easily corrected. To solve the first problem, ramp off the density spherically from the center of the top of the tea. This will confine the steam within the radius of the cup and make the steam rise higher over the center of the cup. The following *steam_slab1* procedure incorporates these changes into the *basic_gas* procedure:

```
steam_slab1(pnt, pnt_world, density,parms, vol)
    xyz_td  pnt, pnt_world;
    float   *density,*parms;
    vol_td  vol;
{
  float         turb, dist_sq,density_max;
```

```
int            i, indx;
xyz_td         diff;
static float pow_table[POW_TABLE_SIZE], ramp[RAMP_SIZE],
             offset[OFFSET_SIZE];
static int    calcd=1;
if(calcd)
   { calcd=0;
     for(i=POW_TABLE_SIZE-1; i>=0; i--)
        pow_table[i] = (float)pow(((double)(i))/(POW_TABLE_SIZE-1)*
                          parms[1]*2.0,(double)parms[2]);
     make_tables(ramp);
   }
turb =fast_turbulence(pnt, pixel_size);
*density = pow_table[(int)(turb*0.5*(POW_TABLE_SIZE-1))];

/* determine distance from center of the slab ^2. */
XYZ_SUB(diff,vol.shape.center, pnt_world);
dist_sq = DOT_XYZ(diff,diff);
density_max = dist_sq*vol.shape.inv_rad_sq.y;
indx = (int)((pnt.x+pnt.y+pnt.z)*100) & (OFFSET_SIZE -1);
density_max += parms[3]*offset[indx];

if(density_max >= .25) /* ramp off if > 25% from center */
   { /* get table index 0:RAMP_SIZE-1 */
     i = (density_max -.25)*4/3*RAMP_SIZE;
     i=MIN(i,RAMP_SIZE-1);
     density_max = ramp[i];
     *density *=density_max;
   }
}
make_tables(ramp, offset)
     float *ramp, *offset;
{
  int    i;
  float dist, result;
  srand48(42);
  for(i=0; i < OFFSET_SIZE; i++)
    {
     offset[i]=(float)drand48();
    }
 for(i = 0; i < RAMP_SIZE; i++)
    { dist =i/(RAMP_SIZE -1.0);
      ramp[i]=(cos(dist*M_PI) +1.0)/2.0;
    }
}
```

These modifications produce the more realistic image seen in Color Plate 4.2 (b). Two additional parameters are used in this new procedure: *pnt_world* and *vol. pnt_world* is the location of the point in world space. *vol* is a structure containing information on the volume being rendered. Table 1 clarifies the use of the various variables.

Table I. Variables for Steam Procedure

Variable	Description
pnt	location of the point in the solid texture space
pnt_world	location of the point in world space
density	the value returned from the function
parms[1]	maximum density of the gas
parms[2]	exponent for the power function for gas shaping
parms[3]	amount of randomness to use in falloff
parms[4]	distance at which to start ramping off the gas density
vol.shape.center	center of the volume
vol.shape.inv_rad_sq	1/radius squared of the slab
dist_sq	point's distance squared from the center of the volume
density_max	density scaling factor based on distance squared from the center
indx	an index into a random number table
offset	a precomputed table of random numbers used to add noise to the ramp off of the density
ramp	a table used for cosine falloff of the density values

The procedure now ramps off the density spherically using a cosine falloff function. If the distance from the center squared is greater than 25%, the cosine falloff is applied. The resulting image can be seen in Color Plate 4.2(b). This image is better than Color Plate 4.2 (a), but still lacking.

To solve the second problem, the gas density decreasing as it rises, the density of the gas needs to be ramped off as it rises to get a more natural look. The following addition to the end of the *steam_slab1* procedure will accomplish this:

```
dist = pnt_world.y - vol.shape.center.y;
if(dist > 0.0)
   { dist = (dist +offset[indx]*.1)*vol.shape.inv_rad.y;
     if(dist > .05)
       { offset2 = (dist -.05)*1.111111;
         offset2 = 1 - (exp(offset2)-1.0)/1.718282;
         offset2 *=parms[1];
         *density *= offset;
       }
   }
```

This procedure uses the e^x function to decrease the density as the gas rises. If the vertical distance above the center is greater than 5% of the total distance, the density is exponentially ramped off to 0. The result of this addition to the above procedure can be seen in Color Plate 4.3. As can be seen in this image, the resulting steam is very convincing. In the next chapter, animation effects using this basic steam model will be presented.

A Single Column of Smoke

The final example procedure creates a single column of rising smoke. The basis of the smoke shape is a vertical cylinder. Two observations can make the resulting image look realistic. First, smoke disperses as it rises. Second, the smoke column is initially fairly smooth, but as the smoke rises, turbulent behavior becomes the dominant characteristic of the flow. In order to reproduce these observations, turbulence is added to the cylinder's center to make the column of smoke look more natural. To simulate air currents and general turbulent effects, more turbulence is added as the height from the bottom of the smoke column increases. To simulate dispersion, the density of the gas is ramped off to zero as the gas rises.

These ideas will produce a very straight column of smoke. The following additional observation will make the image more realistic: smoke tends to bend and swirl as it rises. The swirling of the smoke is created by displacing each point by a vertical spiral (helix). The x and z coordinates of the point are displaced by the cosine and sine of the angle of rotation. The y coordinate of the point is displaced by the turbulence of the point. The procedure below produces a single column of smoke based on these observations.

```
/*
*******************************************************************************
*                              Smoke_stream                                  *
*******************************************************************************
* parms[1] = Maximum density value - density scaling factor                  *
* parms[2] = height for 0 density (end of ramping it off)                    *
* parms[3] = height to start adding turbulence                               *
* parms[4] = height(length) for maximum turbulence;                          *
* parms[5] = height to start ramping density off                             *
* parms[6] = center.y                                                        *
* parms[7] = speed for rising                                                *
* parms[8] = radius                                                          *
* parms[9] = max radius of swirling                                          *
*******************************************************************************
*/

smoke_stream(pnt,density,parms, pnt_world, vol)
     xyz_td   pnt, pnt_world;
     float    *density,*parms;
     vol_td   *vol;
{
 float             dist_sq;
 extern float      offset[OFFSET_SIZE];
 xyz_td            diff;
 xyz_td            hel_path, new_path, direction2, center;
 double            ease(), turb_amount, theta_swirl, cos_theta, sin_theta;
 static int        calcd=1;
 static float      cos_theta2, sin_theta2;
```

```
static xyz_td    bottom;
static double    rad_sq, max_turb_length, radius, big_radius,
                 st_d_ramp, d_ramp_length, end_d_ramp,
                 inv_max_turb_length;
double           height, fast_turb, t_ease, path_turb, rad_sq2;

if(calcd)
  { bottom.x=0; bottom.z = 0;
    bottom.y = parms[6];
    radius   = parms[8];
    big_radius = parms[9];
    rad_sq   = radius*radius;
    max_turb_length = parms[4];
    inv_max_turb_length = 1/max_turb_length;
    st_d_ramp = parms[5];
    end_d_ramp = parms[2];
    d_ramp_length = end_d_ramp - st_d_ramp;
    theta_swirl = 45.0*M_PI/180.0; /* swirling effect */
    cos_theta  = cos(theta_swirl);
    sin_theta  = sin(theta_swirl);
    cos_theta2 = .01*cos_theta;
    sin_theta2 = .0075*sin_theta;
    calcd=0;
  }

height = pnt_world.y - bottom.y + fast_noise(pnt)*radius;
  /* We don't want smoke below the bottom of the column */
if(height < 0)
  { *density =0;   return;}
height -= parms[3];
if (height < 0.0)
  height =0.0;
/* calculate the eased turbulence, taking into account the value may be
 *  greater than 1, which ease won't handle.
 */
t_ease = height* inv_max_turb_length;
if(t_ease > 1.0)
  { t_ease = ((int)(t_ease)) +ease( (t_ease - ((int)t_ease)), .001, .999);
    if( t_ease > 2.5)
      t_ease = 2.5;
  }
else
  t_ease = ease(t_ease, .5, .999);

/* Calculate the amount of turbulence to add in */
fast_turb= fast_turbulence(pnt);
turb_amount = (fast_turb -0.875)* (.2 + .8*t_ease);
path_turb = fast_turb*(.2 + .8*t_ease);

/* add turbulence to the height and see if it is above the top */
height +=0.1*turb_amount;
```

```
if(height > end_d_ramp)
  { *density=0; return; }
/* increase the radius of the column as the smoke rises */
if(height <=0)
  rad_sq2 = rad_sq*.25;
else if (height <=end_d_ramp)
  { rad_sq2 = (.5 + .5*(ease( height/(1.75*end_d_ramp), .5, .5)))*radius;
    rad_sq2 *=rad_sq2;
  }

/*
***********************************************************************
* move along a helical path
***********************************************************************
*

 /*
  * calculate the path based on the unperturbed flow: helical path
  */
hel_path.x = cos_theta2 *(1+ path_turb)*(1+cos(pnt_world.y*M_PI*2)*.11)
  *(1+ t_ease*.1)  + big_radius*path_turb;
hel_path.z = sin_theta2 *(1+path_turb)*
  (1+sin(pnt_world.y*M_PI*2)*.085)* (1+ t_ease*.1) + .03*path_turb;
hel_path.y =  - path_turb;
XYZ_ADD(direction2, pnt_world, hel_path);

/* adjusting the center point for ramping off the density based on the
 * turbulence of the moved point
 */
turb_amount *= big_radius;
center.x = bottom.x - turb_amount;
center.z = bottom.z + .75*turb_amount;

/* calculate the radial distance from the center and ramp off the density
 * based on this distance squared.
 */
diff.x = center.x - direction2.x;
diff.z = center.z - direction2.z;
dist_sq = diff.x*diff.x + diff.z*diff.z;
if(dist_sq > rad_sq2)
  {*density=0; return;}
*density = (1-dist_sq/rad_sq2 + fast_turb*.05) * parms[1];
if(height > st_d_ramp)
  *density *=  (1- ease( (height - st_d_ramp)/(d_ramp_length), .5 , .5));
}
```

The result of the above procedure can be seen in Color Plate 4.4. In this procedure, turbulence is added to many variables before doing tests and computing paths. The addition of the turbulence produces a more natural appearance to the column of smoke. This procedure uses the same *offset* table as in the *steam_slab1*

Table 2.   Parameters for Smoke Column Procedure

Parm	Value	Description
1	0.93	density scaling factor
2	1.6	height for 0 density (end of ramping it off)
3	0.175	height to start adding turbulence
4	0.685	height for maximum turbulence
5	0.0	height to start ramping density off
6	-0.88	center.y
7	2.0	speed for rising
8	0.04	radius
9	0.08	maximum radius of swirling

procedure. An *ease* procedure is also used to perform ease-in and ease-out of the turbulence addition and density ramping. The helical path that is used is actually the multiplication of two helical paths with the addition of turbulence. This calculation provides better results than a single helical path. The parameter values and their description can be found in Table 2.

Animating Solid Spaces 7

David S. Ebert

The previous chapter discussed modeling the geometry of gases. This chapter discusses animating gases and other procedurally defined solid spaces. There are several ways that solid spaces can be animated. This chapter will consider two approaches:

1. Changing the solid space over time.
2. Moving the point being rendered through the solid space.

The first approach has time as a parameter that changes the definition of the space over time, a very natural and obvious way to animate procedural techniques. The second approach does not change the solid space, but actually moves the point in the volume or object over time through the space. The movement of the gas (solid texture, hypertexture) is created by moving the fixed three-dimensional screen space point along a path over time through the solid space before evaluating the turbulence function. Each three-dimensional screen space point is inversely mapped back to world space. From world space, it is mapped into the gas and turbulence space through the use of simple affine transformations. Finally, it is moved through the turbulence space over time to create the movement. Therefore, the path direction will have the reverse visual effect. For example, a *downward* path applied to the screen space point will show the texture or volume object *rising*. Figure 1 illustrates this process.

Both of these techniques can be applied to solid texturing, gases, and hypertextures. After a brief discussion on animation paths, the application of these two techniques to solid texturing will be discussed, followed by the use of these

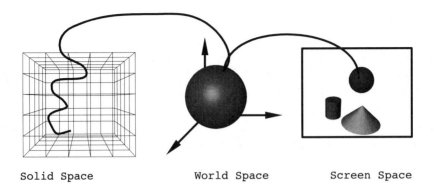

Solid Space   World Space   Screen Space

Figure I.   Moving a screen space point through the solid space.

techniques for gas animation, and finally, the use of these techniques for hyper-textures, including liquids.

Animation Paths

Throughout this chapter, I will describe various ways of creating animation paths for movement through the solid space. For many examples, I will use a helical (spiral) path. There are two reasons for using helical paths. First, most gases do not move along a linear path. Turbulence, convection, wind, etc., change the path movement. From my observations, smoke, steam, and fog tend to swirl while moving in a given direction. A helical path can capture this general sense of motion. Second, helical paths are very simple to calculate. The calculation involves rotation around the axis of the helix (direction of motion) and movement along the axis. To create the rotation, the sine and cosine functions will be used. The angle for these functions will be based on the frame number to produce the rotation over time. The rate of rotation can be controlled by taking the frame number modulo a constant. Linear motion, again based on the frame number, will be used to create the movement along the axis.

The code segment below creates a helical path that rotates about the axis once every 100 frames. The speed of movement along the axis is controlled by the variable *linear_speed*.

```
theta = (frame_number%100)*(2*M_PI/100);
```

```
path.x = cos(theta);
path.y = sin(theta);
path.z = theta*linear_speed;
```

One final point will clarify the procedures given in this chapter. To get smooth transitions between values and smooth acceleration and deceleration, *ease-in* and *ease-out* procedures are used. These are the standard routines used by animators to stop a moving object from jumping instantaneously from a speed of 0 to a constant velocity. One simple implementation of these functions assumes a sine curve for the acceleration and integrates this curve over one-half of its period.

Animating Solid Textures

This section will show how the previous two animation approaches can be used for solid texturing. Applying these techniques to color solid texturing will be discussed first, followed by solid textured transparency.

A marble procedure will be used as an example of color solid texture animation. A simple marble procedure based on Perlin's marble function is given below (Perlin 1985) .

```
rgb_td marble(pnt)
      xyz_td   pnt;
{
 float y;
 y = pnt.y + 3.0*turbulence(pnt, .0125);
 y = sin(y*M_PI);
 return (marble_color(y));
}

rgb_td marble_color(x)
      float x;
{
  rgb_td   clr;
  x = sqrt(x+1.0)*.7071;
  clr.g = .30 + .8*x;
  x=sqrt(x);
  clr.r = .30 + .6*x;
  clr.b = .60 + .4*x;
  return (clr);
}
```

This procedure applies a sine function to the turbulence of the point. The resulting value is then mapped to the color. The results achievable by this procedure can be seen in Color Plate 6.1(d).

Marble Forming

The application of the previous two animation approaches to this function has very different effects. When the first approach is used, changing the solid space over time, the formation of marble from banded rock can be achieved. Marble is formed from the turbulent mixing of different bands of rock. To simulate this process, initially, no turbulence is added to the point, therefore, the sine function determines the color. Basing the color on the sine function produces banded material. As the frame number increases, the amount of turbulence added to the point is increased, deforming the bands into the marble vein pattern. The resulting procedure is given below.

```
rgb_td marble_forming(pnt, frame_num, start_frame, end_frame)
        xyz_td   pnt;
        int      frame_num, start_frame, end_frame;
   {
    float x, turb_percent, displacement;

    if(frame_num < start_frame)
       { turb_percent=0;
         displacement=0;
       }
      else if (frame_num >= end_frame)
         { turb_percent=1;
           displacement= 3;
         }
      else
         { turb_percent= ((float)(frame_num-start_frame))/
                                  (end_frame-start_frame);
           displacement = 3*turb_percent;
         }

    x = pnt.x + turb_percent*3.0*turbulence(pnt, .0125) - displacement;
    x = sin(x*M_PI);
    return (marble_color(x));
 }
```

The *displacement* value in the above procedure is used to stop the entire texture from moving. Without the *displacement* value, the entire banded pattern moves horizontally to the left of the image, instead of the veins forming in place.

This procedure produces the desired effect, but the realism of the results can be increased by a few small changes. First of all, ease-in and ease-out of the rate of adding turbulence will give more natural motion. Second, the color of the marble can be changed to simulate heating before and during the deformation, and to simulate cooling after the deformation. The marble color is blended with a "glowing" marble color to simulate the heating and cooling. (Even though this may not be physically accurate, it produces a nice effect.) This can be achieved by the following procedure:

```
rgb_td marble_forming2(pnt, frame_num, start_frame, end_frame,heat_length)
      xyz_td  pnt;
      int     frame_num, start_frame, end_frame, heat_length;
  {
    float       x, turb_percent, displacement, glow_percent;
    rgb_td      m_color;

    if(frame_num < (start_frame-heat_length/2) ||
       frame_num > end_frame+heat_length/2)
      glow_percent=0;
    else if (frame_num < start_frame + heat_length/2)
      glow_percent= 1.0 - ease( ((start_frame+heat_length/2-frame_num)/
                              heat_length),0.4,0.6);
    else if (frame_num > end_frame-heat_length/2)
      glow_percent =  ease( ((frame_num-(end_frame-heat_length/2))/
                              heat_length),0.4,0.6);
    else
       glow_percent=1.0;

    if(frame_num < start_frame)
      { turb_percent=0; displacement=0;
      }
    else if (frame_num >= end_frame)
      { turb_percent=1;
        displacement= 3;
      }
    else
      { turb_percent= ((float)(frame_num-start_frame))/
                          (end_frame-start_frame);
        turb_percent=ease(turb_percent, 0.3, 0.7);
        displacement = 3*turb_percent;
       }
    x = pnt.y + turb_percent*3.0*turbulence(pnt, .0125) - displacement;
    x = sin(x*M_PI);
    m_color=marble_color(x);
    glow_percent= .5* glow_percent;
    m_color.r= glow_percent*(1.0)+ (1-glow_percent)*m_color.r;
    m_color.g= glow_percent*(0.4)+ (1-glow_percent)*m_color.g;
    m_color.b= glow_percent*(0.8)+ (1-glow_percent)*m_color.b;
    return(m_color);
  }
```

The resulting images can be seen in Color Plate 6.1. This figure shows four images of the change in the marble from banded rock (upper-left image) to the final marbled rock (lower-right image). Of course, the resulting sequence would be even more realistic if the material actually deformed, instead of the color simply changing. This effect will be described in the section on animating hyper-textures.

Marble Moving

A different effect can be achieved by the second animation approach, moving the point through the solid space. Any path can be used for movement through the marble space. A simple, obvious choice would be a linear path. Another choice, which produces very ethereal patterns in the material, is to use a turbulent path. The procedure below uses yet another choice for the path. This procedure moves the point along a horizontal helical path before evaluating the turbulence function, producing the effect of the marble pattern moving through the object. The helical path provides a more interesting result than the linear path, but does not change the general marble patterns as does using a turbulent path through the turbulence space. This technique can be used to determine the portion of marble from which to "cut" the object in order to achieve the most pleasing vein patterns. (You are in essence moving the object through a three-dimensional volume of marble.)

```
rgb_td moving_marble(pnt, frame_num)
      xyz_td   pnt;
      int      frame_num;
{
 float            x, tmp, tmp2;
 static float down, theta, sin_theta, cos_theta;
 xyz_td           hel_path, direction;
 static int    calcd=1;
 if(calcd)

      { theta=(frame_num%SWIRL_FRAMES)*SWIRL_AMOUNT; /*swirling effect*/
        cos_theta = RAD1 * cos(theta) + 0.5;
        sin_theta = RAD2 * sin(theta) - 2.0;
        down = (float)frame_num*DOWN_AMOUNT+2.0;
        calcd=0;
      }
 tmp = fast_noise(pnt); /* add some randomness */
 tmp2 = tmp*1.75;
 /* calculate the helical path */
 hel_path.y = cos_theta + tmp;
 hel_path.x = (- down)  + tmp2;
 hel_path.z = sin_theta - tmp2;
 XYZ_ADD(direction, pnt, hel_path);

 x = pnt.y + 3.0*turbulence(direction, .0125);
 x = sin(x*M_PI);
 return (marble_color(x));
}
```

In the above procedure, *SWIRL_FRAMES* and *SWIRL_AMOUNT* determine the number of frames for one complete rotation of the helical path. By choosing

SWIRL_FRAMES = 126 and *SWIRL_AMOUNT* = 2∗ π/126, the path swirls every 126 frames. *DOWN_AMOUNT* controls the speed of the downward movement along the helical path. A reasonable speed for downward movement for a unit sized object is to use *DOWN_AMOUNT* = 0.0095. *RAD1* and *RAD2* are the *y* and *z* radii of the helical path.

Animating Solid Textured Transparency

This section describes the use of the second solid-space animation technique, moving the point through the solid space, for animating solid textured transparency.

This animation technique is the one that I originally used for animating gases, and is still the main technique that I use for gases. The results of this technique applied to solid textured transparency can be seen in Ebert *et al.* 1989). The *fog* procedure given next is similar in its animation approach to the above *moving_marble* procedure. It produces fog moving through the surface of an object, and can be used as a surface-based approach to simulate fog or clouds. Again in this procedure, a downward helical path is used for the movement through the space, which produces an upward swirling to the gas movement.

```
void fog(pnt,transp, frame_num)
      xyz_td   pnt;
      float    *transp;
      int      frame_num;
{
 float tmp;
 xyz_td direction,cyl;
 double theta;

 pnt.x += 2.0 +turbulence(pnt, .1);
 tmp = noise_it(pnt);
 pnt.y +=   4+tmp;
 pnt.z += -2 - tmp;

 theta =(frame_num%SWIRL_FRAMES)*SWIRL_AMOUNT;
 cyl.x =RAD1 * cos(theta);
 cyl.z =RAD2 * sin(theta);

 direction.x = pnt.x + cyl.x;
 direction.y = pnt.y - frame_num*DOWN_AMOUNT;
 direction.z = pnt.z + cyl.z;

 *transp = turbulence(direction, .015);
 *transp = (1.0 -(*transp)*(*transp)*.275);
 *transp =(*transp)*(*transp)*(*transp);
 }
```

An image showing this procedure applied to a cube can be seen in Figure 2. The values used for this image can be found in Table 1.

Table 1. Values for Fog Procedure.

Parameter	Value
DOWN_AMOUNT	0.0095
SWIRL_FRAMES	126
SWIRL_AMOUNT	$2*\pi/126$
RAD1	0.12
RAD2	0.08

Another example of the use of solid textured transparency animation can be seen in Color Plate 7.1, which contains a still from an animation entitled *Once a Pawn a Foggy Knight...* (Ebert *et al.* 1989). In this scene, three planes are positioned to give a two-dimensional approximation of three-dimensional fog. One plane is in front of the scene, one plane is approximately in the middle, and the final plane is behind all the objects in the scene.

This technique is similar to Gardner's technique for producing images of clouds (Gardner 1985), except that it uses turbulence to control the transparency instead of Fourier synthesis. As with any surface-based approach to modeling gases, including Gardner's, this technique cannot produce three-dimensional volumes of fog or accurate shadowing from the fog.

Animation of Gaseous Volumes

As described in the previous section, animation technique 2, moving the point through the solid space, is the technique that I use to animate gases. This technique will be used in all the examples in this section. The gas movement is created by moving each fixed three-dimensional screen space point along a path over time through the solid space before evaluating the turbulence function. First, each three-dimensional screen space point is inversely mapped back to world space. Second, it is mapped from world space into the gas and turbulence space through the use of simple affine transformations. Finally, it is moved through the turbulence space over time to create the movement of the gas. Therefore, the path direction will have the reverse visual effect. For example, a downward path applied to the screen space point will cause the gas to rise.

This gas animation technique can be considered to be the inverse of particle systems because each point in three-dimensional screen space is moved through the gas space to see which portion of the gas occupies the current location in

Figure 2.   Solid textured transparency based fog. Copyright © 1994 David S. Ebert.

screen space. The main advantage of this approach over particle systems is that extremely large geometric databases of particles are not required to get realistic images. The complexity is always controlled by the number of screen space points in which the gas is potentially visible.

Several interesting animation effects can be achieved through the use of helical paths for movement through the solid space. These helical path effects will be described first, followed by the use of three-dimensional tables for controlling the gas movement. Finally, several additional primitives for creating gas animation will be presented.

Helical Path Effects

Helical paths can be used to create several different animation effects for gases. In this chapter, three examples of helical path effects will be presented: steam rising from a teacup, rolling fog, and a rising column of smoke.

Steam Rising from a Teacup

In the previous chapter, a procedure for producing a still image of steam rising from a teacup was described. This procedure can be modified to produce convincing animations of steam rising from the teacup by the addition of helical paths for motion. Each point in the volume is moved downward along a helical path to produce the steam rising and swirling in the opposite direction. The modification needed is given below. This animation technique is the same technique that was used in the *moving_marble* procedure.

```
       steam_moving(pnt, pnt_world, density,parms, vol)
            xyz_td   pnt, pnt_world;
            float    *density,*parms;
            vol_td   vol;
       {
*      float   noise_amt,turb, dist_sq, density_max, offset2, theta, dist;
       static float pow_table[POW_TABLE_SIZE], ramp[RAMP_SIZE],
                        offset[OFFSET_SIZE];
       extern int frame_num;
       xyz_td direction, diff;
       int i, indx;
       static int calcd=1;
*      static float down, cos_theta, sin_theta;

       if(calcd)
         { calcd=0;
          /* determine how to move the point through space(helical path) */
*           theta =(frame_num%SWIRL_FRAMES)*SWIRL;
*           down = (float)frame_num*DOWN*3.0 +4.0;
*           cos_theta = RAD1*cos(theta) +2.0;
*           sin_theta = RAD2*sin(theta) -2.0;

            for(i=POW_TABLE_SIZE-1; i>=0; i--)
               pow_table[i] = (float)pow(((double)(i))/(POW_TABLE_SIZE-1)*
                                parms[1]*2.0,(double)parms[2]);
            make_tables(ramp);
          }
         /* move the point along the helical path */
*      noise_amt = fast_noise(pnt);
*      direction.x = pnt.x + cos_theta + noise_amt;
*      direction.y = pnt.y - down + noise_amt;
*      direction.z = pnt.z +sin_theta + noise_amt;
       turb =fast_turbulence(direction);
       *density = pow_table[(int)(turb*0.5*(POW_TABLE_SIZE-1))];

     /* determine distance from center of the slab ^2. */
     XYZ_SUB(diff,vol.shape.center, pnt_world);
     dist_sq = DOT_XYZ(diff,diff);
     density_max = dist_sq*vol.shape.inv_rad_sq.y;
     indx = (int)((pnt.x+pnt.y+pnt.z)*100) & (OFFSET_SIZE -1);
     density_max += parms[3]*offset[indx];

     if(density_max >= .25) /* ramp off if > 25% from center */
```

```
    { /* get table index 0:RAMP_SIZE-1 */
      i = (density_max -.25)*4/3*RAMP_SIZE;
      i=MIN(i,RAMP_SIZE-1);
      density_max = ramp[i];
      *density *=density_max;
    }

  /* ramp it off vertically */
  dist = pnt_world.y - vol.shape.center.y;
  if(dist > 0.0)
    { dist = (dist +offset[indx]*.1)*vol.shape.inv_rad.y;
      if(dist > .05)
        { offset2 = (dist -.05)*1.111111;
          offset2 = 1 - (exp(offset2)-1.0)/1.718282;
          offset2*=parms[1];
          *density *= offset2;
        }
    }
}
```

The lines that have changed from the earlier *steam_slab1* procedure are marked with an asterisk, *. This procedure creates upward swirling movement in the gas, which swirls around 360 degrees every SWIRL_FRAMES frames. Noise is applied to the path to make it appear more random. The parameters RAD1 and RAD2 determine the elliptical shape of the swirling path. Additional variables in this procedure are the angle of rotation about the helical path (*theta*), the frame number (*frame_num*), the cosine of the angle of rotation (*cos_theta*), the sine of the angle of rotation (*sine_theta*), the amount to move along the helical axis (*down*), a noise amount to add to the path (*noise_amt*), and the new location of the point after movement along the path (*direction*).

The downward helical path through the gas space produces the effect of the gas rising and swirling in the opposite direction.

For more realistic steam motion, a simulation of air currents is helpful. This can be approximated by adding turbulence to the helical path. The amount of turbulence added is proportional to the height above the teacup. (This assumes that no turbulence is added at the surface.)

Fog Animation

The next example of helical path effects is the creation of rolling fog. For this animation, a horizontal helical path will be used to create the swirling motion of the fog to the right of the scene. From examining the *volume_fog_animation* procedure below, it is clear that this procedure uses the same animation technique as the above *steam_moving* procedure: move each point along a helical path before evaluating the turbulence function. The value returned by the turbulence function is again multiplied by a density scalar factor, *parms[1],* and raised to a power, *parms[2].* As in the previous procedures, a precomputed table of density values raised to a power is used to speed calculation. A more complete description of the use of helical paths for producing fog animation can be found in (Ebert and Parent 1990).

```
volume_fog_animation(pnt, pnt_world, density, parms, vol)
      xyz_td   pnt, pnt_world;
      float    *density,*parms;
      vol_td   *vol;
 {
  float noise_amt, turb;
  extern int frame_num;
  xyz_td direction;
  int      indx;
  static float pow_table[POW_TABLE_SIZE];
  int      i;
  static int calcd=1;
  static float down, cos_theta, sin_theta, theta;
  if(calcd)
     {
      down = (float)frame_num*SPEED*1.5 +2.0;
      theta =(frame_num%SWIRL_FRAMES)*SWIRL;   /* get swirling effect */
      cos_theta = cos(theta)*.1 + 0.5;         /* use a radius of .1  */
      sin_theta = sin(theta)*.14 - 2.0;        /* use a radius of .14 */
      calcd=0;
      for(i=POW_TABLE_SIZE-1; i>=0; i--)
        {
         pow_table[i] = (float)pow(((double)(i))/(POW_TABLE_SIZE-1)*
                        parms[1]*4.0,(double)parms[2]);
        }
     }

  /* make it move horizontally and add some noise to the movement  */
  noise_amt = fast_noise(pnt);
  direction.x = pnt.x - down + noise_amt*1.5;
  direction.y = pnt.y + cos_theta +noise_amt;
  direction.z = pnt.z + sin_theta -noise_amt*1.5;

  /* base the turbulence on the new point */
  turb =fast_turbulence(direction);
  *density = pow_table[(int)((turb*turb)*(.25*(POW_TABLE_SIZE-1)))];

  /* make sure density isn't greater than 1 */
  if(*density >1)
    *density=1;
 }
```

As in the *fog* and *steam_moving* procedures, the *volume_fog_animation* procedure above uses the same values for *SWIRL_FRAMES,* 126, and *SWIRL,* $2*\pi$ */126. SPEED* controls the rate of horizontal movement, and the value I use to produce gently rolling fog is 0.012. The results achievable by this procedure can be seen in Color Plate 7.2, which is a still from an animation entitled *Getting Into Art* (Ebert *et al.* 1990). For this image, *parms[1] = 0.22* and *parms[2] = 4.0.*

Smoke Rising

The final example of helical path effects is the animation of the *smoke_stream* procedure given earlier to create a single column of smoke. Two different helical paths are used to produce the swirling column of smoke. This *smoke_stream* procedure already used a helical path to displace each point to get a more convincing column of smoke. We will now modify this helical path to make it a downward helical path based on the frame number, creating the rising column of smoke. The second helical path will actually displace the center point of the cylinder, producing a swirling cylinder of smoke (instead of a vertical cylinder as was used in Chapter 6). This second helical path will swirl at a different rate than the first. The same input parameter values can be used for this procedure. Below is the procedure that is the result of these modifications.

```
/*
************************************************************************
*                         Rising_smoke_stream                        *
************************************************************************
* parms[1] = Maximum density value - density scaling factor          *
* parms[2] = height for 0 density (end of ramping it off)            *
* parms[3] = height to start adding turbulence                       *
* parms[4] = height(length) for maximum turbulence;                  *
* parms[5] = height to start ramping density off                     *
* parms[6] = center.y                                                *
* parms[7] = speed for rising                                        *
* parms[8] = radius                                                  *
* parms[9] = max radius of swirling                                  *
************************************************************************
*/

  rising_smoke_stream(pnt,density,parms, pnt_world, vol)
       xyz_td  pnt, pnt_world;
       float   *density,*parms;
       vol_td  *vol;
  {
   float   dist_sq;
   extern  float offset[OFFSET_SIZE];
   extern  int frame_num;
```

```
      static int calcd=1;
      static float down, cos_theta2, sin_theta2;
      xyz_td  hel_path, center, diff, direction2;
      double ease(), turb_amount, theta_swirl, cos_theta, sin_theta;
      static xyz_td   bottom;
      static double   rad_sq, max_turb_length, radius, big_radius,
                        st_d_ramp, d_ramp_length, end_d_ramp, down3,
                        inv_max_turb_length, cos_theta3, sin_theta3;
      double            height, fast_turb, t_ease, path_turb, rad_sq2;

      if(calcd)
        {
          bottom.x = 0; bottom.z = 0;
          bottom.y = parms[6];
          radius    = parms[8];
          big_radius = parms[9];
          rad_sq    = radius*radius;
          max_turb_length = parms[4];
          inv_max_turb_length = 1/max_turb_length;
          st_d_ramp = parms[5];
          st_d_ramp =MIN(st_d_ramp, end_d_ramp);
          end_d_ramp = parms[2];
          d_ramp_length = end_d_ramp - st_d_ramp;
          /* calculate rotation about the helix axis based on the fram_number
           */
*         theta_swirl=(frame_num%SWIRL_FRAMES_SMOKE)*SWIRL_SMOKE; /*swirling*/
*         cos_theta  = cos(theta_swirl);
*         sin_theta  = sin(theta_swirl);
*         down = (float)(frame_num)*DOWN_SMOKE*.75 * parms[7];
          /* Calculate sine and cosine of the different radii of the
           * two helical helical paths
           */
*         cos_theta2 = .01*cos_theta;
*         sin_theta2 = .0075*sin_theta;
*         cos_theta3= cos_theta2*2.25;
*         sin_theta3= sin_theta2*4.5;
*         down3= down*2.25;
          calcd=0;
        }

    height = pnt_world.y - bottom.y + fast_noise(pnt)*radius;
      /* We don't want smoke below the bottom of the column */
    if(height < 0)
      { *density =0;   return;}
    height -= parms[3];
    if (height < 0.0)
      height =0.0;

    /* calculate the eased turbulence, taking into account the value may be
     *  greater than 1, which ease won't handle.
     */
```

```
   t_ease = height* inv_max_turb_length;
   if(t_ease > 1.0)
     { t_ease =((int)(t_ease)) +ease((t_ease - ((int)t_ease)), .001, .999);
        if( t_ease > 2.5)
           t_ease = 2.5;
     }
   else

     t_ease = ease(t_ease, .5, .999);
   /* move the point along the helical path before evaluating turbulence */
* pnt.x += cos_theta3;
* pnt.y -= down3;
* pnt.z += sin_theta3;

   fast_turb= fast_turbulence_three(pnt);
   turb_amount = (fast_turb -0.875)* (.2 + .8*t_ease);
   path_turb = fast_turb*(.2 + .8*t_ease);
  /* add turbulence to the height and see if it is above the top */
   height +=0.1*turb_amount;
   if(height > end_d_ramp)
    { *density=0; return; }

   /* increase the radius of the column as the smoke rises */
   if(height <=0)
     rad_sq2 = rad_sq*.25;
   else if (height <=end_d_ramp)
     {
       rad_sq2 = (.5 + .5*(ease( height/(1.75*end_d_ramp), .5, .5)))*radius;
        rad_sq2 *=rad_sq2;
     }
   else
     rad_sq2 = rad_sq;
/*
************************************************************************
* move along a helical path plus add the ability to use tables
************************************************************************
*/
/*
* calculate the path base on the unperturbed flow: helical path
*/
* hel_path.x = cos_theta2 * (1+path_turb)*(1+ t_ease*.1)*
    (1+cos((pnt_world.y+down*.5)*M_PI*2)*.11)  + big_radius*path_turb;

* hel_path.z = sin_theta2 * (1+path_turb)*(1+ t_ease*.1)*
    (1+sin((pnt_world.y +down*.5)*M_PI*2)*.085) + .03*path_turb;

* hel_path.y = (- down) - path_turb;
   XYZ_ADD(direction2, pnt_world, hel_path);
/* adjusting the center point for ramping off the density based on the
*  turbulence of the moved point
*/
```

```
turb_amount *= big_radius;
center.x = bottom.x - turb_amount;

center.z = bottom.z + .75*turb_amount;
/* calculate the radial distance from the center and ramp off the
 * density based on this distance squared.
 */
diff.x = center.x - direction2.x;
diff.z = center.z - direction2.z;
dist_sq = diff.x*diff.x + diff.z*diff.z;
if(dist_sq > rad_sq2)
  {*density=0;
   return;}
*density = (1-dist_sq/rad_sq2 + fast_turb*.05) * parms[1];
if(height > st_d_ramp)
  *density *= (1- ease( (height - st_d_ramp)/(d_ramp_length), .5 , .5));
}
```

The statements that have been changed from the *smoke_stream* procedure are marked with an asterisk. As can be seen, the main changes are in calculating and using two helical paths based on the frame number. One path displaces the center of the cylinder, and the point being rendered is moved along the other path. After trials with only one helical path, it becomes clear that two helical paths give a better effect. Color Plate 7.3 shows the results of this *rising_smoke_stream* procedure. This figure contains three images from an animation of rising smoke.

Three-Dimensional Tables

As shown above, a wide variety of effects can be achieved through the use of helical paths. These aforementioned procedures require the same type of path to be used for movement throughout the entire volume of gas. Obviously, more complex motion can be achieved by having different paths motions for different locations within the gas. A three-dimensional table specifying different procedures for different locations within the volume is a good, flexible solution for creating complex motion in this manner.

The use of three-dimensional tables (solid spaces) to control the animation of the gases is an extension to my previous use of solid spaces in which three-dimensional tables were used for volume shadowing effects (Ebert and Parent).

The three-dimensional tables are handled in the following manner: the table surrounds the gas volume in world space and values are stored at each of the lattice points in the table (see Figure 3). These values represent the calculated values for that specific location in the volume. To determine the values for other locations in the volume, the eight table entries forming the parallelepiped surrounding the point are interpolated. For speed in accessing the table values, I

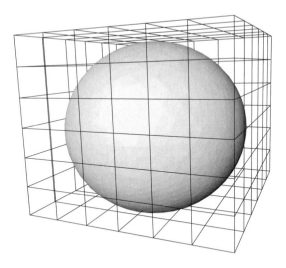

Figure 3.   Three-dimensional table surrounding a sphere.

currently require table dimensions to be powers of 2 and actually store the three-dimensional table as a one-dimensional array. This restriction allows the use of simple bit-shifting operations in determining the array index. These tables could be extended to have nonuniform spacing between table entries within each dimension, creating an octree-like structure; however, this would greatly increase the time necessary to access values from the table, as this fast bit-shifting approach could no longer be used. Table dimensions are commonly of the order of 64 x 64 x 64 or 128 x 64 x 32.

I use two types of tables for controlling the motion of the gases: vector field tables and functional flow field tables. The vector field tables store direction vectors, density scaling factors, and other information for their use at each point in the lattice. Therefore, these tables are suited for visualizing computational fluid dynamics simulations or using external programs for controlling the gas motion. The vector field tables will not be described in this chapter. A thorough description of their use and merits can be found in (Ebert 1991). This chapter concentrates on the use of functional flow field tables for animation control.

The functional flow field and vector field tables are incorporated into the volume density functions for controlling the shape and movement of the gas. Each volume density function has a default path and velocity for the gas movement. First, the default path and velocity are calculated; second, the vector field tables are evaluated; and, finally, functions that calculate direction vectors, density scaling factors, etc., from the functional flow field tables are applied. The default path vector, the vector from the vector field table, and the vector from the flow field function are combined to produce the new path for the movement through the gas space.

Accessing the Table Entries

When values are accessed from these tables during rendering, the location of the sample point within the table is determined. As mentioned earlier, this point will lie within a parallelepiped formed by the eight table entries that surround the point. The values at these eight points are interpolated to determine the final value. The location within the table is determined by first mapping the three-dimensional screen space point back into world space. The following formula is then used to find the location of the point within the table:

$$ptable.x = (point.x—table\_start.x) * table\_inv\_step.x$$
$$ptable.y = (point.y—table\_start.y) * table\_inv\_step.y$$
$$ptable.z = (point.z—table\_start.z) * table\_inv\_step.z$$

Ptable is the location of the point within the three-dimensional table, which is determined from *point*, the location of the point in world space. *Table_start* is the location in world space of the starting table entry, and *table_inv_step* is the inverse of the step size between table elements in each dimension. Once the location within the table is determined, the values corresponding to the eight surrounding table entries are then interpolated (trilinear interpolation should suffice).

Functional Flow Field Tables

Functional flow field tables are a valuable tool for choreographing gas animation. These tables define, for each region of the gas, which functions to evaluate to control the gas movement. Each flow field table entry can either contain one specific function to evaluate, or a list of functions to evaluate to determine the path for the gas motion (path through the gas space). For each function, a file is specified which contains the type of function and parameters for that function. The functions evaluated by the flow field tables return the following information:

Flow Field Function Values

- direction vector

- density scaling value

- percent of vector to use

- velocity

The advantage of using flow field functions is that they can provide infinite detail in the motion of the gas. They are not stored at a fixed resolution, but are evaluated for each point that is volume rendered. The disadvantage is that the functions are much more expensive to evaluate than simply interpolating values from the vector field table.

The "percent of vector to use" value in the above table is used to provide a smooth transition between control of the gas movement by the flow field functions, the vector field tables, and the default path of the gas. This value is also used to allow a smooth transition between control of the gas by different flow field functions. This value will decrease as the distance from the center of control of a given flow field function increases.

Functional Flow Field Functions

Two powerful types of functions for controlling the movement of the gases are attractors/repulsors and vortex functions. Repulsors are the *exact* opposite of attractors, so only attractors will be described here. To create a repulsor from an attractor, simply negate the direction vector.

All of the following procedures will take as input the location of the point in the solid space (*pnt*), and a structure containing parameters for each instance of the function (*ff*). These procedures will return a density scaling factor (*density_scaling*), the direction vector for movement through the gas space (*direction*), the percent of this vector to use in determining the motion through the gas space (*percent_to_use*), and a velocity scaling factor (*velocity*). The *density_scaling* parameter allows these procedures to decrease or increase the gas density as it moves through a region of space. The *velocity* parameter similarly allows these procedures to change the velocity of the gas as it moves through a region of space. The most important parameters, though, are the *direction* and *percent_to_use* parameters, which are used to determine the path motion through the solid space.

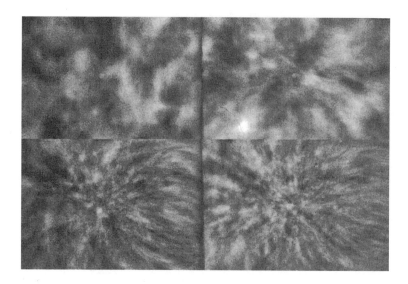

Figure 4. Effect of a spherical attractor increasing over time. Images are every 45 frames. The top-left image has 0 attraction. The lower-right image has the maximum attraction. Copyright © 1992 David S. Ebert.

Attractors

Attractors are primitive functions that can provide a wide range of effects. Figure 4 shows several frames of an attractor whose attraction increases in strength over time. Each attractor has a minimum and maximum attraction value. In this figure, the interpolation varies over time between the minimum and maximum attraction values of the attractor. By animating the location and strength of an attractor, many different effects can be achieved. Effects such as a breeze blowing (see Color Plate 7.4) and the wake of a moving object are easy to create. Spherical attractors create paths radially away from the center of attraction (as stated previously, path movement needs to be in the opposite direction of the desired visual effect). The following is an example of a simple spherical attractor function:

```
spherical_attractor(point, ff, direction, density_scaling,
                    velocity, percent_to_use)
    xyz_td        point, *direction;
    flow_func_td ff;
    float         *density_scaling, *velocity, *percent_to_use;
{
    float         dist, d2;
```

```
/*calculate distance and direction from center of attractor  */
    XYZ_SUB(*direction, point, ff.center);
    dist=sqrt(DOT_XYZ(*direction,*direction));

    /* set the density scaling and the velocity to 1 */
    *density_scaling=1.0;
    *velocity=1.0;

    /* calculate the falloff factor (cosine) */
    if(dist > ff.distance)
        *percent_to_use=0;
    else if (dist < ff.falloff_start)
        *percent_to_use=1.0;
    else
      { d2 =(dist-ff.falloff_start)/(ff.distance-ff.falloff_start);
        *percent_to_use = (cos(d2*M_PI)+1.0)*.5;
      }
  }
```

The *flow_func_td* structure contains parameters for each instance of the spherical attractor. The parameters include the center of the attractor (*ff.center*), the effective distance of attraction (*ff.distance*), and the location to begin the falloff from the attractor path to the default path (*ff.falloff_start*). This function ramps the use of the attractor path from *ff.falloff_start* to *ff.distance*. A cosine function is used for a smooth transition between the path defined by the attractor and the default path of the gas.

Extensions of Spherical Attractors

Variations on this simple spherical attractor include moving attractors, angle limited attractors, attractors with variable maximum attraction, nonspherical attractors, and, of course, combinations of any or all of these types.

One variation on the above spherical attractor procedure is to animate the location of the center of attraction. This allows for dynamic animation control of the gas. Another useful variation is angle-limited attractors. As opposed to having the range of the attraction being 360 degrees, an axis and an angle for the range of attraction can be specified. This can be implemented in a manner very similar to angle-limited light sources and can be animated over time. These two variations can be combined to produce interesting effects. For example, a wake from a moving object can be created by an angle-limited attractor following the movement of the object. This attractor will cause the gas behind the object to be displaced and pulled in the direction of the moving object. The minimum and maximum attraction of the attractor can also be animated over time to produce nice effects as seen in Figure 4 and Color Plate 7.4. Figure 4 shows an attractor increasing in strength over time and Color Plate 7.4 shows a breeze blowing the steam rising from a teacup. As will be described later, the breeze is simulated with an animated attractor.

The geometry of the attraction can be not only spherical, but also planar or linear. A linear attractor can be used for creating the flow of a gas along a wall, as will be explained in a later section.

Spiral Vortex Functions

Vortex functions have a variety of uses, from simulating actual physical vortices to creating interesting disturbances in flow patterns as an approximation of turbulent flow. The procedures described are not attempts at a physical simulation of vortices, an extremely complex procedure requiring large amounts of super-computer time for approximation models.

One vortex function is based on the simple 2D polar coordinate function:

$$r = \theta$$

which translates into three-dimensional coordinates as

$$x = \theta \times \cos(\theta)$$
$$y = \theta \times \sin(\theta)$$

The third dimension is normally linear movement over time along the third axis. To animate this function, θ is based on the frame number. To increase the vortex action, a scalar multiplier for the sine and cosine terms based on the distance from the vortex's axis is added. This polar equation alone produces swirling motion; however, more convincing vortices can be created by the modifications described below, which base the angle of rotation on both the frame number and the distance from the center of the vortex.

The resulting vortex procedure is the following:

```
calc_vortex(pt, ff, direction, velocity, percent_to_use, frame_num)
     xyz_td          *pt, *direction;
     flow_func_td *ff;
     float           *percent_to_use, *velocity;
     int             frame_num;
  {
    static tran_mat_td  mat={0,0,0,0,0,0,0,0,0,0,0,0,0,0,0,0};
    xyz_td                dir, pt2, diff;
    float                 theta, dist, d2, dist2;
    float                 cos_theta,sin_theta,compl_cos, ratio_mult;

     /*calculate distance from center of vortex */
    XYZ_SUB(diff,(*pt), ff->center);
    dist=sqrt(DOT_XYZ(diff,diff));
```

```
dist2 = dist/ff->distance;
 /* calculate angle of rotation about the axis */
theta = (ff->parms[0]*(1+.001*(frame_num)))/
        (pow((.1+dist2*.9), ff->parms[1]));

 /* calculate the matrix for rotating about the cylinder's axis */
calc_rot_mat(theta, ff->axis, mat);
transform_XYZ((long)1,mat,pt,&pt2);
XYZ_SUB(dir,pt2,(*pt));
direction->x = dir.x;
direction->y = dir.y;
direction->z = dir.z;

 /* Have the maximum strength increase from frame parms[4] to
  * parms[5] to a maximum of parms[2]   */
if(frame_num < ff->parms[4])
  ratio_mult=0;
else if (frame_num <= ff->parms[5])
   ratio_mult = (frame_num - ff->parms[4])/
                (ff->parms[5] - ff->parms[4])* ff->parms[2];
else
  ratio_mult = ff->parms[2];

 /* calculate the falloff factor */
if(dist > ff->distance)
  { *percent_to_use=0;
    *velocity=1;
  }
else if (dist < ff->falloff_start)
  { *percent_to_use=1.0 *ratio_mult;
    /*calc velocity  */
    *velocity= 1.0+(1.0 - (dist/ff->falloff_start));
  }
else
  { d2 =(dist-ff->falloff_start)/(ff->distance -ff->falloff_start);
    *percent_to_use = (cos(d2*M_PI)+1.0)*.5*ratio_mult;
    *velocity= 1.0+(1.0 - (dist/ff->falloff_start));
  }
}
```

This procedure uses the above polar function in combination with suggestions from Karl Sims (Simms 1990) to produce the vortex motion. For these vortices, the angle of rotation about the axis is determined by both the frame number and the relative distance of the point from the center (or axis) of rotation. The direction vector is then the vector difference of the transformed point and the original point. The *calc_vortex* procedure also allows the animation of the strength of the vortex action.

A third type of vortex function is based on the conservation of angular momentum: $r * q = constant$, where r is the distance from the center of the vortex. This formula can be used in the above vortex procedure to calculate the angle of rotation about the axis of the vortex: $\theta = \textit{(time} * \textit{constant)/r}$. The angular momentum will be conserved, producing more realistic motion.

An example of the effects achievable by the above vortex procedure can be seen in Color Plate 7.5. Animating the location of these vortices produces interesting effects, especially when coordinating their movement with the movement of objects in the scene, such as a swirling wake created by an object moving through the gas.

Combinations of Functions

The real power of flow field functions is the ability to combine these primitive functions to control the gas movement through different volumes of space. The combination of flow field functions provides very interesting and complex gas motion. Two examples of the combination of flow field functions, wind blowing and flow into a hole, are presented next to illustrate the power of this technique.

Wind Effects

The first complex gas motion example is wind blowing the steam rising from a teacup. A spherical attractor is used to create the wind effect. Color Plate 7.4 shows frames of an animation of a breeze blowing the steam from the left of the image. To produce this effect, an attractor was placed to the upper right of the teacup and the strength of attraction was increased over time. The maximum attraction was only 30%, producing a light breeze. An increase in the maximum attraction would simulate an increase in the strength of the wind. The top-left image shows the steam rising vertically with no effect of the wind. The sequence of images (top-right image to bottom-right image) shows the effect on the steam as the breeze starts blowing toward the right of the image. This is a simple combination of helical motion with an attractor. Notice how the volume of the steam as well as the motion of the individual plumes is "blown" toward the upper right. This effect was created by moving the center of the volume point for the ramping of the density over time. The x-value of the center point is increased, based on the height from the cup and the frame number. By changing the *spherical_attractor* flow function and the *steam_moving* procedure given above, the blowing effect can be implemented. The following is the addition needed to the *spherical_attractor* procedure:

```
/*
 ************************************************************************
 * Move the Volume of the Steam
 ************************************************************************
```

```
 * Shifting is based on the height above the cup(parms[6]->parms[7])
 * and the frame range for increasing the strength of the attractor.
 * This is from ratio_mult that is calculated above in calc_vortex.
 ********************************************************************
 * Have the maximum strength increase from frame parms[4] to
 * parms[5] to a maximum of parms[2]
 */
if(frame_num < ff->parms[4])
  ratio_mult=0;
else if (frame_num <= ff->parms[5])
   ratio_mult = (frame_num - ff->parms[4])/
                 (ff->parms[5] - ff->parms[4]) * ff->parms[2];
if(point.y < ff->parms[6])
   x_disp=0;
else
  {if(point.y <= ff->parms[7])
     d2=COS_ERP((point.y-ff->parms[6])/(ff->parms[7]-ff->parms[6]));
   else
     d2=0;
   x_disp=(1-d2)*ratio_mult*parms[8]+fast_noise(point)*ff->parms[9];
   }
return(x_disp);
```

Table 2 clarifies the use of all the parameters. The *ratio_mult* value for increasing the strength of the attraction is calculated in the same way as in the *calc_vortex* procedure. The *x_disp* value needs to be returned to the *steam_rising* function. This value is then added to the *center* variable before the density is ramped off. The following addition to the *steam_rising* procedure will accomplish this:

```
center = vol.shape.center;
center.x += x_disp;
```

Table 2.   Parameters for wind effects.

Variable	Description
point	location of the point in world space
ff → parms[2]	maximum strength of attraction
ff → parms[4]	starting frame for attraction increasing
ff → parms[5]	ending strength for attraction increasing
ff → parms[6]	minimum y-value for steam displacement
ff → parms[7]	maximum y-value for steam displacement
ff → parms[8]	maximum amount of steam displacement
ff → parms[9]	amount of noise to add in

Flow into a Hole in a Wall

The next example of combining flow field functions constrains the flow into an opening in a wall. The resulting images are shown in Color Plate 7.6(a) and (b). Color Plate 7.6(a) shows gas flow into an opening in a wall on the right of the image. Color Plate 7.6(b) shows liquid flow into the opening. For this example, three types of functions are used. The first function is an angle-limited spherical attractor placed at the center of the hole. This attractor has a range of 180 degrees from the axis of the hole toward the left. The next function is an angle-limited repulsor placed at the same location, again with a range of repulsion of 180 degrees, but to the right of the hole. These two functions create the flow into the hole and through the hole. The final type of function creates the tangential flow along the walls. This function can be considered a linear attraction field on the left side of the hole. The line in this case would be through the hole and perpendicular to the wall (horizontal). This attractor has maximum attraction near the wall, with the attraction decreasing as the distance from the wall increases. As can be seen from the flow patterns toward the hole and along the wall in Color Plate 7.6, the effect is very convincing. This figure also shows how these techniques can be applied to hypertextures. The right image is rendered as a hypertexture to simulate a (compressible) liquid flowing into the opening.

Animating Hypertextures

All of the animation techniques described above can be applied to hypertextures; only the rendering algorithm needs to be changed. The volume density functions that I use for gases are, in reality, hypertexture functions. The difference is that an atmospheric rendering model is used. Therefore, by using a nongaseous model for illumination and for converting densities to opacities, the techniques described above will produce hypertexture animations. An example of this is Color Plate 7.6(b). The geometry and motion procedures are the same for both of the images in Color Plate 7.6.

Volumetric Marble Formation

One other example of hypertexture animation will be explored: simulating marble formation. The addition of hypertexture animation to the solid texture animation discussed earlier will increase the realism of the animation considerably.

One approach is to base the density changes on the color of the marble. Initially, no turbulence will be added to the "fluid": density values will be determined in a manner similar to the marble color values, giving the different bands different densities. Just as in the earlier *marble_forming* procedure, turbulence will be added over time. In the procedure below, these changes are achieved by returning the amount of turbulence, *turb_amount*, from the solid texture function, *marble_forming*, described earlier. The density is based on the turbulence amount from the solid texture function. This is then shaped using the power function in a similar manner to the gas functions given before. Finally, a trick by Perlin (subtracting .5, multiplying by a scalar, adding .5, and limiting the result to the range of .2 and 1.0) (Perlin 1992) is used to form a hard surface more quickly. The result of this function can be seen in Color Plate 7.7.

```
/*
*****************************************************************
* parms[1] = maximum density value: density scaling factor    *
* parms[2] = exponent for  density scaling                    *
* parms[3] = x resolution for Perlin's trick (0-640)          *
* parms[8] = 1/radius of fuzzy area for perlin's trick (> 1.0) *
*****************************************************************
*/
molten_marble(pnt, density, parms,vol)
     xyz_td  pnt;
     float   *density,*parms;
     vol_td  vol;
{
  float  parms_scalar, turb_amount;
  turb_amount = solid_txt(pnt,vol);
  *density = (pow(turb_amount, parms[2]) )*0.35 +.65;
   /* Introduce harder surface quicker. parms[3] multiplied by 1/640*/
  *density *=parms[1];
  parms_scalar = (parms[3]*.0015625)*parms[8];
  *density= (*density-.5)*parms_scalar +.5;
  *density = MAX(0.2, MIN(1.0,*density));
  }
```

Volumetric Cloud Modeling with Implicit Functions 8

David S. Ebert

Modeling clouds is a very difficult task because of their complex, amorphous structure and because even an untrained eye can judge the realism of a cloud model. Their ubiquitous nature makes them an important modeling and animation task. This chapter describes a new volumetric procedural approach for cloud modeling and animation that allows easy, natural specification and animation of the clouds, provides the flexibility to include as much physics or art as desired into the model, unburdens the user from detailed geometry specification, and produces realistic volumetric cloud models. This technique combines the flexibility of volumetric procedural modeling with the smooth blending and ease of control of primitive-based implicit functions (metaballs, blobs) to create a powerful new modeling technique. This technique also demonstrates the advantages of primitive-based implicit functions for modeling semitransparent volumetric objects.

Background

Modeling clouds in computer graphics has been a challenge for nearly twenty years (Dungan, Jr. 1979). Many previous approaches have used semi-transparent surfaces to produce convincing images of clouds (Gardner 1984,Gardner 1985, Gardner 1990, Voss 1983). Although these techniques can produce realistic images of clouds viewed from a distance, these cloud models are hollow and do not allow the user to seamlessly enter, travel through, and inspect the interior of the cloud model. To capture the three-dimensional structure of a cloud, volumetric density-based models must be used. Kajiya (Kajiya and Von Herzen 1984) produced the first volumetric cloud model in computer graphics, but the results are not photo-realistic. Stam (Stam and Fiume 1995), Foster (Foster and Metaxas 1997), and Ebert (Ebert *et al.* 1994b) have produced convincing volumetric models of smoke and steam but have not done substantial work on modeling clouds. Neyret (Neyret 1997) has recently produced some preliminary results of a convective cloud model based on general physical characteristics. This model may be promising for simulating convective clouds; however, it currently uses surfaces (large particles) to model the cloud structure. A general, flexible, easy-to-use, realistic volumetric cloud model is still needed in computer graphics.

In developing this new cloud modeling and animation system, I have chosen to build upon the recent work in advanced modeling techniques and volumetric procedural modeling. As mentioned in Chapter 1, many advanced geometric modeling techniques, such as fractals (Peitgen *et al.* 1992), implicit surfaces (Blinn 1982b, Wyvill *et al.* 1986a, Nishimura *et al.* 1985), grammar-based modeling (Smith 1984, Prusinkiewicz and Lindenmayer 1990), and volumetric procedural models/hypertextures (Perlin 1985, Ebert *et al.* 1994b) use procedural abstraction of detail to allow the designer to control and animate objects at a high level. Their inherent procedural nature provides flexibility, data amplification, abstraction of detail, and ease of parametric control. When modeling complex volumetric phenomena, such as clouds, this abstraction of detail and data amplification are necessary to make the modeling and animation tractable. It would be impractical for an animator to specify and control the detailed three-dimensional density of a cloud model. This system does not use a physics-based approach because it is computationally prohibitive and nonintuitive to use for many animators and modelers. Setting and animating correct physics parameters for dew point, particulate distributions, temperature and pressure gradients, and so forth is a time-consuming, detailed task. This model was developed to allow the modeler and animator to work at a much higher level. I also didn't want to restrict the results by the laws of physics but to allow for artistic expression.

Volumetric procedural models have all of the advantages of procedural techniques and are a natural choice for cloud modeling because they are the most flexible advanced modeling technique. Since a procedure is evaluated to determine the object's density, any advanced modeling technique, simple physics simulation, mathematical function, or artistic algorithm can be included in the model.

Combining traditional volumetric procedural models with implicit functions creates a model that has the advantages of both techniques. Implicit functions have been used for many years as a modeling tool for creating solid objects and smoothly blended surfaces (Bloomenthal *et al.* 1997). However, little work has been done to explore their potential for modeling volumetric density distributions of semitransparent volumes. Nishita (Nishita *et al.* 1996) has used volume rendered implicits as a basic cloud model in his work on multiple scattering illumination models; however, this work has concentrated on illumination effects and not on realistic modeling of the cloud geometry. Stam has also used volumetric blobbies to create his models of smoke and clouds (Stam and Fiume 1991, Stam and Fiume 1993, Stam and Fiume 1995). His work is related to the approach described in this chapter. My early work on using volume rendered implicit spheres to produce a fly-through of a volumetric cloud was described in (Ebert 1997). This work has been developed further to use implicits to provide a natural way of specifying and animating the global structure of the cloud, while using more traditional procedural techniques to model the detailed structure.

Volumetric Procedural Modeling with Implicit Functions

The volumetric cloud model uses a two-level model: the cloud macrostructure and the cloud microstructure. These are modeled by implicit functions and turbulent volume densities, respectively. The basic structure of the cloud model combines these two components to determine the final density of the cloud.

The cloud's microstructure is created by using procedural *turbulence* and *noise* functions, in a manner similar to the *basic_gas* function (see Chapter 7). This allows the procedural simulation of natural detail to the level needed. Simple mathematical functions are added to allow shaping of the density distributions and control over the sharpness of the density falloff.

Implicit functions were chosen to model the cloud macrostructure because of their ease of specification and smoothly blending density distributions. The user simply specifies the location, type, and weight of the implicit primitives to create the overall cloud shape. Any implicit primitive, including spheres, cylinders, ellipsoids, and skeletal implicits can be used to model the cloud macrostructure. Since these are volume rendered as a semitransparent medium, the whole volumetric field function is being rendered, as compared to implicit surface rendering where only a small range of values of the field are used to create the objects. The implicit density functions are primitive-based density functions: They are defined by summed, weighted, parameterized, primitive implicit surfaces. A simple example of the implicit formulation of a sphere centered at the point *center* with radius *r* is the following:

$$F(x,y,z) : (x - \text{center}.x)^2 + (y - \text{center}.y)^2 + (z - \text{center}.z)^2 - r^2 = 0.$$

The real power of implicit functions is the smooth blending of the density fields from separate primitive sources. I chose to use Wyvill's standard cubic function (Wyvill *et al.* 1986) as the density (blending) function for the implicit primitives:

$$F_{cub}(r) = \frac{4}{9}\frac{r^6}{R^6} + \frac{17}{9}\frac{r^4}{R^4} - \frac{22}{9}\frac{r^2}{R^2} + 1.$$

In the above equation, r is the distance from the primitive. This density function is a cubic in the distance squared, and its value ranges from 1 when $r = 0$ (within the primitive) to 0 at $r = R$. This density function has several advantages. First, its value drops off quickly to zero (at the distance R), reducing the number of primitives that must be considered in creating the final surface. Second, it has zero derivatives at $r = 0$ and $r = R$ and is symmetrical about the contour value 0.5, providing for smooth blends between primitives. The final implicit density value is then the weighted sum of the density field values of each primitive:

$$Density_{implicit}(p) = \sum_i \left(w_i F_{cub_i}(p-q) \right)$$

where w_i is the weight of the ith primitive and q is the closest point on element i from p.

To create nonsolid implicit primitives, the location of the point is procedurally altered before the evaluation of the blending functions. This alteration can be the product of the procedure and the implicit function and/or a warping of the implicit space.

These techniques are combined into a simple cloud model as shown below:

```
volumetric_procedural_implicit_function(pnt, blend%, pixel_size)
    perturbed_point  =  procedurally alter pnt
                        using noise and turbulence
    density1  =  implicit_function(perturbed_point)
    density2  =  turbulence(pnt, pixel_size)
    blend  =  blend% * density1 +
              (1 - blend%) * density2
    density  =  shape resulting density based on user
                controls for wispiness and denseness
                (e.g., use pow and exponential function)
    return(density)
```

The density from the implicit primitives is combined with a pure turbulence based density using a user specified *blend%* (60% to 80% gives good results). The blending of the two densities allows the creation of clouds that range from entirely determined by the implicit function density to entirely determined by the procedural turbulence function. When the clouds are completely determined by the implicit functions, they will tend to look more like cotton balls. The addition of the procedural alteration and turbulence is what gives them their naturalistic look.

Volumetric Cloud Modeling

The volumetric procedural implicit algorithm given above forms the basis of a flexible system for the modeling of volumetric objects. This chapter focuses on the use of these techniques for modeling and animating realistic clouds. The volume rendering of the clouds is not discussed in detail. For a description of the volume rendering system that was used to make my images of clouds in this book, please see Chapter 6. Any volume rendering system can be used with these volumetric cloud procedures; however, to get realistic effects, the system should accumulate densities using atmospheric attenuation, and a physics-based illumination algorithm should be used. For accurate images of cumulus clouds, a high-albedo illumination algorithm (e.g., (Max 1994, Nishita *et al.* 1996)) is needed.

Cumulus Clouds

Cumulus clouds are very common in nature and can be easily simulated using spherical or elliptical implicit primitives. Color Plate 8.1 shows the type of result that can be achieved by using nine implicit spheres to model a cumulus cloud. The animator/modeler simply positions the implicit spheres to produce the general cloud structure. Procedural modification then alters the density distribution to create the detailed wisps. The algorithm used to create the clouds in Color Plates 8.1 and 8.2 is the following:

```
cumulus(pnt,density,parms, pnt_w, vol)
     xyz_td   pnt;                /* location of point in cloud space */
     xyz_td   pnt_w;              /* location of point in world space */
     float    *density,*parms;
     vol_td   vol;
{
  float new_turbulence();        /* my turbulence function */
  float peachey_noise();         /* Darwyn Peachey's noise function */
  float metaball_evaluate();   /* function for evaluating the metaball primitives*/
  float mdens,                   /* metaball density value */
        turb, turb_amount          /* turbulence amount */
        peach;                     /* Peachey noise value */
```

```
xyz_td path;                      /* path for swirling the point */
extern int frame_num;
static int ncalcd = 1;
static float sin_theta_cloud, cos_theta_cloud, theta,
        path_x, path_y, path_z, scalar_x, scalar_y, scalar_z;

/* calculate values that only depend on the frame number
 *   once per frame
 */
if(ncalcd)
  {
    ncalcd = 0;
    /* create gentle swirling in the cloud */
    theta  = (frame_num%600)*.01047196; /* swirling effect */
    cos_theta_cloud  =  cos(theta);
    sin_theta_cloud  =  sin(theta);
    path_x  =  sin_theta_cloud*.005*frame_num;
    path_y  =  .01215*(float)frame_num;
    path_z =  sin_theta_cloud*.0035*frame_num;
    scalar_x  =  (.5+(float)frame_num*0.010);
    scalar_z  =  (float)frame_num*.0073;
  }

/* Add some noise to the point's location
 */
peach  =  peachey_noise(pnt); /* Use Darwyn Peachey's noise function */
pnt.x - =  path_x -peach*scalar_x;
pnt.y  =  pnt.y - path_y +.5*peach;
pnt.z + =  path_z - peach*scalar_z;

/* Perturb the location of the point before evaluating the implicit
 * primitives.
 */
turb = fast_turbulence(pnt);
turb_amount = parms[4]*turb;
pnt_w.x + =  turb_amount;
pnt_w.y - =  turb_amount;
pnt_w.z + =  turb_amount;

mdens = (float)metaball_evaluate((double)pnt_w.x, (double)pnt_w.y,
(double)pnt_w.z, (vol.metaball));

*density =  parms[1]*(parms[3]*mdens + (1.0 - parms[3])*turb*mdens);
*density =  pow(*density,(double)parms[2]);
}
```

Parms[3] is the blending function value between implicit (metaball) density and the product of the turbulence density and the implicit density. This method of blending ensures that the entire cloud density is a product of the implicit field values, preventing cloud pieces from occurring outside the defining primitives.

Using a large *parms*[3] generates clouds that are mainly defined by their implicit primitives and are, therefore, "smoother" and less turbulent. *Parms*[1] is a density scaling factor, *parms*[2] is the exponent for the *pow*() function, and *parms*[4] controls the amount of turbulence to use in displacing the point before evaluation of the implicit primitives. For good images of cumulus clouds, useful values are the following: $0.2 < parms[1] < 0.4$, $parms[2] = 0.5$, $parms[3] = 0.4$, and $parms[4] = 0.7$.

Cirrus and Stratus Clouds

Cirrus clouds differ greatly from cumulus clouds in their density, thickness, and falloff. In general, cirrus clouds are thinner, less dense, and wispier. These effects can be created by altering the parameters to the *cumulus* cloud procedure and also by changing the implicit primitives. The density value parameter for a cirrus cloud is normally chosen as a smaller value and the exponent is chosen larger, producing larger areas of no clouds and a greater number of individual clouds. To create cirrus clouds, the user can simply specify the global shape (envelope) of the clouds with a few implicit primitives or specify implicit primitives to determine the location and shape of each cloud. In the former case, the shape of each cloud is mainly controlled by the volumetric procedural function and turbulence simulation, as opposed to cumulus clouds where the implicit functions are the main shape control. It is also useful to modulate the densities along the direction of the jet stream to produce more natural wisps. This can be created by the user specifying a predominant direction of wind flow and using a turbulent version of this vector in controlling the densities as follows:

```
Cirrus(pnt,density,parms, pnt_w, vol, jet_stream)
     xyz_td  pnt;               /* location of point in cloud space */
     xyz_td  pnt_w;             /* location of point in world space */
     xyz_td  jet_stream;
     float   *density,*parms;
     vol_td  vol;
{
  float new_turbulence();      /* my turbulence function */
  float peachey_noise();       /* Darwyn Peachey's noise function */
  float metaball_evaluate();   /* function for evaluating the metaball
                                     primitives*/
  float mdens,                 /* metaball density value */
        turb,turb_amount       /* turbulence amount */
        peach;                 /* Peachey noise value */
  xyz_td path;                 /* path for swirling the point */
  extern int frame_num;
  static int ncalcd = 1;
  static float sin_theta_cloud, cos_theta_cloud, theta,
        path_x, path_y, path_z, scalar_x, scalar_y, scalar_z;
```

```
/* calculate values that only depend on the frame number
 *   once per frame
 */
if(ncalcd)
  {
    ncalcd = 0;
    /* create gentle swirling in the cloud */
    theta  = (frame_num%600)*.01047196; /* swirling effect */
    cos_theta_cloud =  cos(theta);
    sin_theta_cloud =  sin(theta);
    path_x  =  sin_theta_cloud*.005*frame_num;
    path_y  =  .01215*(float)frame_num;
    path_z =  sin_theta_cloud*.0035*frame_num;
    scalar_x  =  (.5+(float)frame_num*0.010);
    scalar_z  =  (float)frame_num*.0073;
  }

/* Add some noise to the point's location
 */
peach  =  peachey_noise(pnt); /* Use Darwyn Peachey's noise function */
pnt.x - =  path_x -peach*scalar_x;
pnt.y  =  pnt.y - path_y +.5*peach;
pnt.z + =  path_z - peach*scalar_z;

/* Perturb the location of the point before evaluating the implicit
 * primitives.
 */
turb = fast_turbulence(pnt);
turb_amount = parms[4]*turb;
pnt_w.x + =  turb_amount;
pnt_w.y - =  turb_amount;
pnt_w.z + =  turb_amount;
/* make the jet stream turbulent */
jet_stream.x +  = .2*turb;
jet_stream.y +  = .3*turb;
jet_stream.z +  = .25*turb;

/* warp point along the jet stream vector */
pnt_w  =  warp(jet_stream, pnt_w);

mdens = (float)metaball_evaluate((double)pnt_w.x, (double)pnt_w.y,
  (double)pnt_w.z, (vol.metaball));

*density =  parms[1]*(parms[3]*mdens + (1.0 - parms[3])*turb*mdens);
*density =  pow(*density,(double)parms[2]);
}
```

Several examples of cirrus cloud formations created using these techniques can be seen in Color Plates 8.3 and 8.4. Color Plate 8.4 shows a higher cirro-stratus layer created by a large elliptical primitive and a few individual lower cirrus clouds created with cylindrical primitives.

Stratus clouds can also be modeled by using a few implicits to create the global shape or extent of the stratus layer, while using volumetric procedural functions to define the detailed structure of all of the clouds within this layer. Stratus cloud layers are normally thicker and less wispy, as compared with cirrus clouds. This effect can be created by adjusting the size of the turbulent space (smaller/fewer wisps), using a smaller exponent value (creates more of a cloud layer effect), and increasing the density of the cloud. Some of the more interesting stratus effects, such as a mackerel sky, can be created by using simple mathematical functions to shape the densities. The mackerel stratus cloud layer in Color Plate 8.5 was created by modulating the densities with turbulent sine waves in the x and y directions.

Cloud Creatures

The combination of implicit functions with volumetric procedural models provides an easy to use system for creating realistic clouds, artistic clouds, and cloud creatures. Some examples of cloud creatures created using a simple graphical user interface (GUI) to position nine implicit spheres can be seen in Color Plate 8.2. They were designed in less than 15 minutes each, and a straw poll shows that viewers have seen many different objects in them (similar to real cloud shapes). Currently, the simple GUI only allows access to a small portion of the system. The rest of the controls are available through a text-based interface. More complex shapes, time-based deformations, and animations can be created by allowing the user access to more of the controls, implicit primitives, and parameters of the full cloud modeling system. These cloud creatures are easily designed and animated by controlling the implicit primitives and procedural parameters. The implicit primitives blend and deform smoothly, allowing the specification and animation of skeletal structures, and provide an intuitive interface to modeling amorphous volumetric creatures.

User Specification and Control

Since the system uses implicit primitives for the cloud macrostructure, the user creates the general cloud structure by specifying the location, type, and weight of each implicit primitive. For the image in Color Plate Figure 8.1, nine implicit spheres were positioned to create the cumulus cloud. Figure Color Plate 8.2 shows the wide range of cloud shapes and creatures that can be created by simply adjusting the location of each primitive and the overall density of the model through a simple GUI. The use of implicit primitives makes this a much more natural interface than with traditional procedural techniques. Each of the cloud models in this chapter was created in less than 30 minutes of design time.

The user of the system also specifies a density scaling factor, a power exponent for the density distribution (controls amount of wispiness), any warping procedures to apply to the cloud, and the name of the volumetric procedural function so that special effects can be programmed into the system.

Animating Volumetric Procedural Clouds

The volumetric cloud models described above produce nice still images of clouds and also clouds that gently evolve over time. The models can be animated using the procedural animation techniques in Chapter 7 or by animating the implicit primitives. Procedural animation is the most flexible and powerful technique since any deformation, warp or physical simulation can be added to the procedure. Animating the implicit primitives can be done by an animator using key frames or dynamics simulations. Several examples of applying these two animation techniques for various effects are described below.

Procedural Animation

Both the implicit primitives and the procedural cloud space can be animated algorithmically. One of most useful forms of implicit primitive animation is warping. A time varying warp function can be used to gradually warp the shape of the cloud over time to simulate the formation of clouds, their movement, and their deformation by wind and other forces. Cloud formations are usually altered based on the jet stream. To simulate this effect, all that is needed is to warp the primitives along a vector representing the jet stream. This can be done by warping the points before evaluating the implicit functions. The amount of warping can be controlled by the wind velocity, or gradually added in over time to simulate the initial cloud development. Implicits can be warped along the jet stream as follows:

```
perturb_pnt  =  procedurally alter pnt
                    using noise and turbulence
height  =  relative height of perturb_pnt
vector  =  jet_stream + turbulence(pnt)
perturb_pnt  =  warp(perturb_pnt, vector, height)
density1  =  implicit_function(perturbed_pnt)
...
```

To get more natural effects, it is useful to alter each point by a small amount of turbulence before warping it. Several frames from an animation of a cumulus cloud warping along the jet stream can be seen in Color Plate 8.6. To create this effect, ease-in and ease-out based on the frame number was used to animate the warp amount. The implicit primitives' locations do not move in this animation, but the warping function animates the space to move and distort the cloud along the jet stream vector. Other warping functions to simulate squash and stretch (Bloomenthal *et al.* 1997) and other effects can also be used. Instead of a single vector and velocity, a vector field is input into the program to define more complex weather patterns. The current system allows the specification of vector flow tables and tables of functional primitives (attractors, vortices) to control the motion and deformation of the clouds. This procedural warping technique was used successfully by Stam in animating gases (Stam 1995).

Implicit Primitive Animation

The implicit primitives can be animated in the same manner as implicit surfaces: Each primitive's location, parameters (e.g., radii), and weight can be animated over time. This provides an easy to use, high-level animation interface for cloud animation. This technique was used in the animation, "A Cloud is Born" (Ebert *et. al.* 1997), showing the birth of a cumulus cloud followed by a fly-through of it. Several stills from the formation sequence can be seen in Color Plate 8.7. For this animation, the centers of the implicit spheres were moved over time to simulate three separate cloud elements merging and growing into a full cumulus cloud. The radii of the spheres were also increased over time. Finally, to create animation in the detailed cloud structure, each point was moved along a turbulent path over time before evaluation of the turbulence function, as illustrated in the *cumulus* procedure.

A powerful animation tool for volumetric procedural implicit functions is the use of dynamics and physics-based simulations to control the movement of the implicits and the deformation of space. Since the implicits are modeling the macrostructure of the cloud while procedural techniques are modeling the microstructure, fewer primitives are needed to achieve complex cloud models. Dynamics simulations can be applied to the clouds by using particle system techniques, with each particle representing a volumetric implicit primitive. The smooth blending and procedurally generated detail allow complex results with less than a few hundred primitives, a factor of 100 to 1000 less than needed with traditional particle systems. I have implemented a simple particle system for volumetric procedural implicit particles. The user specifies a few initial implicit primitives, dynamics information, such as speed, initial velocity, force function, and lifetime, and the system generates the location, number, size, and type of implicit for each frame. In our initial tests, it took less than one minute to generate and animate the implicit particles for 200 frames. Unlike traditional particle systems, cloud implicit particles never die—they just become dormant.

Cumulus clouds created through this volumetric procedural implicit particle system can be seen in Color Plate 8.8. The stills in Color Plate 8.8 show a cloud created by an upward turbulent force. The number of children created from a particle was also controlled by the turbulence of the particle's location. For the animations in this figure, the initial number of implicit primitives was 12 and the final number was approximately 50.

The animation and formation of cirrus and stratus clouds can also be controlled by the use of a volumetric procedural implicit particle system. For the formation of a large area of cirrus or cirro-stratus clouds, the particle system can randomly seed space and then use turbulence to grow the clouds from the creation of new implicit primitives, as can be seen in Color Plate 8.9. The cirro-stratus layer in this image contains 150 implicit primitives that were generated from the user specifying 5 seed primitives.

To control the dynamics of the cloud particle system, any commercial particle animation program can also be used. A useful approach for cloud dynamics is to use *qualitative dynamics*: simple simulations of the observed properties and formation of clouds. The underlying physical forces that create a wide range of cloud formations are extremely complex to simulate, computationally expensive, and very restrictive. The incorporation of simple, parameterized rules that simulate observable cloud behavior will produce a powerful cloud animation system.

Conclusion

The goal of these three chapters has been to describe several techniques used to create realistic images and animations of gases and fluids, as well as provide insight into the development of these techniques. I have shown a useful approach to modeling gases, as well as animation techniques for procedural modeling. To aid in reproducing and expanding the results presented here, all of the images are accompanied by detailed descriptions of the procedures used to create them. This gives the reader not only the opportunity to reproduce the results, but also the challenge to expand upon the techniques presented. These chapters also provide insight into the procedural design approach that I use and will, hopefully, inspire others to explore and expand procedural modeling and animation techniques.

Noise, Hypertexture, Antialiasing, and Gesture 9

Ken Perlin

Introduction

In this first section I touch on several topics that relate to the work I've done in procedural modeling.

In this introduction I give a brief introduction to hypertexture and review its fundamental concepts. Then I discuss the essential functions needed in order to be able to easily tweak procedural models.

The second section is a short tutorial on how the *noise* function is constructed. After this I talk about how raymarching for hypertexture works. I continue on with some examples of hypertexture. I follow this with a discussion about an interesting possible approach for antialiasing procedurally defined images. Then I talk about a surface representation based on sparse wavelets. Finally, I apply notions from procedural modeling to human figure motion.

Shape, Solid Texture, and Hypertexture

The precursor to hypertexture was *solid texture*, described by Darwyn Peachey in Chapter 2 of this book. Solid texturing is simply the process of evaluating a function over R^3 at each visible surface point of a rendered computer graphic (CG) model. The function over R^3 then becomes a sort of solid material, out of which the CG model shape appears to be "carved."

I became interested in what happens when you start extending these texture functions off of the CG surface. What do they look like as space-filling functions? So I developed a simple formalism that allowed me to play with this idea, by extending the notion of *characteristic function*.

Traditionally, the shape of any object in a computer graphic simulation is described by a characteristic function—a mapping from each point in R^3 to the boolean values **true** (for points inside the object) or **false** (for points outside the object). This is a point set. The boundary of this point set is the surface of the object.

I replaced the boolean characteristic function by a continuous one. We define for any object a characteristic function which is a mapping from $f : R^3 \rightarrow [0...1]$. All points $\vec{x}$ for which $f(\vec{x})$ is zero are said to be *outside* the object. All points $\vec{x}$ for which $f(\vec{x})$ is one are said to be *strictly inside* the object. Finally, all points $\vec{x}$ for which $0 < f(\vec{x}) < 1$ are said to be in the object's *fuzzy region*.

This formulation gives the object surface an appreciable thickness. We can now combine solid texture functions with the function that describes the object's fuzzy region. In this way shape and solid texture become unified—a shape can be seen as just a particular solid texture function. I refer to this flavor of texture modeling as *hypertexture*, since we are texturing in a higher dimension (the full three-dimensional object space), and also because it's a really atrocious pun.

Two Basic Paradigms

There are two distinct ways that solid textures can be combined with fuzzy shapes. You can either use the texture to distort the space before evaluating the shape, or add the texture value to a fairly soft shape function, then apply a "sharpening" function to the result.

The first approach involves calculations of the form:

$$f(\vec{x}) = \text{shape}(\vec{x} + \text{texture}(\vec{x})\vec{v})$$

where $\vec{v}$ is a simple vector expression. The second approach involves calculations of the form:

$$f(\vec{x}) = \text{sharpen}(\text{shape}(\vec{x}) + \text{texture}(\vec{x}))$$

Bias, Gain, and so Forth

The secret to making good procedural textures is an interface that allows you to tune things in a way that makes sense to you. For example, let's say that there is

Plate 2.1.
Knickknack
copyright © 1989
Pixar.

Plate 2.2.
Lifesavers
"At the Beach."
Image by Pixar.
copyright © 1991
FCB/Leber Katz
Partners.

Plate 2.3.
Carefree Gum
"Bursting."
Image by Pixar,
copyright © 1993
FCB/Leber Katz
Partners.

Plate 2.4.
Listerine "Knight."
Image by Pixar,
copyright © 1991
J. Walter
Thompson.

Plate 2.5.
Listerine "Arrows."
Image by Pixar,
copyright © 1994
J. Walter Thompson.

Plate 2.6.
Listerine "Arrows."
Image by Pixar,
copyright © 1994
J. Walter Thompson.

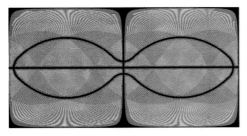

Plate 3.1. A 2D basketball image map.

Plate 3.2. The seamless wrapped ball.

Plate 4.2.
Preliminary steam rising from a teacup. (a) has no shaping of the steam. (b) has only spherical attenuation.
Copyright © 1992 David S. Ebert.

Plate 4.3.
Final image of steam rising from a teacup, with both spherical and height density attenuation. Copyright © 1991 David S. Ebert.

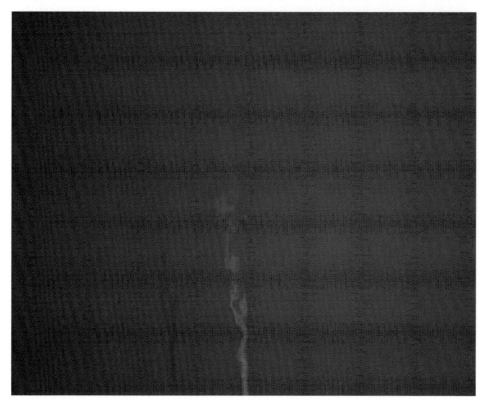

Plate 4.4.
A rising column of smoke. Copyright © 1994 David S. Ebert.

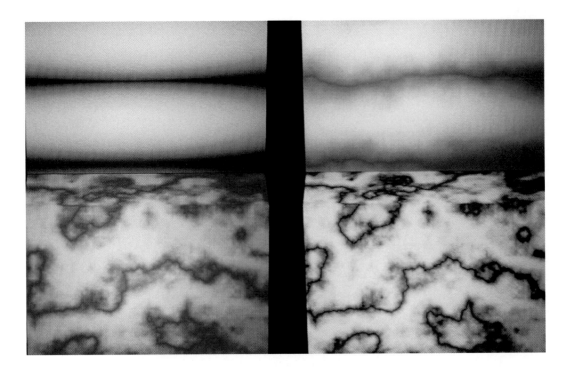

Plate 6.1. (a,b,c,d). Marble forming. The images show the banded material heating, deforming, then cooling and solidifying. Copyright © 1992 David S. Ebert.

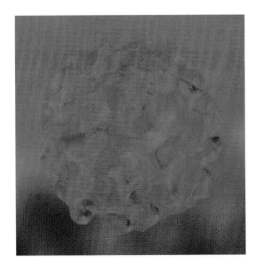

Plate 6.1. Blue glass.

Plate 6.2. Fireball.

Plate 6.3. New York University torch.

Plate 7.1.
A scene from *Once a Pawn a Foggy Knight...* showing solid textured transparency used to simulate fog. Copyright © 1989 David S. Ebert.

Plate 7.2.
A scene from *Getting Into Art*, showing volume rendered fog animation created by horizontal helical paths. Copyright © 1990 David S. Ebert.

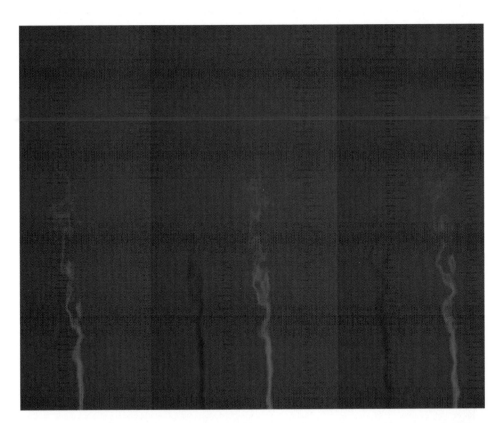

Plate 7.3.
Rising column of
smoke animation.
Images are every
30 frames.
Copyright © 1994
David S. Ebert.

Plate 7.4.
An increasing
breeze blowing
toward the right
created by an
attractor.
Copyright © 1991
David S. Ebert.

Plate 7.5.
Spiral vortex.
Images are every 21
frames. The top-left
image is the default
motion of the gas.
The remaining
images show the
effects of the spiral
vortex.
Copyright © 1994
David S. Ebert.

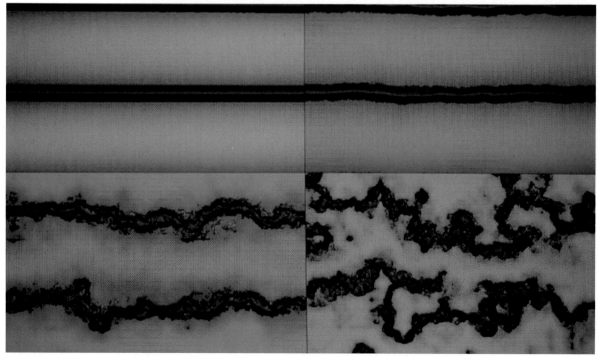

Plate 7.7. Liquid marble forming. Copyright © 1993 David S. Ebert.

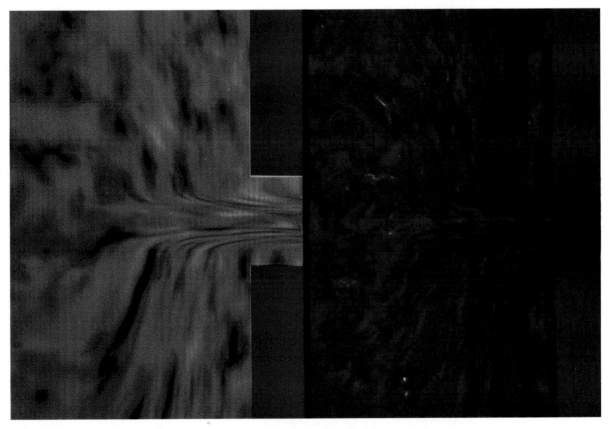

Plate 7.6. (a) Gas flowing into a hole in the wall. (b) Liquid flowing into a hole in the wall. Copyright © 1991 David S. Ebert.

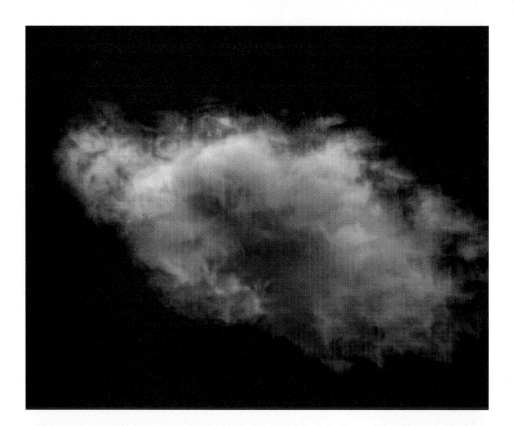

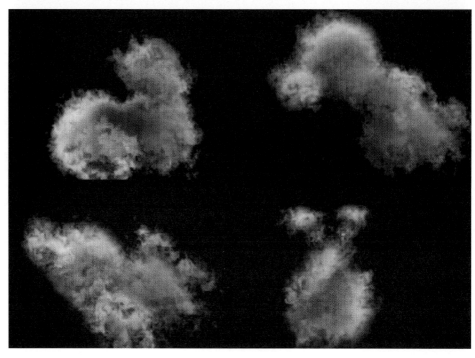

Plate 8.3.
Cirrus clouds.
Copyright © 1998
David S. Ebert.

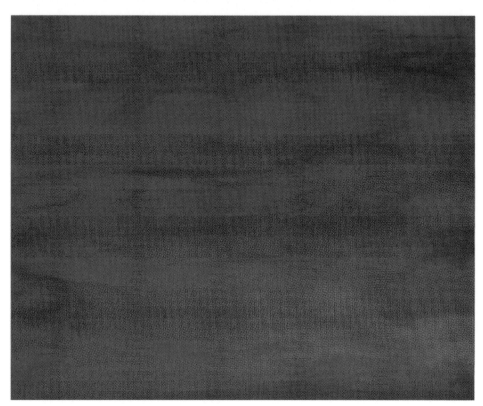

Plate 8.4.
Another example
of cirrus and
cirrostratus clouds.
Copyright © 1998
David S. Ebert.

Plate 8.5.
A mackerel
stratus layer.
Copyright © 1998
David S. Ebert.

Plate 8.6.
Cloud warping
along the jet stream.
Copyright © 1998
David S. Ebert.
.

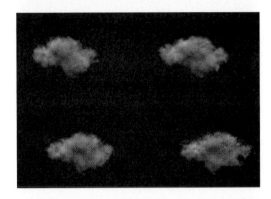

Plate 8.7.
Several stills from
"A Cloud is Born"
showing the
formation of the
cloud.
Copyright © 1998
David S. Ebert.

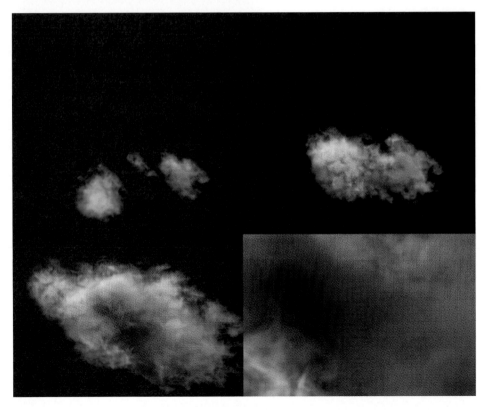

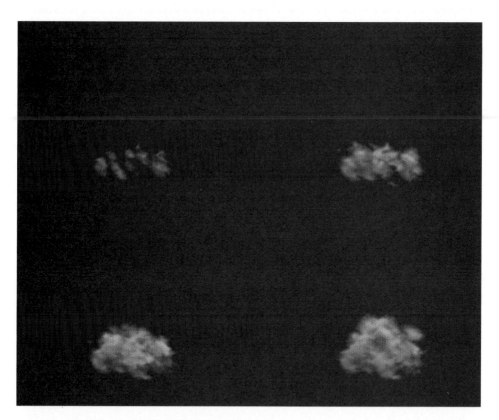

Plate 8.8.
Volumetric procedural implicit particle system formation of a cumulus cloud. Copyright © 1998 David S. Ebert.

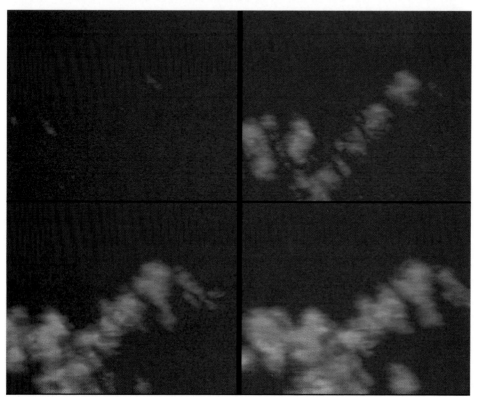

Plate 8.9.
Formation of a cirrostratus cloud layer using volumetric procedural implicit particles. Copyright © 1998 David S. Ebert.

Plate 11.1. *Zabriskie Point* illustrates distorted fBm-clouds and the rounded character of terrains constructed from the noise function. A vector-valued fBm function, with the vector interpreted as an rgb color value, has been used to perturb the color of the terrain. Such coloring is also seen in Plate 13.3. It is a prototype of the more sophisticated coloring seen in Plates 11.13–14 and 12.1–2. Copyright © F. Kenton Musgrave.

Plate 11.2.
Gaea & Selene
shows two procedur-
al planet models.
The clouds are the
same ones seen in
Plate 11.1. Note the
multifractal coast-
line: At some places
it is quite smooth,
while at others it is
quite convoluted,
with many islands.
Copyright ©
F. Kenton Musgrave.

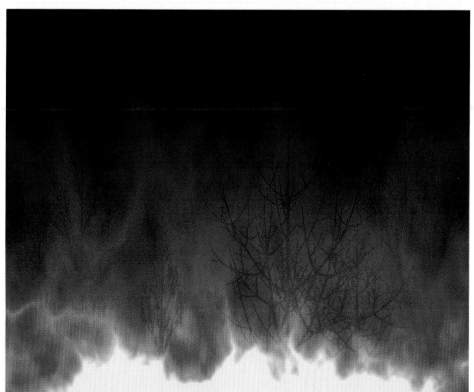

Plate 11.3.
Forest Fire illustrates a fire texture. Color is critical in getting the look of fire. Note that the 1-abs(noise) basis function gives rise to the sinews in the flames.
Copyright ©
F. Kenton Musgrave.

Plate 11.4.
Blessed State is also a polygon-subdivision terrain—compare it to the terrain models seen in Plates 11.1 and 11.9. The water is the "ripples" texture. The moon is a very simple fBm bump map applied to a white sphere; a more realistic moon model would be too busy for the visual composition.
Copyright ©
F. Kenton Musgrave.

Plate 11.5.

Bryce illustrates a sedimentary rock strata texture. Note the red and yellow strata which provide visual interest. The terrain model is a polygon-subdivision erosion model described by Mandelbrot (Peitgen and Saupe 1988). Copyright © F. Kenton Musgrave.

Plate 11.6.

A sequence of stages in the development of a planetary structure. Copyright © F. Kenton Musgrave.

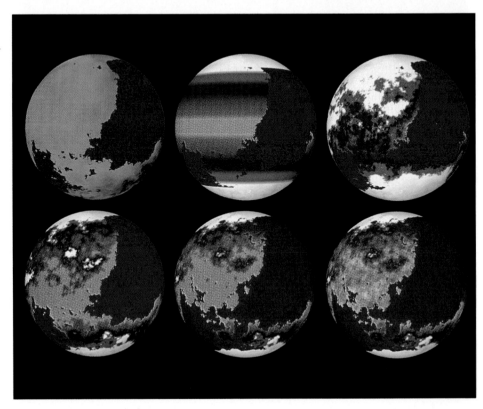

Plate 11.7. A GIT-processed image of Beth Musgrave skating, by Myeong Lim. The GIT processing adds random colors and the painterly quality. Copyright © F. Kenton Musgrave.

Plate 11.8.
The "multicolor" texture attempts to capture some of the richness of color juxtaposition seen in paintings. Copyright © F. Kenton Musgrave.

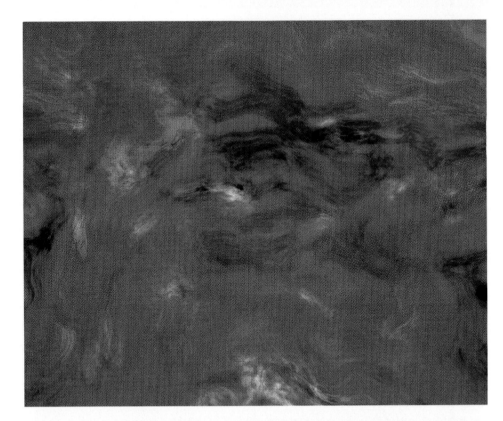

Plate 11.9.
Spirit Lake shows a noise-based water bump map. The terrain model is the first multifractal model described in Chapter 12. Copyright © F. Kenton Musgrave.

Plate 11.10. *Lethe* is a polygon-subdivision terrain model, hence the jagged appearance. It illustrates the water, sedimentary rock strata, and moon textures described in Chapter 11. Copyright © F. Kenton Musgrave.

Plate 11.11. *Other State* features a procedural model of Saturn in place of the moon in *Blessed State*. Copyright © F. Kenton Musgrave.

Plate 11.12.
Slickrock I features a procedural terrain with adaptive level of detail and a terrain model constructed from a ridged basis function—hence the ridges everywhere and at all scales. The same subtle color perturbation has been applied to the surface as in Plate 11.1, but it has been "squashed down" vertically to make it resemble sedimentary rock strata. Copyright © F. Kenton Musgrave.

Plate 11.13.
Slickrock III illustrates a GIT texture applied to a terrain. Both the terrain and the texture feature adaptive level of detail, as described in Chapter 13. Copyright © F. Kenton Musgrave.

Plate 11.14.
Slickrock II.V is actually situated on the surface of the planet *Gaea* seen in Plate 11.2, which scaled to be about the size of Earth. The moon is outside the atmosphere as in Plate 11.2; the atmosphere model is described in Chapter 14. Copyright © F. Kenton Musgrave.

Plate 12.1.
Emil is a QAEB-traced terrain with a GIT texture and a multifractal texture representing the Milky Way in the background. The terrain is the "ridged multifractal" function. Copyright © F. Kenton Musgrave.

Plate 12.2.
Parabolic Curves in the Plane of the Ecliptic employs most of the tricks described in Chapters 10–14, from multifractals to GIT textures to QAEB tracing. There are parabolas in the terrain, in the central valley, in the clouds, and in depth. Copyright © F. Kenton Musgrave.

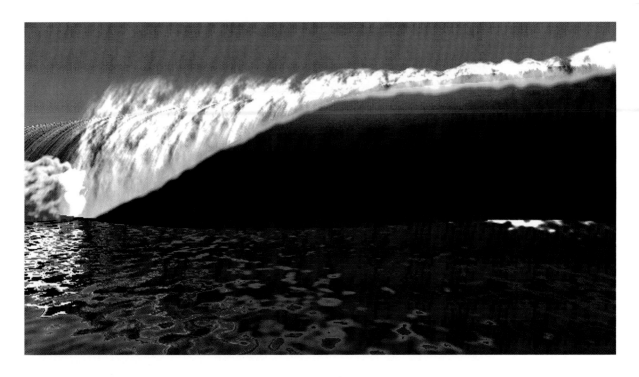

Plate 13.1. A QAEB-traced non-heightfield model of a wave, modeled and rendered by Manuel Gamito. The spray and foam are QAEB hypertextures.

Plate 13.2.
A QAEB-traced hypertexture cloud, with a radiosity solution for high-albedo anistropic multiple scattering, by Sang Yoon Lee. The radiosity model is by Nelson Max.

Plate 13.3.
Comet Leary is a whimsical rendering of Timothy's final return to Earth. It is a QAEB cloud with coloring by a vector-valued fBm. Copyright © F. Kenton Musgrave.

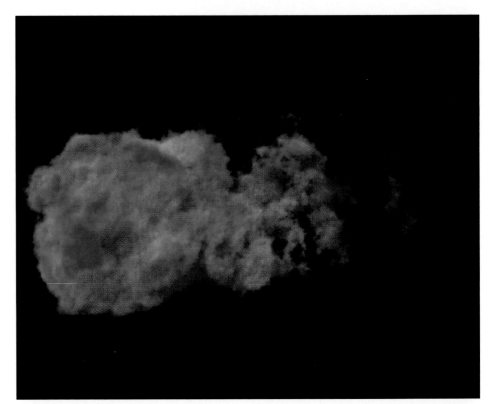

Plate 14.1.
Fractal Mandala illustrates an alternative use of the planetary atmosphere and minimal Rayleigh scattering model. The color is obtained by changing values in the extinction coefficient vector from those used for Rayleigh scattering. Copyright © F. Kenton Musgrave.

Plate 14.2.
Carolina illustrates both the exponential atmosphere and color perspective. Copyright © F. Kenton Musgrave.

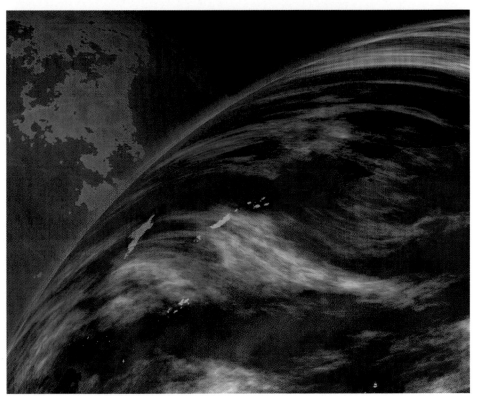

Plate 14.3.
A detail of Plate 11.2 illustrates color perspective in a planetary atmosphere. This is the e^{-r^2} atmosphere model. Copyright © F. Kenton Musgrave.

Plate 14.4.
Himalayas shows
color perspective
over a long distance.
Note that the white
peaks turn red, while
the dark areas turn
blue with distance.
Copyright ©
F. Kenton Musgrave.

Plate 14.5. Color perspective in raw form. Two parallel vertical planes, one black and one white, illustrate how color changes with distance. The atmosphere is an exponential mist. Copyright © F. Kenton Musgrave.

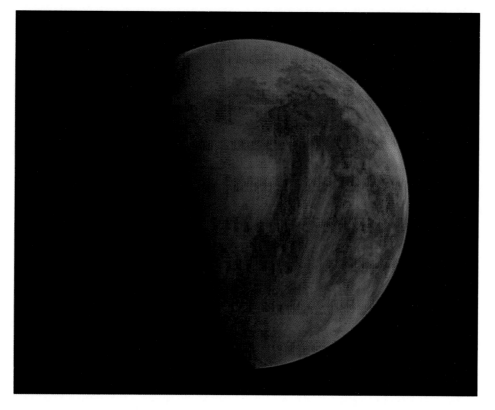

Plate 14.6.
A ray-marched e^{-r} planetary atmosphere model, implemented as a RenderMan shader. Such a model can yield more realistic coloring by including color extinction in the illumination. Copyright © F. Kenton Musgrave.

Plate 15.1 and 15.2
Images generated by
the genetic program
"Dr Mutatis." Note
the rich visual com-
plexity that arises
through the automat-
ed evolution of a
procedural texture.
Copyright ©
F. Kenton Musgrave.

**Chapter 13,
Figure 3**
The very first
QAEB-traced
terrain. The terrain
model is the "ridged
multifractal" func-
tion described in
Chapter 12.
Copyright ©
F. Kenton Musgrave.

**Chapter 13,
Figure 4**
The first QAEB
rendering demon-
strating shadows
from a light source
at infinity.
Copyright ©
F. Kenton Musgrave.

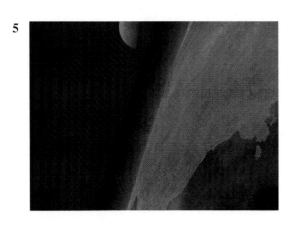

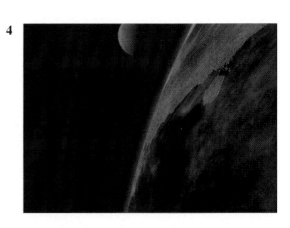

Chapter 12, Figure 3
A series of frames from the Gaea Zoom animation demonstrate the kind of continuous adaptive level of detail possible with the models presented in the text. The MPEG animation is available at www.metacreations/people/musgrave/animations.html.
Copyright © F. Kenton Musgrave.

6

7

8

9

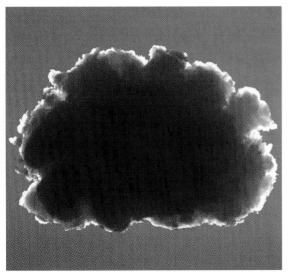 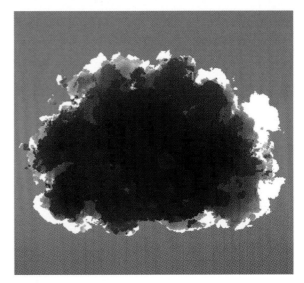

A. B.

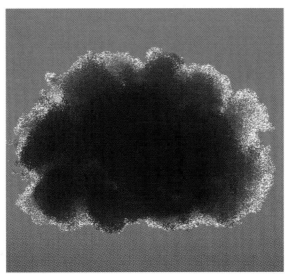

**Chapter 13,
Figure 6**
A QAEB-traced
cloud.
(A) Rendered with a
stride of 2 pixels.
(B) Quantization
artifacts from long
stride with regular
sampling.
(C) Same long
stride, with jittered
sampling.
Copyright ©
F. Kenton Musgrave.

C.

some region over which a function value is varying from 0.0 to 1.1. Perhaps you realize that this function should be "pushed up" so that it takes on higher values in its middle range. Or maybe you want to push its values a bit toward its high and low values, and away from the middle.

You could do these things with spline functions or with power functions. For example, let's say that $f(t): \to [0...1]$. Then $pow(f(t), 0.8)$ will push the values of f up toward 1.0. But this is not intuitive to use, because it's hard to figure out what values to put into the second argument to produce a particular visual result.

For this reason, I've built two functions that I use constantly, just to do these little continuous tweaks.

Bias

To get the same functionality provided by the power function, but with a more intuitive interface, I've defined the function $bias_b$, which is a power curve defined over the unit interval such that $bias_b(0.0) = 0.0$, $bias_b(0.5) = b$, and $bias_b(1.0) = 1.0$. By increasing or decreasing b, we can thus bias the values in an object's fuzzy region up or down. Note that $bias_{0.5}$ is the identity function.

Bias is defined by $t^{\frac{\ln(b)}{\ln(0.5)}}$.

Gain

Similarly, we often want an intuitive way to control whether a function spends most of its time near its middle range, or, conversely, near its extremes. It's sort of like having a gain knob on your TV set. You can force all the intensities toward middle gray (low gain) or, conversely, force a rapid transition from black to white (high gain).

We want to define $gain_g$ over the unit interval such that:

$$gain_g(0.0) = 0.0,$$
$$gain_g(0.25) = 0.5 - g/2,$$
$$gain_g(0.5) = 0.5,$$
$$gain_g(0.75) = 0.5 + g/2,$$
$$gain_g(0.1) = 1.0.$$

By increasing or decreasing g, we can thus increase or decrease the rate at which the midrange of a object's fuzzy region goes from 0.0 to 1.0. Note that $gain_{0.5}$ is the identity function.

Motivated by the above, I've defined gain by:

$$\text{if } t > 0.5 \text{ then } \frac{bias_{1-g}(2t)}{2} \text{ else } \frac{2 - bias_{1-g}(2 - 2t)}{2}.$$

The above two functions provide a surprisingly complete set of tools for tweaking things. If you want to make something look "darker" or "more transparent" you would generally use $bias_b$ with $b < 0.5$. Conversely, if you want to make something look "brighter" or "more opaque" you would generally use $bias_b$ with $b > 0.5$.

Similarly, if you want to "fuzz out" a texture, you would generally use $gain_g$ with $g < 0.5$. Conversely, if you want to "sharpen" a texture, you would generally use $gain_g$ with $g > 0.5$. Most of the time, you'll want to instrument various numerical parameters with bias and gain settings and tune things to taste.

Constructing the Noise Function

Part of the reason that procedural texture looks any good is that it incorporates randomness in a controlled way. Most of the work involved in achieving this is contained inside the *noise* function, which is an approximation to what you would get if you took white noise (say, every point in some sampling mapped to a random value between −1.0 and 1.0) and blurred it to dampen out frequencies beyond some cutoff.

The key observation here is that, even though you are creating "random" things, you can use *noise* to introduce high frequencies in a controlled way by applying *noise* to an appropriately scaled domain. For example, if $\vec{x}$ is a point in R^3, then $noise(2\vec{x})$ introduces frequencies twice as high as does $noise(\vec{x})$. Another way of saying this is that it introduces details that are twice as small.

Ideally the *noise* function would be constructed by blurring white noise, preferably by convolving with some Gaussian kernel. Unfortunately, this approach would necessitate building a volume of white noise, and then blurring it all at once. This is quite impractical.

Instead we want an approximation that can be evaluated at arbitrary points, without having to precompute anything over some big chunk of volume. The approach described here is the original one I came up with in 1983, which I still use. It's a kind of spline function with pseudorandom knots.

The key to understanding the algorithm is to think of space as being divided into a regular lattice of cubical cels, with one pseudorandom wavelet per lattice point. You shouldn't get scared off by the use of the term "wavelet." A wavelet is simply a function which drops off to zero outside of some region, and which integrates to zero. This latter condition means that the wavelet function has some positive region and some negative region, and that the two regions balance each other out. When I talk about the "radius" of a wavelet, I just mean the distance in its domain space from the wavelet center to where its value drops off to zero.

We will use wavelets that have a radius of one cel. Therefore, any given point in R^3 will be influenced by eight overlapping wavelets—one for each corner of the cel containing the point.

Computation proceeds in three successive steps:

- Compute which cubical "cel" we're in
- Compute the wavelet centered on each of eight vertices
- Sum the wavelets

Computing Which Cubical "Cel" We're In

The "lowest" corner of the cel containing point [x, y, z] is given by:

- [i, j, k] = [[x], [y], [z]]

Then the eight vertices of the cel containing [x, y, z] are

(1) [i, j, k]
(2) [$i + 1, j, k$]
(3) [$i, j + 1, k$]
    . . .
(8) [$i + 1, j + 1, k + 1$].

Finding the Pseudorandom Wavelet at Each Vertex of the Cel

For each of the above lattice points, we want to find what wavelet to apply. Ideally, the mapping from cels to wavelet coefficients would be nonrepeating. It turns out though, that because *noise* has no large-scale structure, the mapping can eventually repeat itself, without this repetition being at all noticeable. This allows us to use a relatively simple table look-up scheme to map vertices to coefficients. I find that a repeat distance of 256 is more than large enough.

The basic idea is to map any [i, j, k] into a unique number between 0 and 255. We precompute a table G of 256 pseudorandom coefficient values, and always index into this fixed set of values.

In the following two sections we will accomplish two things. First, we will discuss what properties we want from the wavelet coefficients and how to precompute G—a table of 256 sets of coefficients that has these properties. Then we will discuss the properties we want in the mapping from $P : [i, j, k] \rightarrow 0 \ldots 255$ and how to achieve these properties.

Wavelet Coefficients

I actually force the *noise* function to take on a value of zero at each lattice point. This ensures that it can't have any appreciable energy at low spatial frequencies. To achieve this, I give a value at its center of zero to each of the overlapping wavelets that are being summed, and then give each wavelet a radius of one—so that each wavelet will reach a value of zero just as it gets to the center of its neighbors.

This means that we can define the wavelet centered at each lattice point as a smooth function with the following properties:

- It has a value of zero at its center
- It has some randomly chosen gradient at its center
- It smoothly drops off to zero a unit distance from its center

So we have to randomly choose a gradient for each wavelet center. I do this via a Monte Carlo method—precompute a table of gradients in uniformly random directions, and then index into this table. To create the gradient table, I need a set of points that are uniformly distributed on the surface of a unit sphere. I ensure that this set of points will be uniformly distributed as follows:

- Choose points uniformly within the cube $[-1 \ldots 1]^3$
- Throw out any points falling outside of the unit sphere
- Project surviving points onto the unit sphere

The pseudocode to do this is

for *i* in [0...255]

repeat

$$x = random(-1. \cdots +1.)$$
$$y = random(-1. \cdots +1.)$$
$$z = random(-1. \cdots +1.$$
until $x^2 + y^2 + z^2 < 1.0$
$G[i] = normalize\ [x, y, z]$

To Quickly Index into G in a Nonbiased Way

Now we need to find a way to answer the following question: If any point in R^3 is in the vicinity of a wavelet, how can it rapidly get the coefficients of that wavelet?

We basically want a really random way to map lattice points $[i, j, k]$ to indices of G. We have to avoid regularities in this mapping, since any regularity would be extremely visible to somebody looking at the final *noise* function.

I use the following method:

- Precompute a "random" permutation table P
- Use this table to "fold" $[i, j, k]$ into a single n

In this section I describe first how to create a suitable permutation table, and then how to use this table to "fold" $[i, j, k]$ into the range $[0 \ldots 255]$.

The permutation table can be precomputed, so that step doesn't need to be especially fast. The pseudorandom permutation table P is created by:

for i in $[0 \ldots 255]$
$\qquad j = random[0 \ldots 255]$
$\qquad$ *exchange* $P[i]$ *with* $P[j]$

The folding function *fold*(i, j, k) is then computed by:

$n = P[\, i_{\mathrm{mod}256}]$
$n = P[(n + j)_{\mathrm{mod}256}]$
$n = P[(n + k)_{\mathrm{mod}256}]$

For added speed, I don't actually do the mod operations. Instead, I precompute P to be twice as long, setting $P[256 \ldots 511] := P[0 \ldots 255]$. Then if $0 \le i, j, k \le 255$, we can just do $P[P[P[i] + j] + k]$ for each wavelet.

Now for each vertex of the unit cube whose "lowest" corner is $[i, j, k]$, we can quickly obtain wavelet coefficients as follows:

(1) $G(fold(i, j, k))$

(2) $G(fold(i + 1, j, k))$

(3) $G(fold(i, j + 1 , k))$

   ...

(4) $G(fold(i + 1, j + 1, k + 1))$

Evaluating the Wavelet Centered at $[i, j, k]$

The remaining steps to finding *noise* (x, y, z) are now as follows:

- Each wavelet is a product of:
  - a cubic weight which drops to zero at radius 1
  - a linear function, which is zero at (i, j, k)

- To compute the wavelet we must:
  - get (x, y, z) relative to the wavelet center
  - compute the weight function
  - multiply the weight by the linear function

First we must get (x, y, z) relative to the wavelet center:

$$[u, v, w] = [x - i, y - j, z - k]$$

Note that u,v,w values are bounded by $-1 \leq u, v, w \leq 1$.

Now we must compute the dropoff $\Omega_{(i,j,k)} (u, v, w)$ about $[i, j, k]$:

$$\Omega_{(i,j,k)} (u, v, w) = drop(u) \times drop(v) \times drop(w)$$

where each component dropoff is given by the cubic approximation:
$drop(t) = 1. - 3|t|^2 + 2|t|^3$
(but zero whenever $|t| > 1$)

and we must multiply this by the linear function that has the desired gradient and a value of zero at the wavelet center:

$$G_{(i, j, k)} \bullet [u, v, w]$$

The value of wavelet$_{(i, j, k)}$ at (x, y, z) is now given by:

$$\Omega_{(i, j, k)} (u, v, w) (G_{(i, j, k)} \bullet [u, v, w])$$

Finally, *noise* (x,y,z) is given by the sum of the eight wavelets near (x, y, z).

Following is a complete implementation of *noise* over R^3:

```
/* noise function over R3-implemented by a pseudorandom tricubic spline */

#include <stdio.h>
#include <math.h>

#define DOT(a,b) (a[0] * b[0] + a[1] * b[1] + a[2] * b[2])

#define B 256

static p[B + B + 2];
static float g[B + B + 2][3];
```

```
static start = 1;
#define setup(i,b0,b1,r0,r1) \
        t = vec[i] + 10000.; \
        b0 = ((int)t) & (B-1); \
        b1 = (b0+1) & (B-1); \
        r0 = t - (int)t; \
        r1 = r0 - 1.;

float noise3(vec)
float vec[3];
{
        int bx0, bx1, by0, by1, bz0, bz1, b00, b10, b01, b11;
        float rx0, rx1, ry0, ry1, rz0, rz1, *q, sy, sz, a, b, c, d, t, u, v;
        register i, j;

        if (start) {
                start = 0;
                init();
        }

        setup(0, bx0,bx1, rx0,rx1);
        setup(1, by0,by1, ry0,ry1);
        setup(2, bz0,bz1, rz0,rz1);

        i = p[ bx0 ];
        j = p[ bx1 ];

        b00 = p[ i + by0 ];
        b10 = p[ j + by0 ];
        b01 = p[ i + by1 ];
        b11 = p[ j + by1 ];

#define at(rx,ry,rz) ( rx * q[0] + ry * q[1] + rz * q[2] )

#define s_curve(t) ( t * t * (3. - 2. * t) )

#define lerp(t, a, b) ( a + t * (b - a) )

        sx = s_curve(rx0);
        sy = s_curve(ry0);
        sz = s_curve(rz0);

        q = g[ b00 + bz0 ] ; u = at(rx0,ry0,rz0);
        q = g[ b10 + bz0 ] ; v = at(rx1,ry0,rz0);
        a = lerp(sx, u, v);

        q = g[ b01 + bz0 ] ; u = at(rx0,ry1,rz0);
        q = g[ b11 + bz0 ] ; v = at(rx1,ry1,rz0);
        b = lerp(sx, u, v);
```

```
    c = lerp(sy, a, b);              /* interpolate in y at low x */
    q = g[ b00 + bz1 ] ; u = at(rx0,ry0,rz1);
    q = g[ b10 + bz1 ] ; v = at(rx1,ry0,rz1);
    a = lerp(sx, u, v);

    q = g[ b01 + bz1 ] ; u = at(rx0,ry1,rz1);
    q = g[ b11 + bz1 ] ; v = at(rx1,ry1,rz1);
    b = lerp(sx, u, v);

    d = lerp(sy, a, b);              /* interpolate in y at high x */

    return 1.5 * lerp(sz, c, d);     /* interpolate in z */
}

static init()
{
    long random();
    int i, j, k;
    float v[3], s;

    /* Create an array of random gradient vectors uniformly on the
       unit sphere */
    srandom(1);
    for (i = 0 ; i $<$ B ; i++) {
        do {                         /* Choose uniformly in a cube */
            for (j=0 ; j<3 ; j++)
                v[j] = (float)((random() % (B + B)) - B) / B;
            s = DOT(v,v);
        } while (s > 1.0);           /* If not in sphere try again */
        s = sqrt(s);
        for (j = 0 ; j < 3 ; j++)        /* Else normalize */
            g[i][j] = v[j] / s;
    }

    /* Create a pseudorandom permutation of [1..B] */
    for (i = 0 ; i $<$ B ; i++)
        p[i] = i;
    for (i = B ; i $>$ 0 ; i -= 2) {
        k = p[i];
        p[i] = p[j = random() % B];
        p[j] = k;
    }

    /* Extend g and p arrays to allow for faster indexing, */
    for (i = 0 ; i < B + 2 ; i++) {
        p[B + i] = p[i];
        for (j = 0 ; j < 3 ; j++)
            g[B + i][j] = g[i][j];
    }
}
```

Raymarching

To see hypertexture, you need a *raymarcher* renderer. I've implemented the ray-marcher in two parts. First I built a system layer—the part that never changes. This renders hypertexture by marching a step at a time along each ray, accumulating density at each sample along the way. There are all kinds of hooks for user interaction built into the raymarcher.

Then, for each type of hypertexture, I construct different "application" code, describing a particular hypertexture. At this point in the process I can safely wear the hat of a "naive user." Everything is structured so that at this level I don't have to worry about any system details. All I really need to worry about is what density to return at any point in R^3. This makes it very painless to try out different types of hypertexture.

System Code: The Raymarcher

I render hypertexture by "raymarching"—stepping front to back along each ray from the eye until either total opacity is reached or the ray hits a back clipping plane. Conceptually, the raymarching is done inside the unit cube: $-0.5 < x,y,z < 0.5$. A 4×4 viewing matrix transforms this cube to the desired view volume.

One ray is fired per pixel; the general procedure is as follows:

```
step = 1.0/resolution;
for (y = -0.5 ; y < 0.5 ; y += step)
for (x = -0.5 ; x < 0.5 ; x += step) {
    [point, point_step]=create_ray([x,y,-0.5], [x,y,-0.5+step], view_matrix);
    previous_density = 0.;
    init_density_function();                      /* User supplied */
    color = [0,0,0,0];
    for (z = -0.5 ; z < 0.5 && color.alpha < 0.999 ; z += step} {

        density = density_function(point);    /* User supplied */
        c = compute_color(density);           /* User supplied */

    /* Do shading only if needed */

        if (is_shaded && density != previous_density) {
            normal = compute_normal(point, density);
            c = compute_shading(c, point, normal);    /* User supplied */
            previous_density = density;
        }
```

```
/* Attenuation varies with resolution */

    c[3] = 1.0 - pow( 1.0 - c[3], 100. * step );

/* Integrate front to back */

    if (c[3] $>$ 0.)} {
        t = c[3] * (1.0 - color.alpha);
        color += [ t*c.red, t*c.green, t*c.blue, t ];
          }

/* March further along the ray */

    point += point_step;
    }
}
```

Application Code: User-Defined Functions

The "user" gets to define four functions to create a particular hypertexture:

```
void init_density_function();
float density_function(float x, float y, float z);
color compute_color(float density);
color compute_shading(color c, vector point, vector normal);
```

What makes things really simple is that as a user you only have to define behavior at any given single point in space—the raymarcher then does the rest for you.

- `init_density_function()`

This function is called once per ray. It gives you a convenient place to compute things that don't change at every sample.

- `density_function()`

This is where you specify the mapping from points to densities. Most of the behavior of the hypertexture is contained in this function.

- `compute_color()`

Here you map densities to colors. This also gives you a chance to calculate a refractive index.

- `compute_shading()`

Nonluminous hypertextures react to light, and must be shaded. The model I use is to treat any substance that has a density gradient as a translucent surface, with the gradient direction acting as normal vector, as though the substance consists of small, shiny, suspended spheres.

In the raymarcher library I've included a Phong shading routine. I usually just call that with the desired light direction, highlight power, etc.

Shading is relatively expensive, since it requires a normal calculation. Also, in many cases (e.g., self-luminous gases) shading is not necessary. For this reason, shading is only done if the user sets an `is_shaded` flag.

The raymarcher computes normals for shading by calling the user's density function three extra times:

```
vector = compute_normal(point, density) {
   vector d = = [
       density_function[point.x - epsilon, point.y, point.z] - density,
       density_function[point.x, point.y - epsilon, point.z] - density,
       density_function[point.x, point.y, point.z - epsilon] - density ];
   return d / |d|;
}
```

The above is the basic raymarcher. Two features have not been shown—refraction and shadows. Shadows are done by shooting secondary rays at each ray step where density ! = 0. They are prohibitively expensive except for hypertextures with "hard," fairly sharpened surfaces. In this case the accumulated opacity reaches totality in only a few steps, and so relatively few shadow rays need be followed.

Of course if we used a large shared memory to store a shadow volume, then cast shadows would only involve an additional raymarch pass. Unfortunately, the AT&T Pixel Machine architecture does not support large shared memory.

Refraction is done by adding a fifth component to the color vector—an index of refraction. The user sets `c.irefract` (usually from density) in the `compute_color` function. The raymarcher then uses Snell's law to shift the direction of `point_step` whenever `c.irefract` changes from one step along the ray to the next. An example of this is shown in Color Plate 6.1.

Since the density can change from one sample point to the next, it follows that the normal vector can also change continuously. This means that refraction can occur continuously. In other words, light can travel in curved paths inside a hypertexture. This raises some interesting possibilities. For example, imagine a manufacturing process that creates wafers whose index of refraction varies linearly from one face to the other (probably by some diffusion process). By carving such a material, one could create optical components within which light travels in curved paths. It might be possible to do things this way that would be very difficult or impossible to do with traditional optical components (in which light only bends at discrete surfaces between materials). The results of such components should be quite straightforward to visualize using refractive hypertexture.

Interaction

Levels of Editing: Changing Algorithms to Tweaking Knobs

There are three levels of changes you can make. I describe them in order of slowest to implement(and most sweeping in effect) to fastest to implement.

- Semantic changes—changing the user functions

    This is redefining your hypertexture methods. This type of change is covered in detail in the next section.

- Parameters you change by editing an input file of numeric parameters

    This saves the time of recompiling the user functions, when all you want to change is some numeric value. The raymarcher has a mechanism built into it that lets you refer to a file that binds symbols to floating point values when you run the program. These bindings are made accessible to the hypertexture designer at the inner rendering loop.

    In the following examples, I will adopt the following convention: any symbol that begins with a capital letter refers to a parameter whose value has been set in this input file. Symbols beginning with lowercase letters refer to variables that are computed within the individual rays and samples.

- Parameters you change from the command line

    These override any parameters with the same name in the input file. They are used to make animations showing things changing. For example, let's say you want to create an animation of a sphere with an expanding `Radius`, and you are working in the UNIX csh shell:

```
set i = 0
while (= $i $<$ 100)
    $rm hypertexture -Radius$ $i sphere $>$ $i
    @ i++
end
```

There are also some special parameters: XFORM for the view matrix, RES for image resolution, CLIP for image clipping (when you just want to recalculate part of an image). These can be set either from the command line or as an environment variable (the former overrides the latter, of course).

In these notes, I have hard-wired numerical parameters into a number of expressions. These are just there to "tune" the model in various useful ways. For example, the expression "100 * step" appearing above in the attenuation step of the raymarcher has the effect of scaling the integrated density so that the user can get good results by specifying densities in the convenient range [0.0 . . . 1.0].

z-Slicing

For much of the time when designing hypertextures, you just need a general sense of the shape and position of the textured object. In this case it is useful to evaluate only at a fixed z—setting the value of a ray to the density at only one sample point a fixed distance away. This obviously runs many times faster than a full raymarch. I use z-slicing for general sizing and placement, often going through many fast iterations in z-slice mode to get those things just right.

Some Simple Shapes to Play With

Sphere

Start with a sphere with *inner_radius* and *outer_radius* defined. Inside *inner_radius*, density is everywhere 1.0. Beyond *outer_radius*, density has dropped completely to 0.0. The interesting part is the hollow shell in between:

```
/* (1) Precompute (only once) */

    rr0 = outer_radius * outer_radius;
    rr1 = inner_radius * inner_radius;

/* (2) radius squared */

    t = x * x + y * y + z * z;

/* (3) compute dropoff */

    if (t > rr0)
        return 0.;
    else if (t < rr1)
        return  1.;
    else
        return (t - rr0) / (rr1 - rr0);
```

Egg

To create an egg, you start with a sphere, but distort it by making it narrower at the top. A good maximal "narrowing" value is 2/3, which is obtained by inserting the following step to the sphere procedure:

```
/* (1.5) introduce eccentricity */

        e = (5. - y / outer_radius) / 6.;
        x = x / e;
        z = z / e;
```

Notice that we must divide, not multiply, by the scale factor. This is because x and z are the arguments to a shape defining function—to make the egg thinner at the top, we must increase (not decrease) the scale of x and z.

Examples of Hypertexture

Explosions

The texture component here is turbulence uniformly positioned throughout space.

```
t = 0.5  +  Ampl * turbulence(x, y, z);
return max(0., min(1. t));
```

Shape is just a sphere with *inner_radius* = 0.0, which ensures that the fuzzy region will consist of the entire sphere interior.

The density function is:

```
d = shape(x, y, z);
if (d > 0.)
        d = d * texture(x, y, z);
 return d;
```

You can animate an explosion by increasing the sphere *outer_radius* over time. Figure 1 shows an explosion with *outer_radius* set to 0.4. Figure 2 shows the same explosion with *outer_radius* set to 0.8.

To create these explosions I oriented the cusps of the texture inward, creating the effect of locally expanding balls of flame on the surface. Contrast this with Color Plate 6.2 (Perlin and Hoffert 1989) , where the cusps were oriented outward to create a licking flame effect.

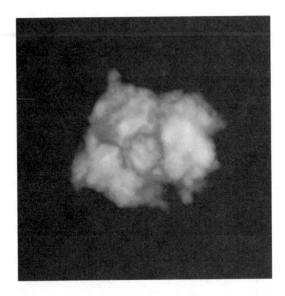

Figure 1.

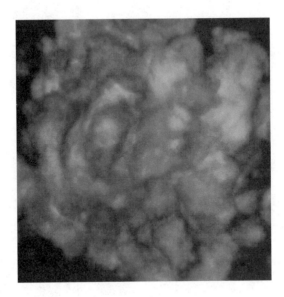

Figure 2.

Lifeforms

Just for fun, I placed a shape similar to the above explosions inside of an egg shape of constant density, as in Figure 3. By pulsing the *outer_radius* and *Ampl* rhythmically, while rotating slightly over time, I managed to hatch some rather intriguing simulations.

Space Filling Fractals

Figures 4 through 7 show steps in the simulation of a sparsely fractal material. At each step, *noise()* is used to carve volume away from the egg. Then *noise()* of twice the frequency is carved away from the remainder, and so on.

Figure 8 shows one possible result of such a process, a shape having infinite surface area and zero volume.

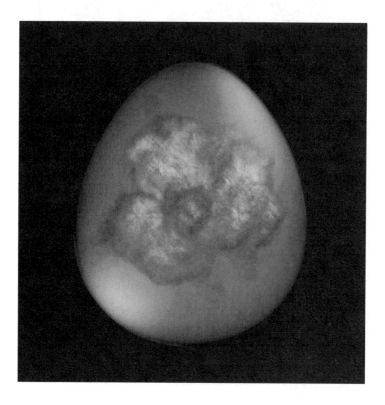

Figure 3.

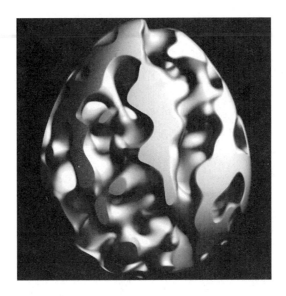

Figure 4.

Figure 5.

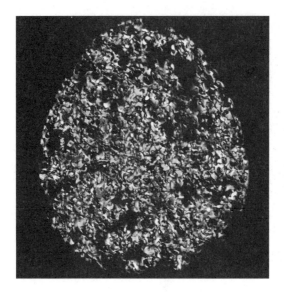

Figure 6.

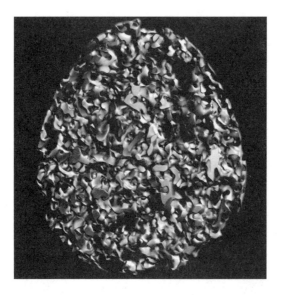

Figure 7.

Figure 8.

Woven Cloth

Cloth is defined by the perpendicular interweaving of warp threads and woof threads. We define a warp function: *warp(x, y, z)*, where *y* is the direction perpendicular to the cloth:

```
/* (1) make an undulating slab */

    if (fabs(y) > PI)
        return 0.;

    y = y + PI/2 * cos(x) * cos(z);
    if (fabs(y) > PI/2)
        return 0.;

    density = cos(y);

/* (2) separate the undulating slab into fibers via cos(z) */

    density = density * cos(z);

/* (3) shape the boundary into a hard surface */
```

```
density = density * density;
density = bias(density, Bias);
density = gain(density, Gain);
return density;
```

We can then define a woof function by rotating 90 degrees in *z*, *x* and flipping in *y*. The complete cloth function is then:

```
cloth(x, y, z) = warp(x, y, z)  +  warp(z, -y, x);
```

You can make the cloth wrinkle, fold, etc., by transforming *x*, *y*, and *z* before applying the cloth function. You can also add high frequency *noise()* to x,y,z before applying cloth(), to simulate the appearance of roughly formed fibers. In the examples shown I have done both sorts of things.

In the cloth examples shown here, I "sharpen" the surface by applying the *bias()* and *gain()* functions. Figures 9 through 12 are extreme closeups of cloth with various bias and gain settings. Figure 9 has low bias and gain. In Figure 10 I increase gain, which "sharpens" the surface. In Figure 11 I increase bias, which expands the surface, in effect fattening the individual threads. In Figure 12 I increase both bias and gain. Figure 13 shows a high-resolution rendering of a low-bias, high-gain cloth, which gives a "thread" effect. Conversely, a high-bias, low-gain would give a "woolen" effect.

Architexture

Now let's take an architectural sketch and "grow" solid texture around it, ending up with hard textured surfaces. This is similar in spirit to Ned Greene's voxel automata algorithm. The difference is that whereas he literally "grows" a volume from a defining skeleton, one progressive voxel layer at a time, the hypertexture approach directly evaluates its result independently at each point in space.

I start with a skeleton of architectural elements. This can be supplied by free-hand drawing or, alternatively, generated from a CAD program. Each architectural element is a "path" in space formed by consecutive points P_i.

Each path defines an influence region around it, which gives the architexture its shape component. This region is created by "blurring" the path. To do this I treat each point along the path as the center of a low density soft sphere of radius *R*. The shape density at a given point $\vec{x}$ is given by:

$$path\_shape(\vec{x}) = \frac{1}{KR^2} \sum_i \max(0, R^2 - |P_i - \vec{x}|^2),$$

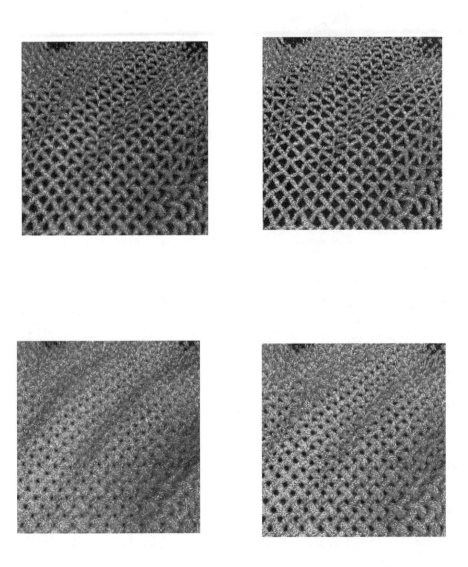

Figures 9–12.

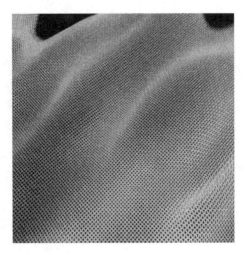

Figure 13.

where the normalizing constant K is the distance between successive points on the path. For each volume sample, the cost per path point is a dot product and some adds, which is fairly expensive. To speed things up I maintain a bounding box around each path, which eliminates most paths from consideration for any given sample point.

I've only played so far with rocklike textures for architexture. The texture component of this is given by a simple noise-based fractal generator:

$$\text{rock\_texture}(\vec{x}) = \sum_{f=\log base\_freq}^{\log resolution} 2^{-f} \, noise(2^f \, \vec{x})$$

and I define the final density by:

$$\text{sharpen}(\text{path\_shape}(\vec{x}) + \text{rock\_texture}(\vec{x}))$$

where I use the sharpening function to reduce the effective fuzzy region size about one volume sample. For a given image resolution and shape radius R, correct sharpen is done by:

- scaling the density gradient about 0.5 by a factor of $1/R$ (adjusting also for variable image resolution)
- clipping the resulting density to between 0.0 and 1.0.

The idea of the above is that the larger R becomes, the smaller will be the gradient of density within the fuzzy region, so the more sharpening is needed. The actual code I use to do this is:

```
density = (density - 0.5) * (resolution / 600) / R  +  0.5;
density = max(0.0, min(1.0, density));
```

I also decrease the shape's radius R with height (y coordinate), which gives architectural elements a sense of being more massive in their lower, weight supporting, regions.

In Figures 14 and 15 I show a typical arch (which I suppose could archly be called archetypical architexture). This started out as a simple curved line tracing the inner skeleton, which was then processed as described above.

Figure 14 shows a sequence where three parameters are being varied. From left to right the width of the arch at the base increases. From top to bottom the thickness enhancement toward the base increases. These two parameters act in concert to add a "weight-supporting" character to architectural elements. Finally, the amplitude of the texture is increased linearly from the first image in the sequence to the last.

Figure 15 shows a high-resolution version of the bottom right image in the sequence.

Figure 14.   Arch with varying parameter values.

Figure 15.

The NYU Torch

In Color Plate 6.3, a number of hypertextures were used for various parts of the same object to build an impression of this well-known New York University icon. The various amounts of violet reflected down from the flame to the torch handle were just added manually, as a function of y.

Smoke

In a recent experiment we tried to create the look of an animating smoke column, using as simple a hypertexture as possible. This work was done in collaboration with Ajay Rajkumar at NYU.

The basic approach was to create a smooth smoke "column" along the y axis, and then to perturb this column in x, z—increasing the perturbation at greater y values. We added knobs for such things as column opacity and width. These "shaping" knobs can have a great effect on the final result. For example, Figures 16 and 17 vary only in their column width. Yet the difference in appearance between them is drastic.

Figure 16.

Figure 17.

Time Dependency

We make the smoke appear to "drift" in any direction over time by moving the domain of the turbulence in the *opposite* direction. In the example below, we do this domain shift in both x and y.

We move y linearly downward, to give the impression of a rising current. We move x to the left but increase the rate of movement at greater y values. This creates the impression that the smoke starts out moving vertically, but then drifts off to the right as it dissipates near the top.

The particular shape of the smoke can vary dramatically over time, yet the general *feel* of the smoke stays the same. Compare, for example, the two images in Figures 18 and 19, which are two frames from the same smoke animation.

Smoke Rings

Figure 20 shows the formation over time of a smoke ring. Smoke rings will occur when the turbulence function distorts the space sufficiently so that the column appears to double over on itself horizontally. We need to let this happen only fairly high up on the column. If it happens too low, then the rings will appear to be forming somewhere off in space, not out of the column itself.

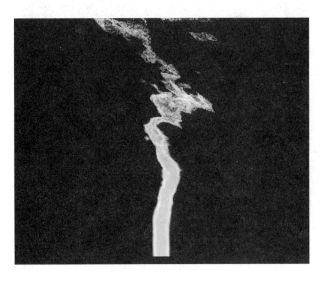

Figure 18.

Figure 19.

For this reason, we employ two different gain curves. One controls turbulence amplitude near the column as a function of y, and the other controls turbulence amplitude far from the column as a function of y. The latter curve always lags behind the former, thereby preventing low-lying smoke rings.

Optimization

Since smoke is quite sparse within its sampled volume, it is a good candidate for optimization based on judicious presampling. Tests on the AT&T Pixel Machine with 64 DSP32 processors showed that it took about 8 hours to compute a single frame of a $640 \times 480 \times 640$ volume. This is rather impractical for animation. To speed this up, we pre-compute the image at a smaller resolution to find out where the smoke lives within the volume. We then do the final computation only within those parts of the volume.

More specifically, we do a preliminary ray-march at one-fourth the final x, y, z resolution. Note that this requires only 1/64 as many density evaluations as would a full computation. At each 4×4 pixel, we save the interval along z which bounds all nonzero densities. For many pixels, this will be a null interval. Then to be conservative, at each pixel we extend this interval to be its union with the intervals at all neighbor pixels.

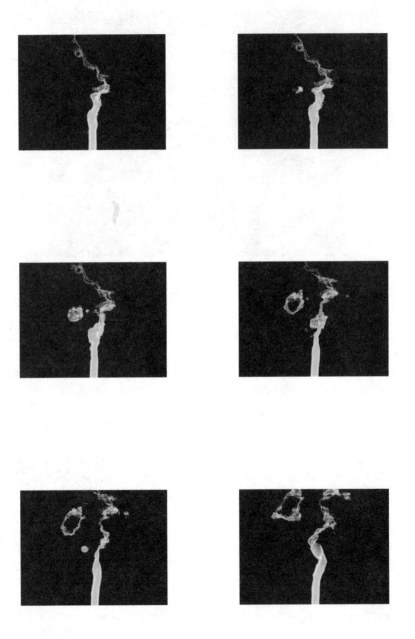

Figure 20.

We use this image of bounding z intervals to restrict the domain of the final ray-marching. We have found about a 30-fold speed-up using this method—each image now takes about 16 minutes to compute (including the time for the sub-sampled prepass). Smoke is optimal for this type of speedup for two reasons: (1) since it is sparse, the speedup is great, and (2) since density takes many sample widths to fall off to zero, tiny details are not inadvertently skipped over.

Here is pseudocode for the smoke density function. It's mostly just C code with some unimportant details and declarations left out.

```
smoke_density_function(x, y, z)
{
     /* k1, k2, etc. are the column shape knobs */

     /* rotate z randomly about y, based on noise function */
     /* this creates the impression of random ''swirls'' */

     t = noise(x,y,z);
     s = sin(t / 180. * PI);
     c = cos(t / 180. * PI);
     z = x * s + z * c;

     /* once the space is ''swirled'', create the column of smoke */

     /* 1) phase shift x and z using turbulence; this varies with time */

     x += k1 * phase_shift(x, y, z);
     z += k2 * phase_shift(x, y, z + k3);

     /* 2) define column by distance from the y-axis */

     rx = (x * x + z * z) * k4;

     /* 3) if inside the column, make smoke */

     if (rx < =1.) {
         rx = bias(rx, k5); /* the basic column shape is */
         s = sin(PI * rx);  /* a tube with hollow core */
         return s * s;
     }
     else
         return 0.;
}

phase_shift(x, y, z)
float x, y, z;
{
     /* c1, c2, etc. are the ''texture'' knobs */
```

```
p[0] = c1 * x + bias(y + .5, .3) * TIME; /* vary with time */
p[1] = c1 * y + TIME;
p[2] = c1 * z + c2;
g = gain(y + .5, c3);              /* dropoff with y */

/* these 3 lines remove smoke rings that are */
/* too low in y to be physically plausible */

r = max(0., 1. - (x * x + z * z) * c5);
gl = gain(bias(y + .5, c4), c3); /* smoke ring dropoff with y */
g = g * LERP(gl, r, 1.);

return g * (turbulence(p, 1., RES) + c6); /* c6 recenters the column */
}
```

Turbulence

The turbulence function, which you use to make marble, clouds, explosions, etc., is just a simple fractal generating loop built on top of the *noise* function. It is not a real turbulence model at all. The key trick is the use of the *fabs()* function, which makes the function have gradient discontinuity "fault lines" at all scales. This fools the eye into thinking it is seeing the results of turbulent flow. The *turbulence()* function gives the best results when used as a phase shift, as in the familiar marble trick:

```
sin(point  +  turbulence(point) * point.x);
```

Note the second argument below, *lofreq*, which sets the lowest desired frequency component of the turbulence. The third argument, *hifreq*, is used by the function to ensure that the turbulence effect reaches down to the single pixel level, but no further. I usually set this argument equal to the image resolution.

```
float turbulence(point, lofreq, hifreq)
float point[3], freq, resolution;
{
    float noise3(), freq, t, p[3];

    p[0] = point[0] + 123.456;
    p[1] = point[1];
    p[2] = point[2];

    t = 0;
    for (freq = lofreq ; freq < hifreq ; freq *= 2.) {
        t += fabs(noise3(p)) / freq;
```

```
        p[0] *= 2.;
        p[1] *= 2.;
        p[2] *= 2.;
    }
    return t - 0.3; /* readjust so that mean returned value is 0.0 */
}
```

Antialiased Rendering of Procedural Textures

In this section I describe a way of antialiasing edges antialiasing edges that result from conditionals in procedurally defined images, at a cost of one sample per pixel, wherever there are no other sources of high frequencies. The method proceeds by bifurcating the calculation over the image at conditional statements. Where a pixel straddles both true and false branches under its convolution area, both branches are followed and then linearly combined. A neighbor-comparing, antialiased, high-contrast filter is used to define regions of bifurcation. The method proceeds recursively for nested conditionals.

Background

If an image is described by an algorithmic procedure, then in principle there are cases where antialiasing can be done analytically, without supersampling, just by examining the procedure itself.

Generally speaking, there are two sources of high frequencies for procedurally generated images. *Edge events* are caused by conditional statements, which do boolean operations on continuous quantities. For example, there are infinitely high frequencies on the image of a circular disk formed by the following conditional statement when sampled over the unit square:

$$\text{if } (x - .5)^2 + (y - .5)^2 < .25 \text{ then } \textbf{white} \text{ else } \textbf{black}$$

The edges of discontinuity in this image can, in principle, be detected by analyzing the statement itself. Nonedge high-frequency events cannot be detected in this way. For example, to render the image represented by

$$\text{if } \sin(10^5\, x) \sin(10^5\, y) > 0 \text{ then } \textbf{white} \text{ else } \textbf{black}$$

we need to resort to statistical oversampling or other numerical quadrature methods, since this expression has *inherently* high frequencies.

The Basic Idea

As in (Perlin 1985), consider any procedure that takes a position (x, y) in an image as its argument, and returns a color. Usually we create an image from such a procedure by running the procedure at enough samples to create an antialiased image. Where the results produce high variance, we sample more finely and then apply a weighted sum of the results to convolve with a pixel reconstruction kernel.

One common source of this high local variance is that fact that at neighboring samples the procedure follows different paths at conditional statements. No matter how finely we oversample, we are faced with an infinitely thin edge on the image—a step function—between the **true** and **false** regions of this conditional.

Our method is to identify those edges on the image caused by conditional expressions. We do this by comparing neighboring sample values at each conditional expression in the computation. We use the results of this comparison to create an antialiased filter that represents the resulting step function as though it had been properly sampled.

To do this, we can view the procedure as a single-instruction-multiple-data (SIMD) parallel operation over all samples of the image. More precisely, we view the computation as a reverse polish stack machine. Items on the stack are entire images. For example, the "+" operator takes two images from the stack, adds them sample by sample, and puts the result back on the stack.

This calculation proceeds in lock-step for all samples. When a conditional is reached, we can evaluate both sides of the conditional, and then just disregard the results from one of the branches.

Obviously this approach is wasteful. Instead we would like to go down only one path wherever possible. We arrange to do this as follows. We recast each conditional expression using a pseudofunction $if pos$, so that $expr\ if pos$ evaluates to 1 when $expr > 0$ and 0 otherwise. Using the $if\ pos$ operator we can recast any function containing conditionals into an expression:

$$expr\ if\ pos\ [ToDoIfFalse, ToDoIfTrue]\ LERP$$

where $t\ [a, b]\ LERP$ is a linear interpolation operation defined as follows: when $t \leq 0$ or $t \geq 1$, LERP returns a or b, respectively. When $0 < t < 1$, LERP returns $a + t(b - a)$. For example:

$$abs(x) = if\ x < 0\ then\ -x\ else\ x$$

can be expressed as:

$$x \ if pos \ [-x, x] \ LERP.$$

Over the convolution kernel of any pixel, *if pos* will return **true** for some samples and **false** for others, creating a step function over the image. We actually return a floating point value between 0.0 and 1.0 to express the convolution of this step function with each sample's reconstruction kernel. Now the problem of properly sampling edges that have been formed from conditions is completely contained within one pseudofunction.

This is done as follows. When execution of our SIMD stack machine gets to an *if pos* function, it looks at the image on top of the stack, and runs a high-contrast filter *h* on this image, which examines the neighbors of each sample. If the sample and its neighbors are all positive or all negative, then *h* returns 1 or 0, respectively. Otherwise, *h* approximates the gradient near the sample by fitting a plane to the values at neighboring samples. Where there is a large variance from this plane, then supersampling must be done—the procedure must be run at more samples.

But where there is a low variance, then just from the available samples, *h* can produce a linear approximation to the argument of *if pos* in the neighborhood of the sample. It uses this to construct a step function, which it then convolves with the sample's reconstruction kernel. As we shall see, this is a fairly inexpensive procedure.

After the *h* function is run, the samples of the image on the stack will fall into one of three subsets:

> *value* $\equiv$ 0.
> 0 < *value* < 1.
> *value* $\equiv$ 1.

We label these subsets *F*, *M*, and *T* (for "false," "midway," and "true"), respectively.

Once *h* is run, we gather up all samples in (*F* union *M*) and run the *ToDoIfFalse* statements on these. Then we gather up all samples in (*T* union *M*) and run the *ToDoIfTrue* statements on these. Finally we do a linear interpolation between the two branches over the samples in *M*, and place the reconstructed image on the stack.

Because each conditional splits the image into subsets some of a sample's neighbors may be undefined inside a conditional. This means that within nested conditionals, *h* may not be faced with a full complement of neighbors. This happens near samples of the image where several conditional edges intersect. As long as there is at least one horizontal and one vertical neighbor, *h* can recreate the gradient it needs. When there are no longer enough neighbors, *h* flags a "high-variance" condition, and supersampling is then invoked.

More Detailed Description

In this section we describe the flow of control of the algorithm. We maintain a stack of lists of *it current_samples*. We start with *current_samples* = ALL samples. At any given moment during execution, samples are examined only if they are in the current list.

(I)   When the *i f pos* token is encountered:
         Evaluate hicon for all samples in *current_samples*.
         Use the result to make the three sublists: F,M,T.
         Push these sublists onto an FMT stack.
         Push a new *current_samples* list (M union T).

(II)   Continue to evaluate normally, over samples in *current_samples*.
         If the *i f pos* code is encountered, recurse to (I).

(III) When the beginning of the *ToDoIfFalse* code is encountered:
         Pop the *current_samples* stack.
         Push a new *current_samples* list (F union M).
         Evaluate normally until matching LERP token is encountered.
         If the *i f pos* token is encountered first, recurse to (I).

(IV) When the *LERP* token is encountered:
         Pop the *current_samples* stack.
         For all samples in *current_samples*:
                 stacktop[1] := LERP(stacktop[1], stacktop[−1], stacktop[0])
         Pop the FMT stack.

The High Contrast Filter

Given a large enough subset of the eight neighbors around a sample, we can use the value at the sample and its neighbors to construct an approximation to the integral under the sample's reconstruction kernel in the area where *i f pos* evaluates to 1.

Let $f(x, y)$ denote the value of the expression at any small offset (x, y) from the sample. First we do a least squares fit of the differences in value between the sample and its neighbors to approximate the x and y partials. If the variance is high for either of these two computations, then we give up and resort to supersampling the procedure in the neighborhood of the sample.

Otherwise we can use the linear approximation function $ax + by + c = 0$ near the sample, where $c = f(0,0,)$ and a and b approximate the x and y partials of f, respectively.

We want to find out the integral under the sample's reconstruction kernel of the step function:

$$\text{if } f(x, y) > 0 \text{ then } 1 \text{ else } 0.$$

We assume a circularly symmetric reconstruction kernel.

The problem at this stage is illustrated in Figure 21. Figure 21(a) shows the sample reconstruction kernel, Figure 21(b) shows the intersection of this kernel with a linear approximation of the function near the sample, Figure 21(c) shows the step function induced by this linear function, and Figure 21(d) shows the region under the kernel where this step function is positive.

Since we assume the kernel is circularly symmetric, finding the convolution reduces to a one-dimensional problem. We need only to compute the perpendicular distance from the sample to the step, and then use a spline fit to approximate the integral under the kernel in the positive region of the step function.

To do this, we compute the magnitude of the linear gradient $|f'| = \sqrt{(a^2 + b^2)}$. Then we calculate the distance from the sample to the line of the image where this function equals zero by $d = f(x, y)/|f'|$. Finally, we approximate the integral of the reconstruction kernel by a cubic spline:

$$\text{if } t < -.5 \text{ then } 0 \text{ else if } t > .5 \text{ then } 1 \text{ else } 3(t + .5)^2 - 2(t + .5)^3$$

Examples

Figures 22 through 27 show a succession of steps in the creation of a simple procedural image that requires two levels of nested conditionals. Each image is on the top of the stack during a particular snapshot of execution.

The image is formed by doing a conditional evaluation of the circular disk (Figure 22):

$$(x - .5)^2 + (y - .5)^2$$

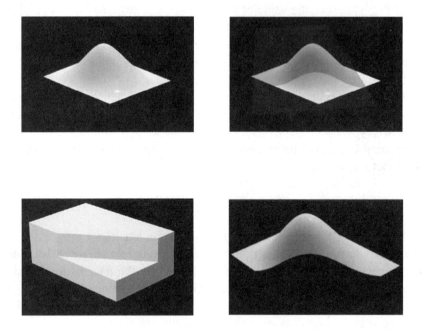

Figure 21. Reconstruction kernel.

Then $.3^2$ is subtracted, a conditional is done, execution bifurcates, and *noise* (Perlin 1985) is applied to the outside of the disk (Figure 23). Then $\sin(10x + noise(x, y)/10)$ $\sin(10y + noise(x,y)/10)$ is evaluated inside the disk (Figure 24), and another conditional is done. A constant is applied to the negative areas, and $.5 + noise(3x,y)$ is applied to the positive areas (Figure 25). Finally, Figure 26 and Figure 27 show the successive reconstruction of the two nested levels of conditionals.

To Sum Up

The above method recasts image synthesis as a set of recursively bifurcating SIMD processes over image samples. In this way we were able to do true procedural antialiasing of edges.

This approach differs from previous approaches in that it finds and resolves sampling problems by using information contained in the image synthesis algorithm itself, usually without resorting to supersampling. Whether such methods can be applied to the general image synthesis problem is an open question.

Figures 22–27.

Surflets

Instead of regenerating hypertexture procedurally all the time, it is sometimes useful to "cache" it in some format for display. For this purpose we want rapid and accurate display, as well as a good ability to do light propagation—including self-shadowing and diffuse penumbra.

In this section I describe a useful intermediate representation for procedurally generated volumes. The approach is based on a sparse wavelet representation, and is particularly suitable for the sorts of free-form surfaces generated by hypertextural algorithms.

Other sorts of complex volumetric data can also be conveniently represented using this approach, including medical data (CT and MR), and meteorological, geological, or molecular surface data.

A "surflet" is a flavor of wavelet that can be used to construct free-form surfaces. Surfaces obtained by evaluating scalar volumes or procedural volumetric models such as hypertexture can be stored in the intermediate form of surflets. This allows us when rendering such surfaces to (1) do self-shadowing, including penumbras, from multiple light sources, and (2) have the option at rendering time to either (a) further refine the surface locally from the volume data, or (b) do a bump-texture approximation, or any mixture of (a) and (b). Thus issues of lighting placement and level-of-details differences can be resolved at a postprocessing stage, after the bulk of the computation is completed. This is work I did mainly with Benjamin Zhu, and is based in part on earlier work that I did together with Xue Dong Yang.

First I will define the surflet model and show a particular implementation. Then I will talk about how to find visible surfaces. I will show how by using surflets we can decide locally at rendering time whether true volumetric surface refinement or shading approximation should be performed. Finally I will introduce a multiresolution, hierarchical modeling of surflets, and describe a way to do self-shadowing with penumbra.

Introduction to Surflets

Volume visualization studies the manipulation and display of volume data. Depending on the intermediate representation between raw data and final display, volume visualization techniques can be classified as surface-based techniques (or surface modeling) [(Lorensen and Cline 1987), (Lorensen and Cline 1990), (Wywill *et al.* 1986)] and rendering [(Drebin *et al.* 1988), (Hanrahan 1990), (Kajiya and Von Herzen 1984), (Levoy 1988), (Levoy 1990c), (Levoy 1990b),

(Levoy 1990a), (Sabella 1988), (Westover 1990)]. Methods in the first category approximate surfaces of interest (determined by thresholds) by geometric primitives and then display these primitives, whereas volume rendering directly operates on the volume data and renders the scenes.

Surface modeling is the main topic of this discussion. Since surfaces offer a better understanding of the external structure of volumes, accurately reconstructing surfaces from volumes and subsequently rendering the surfaces efficiently is very important in practice. Surface modeling techniques differ from one another in that different primitives can be used to approximate the surfaces of interest. (Keppel 1975) and (Fuchs *et al.* 1977) construct contours on each 2D slice, and connect contours on subsequent slices with triangles. The cuberille model uses parallel planes to create surfaces [(Chen *et al.* 1985), (Gordon and Reynolds 1985), (Hoehne *et al.* 1990)]. The marching-cube algorithm uses voxel-sized triangles to approximate surfaces (Cline *et al.* 1988), (Lorensen and Cline 1987), (Lorensen and Cline 1990), (Wywill *et al.* 1986)]. Bicubic patches can also be used to reconstruct surfaces (Gallagher and Nagtegaal 1989).

All of these techniques share a common characteristic: the geometric primitives involved in surface reconstruction are in an explicit form. This leads to an interesting question: can we define the surfaces of interest in an implicit form? If so, what are the advantages of using the implicit representation?

In the following sections, a "surflet" model is introduced to define free-form surfaces. Methods to find visible surfaces, perform selective surface refinement, and do self-shadowing with penumbra are described. A multiresolution, hierarchical modeling of isosurfaces is sketched. Experimental results are shown to demonstrate the benefits of adopting this new model.

Surflets as Wavelets

As I've discussed earlier in the section on *noise*, a wavelet [(Mallat 1989a), (Mallat 1989b)] is a function that is finite in extent and integrates to zero. Decomposing signals or images into wavelets, and then doing analysis on the wavelet decomposition, is a powerful tool in signal and image recognition.

We use a specific kind of continuous wavelets, which we call surflets, to approximate surfaces. We use a summation of surflets that together define a function over R^3 so that the desired surface is closely approximated by the locus of points where (i) the summation function is zero but where (ii) the function's gradient magnitude is nonzero. The general intuition here is that each surflet is used as a free-form spline that approximates a little piece of localized surface. All of these surflets sum together to form isosurfaces of interest.

We define each surflet as follows: let $\bar{p}$ = [x, y, z] be a sampled location in space and let r be its sampling radius. Then if the sample at $\bar{p}$ has a value of d and a gradient vector of $\vec{n}$, we define a wavelet approximtion to the sample at $\vec{x}$ = [x, y, z] near $\bar{p}$ by:

$$\prod drop\left(\frac{x_i - p_i}{r}\right) \times \sum n_i(x_i - p_i)$$

where:

- $\vec{x}$ is any point in R^3
- $\bar{p}$ is the wavelet center
- $\vec{n}$ is the wavelet gradient
- r is the wavelet radius
- i varies over the three coordinates
- $drop(t)$ defined as for the *noise* function: $2\ t^3 - 3\ t^2$.

At points with distance greater than r from $\bar{p}$ we assign a value of zero.

[$\bar{p}$, d, $\vec{n}$] defines a surflet. Since each sample at p cannot affect any sampled location farther than r away from its center, the wavelet contribution is localized.

It should be pointed out that other continuous functions might also work well, as long as each surflet has a limited extent in terms of its wavelet contribution, and this contribution drops from 1.0 down to 0.0 monotonically. The cubic drop-off function is chosen due to its simplicity.

In practice, we define the surflets on a rectangular grid. When surflets are refined (see ahead), the size of the sampling grid is successively halved. We generate surflets from a functional sampling with the following steps:

- Subtract the desired isovalue from all samples.
- Find samples that have any six-connected neighbor with density of opposite sign.
- Approximate surflet normal $\vec{n}$ by density difference between neighbors.
- Approximate surflet normal $\vec{n}$:.
- Use $\vec{n}$ to locate center $\bar{p}$ near the sample.

We use the normal to locate the surflet center as follows:

- Approximate surflet normal $\vec{n}$ by taking density difference between neighbor samples along each coordinate axis.
- Use $\vec{n}$ to locate surflet center $\bar{p}$

$$\vec{p} = \vec{x}_{sample} - d_{sample}\vec{n}.$$

Note that we end up with something very closely related to the *noise* function (Perlin 1985). In fact, the *noise* function can be viewed as the surflet decomposition of a random density function sampled at a rectangular grid.

Finding Visible Surfaces

Because surflets are well-defined analytic functions, it is possible to find the intersection of a ray with the zero surface of a summation-of-surflets function.

Since the contribution from each surflet has a limited extent, for each point $\vec{x}$ in R^3 only a finite number of surflets will have a nonzero wavelet contribution to $\vec{x}$. Two alternatives are possible for finding a ray-surface intersection. A numerical method such as binary division or Newton iteration can guarantee convergence to the true intersection, given initial guesses close to the actual solution. However, since all these numerical methods involve iterative root-finding, they can be quite slow. We instead use a faster approximation method.

As in cone-tracing (Amanatides 1984), we trace a fat ray (a cone) into the scene. We represent each surflet by a sphere whose radius is the surflet's r times a constant factor, and whose center is $\vec{p}$. We shrink the cone ray into a thin line, and grow all the spheres by the cross-sectional width of the cone at the surflet. This is equivalent to the computation in (Amanatides 1984). Since perspective projection is used, the spheres that approximate the surflets become variously sized. Each sphere is given a weight according to how far along its radius it intersects the ray as well as the magnitude of its gradient. Spheres that mutually intersect each other within the ray form a local bit of surface. We use a scheme similar to the fragment-merging in Carpenter's A-buffer algorithm (Carpenter 1984), and use the weighted average of the surflet normals as the surface fragment normal. All such surface fragments are evaluated from front to back along the ray as opacity accumulates.

Shading is done as in (Duff 1985). We stop ray-marching when the opacity reaches totality. Because we render one surflet at a time (as opposed to one ray at a time), our surface approximation method is view-dependent, in contrast to the numerical approach, which is view-independent.

Visible surfaces can be rendered efficiently by using a depth-sorting algorithm similar to the Z-buffer algorithm. More efficiency can be derived by using the selective surface refinement described in the following section and the hierarchical surflet modeling described in the section "Constructing a Surflet Hierarchy."

Selective Surface Refinement

A sampled location is defined as a singularity if along any coordinate axis, it is inside the surface while its two neighbors are outside the surface; or it is outside the surface while its two neighbors are inside the surface.

We generally need to refine a surflet only when any one of the following conditions is true:

- Due to perspective, the surflet is large with respect to a pixel on the viewing plane.
- The surflet normal is nearly perpendicular to the line of sight, thus presenting a silhouette edge.
- The surflet is a singularity.

However, if only the first condition is satisfied, then a surflet, no matter how large, can be visually approximated by normal perturbation alone.

By using selective surface refinement, we can greatly reduce the rendering time. Since surface refinement adapts to the complexity of a scene, different parts of the scene can be rendered at different resolutions. This is very attractive in practice. We have observed that the number of surflets involved in rendering decreases by more than 50% when we start at a low resolution and perform selective surface refinement at next higher resolution than when we start directly at the next resolution level.

A Surflet Generator

Surflets can be generated from either sampled scalar data or procedural volumetric functions such as hypertexture. In the first case, we read in digitized samples from a regular grid, whereas in the latter case, we evaluate samples on a regular grid. One orthogonal 2D slice is processed at a time. We always keep three slices, which helps us detect surflets as well as singularities.

After each slice has been processed, we find those samples that have any neighbors with density value on the opposite side of the isosurface density. At a candidate sample located at point $\bar{p}$, we approximate the normal gradient $\bar{n}$ by the density difference d between the samples and its neighboring samples along each coordinate axis. Forward difference, central difference, or a mixture of both (Hoehne *et al.* 1990) can be applied to get gradients. If the distance from the sample to the surface is less than 0.5, then [$\bar{p}$, d, $\bar{n}$] defines a surflet. This 0.5 bias is determined empirically to compromise between two constraints: (1) If the distance is too small, we do not have enough surflets to interlock with each other, and consequently we might get undersampling. (2) If the distance is too big, then we will have too many surflets. This will create a huge intermediate structure to store surflets, and the rendering time will be too high.

For those samples that are singularities, each one is treated as eight different samples in eight octants; their gradient vectors and distances to the isosurface are evaluated. Therefore, a maximum number of eight surflets can be generated. Each singular surflet will have an appropriate flag tagged in its data structure, indicating which octant it contributes to.

Constructing a Surflet Hierarchy

Up to now we have described surflets limited to a single resolution. However, it would be more desirable to create surflets iteratively from lower resolutions to higher resolutions. A hierarchical surflet model can not only provide the freedom to render surfaces at arbitrary details, but can also avoid unnecessary details which would be washed out due to shadowing, etc.

We construct a surflet hierarchy as follows: since only the isosurfaces are interesting to us, a candidate set of potential surflets is created at each resolution as in the previous section. Each candidate set is generally very small as compared to the number of samples in the volume. All surflets at the lowest resolution level are detected and collected. We compute the image at this resolution based on the wavelet approximation formula. Then we precede to the next higher level, and subtract the image at this level from the image at the previous level. Because we have precomputed the surflet candidate set at this level, the computation only involves those potential surflets. Those samples less than $r/2$ away from the isosurface are classified as surflets, where r is the sampling radius at this resolution. We repeat the same procedure and subtract images at lower resolutions from higher resolutions. When the sampling resolution equals the size of the sampling grid, a surflet hierarchy is created.

Self-Shadowing with Penumbra

Let us assume for simplicity that there is a single light source in the scene. We can then handle multiple light sources as the summation of the shading contribution from each light source.

We want to render surfaces with self-shadowing and penumbra. It is theoretically impossible to use a point source to create true penumbra, although some filtering techniques might create quite vivid penumbra effects (Reeves *et al.* 1987). We instead use a light source of a certain shape, such as a spherical light source (or a rectangular light source). The portion of light source visible from any surflet is computed and used to determine the brightness at a surflet. An approximation of this portion is sketched here.

Each surflet in the scene is approximated by a sphere whose radius r is the sampling radius, and whose center is given by $\bar{p}$. For each visible surflet, we trace a fat shadow ray from the surflet center to the light source. The spread angle of the fat ray is approximated by R/D, where R is the radius of the spherical light source, and D is the distance from the surflet center to the center of the light source. We perform cone-tracing to determine shadowing and penumbra in the same way that we found visible surfaces. We shrink the cone ray into a thin line, and grow the spheres accordingly. The portion of the shadow ray that any surflet blocks is determined by how far along its radius the surflet intersects the ray. To make the approximation more accurate, spheres that mutually intersect each other within the ray are split into small, disjoint fragments. Portions of the shadow ray blocked by all these small segments are computed and summed to find the proportion of light blocked by this piece of surface.

We compose the portion of the shadow ray blocked by isosurfaces by a method similar to the image composition scheme in (Duff 1985). The shadow ray marches through the scene until (1) the blocked portion reaches totality, or (2) the shadow ray reaches the light source. In the first case, the surflet that initiates the shadow ray is in full umbra. In the latter case, we subtract this blocked portion from 1.0 to get the surflet illumination. Clearly, the surflet is in penumbra if its illumination level is less than 1.0, and the surflet is not in shadow if its illumination equals 1.0.

To speed up the rendering, we can render surflets in shadow at lower resolutions. For example, we can do shadow detection at low resolutions, and do selective surface refinement only for those visible surflets not in shadow. A major advantage of this scheme is that important surface details are not left out, while unnecessary details hidden by the shadow are not given much attention. This can produce softer shadows, as well as increase rendering speed.

Discussion

The surflet model has a number of advantages over other surface-based techniques. First, it has an implicit form. Although we approximate surflets with spheres in our implementation, it does not mean that this is the only choice. On the contrary, it is not clear to us whether this is the best way. For example, with special hardware, numerical root-finding can be more accurate and more promising. We have also started to experiment with ellipsoid-like primitives to approximate surflets.

Second, the surflet model provides a convenient way to do hierarchical modeling of surfaces and selective surface refinement due to its implicit form. This feature cannot be found in many existing surface modeling methods. Adaptive sampling gives us the power to avoid unnecessary details while preserving important surface subtleties.

Third, the representation has a compact structure. Our experiments indicated that using surflets takes only 25% to 50% of the storage of marching-cubes at the same resolution. Fourth, isosurfaces can be rendered in parallel with surflets. Since for any point on the isosurfaces, there are only a limited number of surflets determining the zero crossing, surflets are amenable to either a parallel implementation or an implementation with distributed computing.

Fifth, surflets can be integrated with wavelets in a straightforward manner to yield a combined model of surface modeling and volume rendering. If we delay thresholding until the rendering stage, we can generate wavelets by subtracting the low resolution signals from the high resolution signals with the same kind of hierarchical modeling as in the section "Constructing a Surflet Hierarchy." Depending on our need, we can do either volume rendering or thresholding followed by surface rendering at rendering time. This integrated approach is attractive, since it reduces the difference between rendering surfaces and rendering volumes. However, it differs from conventional volume rendering (Drebin *et al.* 1988, Levoy 1988, Levoy 1990c) in that an intermediate data structure, as well as hiearchical modeling, is introduced to speed up the process. Thresholding can still be used at rendering time to distinguish the rendering form volume rendering. Moreover, it is possible to have volume details and surface details in the same scene.

Conclusion

Surflets are a free-form modeling of isosurfaces. This model is attractive in that it prides a convenient way to do shadowing, seletive surface refinement, and hierarchical modeling. Moreoever, it requires mauh less stroage than other volumne-to-surface methofs, and allows considerable freedom for a particular implementation. Finally, it encourages an integreaated approach for surface modeling and volume rendering.

This surflet model is still quite empirical. Although it is quite intuitive and supported by image synthesis theory [(Grossman and Morlet 1984), (Mallat 1989a), (Mallat 1989b)], in many places we have had to tune the parameters to make the rendered images more realistic.

We are currently integrating surface modeling with column modeling. This step is very likely to provide us answers to the trade-offs in hierarchical modeling of surfaces, since heirachical modeling of volumes is more general than that of surfaces.

Textual Limb Animation

In this section I borrow notions from procedural texture synthesis and ise them to control affect of human-like figures. I apply stochastic *noise* to create time-varying parameters with well-controlled statistics. I then linearly blend these parameters, and feed the results into a motion system. Potential uses of this technique include role playing games, simulated conferences, "clip animation," and simulated dance.

Introduction to Textural Limb Motion

In simulated environments we often want synthetic cooperating characters to respond to each other and to a changing environment in real time. Because simulated worlds are often used primarily as a means of communication (in contrast to, say, robotics simulation), we are often not so concerned with specific task completion, as with conveying emotional messages through motion or gesture.

This situation comes up in role playing games, where game players want their "Avatars" (Stephenson 1992) to show a particular affective response to a person or event in the immediate environment.

Similarly, emotive gesturing would be useful for monitoring a shared electronic "talk" conference. One could model the participants as physical gesturing characters around a conference table. At a glance one could tell who is talking to whom, who is entering and leaving the discussion, and who is paying attention to whom.

Also, it is useful to have "clip animation," much like clip art, where for example an entire crowd of people reacts in a particular way to a character or event. We are not so concerned with their particular motions, but with the sense that "the crowd went wild," or "they respectfully parted to let her pass."

Dance is another instance where we're primarily interested in the *affect* of gesture. Music conveys emotional meaning, not literal meaning. It would be useful to be able to generate simulated dancing characters to music, by working on the level of, "Now I want the dancer to convey this combination of emotions and reactions to the other dancers."

The system described here aims at allowing the building of and use of gesture on the level of affective communication. It sidesteps many difficult issues faced by systems that address robotic problems such as "Pick up the glass of water and drink it." The work described here can be plugged into such systems as a modifying filter, but is independent of them.

Roadmap

The structure of this section is as follows. First I'll describe some prior and related work by others. Then I'll outline the basic approach, which I'll illustrate with a simple example.

After this I'll describe textural gesture and the structure of the system, what the different layers and modules are, and how they communicate. I'll follow this with some examples of the system in use. Finally, I'll discuss future and ongoing work.

Related Work

A number of researchers have done work complementary to that described in this section. Badler has specified movements in a goal-driven way and then fed those goals to a simulator (Badler *et al.* 1980). Calvert sampled human figure motion and used Labanotation (a form of dance notation) to create an animated deterministic stick figure (Calvert *et al.* 1980). Miller has applied synthesis techniques to worms (Miller 1988).

Waters did procedural modeling of faces (Waters 1987). Deterministic methods for dance have been described by (Yang 1988). Actor/Script-based systems for crowds (flocks and herds) were first described by (Reynolds 1987). Goal-based movement was described by (Badler *et al.* 1980) .

Physically based systems for jointed motion are very powerful, although they but can be difficult to control and specify (Girard and Maciejewski 1985). Fusco *et al.* take a sampling approach, digitizing sequences of actual human movement and using those to drive animated figures (Fusco and Tice 1993).

Basic Notions

The basic idea is that often we don't care what a gesture is actually doing, so long as it is conveying particular emotional information. For example, when someone is explaining something, his or her arms will wave about in a particular way. Different people, and the same people in different emotional states, will do this in a way that can be defined statistically. Those watching do not care exactly where the hands or arms of the speaker are at any given moment. Instead they watch the rhythm, the range of motion, the average posture, and the degree of regularity or irregularity of movement.

Our approach is to create a nondeterministic "texture" as a synthesis of scalar control parameters and to use these parameters to drive a motion description subsystem.

Stochastic Control of Gesture

The key innovation is the use of stochastic controls to specify gestural affect. But this needs to be placed in an appropriate system to be useful. This section consists of two parts. First I'll describe stochastically defined gestures, and then the system in which this technique is embedded.

Any animatable character has some N input parameters that control its motion. At any moment, the character can be thought of as residing at a point in an N dimensional unit cube. Each dimension spans the lowest to the highest value of one parameter.

We define a *textural gesture* as a stochastically defined path of motion within this cube that has constant statistical properties. Many gestures of a human figure can be defined by assigning to each joint angle a value for the triple [*center, amplitude, frequency*] and using the following procedure at the *time* of each frame:

```
center  +  amplitude * noise (frequency * time)
```

The above procedure was used for most of the gestures in this section. It allows control over average position, and frequency of undulation, while conveying a "natural" quality to all motion. This procedure has a constant statistical quality over time and therefore can be thought of as a fixed point in a gesture space induced over the N-cube space.

Several specific and interesting relationships came out of playing with these parameters. For example, I found that natural arm gestures generally resulted when elbow joints were moved with twice the frequency of shoulder joints. Varying too far from this ratio produced unnatural and artificial looking gestures. This might be related to the fact that the weight of the entire arm is approximately twice the weight of the lower arm alone.

The output of these procedures are combined via linear blending and fed into a kinematic model. In this way the single gestural "points" of the induced gesture space are used to traverse convex regions in this space.

The system provides the user with a general-purpose interpreted language for defining new gesture textures, in the spirit of (Stephenson 1992). Surprisingly, almost all gestures built using the system could be defined by linearly transformed *noise* of the various joint angles. For example, the bottom row of Figure 28 shows a transition from a "fencing" gesture to a "conducting" gesture. This illustrates sliding along a line within the induced gesture space.

The System

The texturally defined parameters feed into "scene description modules" (SDMs). An SDM can represent an animated character, a group of animated characters, or some physical object(s) in the scene. Each SDM knows about kinematics, static constraints, dynamics, etc. (whereas the texture module does not). This separation allows a very simple, high-level control of emotive qualities, and makes those qualities very easy to modify.

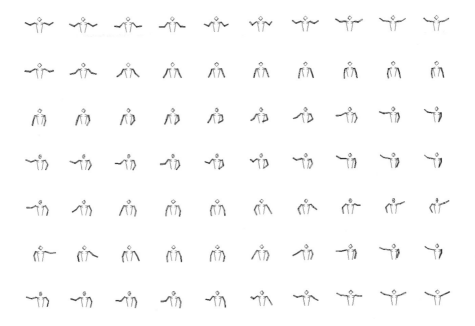

Figure 28.   Gesturing man.

An SDM can take as input a set of scalar parameters, and generally outputs scene transformations (matrices) and geometry to be rendered. Also, one SDM can be dependent on the matrices computed by another. For clarity in this section, I'll define a *parameter* as a scalar value that controls the movement of an SDM, and a *gesture* as a procedure that outputs varying values over time of a set of scalar parameters that feed into an SDM.

The system evaluates a frame of animation in several layers. At the top is a goal determination module (GDM). The GDM is responsible for determining, at each frame of animation, a weight for each gesture.

Below this we have the stochastic procedures for creating individual gestures. A gesture g is invoked if its weight is non-zero. Each gesture creates values over time for some set of parameters, as described in the previous section.

Once all gestures have been evaluated, we perform for each parameter a weighted sum of its values within each gesture for which it is defined. All parameter values are then normalized by their respective accumulated weights.

Finally, all SDMs are run for this frame.

The transformation matrices produced by the various SDM1s are available to an analyzer, which uses them to produce scalar variables that can be fed back into the GDM. For example, as character B physically approaches character A, the analyzer can evaluate their mutual distance, and feed this back to the GDM to influence character A to increase the weight of a gesture that conveys a sense of, say, "being sad," or "waving to character B."

Examples

Figure 28 shows a gesticulating man at various points in his gesture space. The top row shows him at a fixed "conducting" gesture point. If held at this point, he will continue to convey exactly the same affect forever, while never actually repeating the same movement twice. The second row shows a transition between this point and a "sad" gesture point—downcast with relatively slow movement, sloping shoulders, and low energy.

The third row shows a linear transition to a "fencing" gesture point. This point is held throughout the fourth row. In the fifth and sixth rows the man switches to fencing the other way and then back again. Finally in the bottom row he transitions back to the original gesture point.

One important thing to note is that every point in the transition between gestures produces reasonable motion. This is logical, since the statistical properties of motion during these transitions are still under tight control.

A reasonable use to this approach would be to do statistical analysis/resynthesis of human motion. This would involve analyzing statistics from real human figure motion, and turning these into sum-of-noise descriptions. These gesture "points" would then be added to the system.

Texture for Facial Movement

In this section I apply texture principles to the interactive animation of facial expression. Here the problems being addressed are: "How does one make an embodied autonomous agent react with appropriate facial expression, without resorting to repetitive prebuilt animations?" and "How does one mix and transition between facial expressions to visually represent shifting moods and attitudes?"

By building up facial expression from component movements, and by approaching combinations of these movements as a texturing problem, it is possible to use controlled *noise* to create convincing impressions of responsiveness and mood.

Background

Much human communication is conveyed by facial expression (Faigin 1990). One of the limitations of computer/human interfaces is their inability to convey the subtleties we take for granted in face to face communication. This concept has been well described in speculative fiction on the subject (Stephenson 1992). Toward this end, Parke (Parke 1982) and others have made good use of the Facial Action Coding System (FACS) (Ekman and Friesen 1978) for designing facially expressive automata, and there has been considerable work on computer generated facial animation (Parke and Waters 1996).

Here I focus in particular on using procedural texture to convey some of the rich, time varying facial expressions that people generally expect of each other. Aggressive, endearing, or otherwise idiosyncratic movements of facial expression convey a lot of our sense of another person's individuality. One inspiration for capturing this individuality can be found in successful animated characters.

For example, the hugely successful and endearing character of *Gromit* in Nick Park's animation (Park 1993) consistently reacts to events first with internal expressions of instinctive surprise or worry, and then, a beat later, with some expression of higher judgement: disgust, realization, suspicion, etc. *Gromit's* reactions become the audience's point of view. This identification creates an emotional payoff that draws in the audience (Park 1996).

It would be good for an interactive character to be able to convey the same sense of a compelling emotional point of view, and to react with appropriate dynamic facial expression, without resorting to predefined expressions, or to repetitive prebuilt animations.

To approach this with procedural textures, I build on (Perlin and Goldberg 1996) , using a parallel layered approach. The key is to allow the author of the animated agent relate lower level facial movements to higher level moods and intentions, through controlled procedural textures. The animator specifies time varying linear combinations and overlays of facial movements. Each such combination becomes a new, derived, set of facial movements.

In this section I will show how to use controlled *noise* (Perlin 1985) to introduce controllable autonomous motion, and I will show a number of examples of autonomous facial animation built with this texturing approach.

Related Work:

Facial movement synthesis by linear motion blending has been around for quite some time. In addition to Parke's work, this basic approach was also used by (DeGraf and Wahrman 1988) to help drive an interactive puppeteered face.

Kalra (Kalra 1991) proposed an abstraction model for building facial animation, for combining vocal articulation with emotion, and for facilitating specification of dialogs in which characters could converse while conveying facial emotion. The model consisted of five abstraction layers:

1. abstract muscles,
2. parameters built from these abstract muscles,
3. poses build by mixing parameters,
4. sequences and attack/sustain/release envelopes of poses, and
5. high level scripts.

Within this structure, the facial-expression textures that I will describe largely contribute between levels *(2)* and *(3)* of Kalra's formalism, by providing a mechanism for combining multiple time-varying layers of successively abstracted facial expression.

Brooks (Brooks 1986) developed autonomous robots having simultaneous different semantic levels of movement and control. In his *subsumption architecture,* longer term goals were placed at higher levels, and immediate goals (such as "don't fall over") were placed at lower levels. When necessary, the lower level controls could temporarily override higher level activities.

Using the basic noise-based procedural texture tools of (Perlin 1985), including *bias* and *gain* controls, I developed a responsive real time dancer whose individual actions were procedurally defined (Perlin 1995). Actions could be layered and smoothly blended together to create convincing responsive body movement, which conveyed varying moods and attitudes. Athomas Goldberg and I later extended this work (Perlin and Goldberg 1996), to create characters that used a more advanced layering system for multiple levels of responsive motion. This continuous movement model was controlled by a discrete stochastic decision system, which allowed authors to create characters that would make choices based on dynamic moods, personalities and social interactions, both with each other and with human participants.

Structure of this Section

This section is structured as follows. First I introduce a simple layered movement model. Then I describe the mechanism that allows animators to build successive abstractions. Finally, I give examples of the use of controlled *noise* to build up elements of autonomous facial movement. Finally I discuss some future work.

The Movement Model

Assume that a face model consists of a set of vertices, together with some surface representation built on those vertices. We can build a component movement as a linear displacement of some subset of vertices. Thus, each movement is a list of [i, x] pairs, where i is a vertex identifier, and x is the displacement vector for that vertex. We add additional movements for the axes of rigid head rotation, which are applied after all vertices have been displaced.

Given K component movements, we can give a state vector for the facial expression, consisting of linear combinations of its component movements. I used this approach to build a face that was as simple as possible, including only vertices that were absolutely necessary (Figure 29).

The goal was to make a model that would be used for working out a facial expression-texture vocabulary. Then the small number of vertices of this model could subsequently be used to drive movement of more elaborate facial geometries.

The face model used throughout this section contains fewer than 80 vertices—including the hair and shoulders. It requires no 3D graphical support, and runs as an interactive Java Applet on the Web (Perlin 1998).

The basic component movements included are:

- Left/Right eye brows
- Left/Right upper eyelids
- Left/Right lower eyelids
- Horizontal/Vertical eyegaze
- Left/Right sneer
- Left/Right smile
- Mouth open

 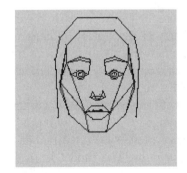

Figure 29.

- Mouth narrowed
- Head rotation

In this chapter I will refer to each of these component movements by the following respective names:

- BROW_L, BROW_R

- WINK_L, WINK_R

- LLID_L, LLID_R

- EYES_R, EYES_UP

- SNEER_L, SNEER_R

- SMILE_L, SMILE_R

- AHH

- OOH

- TURN, NOD

Internally, each component movement is represented by a K dimensional basis vector, each of which has a value of 1 in some dimension j, and a value of 0 in all other dimensions. For example:

```
BROW_L = (1,0,0,0,0,0,0,0,0,0,0,0,0,0,0,0,0)

BROW_R = (0,1,0,0,0,0,0,0,0,0,0,0,0,0,0,0,0)
```

The state space for the face consists of all linear combinations of these basis vectors. Commonly used combinations can be created rather easily. For example:

```
BROWS = BROW_L + BROW_R
BLINK = WINK_L + WINK_R
SNEER = SNEER_L + SNEER_R
```

Figure 30 shows some simple combinations of component movements.

Figure 31 illustrates simple movement combinations, and summation of component movements, first in wire frame and then shaded.

Each component movement also defines its opposite. For example, (−1 ∗ SMILE) creates a frown. By convention, the face is modeled in a neutral expression, with the mouth half open, and the component movements are defined s so that a range of − 1 to + 1 will produce a full range of natural looking expressions.

Clearly, this is an simplified and incomplete model, sufficient just for the current purposes. The model is flexible enough to allow building textural facial expressions, but simple enough that it could be worked with quickly and easily for experiments. For experimental purposes, 16 component movements is just sufficient to allow a emotionally expressive face to be built.

Movements absent from this set include the ability to puff out or suck in the cheeks, to stick out or wave the tongue, to thrust the lower jaw forward or back, to tilt the head to the side, to displace the entire mouth sideways, as well as others. These should certainly be included in a complete facial model, which could either retain our simple abstracted geometry, or else drive a nonlinear muscle/skin model such as that of (Lee *et al.*1995) or (Chadwick *et al.*1989).

Figure 30.

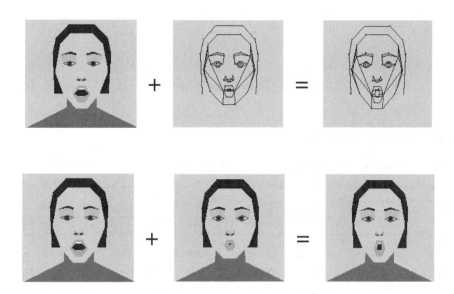

Figure 31.

Movement Layering

The lowest level abstraction is built on top of the primitive movements, using them as a vocabulary. We extend the model for mixing and layering that was described in (Perlin 1995) and (Perlin and Goldberg 1996). As in that model, movement is divided into *layers*. Each layer is a collection of related actions that compete for control of the same movements. Within a layer, one or more actions are always active. When a particular action A_i in a layer is activated, then the weight W_i for that action smoothly rises from zero up to one, and simultaneously, the weights of all other actions in the layer descend smoothly down to zero, with a default transition time of one second.

Each action modulates the value of a set of movements (usually a fairly small set). Action A_i produces a mapping from *Time* to a list of *Component Movement, Value* pairs:

```
Ai : Time- > ((D1 , V1), ... (Dk , Vk))
```

where each V_j is a scalar valued time varying function. In this way, an action influences one or more movements toward particular values. A_i *(Time)[D]* refers to the value in action A_i at *Time* for component movement D.

Generally, more than one action is occurring within a layer. The total effect upon component movement D of all actions that influence it is given by the weighted sum

```
Σi Ai (Time)[D] * Wi (Time)
```

The total effect, or *opacity* upon D from this group is given by

```
Σi Wi (Time)
```

All the groups run simultaneously. At any given moment, at least one action is running in each group. As in an optical compositing model, the groups are layered back-to-front. For each movment D: If the cumulative weight of a *Layer* at some *Time* is *opacity(Layer)(Time)* , then the results of all previous group influences on D are multiplied by $1 - opacity(Layer)(Time)$.

The Bottom Level Movement Vocabulary

At the bottom level are actions which simply pose the face, or else make simple movements. This level has separate layers for head position, facial expression, eye position, and mouth position, respectively. Below are some actions in each layer. All are simple poses, except for *headroll*, *headbob*, and *headshake*. The latter two are controlled by *noise*.

```
//from head position group
action headback      {TURN -0.2 NOD -0.5}
action headbob       {TURN 0 NOD noise(2*Time)}
action headdown      {NOD 1}
action headroll      {TURN cos(Time)  NOD sin(Time)}
action headshake     {TURN noise(2*Time) NOD 0}
//from facial expression group
action angry         {BROWS -1 SMILE -.8}
action distrust      {BROW_L -1 LLID_L 5 WINK_L .5}
action nono          {AHH -.6 OOH 6 BROWS -1 BLINK 1}
action sad           {AHH -1 BROWS 1 SMILE -.8}
action smile         {BLINK .4 LLIDS .5 BROWS 0 SMILE 1 OOH -.6}
action sneeze        {AHH -1 BLINK 1 BROWS 1 LLIDS .7 SNEER .7}
action surprised     {AHH 1 BROWS 1 BLINK -.5 LLIDS 1}
action suspicious    {AHH -.9 BLINK .5 BROW_R -1.2 BROW_L -.5 LLIDS 1.1}
//from mouth position group
action say_a         {AHH 1 OOH 0}
action say_e         {AHH -.6 OOH -.2}
action say_f         {AHH -.9 OOH -.2 SNEER .2}
action say_o         {AHH -.1 OOH .3}
action say_r         {AHH -.6 OOH .2}
action say_u         {AHH -.6 OOH .6}
action say_y         {AHH -.7 OOH -.3}
```

Figure 32 shows the results of some pose actions: (angry, daydreaming, disgusted, distrustful), (fiendish, haughty, head back, disapproving, sad), and (smiling, sneezing, surprised, suspicious).

Painting with Actions

Up to this point, the model mimics that of (Perlin and Goldberg 1996), by allowing simple layered combinations of the primitive movements. It would be useful to go beyond this, treating an action as a texture. For example, the actions defined above can place the face into useful positions, and the layered blending mechanism will make smooth transitions between those positions. Yet the face will appear to move in a fairly lifeless and mechanical way.

To improve on this, we would like to mix some coherent jitter into many component movements, tuned to match the subtle shifting that real faces do. This is done first by defining an action that creates the jitter, and then by "mixing in" amounts of this action as a transparent wash on top of the pre-existing motion.

More generally, an action is a time varying function of some set of movements. This action itself can be viewed as a primitive, which can be added and mixed. Consider the analogy with painting. An artist begins with a set of paints, each having a discrete color. The artist then creates a palette by mixing these colors, to get new colors. The artist can then use each of these new colors without needing to

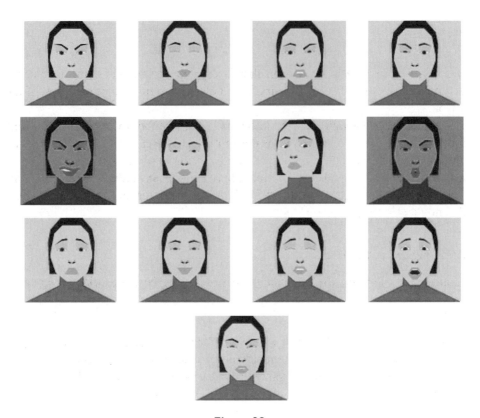

Figure 32.

go back to the original color set. In digital paint systems, the artist can do this with textures as well. The artist can create a texture, and then paint with it, as though painting with a custom-designed textured brush.

Similarly, an action provides a way to encapsulate a time varying function of movements, and to treat this time varying function as though it were itself a primitive movement. If noise-based variation in the action definition creates some motion "texture," then any uses of this action will reflect that texture.

Here is a more sophisticated example, which contains time varying behavior:

```
action sneeze {
    Ah = tspline((0 ,0),(1 ,1),(1.5,0))
    Choo = tspline ((1.2,0),(1.5,1),(2 ,0));
    sneeze  Ah
    headup Ah / 3)
    nono  Choo
```

```
headshake Choo/ 2
headdown Choo / 2
}
```

where *timeCurve(...)* is a function that interpolates a smooth spline between a given sequence of (*time, value*) pairs, based on elapsed time since the onset of the action.

The animator does not need to know the details of the lower level definitions for *sneeze*, *headup*, etc., which frees the animator to concentrate on the details that are important at this level: tuning the time-varying behavior of the sneeze. Note that in this example the derived action inherits, via the *headshake*, a realistic nondeterministic shaking during the "Choo" phase of the sneeze. The animator gets this nondeterminism for free.

Using Noise in Movement

A number of examples will illustrate the use of *noise* in layering facial movement.

blinking

Noise is used to trigger blinking with controlled irregularity. After each blink, we wait for one second. Then we start to check the value of a time-varying *noise*, which ranges smoothly from –1.0 to 1.0. When the value of this *noise* exceeds 0.1, we trigger another blink:

```
action blink {
  if (Time X blink.Time + 1 and noise(Time) X 0.1){
    blink.Time = Time
    BLINK 1    // set BLINK on this frame
  }
}
```

small constant head movements

As we said above, we would like to mix some coherent *noise* into the movement, tuned to match the subtle shifting that real faces do. To do this in a way that works with all other movement, we overlay a transparent layer of random movement over the activities of the bottom abstraction. First we add an action into the bottom abstraction that creates random movements:

```
action jitter {
    T = noise(Time)
  BROWS T
  LLIDS T
```

```
EYES_R  T/2
EYES_UP, T/2
TURN noise(Time + 10)
NOD  noise(Time + 20)
}
```

Then we add an action to the next level of abstraction that creates a transparent mix-in of the lower level jitter:

```
action jitter { jitter 0.3}
```

The effect is subtle, yet essential. It gives a sense of life and movement to whatever the face is doing.

Both blinking and jitter are controlled by *noise*. This allows us to make movements which are unpredictable to the observer, and yet which have tunable statistics that match users' expectations.

simulated talking

We found that we could also use tuned *noise* to create a fairly realistic simulation of the mouth movements a person makes while talking. This would be useful, for example, when an agent or character is pretending to hold a conversation off in the background:

```
action talking {
  T = (1 + noise(2 * Time)) / 2      // noise between 0 and 1

   AHH lerp(gain(.9, bias(.3, T)), -1, .8) // snap open/closed add
  OOH noise(2 * Time + 10.5) );              // vary smoothly add
  SNEER lerp(bias(T, .1), -.1, .6) )      // the "f" phoneme
}
```

In the above implementation, we first define a *noise* process that has a frequency of two beats per second, with values in the range 0 to 1. We also use *bias()* and *gain()* as defined in (Perlin 1985) to shape the *noise*, as well as linear interpolation, defined by: $lerp(t,a,b) = a + t(b - a)$.

We use these tools to do several things simultaneously:

- Snap the mouth open and closed fairly crisply (t*he gain(.9, bias(.3, T))* takes care of this);
- Smoothly make the mouth wider and narrower;
- Occasionally show the upper teeth via a *SNEER*. This gives the visual impression of an occasional "f" or "v" sound.

Once the parameters have been tuned, the result is surprisingly convincing. We use a derived abstraction to smoothly turn this talking action on and off, as when two characters are taking turns during a conversation.

searching

We can also create a lifelike motion to make the agent appear to be addressing an audience. When people do this, they tend to look at particular people in their audience in succession, generally holding each person's gaze for a beat before moving on. We can simulate this with *noise*, by making the head and gaze follow a controlled-random moving target. First we create a target that darts smoothly around, lingering for a moment in each place:

```
T = Time/3 + .3 * sin(2*PI * Time/3)       // make time undulate
Target = noise(T), noise(T + 10) / 2 )     // choose moving target
```

Then we direct the *TURN* , *NOD* , *EYES_R* , and *EYES_UP* movements to follow this target point.

The first line in the above code undulates the domain of the *noise* so that the target point will linger at each location. This is a special case of expressions having the form: $X/S + A * sin(2*PI*F/S)$, with A in the range [0..1], which creates a monotonically increasing function that undulates regularly between slow and fast movement, with an average slope of 1 $/S$. In particular, the function becomes slow every S units on its domain.

By feeding such an undulating function into *noise*, we have specified a smoothly moving point that slows to a near stop at a different random target point every three seconds. We have found this to be quite effective together with the talking simulation, to create a realistic impression of a person addressing an audience.

laughing

Here we create a laugh motion which starts by rearing the head up momentarily, and then settles into a steady state of bobbing and shaking the head while modulating an open "o" sound with a *noise* function:

```
action laugh {
  headshake 0.3
  headbob 0.3
    headup tspline( (0,0) (.5,.5) (1,0) )
  smile 1,
  say_o 0.8 + noise(Time)
}
```

We can then mix this in, as a fleeting action, by deriving a higher level laugh. This more abstracted laugh leaves the face in persistent smiling mood, until some other response causes the laugh action to be turned off:

```
action laugh {
    laugh  tspline ((0,0), (.5,1), (2,0) )
  smile,1
}
```

Same Action in Different Abstractions

We now describe several more actions that have been implemented at multiple semantic levels, within successively derived abstractions.

wink

At the lowest level, we can a wink as just the closing of one eye:

```
action wink { (WINK_L 1)
```

At the next level we can mix-in a sly or distrustful expression with the head slightly turned to one side:

```
action wink {
H = timeCurve( (0,0) (.5,.4) (.6,.5) (.9,.5) (1,.4) (3,0) )
W  = gain(.999, bias(.1, 2 * H))
wink W
distrust H
headright 0.2 * H
}
```

This has consistent but different effects when it is invoked while the face is in different moods: smile, haughty, distrustful (Figure 33).

Note also that the haughty and distrustful facial expressions are more effective than were their lower level equivalents in Figure 33. At this higher level of abstraction they have been combined with the most effective head positions. Because head position and facial expression have been mixed within a higher abstraction layer, each is correctly modulated by the wink.

Talking in Different Moods

Finally, we have created various combinations of the autonomous talking process overlaid with different moods. While these cannot be properly illustrated on paper, they are shown in the accompanying Java applet (Perlin 1998).

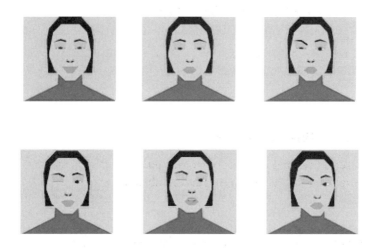

Figure 33.

What Next?

Currently the interface for creating individual actions is entirely script based, although I use simple drawing widgets for defining time-varying splines. There is ongoing work to create a graphic user interface, so that animators can move sliders interactively to modify component movements and mix-in weights.

Beyond this, I'm planning to extend the paint mixing metaphor for blending actions. Within any abstraction, the animator will see a palette of small animated faces that represent the primitives available to that abstraction. The animator can then blend these to modify an action, using a time varying brush.

I'm also continuing to increase the vocabulary of movements, working mostly from direct observation. For example, one movement to add is amused disbelief, which combines eyes looking up, smile, and head shaking from side to side. Another is "you want this, don't you"?, which combines head turned to the side, eyes looking at you, eyes wide upon, and eyebrows up. A third is puzzlement , which combines head tilted to the side (requiring an additional degree of freedom), the lower lids up, and one eyebrow raised.

In near future work, I'd like to categorize idioms that consist of mixing of lower and higher levels. One goal is to implement a *Gromit*-like character by the use of these mixed level idioms. For example, the character can raise one eyebrow and then shake its head a beat later. A test of this would be to attempt to implement some of *Gromit's* basic emotional reaction vocabulary.

A Brief Introduction to Fractals 10

F. Kenton Musgrave

The world we confront every day is visually complex. The pursuit of realism in computer graphics is largely a problem of reproducing that complexity in synthetic images. *Fractal geometry* is our first cogent language of visual complexity; its lexicon, *fractals*, provides a potent vocabulary for complex form, particularly the kinds of forms found in Nature. Fractal geometry can map chaotic complexity into the terse, deterministic idiom of mathematics in a way that, as we shall see, is uniquely suited to the capabilities of the computer. Computer graphics, on the other hand, can map complex synthetic fractal constructions into the form that is best suited to human cognition: images.

Having come into their own during the same years, fractals and computer graphics have fed and inspired one another throughout their brief and recent developments. Indeed, the study of fractals is not possible without computer graphic visualization—they are too complex to comprehend except through pictures, and too tedious to create except with a computer. Thus computers have always been essential to the study of fractals. For their part, fractals have always been the source of much of the visual complexity in realistic computer graphics. Fractals are particularly salient in synthetic images of Nature such as landscapes, while fractal textures often add visual interest to simple geometric models, such as flying logos. Fractals can even comprise abstract art in themselves, as Figure 1 and Plate 15.1 and 15.2 illustrate. It is safe to say that fractals have been the source of much of the beauty in synthetic images, throughout the brief history of computer graphics.

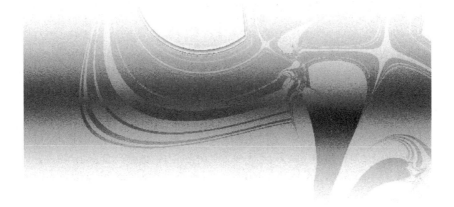

Figure 1. **"Genetic Sand Painting" is a procedural texture "grown" using Karl Sims'**
genetic software. Copyright © 1994 F. Kenton Musgrave.

This chapter is designed to provide you with a thumbnail sketch of fractal geometry. It is designed to be a sort of "fractals for artists" discussion of the relevant issues. I have made every effort to provide accurate detail but also to avoid mathematical technicalities, knowing how stultifying a dry technical presentation can become.

The importance of this chapter lies in the introduction of two fractal constructions and the C code for them. While the second, pure multifractal, function may safely be ignored, the first is *the* primary building block for all of the constructions I will present in later chapters. So, whatever your level of technical and/or mathematical competence, I urge you to read on. I hope you enjoy the discussion; I have attempted to make it provocative as well as informative.

What Is a *Fractal?*

As important as fractals are to computer graphics, there remains much misunderstanding of them in our field. They have even become a source of heated controversy at times. In my view, this arises largely from people's incomplete knowledge of exactly what fractals are and are not. They *are* a potent language of form for shapes and phenomena common in Nature. They are decidedly *not* the end-all for describing all aspects of the world we inhabit, or for creating realistic synthetic images. They are simultaneously more and less than what many people think. I will attempt to illuminate the concept "fractal" below, and also to make a first cut at delineating both the power of fractal geometry and (at least some of) its limitations. Having worked with Benoit Mandelbrot, the father of fractal geometry, for six years, I feel well qualified to present the topic and to address some of the misunderstandings of fractals which seem to be common in our field.

Fractal geometry is mathematics, but it is a particularly user-friendly form of math. In practice, it can be approached entirely heuristically: no understanding of the underlying formulae is required, and the numerical parameters of the user interface may be used intuitively, their exact values being more or less arbitrary "positions of a slider," a slider which controls some aspect of visual behavior. For the purposes of this text, I will develop this heuristic approach to fractals in computer graphics. I refer readers interested in a more mathematical treatment of the topic to the excellent text *The Science of Fractal Images* (Peitgen and Saupe 1988).

What, then, *is* a fractal? Let me define a fractal as *a geometrically complex object, the complexity of which arises through the repetition of form over some range of scale.*[1] Note the simplicity and breadth of this definition. This simple, heuristic definition will be sufficient for our purposes here in this text.[2]

In my current world view there are at least two kinds of complexity: fractal and nonfractal. Nonfractal complexity seems to be characterized by the accumulation of a variety of features through distinct and unrelated events over time—like the scuffs, holes, and stains on an old pair of shoes, for instance. Because of the independence of the events that create the features that characterize such complexity, it is hard to characterize succinctly. Fractal complexity, on the other hand, can be very simple: just keep repeating the same thing over and over, at different scales.

Our heuristic definition is sufficient, but let me explain a little further. Fractals have the peculiar property of *fractal dimension*, which can have noninteger values such as 2.3. We are all familiar with the Euclidean integer-valued dimensions: a dimension of zero corresponds to a point, one to a line, two to a plane, and three to space. The real-valued fractal dimensions, such as 2.3, provide a continuous "slider" for the visual complexity of a fractal construction. The "whole" compo-

---

[1] No tricks here: "scale" simply means "size."

[2] Another easy way to think of fractals is as a new form of symmetry: dilation symmetry. Dilation symmetry is when an object is invariant under change of scale—zooming in or zooming out. This invariance may only be in gross appearance, not in exact details. Thus a small part of a cloud looks like a larger part, but only in a qualitative way.

nent of the fractal dimension—the "2" in 2.3—indicates the underlying Euclidean dimension of the fractal, in this case a plane. The "fractional" part—the ".3" in 2.3—is called the *fractal increment*. As this part varies from .0 to .999. . . , the fractal literally goes from (locally) occupying only its underlying Euclidean dimension, for instance a plane, to densely filling some part of the next higher dimension, such as space. It does this by becoming ever more convoluted as the value of the fractal increment increases.

This is a peculiar property, to be sure. The mathematical definition of this behavior involves infinity; therefore, I claim, the human mind simply cannot fully comprehend it. But one quickly becomes numb to this incomprehensibility, and furthermore, for our purposes it is beside the point. So let us not belabor the technical details here; rather, let us continue in developing an intuitive grasp of fractals.

The source of the convoluted complexity that leads to this intermediate dimensionality is, again, simply the *repetition of some underlying shape*, over a variety of different scales. I refer to this underlying shape as the *basis function*. While that function can be literally anything, for all of my constructions it is (a version of) Ken Perlin's "noise" function.[3] The first procedural fractal function I will present is a variation on, and generalization of, the "chaos" function described by Ken Perlin in his original paper on procedural textures (Perlin 1985). I will describe it in detail a little later. For now, think of the noise function as providing a kind of cottage cheese with lumps all of a particular size. We build a fractal from it, simply by scaling down the lateral size of the lumps, and their height as well, and adding them back in to the original lumps. We do this several times, and presto! We have a fractal.

To be a little more technical: We refer to the lateral size of the lumps as the *frequency* of the function (more specifically, the *spatial frequency*). The height of the lumps we refer to as the *amplitude*. The amount by which we change the lateral size, or frequency, in each step of our iterative addition process, is referred to as the *lacunarity* of the fractal. (Lacunarity is a fancy Latin word for "gap." The gap, in this case, is between successive frequencies in the fractal construction.) In practice, lacunarity is a non-issue, as we almost always leave it set at 2.0 (though in Chapter 3 Steve Worley describes some cases where you might want to change that value slightly). In music, doubling the frequency (which is exactly what a lacunarity value of 2.0 implies) raises a given pitch by exactly one octave; hence we generally speak of the number of *octaves* in our fractals—this corresponds to the number of times we scaled down and added back in, smaller lumps to bigger lumps.

---

[3] The version of the noise function I prefer to use has zero crossings (i.e., its value is zero) at lattice points, and a range of [−1,1]. These properties will have specific importance in certain of my constructions. For more on such properties of the noise function, see Chapters 2, 3, and 6.

There is a well-defined relationship between the amount by which we scale size and the amount by which we scale the height. This relationship is what determines the fractal dimension of our result. (Again, I will decline to get any more technical, and refer the interested reader to *The Science of Fractal Images* for details.) The particular kind of fractal we're building is called *fractional Brownian motion*, or *fBm* for short.

Allow me now to point out two of the most common misconceptions about fractals in our field of computer graphics. The first is that all fractals are variants of fBm. Nothing could be less so! Go back and look at our definition of fractals: it subsumes a far larger class of objects than our scaled-and-added-up cottage-cheese lumps. Many, many things are fractal; more interestingly perhaps, many things are "only sort of" fractal. Fractality is a property which is, believe it or not, best left loosely defined. Think of it as a quality like color: It is hard to define "blue" precisely, and any really precise definition of "blue" is likely to be overly restrictive in certain circumstances. The same goes for fractals.

The second common misconception about fractals is this: that an object must have infinite detail in order to qualify as truly fractal. This is also not so. Benoit Mandelbrot and I agree that to talk about self-similarity over a range of less than three scales is rather vacuous. So we may heuristically constrain fractals to be "objects that display self-similarity at a minimum of three separate scales." This magic number three may not even provide such a great definition of "fractal"— later I will describe a nice model of water that can use only two octaves of noise. Is it fractal, or is it not? One can argue convincingly either way. The main point is this: as long as it displays self-similarity over some, albeit perhaps small, range of scale, an object or phenomenon may qualify as "fractal." Note that *all* fractals in Nature exhibit their fractal behavior over a limited range of scale (the large-scale cosmological structure of the Universe possibly excepted). For example, seen from a distance in space, the Earth is smoother than a marble, yet on smaller scales it has many mountain ranges which are quite fractal. We refer to the size above which self-similarity ceases to manifest itself as the *upper crossover scale*. Similarly, there is a smaller size, below which self-similarity no longer is manifest; this is the *lower crossover scale*. All fractals in Nature, then, are what we call *band-limited*: they are fractal only over some limited range of scales. Mandelbrot makes a striking observation on this: the Himalayas and the runway at JFK have approximately the same fractal dimension (i.e., roughness)—they differ only in their crossover scales!

Finally, I'd like to note that all fractals for computer graphics must also be band-limited, for two reasons: First, spatial frequencies that are higher than half our pixel frequency (the screen width divided by resolution) may violate the

Nyquist sampling limit and cause aliasing (a highly technical point; feel free to ignore it here and when it comes up again later). Second, we generally wish for our computations to terminate, so it's poor programming practice to put in the kind of infinite loop that would be required to construct non-band-limited fractals.

What Are Fractals Good For?

A definitive visual characteristic of the world we inhabit is that it is complex. In synthesizing worlds of our own, *complexity* equals *work*. This work can be on the part of the programmer/artist or the computer; in fact it will always be some of each. But there is a balance to be struck and personally, I prefer to have the computer do most of the work. Usually it seems to have nothing better to do, while I generally feel that *I* do. One of the defining characteristics of procedural modeling in general is that it tends to shift the burden of work from the programmer to the computer. Complexity is vital to realism in synthetic images. We have a long way to come in this area: I claim that you'd be hard put to find any scene in your everyday environment as visually simple as the best, most-detailed synthetic image of the same thing. How, then, can we move to close the gap? To date, fractals are our best tool for synthesizing visual complexity. While not all complexity in Nature arises from the repetition of form over different scales, much of it does. It is not so much true that Nature is fractal, as that fractals are natural. Thus fractal models can be used to construct scenes with good realism and a high degree of visual complexity (as I hope some of my images demonstrate), but they effectively address only a limited range of phenomena. People often ask me if I can model dogs and people with fractals; the answer is "no," dogs and people simply aren't self-similar over a range of scales. Fractals, then, allow us to do certain things well: mountains, clouds, water; even planets. Non-self-similar complexity such as hair and grass require other methods to reproduce. Things not visually complex, obviously, do not require fractal geometry to be reproduced.

My extensive experience with fractals has led me to view them as "the simplest conceivable form of complexity." (If you can think of a simpler way to give rise to complexity than to simply repeat the same thing over and over at a variety of scales, I'd love to hear about it!) This simplicity is a very good thing, since computers are simpletons, and simpler programs are better programs, too: They are quicker to write, (usually) easier to understand, take up less memory, etc.[4]

Now let me answer the question "What are fractals good for?" Many natural phenomena are fractal. Mountains are perhaps the best-known example: a smaller

---

[4] This bias in favor of simplicity is canonized in Occam's Razor: "The simpler model is the preferred model." This principle has guided much of science and engineering through the centuries; more on this later.

part of mountain looks just as mountain-like as a larger part. They're not exactly the same; this is the distinction between *statistical self-similarity*, where only the statistics of a random geometry are similar at different scales, and *exact self-similarity*, where the smaller components are exactly the same as the larger ones, as with the equilateral triangles forming the famous von Koch snowflake fractal. Trees, river systems, lightning, vascular systems in living things; all have the character of statistical self-similarity: smaller branches tend to resemble larger branches quite closely. My final example, on which we capitalize quite heavily in this book, is turbulent flow: The hierarchy of eddies in turbulence was known to be self-similar long before Mandelbrot elucidated the concept of "fractal." There's even a little poem about it:

> "Bigger swirls have smaller swirls, That feed on their velocity,
> And smaller swirls have smaller swirls, And so on, to viscosity"
> —Anonymous

The essential fractal character of turbulence allows us to use fractal models to represent clouds, steam, global atmospheric circulation systems on planets, and soft-sediment deformation in sedimentary rock, among other things. Again, the pictures attest to the success of these models, as well as the limits to that success.[5]

Fractals and Proceduralism

How are fractals and proceduralism related? Very closely indeed. The complexity of computer-generated fractals is inherently procedural: Note that we will describe fBm with an iterative, constructive procedure. The simplicity of fractals resonates well with computers, too, as they are simple-minded devices. The sort of simple, tedious, repetitive operations required to build a fractal are exactly the kind of thing computers do best. As we will see, fractal constructions can provide potentially unlimited visual complexity, all of which issues from a relatively small amount of code.

Alvy Ray Smith called this complexity from simplicity *amplification* (Smith 1984)—a small input provides a wealth of output. This is accomplished through the classic proceduralist method: by shifting the burden of work from the human designer to the computer. In fact, Mandelbrot himself points out that fractals have

---

[5] For instance, as our poem points out, turbulence is actually composed of a hierarchy of *vortices*, not simply lumps like the noise function provides. However, no one has, to date, published a fractal-vortex model of turbulence, other than those which isse from time-consuming numerical simulations using the Navier–Stokes equations.

been evident to mathematicians for some time, but until the advent of the digital computer and computer graphic visualization, they simply did not have the tools necessary to investigate them. This is almost certainly why fractals were only recently "discovered" (more like "fleshed out"), and why it happened be a researcher (Mandelbrot) at IBM (a computer company) who did so. Fractals and computers have always been inextricably linked. The fecundity of this symbiosis is illustrated by the fact that so much of the realistic visual complexity in synthetic imagery issues from fractal models, and by the observation that the rest uniformly issues either from simple nonscaling repetition or the hard labor of constructing detailed models by hand.

Procedural fBm

But enough lecturing already. Let's see exactly how to build the archetypal fractal procedural texture: fBm. It's quite simple:

```
/*
 * Procedural fBm evaluated at "point"; returns value stored in "value".
 *
 * Parameters:
 *     ''H''  is the fractal increment parameter
 *     ''lacunarity''  is the gap between successive frequencies
 *     ''octaves''  is the number of frequencies in the fBm
 */
double
fBm( Vector point, double H, double lacunarity, double octaves )
{
    double          value, frequency, remainder, Noise3();
    int             i;
    static int      first = TRUE;
    static double   *exponent_array;

    /* precompute and store spectral weights */
    if ( first ) {
        /* seize required memory for exponent_array */
        exponent_array =
                (double *)malloc( (octaves+1) * sizeof(double) );
        frequency = 1.0;
        for (i=0; i<=octaves; i++) {
            /* compute weight for each frequency */
            exponent_array[i] = pow( frequency, -H );
            frequency *= lacunarity;
        }
        first = FALSE;
    }
```

```
value = 0.0;                   /* initialize vars to proper values */

frequency = 1.0;
/* inner loop of spectral construction */
for (i=0; i<octaves; i++) {
        value += Noise3( point ) * exponent_array[i];
        point.x *= lacunarity;
        point.y *= lacunarity;
        point.z *= lacunarity;
} /* for */

remainder = octaves - (int)octaves;
if ( remainder )         /* add in ''octaves''  remainder */
        /* ''i''  and spatial freq. are preset in loop above */
        value += remainder * Noise3( point ) * exponent_array[i];

return( value );


} /* fBm() */
```

Note that most of the above code has to do with initialization (computing and storing the exponent array for efficiency) and the picayune point of dealing with the remainder of `octaves`. The fractal itself is constructed in the six-line inner loop.

Again, this is a generalization of Perlin's original "chaos" function. I have provided new parameters to control lacunarity (which in most cases can simply be fixed at 2.0, as Perlin originally did), the fractal increment parameter H, and the number of octaves in the construction. Formally, a properly band-limited fBm (seen from a distance of 1.0) would have:

$$octaves = \log_2 (screen.resolution) - 2$$

or a value of about 6 to 10. (The minus 2 term in this expression has to do with the facts that the Nyquist limit is 1/2 of the screen resolution, and that the highest frequency in the Perlin noise function is ~1/2 of the lattice spacing. Then we have $1/2 * 1/2 = 1/4$, and $\log^2 (1/4) = -2$.) You can use a smaller number of octaves to speed the rendering time of test images.

Note that this function is designed to accommodate real-valued octaves: the fractional part of the value of parameter `octaves` is added in, linearly, after the main loop. This is important for adaptively band-limited textures where, for example, you might want to link the number of octaves to distance to avoid exceeding the Nyquist limit and subsequent aliasing. (We will use this in the QAEB algorithm in Chapter 13.) This trick with the octaves remainder avoids discontinuities in the function where the number of frequencies abruptly changes. If you implement something like adaptive band-limiting, be careful the first time you call the function to compute and store a large enough number of exponents in the exponent array to accommodate the largest number of octaves you'll require at any point in the image. (This is necessary because the exponent array is a static variable, and its contents are fixed the first the time the function is called.)

The exponent array stores the amplitude-scaling values for the various frequencies in the construction. These weights are a function of *H* and the lacunarity; they determine the fractal dimension of the function. (Again, see *The Science of Fractal Images* for details on how.) The fBm function can be made shorter and slightly more efficient by moving the exponent-array part into a separate initialization procedure. If you need to use fBms of different fractal dimensions (i.e., values of *H*), you may want to use such an external procedure and pass different exponent arrays to the fBm function to get different fractal dimensions.

The parameter *H* is equal to 1 minus [the fractal increment]. It corresponds to the H described by Voss in T*he Science of Fractal Images*. When *H* = 1, the fBm is relatively smooth; as *H* goes to 0, the function approaches white noise. Figure 2 shows traces of the function for various values of *H*.

The underlying Euclidean dimension of the function is given by the dimensionality of the vector-valued argument `point`.[6]

Multifractal Functions

The fBm described above is, at least as closely as we can make it (see Chapter 3 for more on that), statistically *homogeneous* and *isotropic*. Homogeneous means "the same everywhere" and isotropic means "the same in all directions" (note that the two do not mean the same thing). Fractal phenomena in Nature are rarely so simple and well behaved. For instance, synthetic fractal mountains constructed with a single, uniform fractal dimension everywhere—as are almost all fractal mountains in computer graphics—have the same roughness everywhere. Real mountains are never like that: they typically rise out of plains and have rolling foothills at their feet. For this and other concerns of realism, we desire some more interesting, heterogeneous fractal functions.

---

[6] A definition of *vector*: an ordered set of numbers, usually three numbers for our purposes, which defines an arrow from the origin (the origin being [0,0,0] in three dimensions) to the point in space which the set of numbers locate. The dimensionality of the space is the same as the number of elements in the vector. Thus the vector [1,-1,1] defines an arrow in three dimensions which points out from the origin at 45 degrees to each of the *x, y,* and *z* axes. Its length is defined as $\sqrt{x^2+y^2+z^2} = \sqrt{1^2+(-1^2)+1^2} = \sqrt{3}$.

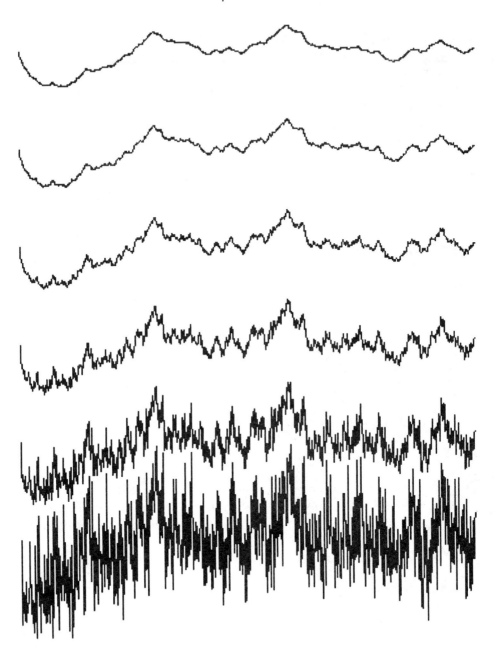

Figure 2.   Traces of fBm for *H* varying from 1.0 to 0.0 in increments of 0.2.

Enter *multifractals*. Multifractals may be heuristically defined as *fractals that require a multiplicity of measures, such as fractal dimension, to characterize them.* Another heuristic definition is *heterogeneous fractals, the heterogeneity of which is invariant with scale.*[7] They are most easily thought of as fractals whose dimension varies with location; the key point is that they are heterogeneous. Later I will demonstrate some terrain models with plains, rolling foothills, and jagged alpine mountains, all of which issue rom a single function that is only a little more complicated than the basic fBm described above.

One mathematical definition of multifractals ties them to *multiplicative cascades* (Evertsz and Mandelbrot 1992). We built our fractal fBm function from an *additive cascade*. The formal difference between an additive and a multiplicative cascade is simply that the addition of frequencies in the inner loop is replaced by a multiplication. Here is a multiplicative-cascade multifractal variation on fBm:

```
/*
 * Procedural multifractal evaluated at "point";
 * returns value stored in "value".
 *
 * Parameters:
 *      ''H''   determines the highest fractal dimension
 *      ''lacunarity''  is gap between successive frequencies
 *      ''octaves''  is the number of frequencies in the fBm
 *      ''offset''  is the zero offset, which determines multifractality
 */
double
multifractal( Vector point, double H, double lacunarity,
              double octaves, double offset )
{
    double          value, frequency, remainder, Noise3();
    int             i;
    static int      first = TRUE;
    static double   *exponent_array;

    /* precompute and store spectral weights */
    if ( first ) {
        /* seize required memory for exponent_array */
        exponent_array =
                (double *)malloc( (octaves+1) * sizeof(double) );
        frequency = 1.0;
        for (i=0; i<=octaves; i++) {
            /* compute weight for each frequency */
            exponent_array[i] = pow( frequency, -H );
            frequency *= lacunarity;
        }
```

[7] The heterogeneity may be, for instance, that peaks on a terrain are rougher than valleys. This can be true at all scales; then we have a multifractal, by this definition.

```
            first = FALSE;
    }

    value = 1.0;                  /* initialize vars to proper values */
    frequency = 1.0;

    /* inner loop of multifractal construction */
    for (i=0; i<octaves; i++) {
            value *= offset + frequency * Noise3( point );
            point.x *= lacunarity;
            point.y *= lacunarity;
            point.z *= lacunarity;
    } /* for */

    return value;

} /* multifractal() */
```

Note the addition of one more argument, `offset`, to the function, over the function for ordinary (*monofractal*) fBm; other than this and the multiplication in the inner loop, this function is nearly identical to `fBm()`. The `offset` argument controls the multifractality, if you will, of the function. When `offset` equals zero, the function is heterogeneous in the extreme; as its value increases the function goes from multi- to monofractal, and then approaches a flat plane as `offset` gets large (i.e., around 100 or so). An `offset` value of ~0.8 yields a very nice, heterogeneous terrain model, as seen in Figure 3. One thing you must know about this function: its range varies widely with changes to the value of `offset` (i.e., by many orders of magnitude!) So if you use this function, you will need to take measures to rescale its output. I have accomplished this by evaluating the function over some finite patch, e.g., a 3 x 3 area sampled at 100 x 100 resolution, and rescaling the functions output by 1/[the maximum value in patch].

The above function has the abstract advantage of following at least one mathematical definition of "multifractal" closely. This is desirable for my ongoing research into multifractals, but it is really pretty much a red herring for those more interested in applications. Therefore I suggest that you just ignore the above construction, and concentrate on the less mathematically well-defined, but better behaved, multifractal functions described in Chapter 9. Those functions are additive/multiplicative hybrids which I don't quite know how to characterize mathematically yet, but which have proven their usefulness in applications.

My multifractal models were developed for terrain models, and I have most often interpreted them as height fields for that purpose. But in fact they are really just more examples of procedural textures, and they can be used as such, though

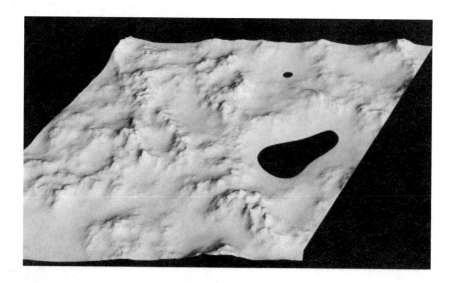

**Figure 3.   A multifractal terrain patch, with *offset* parameter set to 0.8.
Copyright © 1994 F. Kenton Musgrave.**

I personally have yet to have much opportunity to do so. (I encourage *you* to experiment; invent your own new applications—it's a lot of fun! For example, see Color Plate 12.8.) Since they were conceived as terrain models, I will explain them in that context, in the chapter on terrain models. But keep in mind that those models can also be used as textures, should an application arise.

Fractals and Ontogenetic Modeling

Fractal models are sometimes assailed on the grounds that they lack a physical basis in reality. For example, there is no (known) causal basis for the resemblance between fBm and real mountains. Is this a problem? For the reductionist-minded it is, for such a model violates the reductionist principle that true validity can only be established by showing that the model issues from first principles of physical law. This is a narrow view which Mandelbrot and I, among others, would dispute. To wit, Nobel Prize-winning physicist Richard Feynman once said: "A very great deal more truth can become known, than can be proven." (Brown 1983) In practice, both physical and nonphysical modeling have their place in computer graphics. To provoke and focus this argument, I have coined the term *ontogenetic modeling.*

From Webster's Collegiate Dictionary, tenth edition:

> ontogenetic: . . . 2: based on visible morphological characters.

I coined the term deliberately to contrast with Al Barr's "teleological" modeling (Barr 1991). Again, from Webster's:

> teleology: 1 a: the study of evidences of design in nature b: a doctrine (as in vitalism) that ends are immanent in nature c: a doctrine explaining phenomena by final causes 2: the fact or character attributed to nature or natural processes of being directed toward an end or shaped by a purpose 3: the use of design or purposes as an explanation of natural phenomena.

The underlying idea of ontogenetic modeling is that, in the field of image synthesis, it is a legitimate engineering strategy to construct models based on subjective morphological (or other) *semblance.* This as opposed to, for instance, pursuing precise (e.g., mathematical) veracity, as is a goal in scientific models, or constructing them such that they and their behavior issue from first scientific principles, as in the reductionist tradition.

My point is that we computer graphics professionals are engineers, not scientists. The goal of engineering is to construct devices that *do* something desirable. The goal of science is to devise internally consistent models that reflect, and are consistent with, the behavior of (external) systems in Nature. Science informs engineering. But engineering is an ends-driven discipline: If the device accomplishes what it is intended to accomplish, it works and is therefore good. The means by which it accomplishes its end are of secondary importance.

Elegance[8] in the model is nice in engineering, while it is necessary in science. Occam's Razor (i.e., "The simpler solution is the preferred solution") is equally applicable in both science and engineering. Engineers call it the KISS principle: "Keep it simple, stupid."[9]

In engineering—specifically, in computer graphics—Occam's Razor often recommends ontogenetic models. Science is going for Truth and Beauty; we're after pictures that look like things familiar. The degree of preoccupation with accuracy and logical consistency that marks good science is not admissible in our engineering discipline: We have a job to get done (making a picture); getting that job

---

[8] Again from Webster's: "elegance: scientific precision, neatness, and simplicity."

[9] My mentor in landscape photography, Steve Crouch, put it another way: Referring to composing an image in the viewfinder, he said "See what you can get out of the picture," not what you can get into it.

done efficiently takes precedence. Scientific models ("physical" models, in computer graphics parlance) do not generally map well into efficient algorithms for image synthesis. Given the aims and methods of science, this is not surprising: Algorithmic computability and/or efficiency are not considerations in constructing scientific models. Such concerns invoke a new, different set of constraints which may be orthogonal to the considerations that shaped any given scientific model. (For instance, no scientist would hesitate to use an integral with no closed-form solution in a model—the lack of a mechanism to obtain an exact evaluation is orthogonal to, and in no way compromises the validity of, the model.)

As Alain Fournier puts it: When you use a physical model for image synthesis, you often waste time computing the answers to questions about which you care not. That is, they do not contribute to the image. Excessive accuracy in illumination calculations is an example, given the fact that we quantize our illumination values to at most 256 levels in most standard output formats.

Given the serious drawbacks and complications of physically based models of natural phenomena, I claim that the ontogenetic approach remains, for the foreseeable future, a viable alternative approach to engineering the synthesis of realistic images. Ontogenetic models tend to be—indeed *ought* to be—simpler and more efficient, both in programming and execution time, than corresponding physical models.

Conclusions

I hope I've helped you establish an intuitive understanding of fractals. This level of understanding is all that is required to pursue applications. You don't need to be a mathematician to create and use fractals; in fact my experience indicates that an artistic eye is far more important than a quantitative facility, for creating striking fractal models for synthetic imagery. Keep in mind that fractals are the simplest and easiest (for the human operator, at least) way to generate visual complexity, whether it be geometric detail, as in landscapes, or visual detail, as with procedural textures. Fractals represent a first step toward procedurally elegant descriptions of complexity in the natural world.

To work effectively with fractals, you need to be familiar with the heuristic definition of *fractal dimension*—merely that it corresponds to roughness or wiggly-ness. You need to be aware of the idea of *octaves*—the number of scales at which you're adding in smaller details. Also, you may occasionally find it helpful to be familiar with the concept of *lacunarity*—the change in scale between successive levels of detail (though you probably will never have need to use this knowledge).

Finally, it is helpful to understand that most fractal constructions we use in computer graphics are *monofractal*—that is, they are homogeneous, and for that reason, may become a bit monotonous and boring. *Multifractals*, while not yet fully understood in the context of image synthesis, can provide a second step towards capturing more of the true complexity abundantly manifest in Nature. Turbulence, for instance, is a decidedly multifractal phenomenon.

These elements of understanding in place, let us proceed to applications, and see how fractals may be used in procedural models.

Fractal Solid Textures: Some Examples

F. Kenton Musgrave

In this chapter I will describe some fractal procedural textures that serve as models of natural phenomena. I have divided them into the four elements of the ancients: air, fire, water, and earth. I'm switching the presentation format of the code segments, for the most part, from the C programming language to the RenderMan (Upstill 1990) shading language.[1] This is because the fundamental fractal functions described in the previous chapter are to be used as primitive building blocks for the textures we'll develop here, and as such, they should be implemented in the most efficient manner possible, e.g., in compiled C code. If you like any of the textures we develop here enough to make them part of a standard texture library, you might want to translate them to C code and compile them, for efficiency. But in general, it is quicker and easier to develop texture functions in the RenderMan shading language. Again I encourage you to take the texture constructions described here and modify them; do lots of experiments and come up with your own unique textures—after all, such experimentation is how these textures came into being! Nothing here is written in stone; you can have endless fun devising variations.

Let me point out that the textures described ahead were certainly not designed as a whole, a priori, then implemented. Rather, they are generally the result of "hacking": hours and hours of making modifications and extensions, evaluating

---

[1] The translations from C to the RenderMan shading language are provided courtesy of Larry Gritz of Pixar, the author of the shareware RenderMan package Blue Moon Rendering Tools, or BMRT. Larry has kindly updated the shaders for the second edition of this book. They have been tested and verified on both Pixar's PhotoRealistic RenderMan (prman) and BMRT.

the texture to see how it looks, making more changes, etc. It may seem to you that this iterative loop is more artistic than scientific, and I would agree that it is, but it does share with the scientific method what Gregory Nielson calls "the basic loop of scientific discovery" (Nielson 1991): One posits a formal model (nothing, after all, is more formal than the logic of a computer program), one makes observations of the behavior of the model and the system being modeled, one makes modifications to improve the model, then more observations, and so on, in an iterative loop. Perhaps the main difference between science and computer graphics is in the time required per iteration: That time is certainly much shorter when designing procedural textures than when pursuing the physical sciences. The point is, no scientific model was born perfect; neither is any procedural texture. Particularly in ontogenetic modeling, again, we are not concerned with Truth but rather with visual Beauty; we are more interested in semblance than in veracity. When one is more interested in the quality of the final image than in the methodology of its production, one is more an engineer than a scientist. In such an endeavor, whatever gets us the result in a reasonable amount of time, both human and computer, is a viable strategy.

Clouds

Clouds remain one of the most significant challenges in the area of modeling natural phenomena for computer graphics. While some very nice images of clouds have been rendered by Geoffrey Gardner, Richard Voss, David Ebert, Sang Yoon Lee and myself, in general, the modeling and rendering of clouds remains an open problem. I can't claim to have advanced the state of the art in cloud modeling much, but I have devised a few new two-dimensional models[2] which are at least significant *aesthetically*. I'll describe them below, but first I'll describe the most common, quick, and easy cloud texture.

Puffy Clouds

One of the simplest and most often used fractal textures is a simple representation of thin, wispy clouds in a blue sky. All this consists of is a thresholded fBm. If our fBm function outputs values in the range [−1,1], we might specify that any value less than zero represents blue sky. This will accomplish the effect:

---

[2] This may be a little confusing: I call these models 2D because, while they are implemented as 3D solid textures, they are designed to be evaluated on 2D surfaces. In Chapter 13, I'll show how to evaluate them as volumetric hypertextures via the QAEB algorithm.

```
surface
puffyclouds (float Ka = 0, Kd = 0;
            float txtscale = 1;
            color skycolor = color(.15, .15, .6);
            color cloudcolor = color(1,1,1);
            float octaves = 8, omega = 0.5, lambda = 2;
            float threshold = 0;
            )
{
    float value;
    color Ct;        /* Color of the surface */
    point PP;        /* Surface point in shader space */

    PP = txtscale * transform ("shader", P);
    /* Use fractional Brownian motion to compute a value for this point */
    value = fBm (PP, filterwidthp(PP), octaves, lambda, omega);
    Ct = mix (skycolor, cloudcolor, smoothstep (threshold, 1, value));
    /* Shade like matte, but use color Ct */
    Ci = Ct;    /* This makes the color disregard the lighting */
    /* Uncomment the next line if you want the surface to actually be lit */
    /*  Ci = Ct * (Ka * ambient() + Kd * diffuse(faceforward(N,I))); */
}
```

This can make a good background texture for images where the view is looking up toward the sky, as in Jules Bloomenthal's image of the mighty maple (Bloomenthal 1985).

A Variety of fBm

As noted in the previous chapter, our fractals can be constructed from literally *any* basis function; the basis function we choose is the Perlin noise function. For theoretical reasons outlined in the previous chapter, with our usual lacunarity of 2.0, we use at most about 8 to 10 octaves of the basis function in our constructions. It turns out that the character of the basis function shows through clearly in such a small spectral summation. So, if we use a different basis function, we get fBm with a different character, with a different aesthetic "feel" to it. For instance, one of the characteristics of the fBm comprising fractal mountains constructed by the popular polygon-subdivision schemes is that the basis function, implicit in the linear interpolation between the sample points, is a sawtooth wave. Thus the resulting mountains are always quite jagged. When it comes to playing with different basis functions, the possibilities are endless. *Wavelets* (Ruskai 1992) offer an exciting prospect for basis function manipulation; Lewis' "sparse convolution" (Lewis 1989), also called "fractal sum of pulses" in Lovejoy and Mandelbrot (Lovejoy and Mandelbrot 1985), is a theoretically desirable approach which accommodates the use of any finite basis function. Unfortunately, it is slow, in practice.

Let me now describe one trick I sometimes play with the Perlin noise function, to get a variation of it with significantly altered aesthetic "feel." I call it, for lack of a better name, `VLNoise3()`, for *variable lacunarity noise* (not a great characterization or name, but not completely off the mark). As it is a fundamental building-block type function, I present it in C.

```
double
VLNoise3( Vector point, double distortion )
{
        Vector offset, VecNoise3(), AddVectors();
        double Noise3();

        offset.x = point.x +0.5;           /* misregister domain */
        offset.y = point.y +0.5;
        offset.z = point.z +0.5;

        offset = VecNoise3( offset );   /* get a random vector */

        offset.x *= distortion;            /* scale the randomization */
        offset.y *= distortion;
        offset.z *= distortion;

        /* "point" is the domain; distort domain by adding "offset" */
        point = AddVectors( point, offset );

        return Noise3( point );            /* distorted-domain noise */

} /* VLNoise3() */
```

The function `VecNoise3()` is a vector-valued Noise function that takes a 3D vector as an argument and returns a 3D vector that corresponds to three separate noise traces for each of the x, y, and z components of the vector returned. It can be constructed by simply evaluating a noise function at three points in space: the one passed in as the argument and two displaced copies of it, as in the misregistration above. (Note that this is not the same thing as Perlin's `DNoise()`, which is specified to return the three partial derivatives of `Noise3()`, noise over a 3D domain. The latter will be C-2 continuous, while our function is C-3 continuous.)[3] We displace the point passed to `VecNoise3()` by 0.5 in each of x, y, and z, to misregister deliberately the underlying integer lattices upon which `VecNoise3()` and `Noise3()` are evaluated as, at least in my implementations, both functions have value zero at these points in space. We then evaluate `VecNoise3()` at the dis-

---

[3] This business of C-2 and C-3 continuity is a mathematical point about the number of continuous derivatives a function has. If you don't know what a derivative is, just ignore this rigmarole.

placed point and scale the returned vector by the distortion parameter. Next we add the resultant vector to the input point; this has the net effect of distorting the input domain given to the Noise3() function. The output is therefore also distorted.

Figure 1 illustrates the difference between undistorted Noise3() and the distorted VLNoise3(), with the distortion parameter set to 1.0. It also shows the difference between fBms constructed using Noise3() and VLNoise3(), respectively, as the basis function. That difference is subtle, but significant. To my artist's eye, the latter fBm has a sort of wispy character that looks more like certain cirrus clouds than does the "vanilla" fBm, which seems a little bland in comparison. Note, however, that VLNoise3() is about four times as expensive to evaluate as Noise3(), so you pay dearly for this difference. Cost aside, I have used the modified fBm to good effect in clouds, as seen in Color Plates 11.1 and 11.2. Below I will refer to such fBm by the function name VLfBm().

Note that in languages such as C++ or the RenderMan shading language we could write VLNoise3() more tersely:

```
/*
 * C++ version of VLNoise3()
 */
double
VLNoise3( Vector point, double distortion )
{
        return Noise3( point + distortion * VecNoise3( point + 0.5 ) );
} /* VLNoise3() */
```

Note that the shading language looks very much like C++:

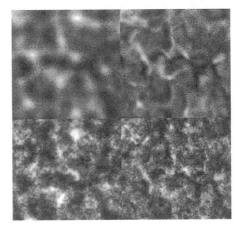

Figure 1. The upper-left square shows Noise3(); the upper-right shows VLNoise3(). **Below appears fBm constructed from each; note the subtle difference.**

```
/*
 * RenderMan version of VLNoise3()
 *
 * Since the noise() function in RenderMan Shading Language has range
 * [0,1], we define a signed noise to be the noise function that Perlin
 * typically uses.
 */

#define snoise(P)  (2*noise(P) - 1)

float VLNoise3( point Pt, float distortion )
{
  point offset = snoise( Pt + point(0.5,0.5,0.5) );
  return snoise( Pt + distortion * offset );
}

/* Alternatively, it can be defined as a macro: */

#define VLNoise3(Pt,distortion) \
    (snoise( Pt + distortion*snoise( Pt+point(0.5,0.5,0.5) ) ) )
```

The terseness of the C++ and RenderMan code is due to the flexibility provided by overloaded operators, which allow us to perform arithmetic on vectors transparently. It's hard to directly compare C code to the RenderMan language, but whether or not C++ is to be recommended over C is debatable at the time of this writing. I personally prefer to sacrifice coding elegance for the portability and nominal speed advantage of C over C++, but it is for you to decide for yourself. The C code *can* get awfully long, tedious, and ugly.

Distortion for Cirrus Clouds and Global Circulation

Note that the above construction is an example of *functional composition,* wherein functions become the arguments to other functions. Such nesting is a powerful procedural technique, as Karl Sims showed in his genetic LISP program (Sims 1991) which creates procedural textures, and which was used to create Figure 1 in Chapter 10 and Color Plates 15.1 and 15.2; we'll investigate this paradigm in detail in the final chapter. The idea of composition of noise functions to provide distortion has proved useful in another aspect of modeling clouds—in emulating the streaming of clouds that are stretched by winds. We can get the kind of distinctive cirrus clouds seen in Color Plate 11.1 from the following specification:

```
/* Use signed, zero-mean Perlin noise */
#define snoise(x)  ((2*noise(x))-1)
/* Should be VecNoise(), but this will do */
#define DNoise(p)  (2*(point noise(p)) - point(1,1,1))
```

```
/* A more up-to-date RenderMan vector-valued Perlin noise */
#define vsnoise(p) (2 * (vector noise(p)) - 1)
/* If we know the filter size, we can crudely antialias snoise by fading
 * to its average value at approximately the Nyquist limit.
 */
#define   filteredsnoise(p,width)   (snoise(p)   *   (1   -   smoothstep
(0.2,0.6,width)))
#define   filteredvsnoise(p,width)   (vsnoise(p)   *   (1-smoothstep
(0.2,0.6,width)))

surface
planetclouds (float Ka = 0.5, Kd = 0.75;
              float distortionscale = 1;
              float omega = 0.7;
              float lambda = 2;
              float octaves = 9;
              float offset = 0;)
{
    vector Pdistortion;         /* "distortion" vector */
    point PP;                   /* Point after distortion */
    float result;               /* Fractal sum is stored here */
    float filtwidth;

    /* Transform to texture coordinates */
    PP = transform ("shader", P);
    filtwidth = filterwidthp (PP);

    /* Add in "distortion" vector */
    Pdistortion = distortionscale * filteredvsnoise (PP, filtwidth);
    PP = PP + Pdistortion;
    filtwidth = filterwidthp (PP);

    /* Compute fBm */
    result = fBm (PP, filtwidth, octaves, lambda, omega);

    /* Adjust zero crossing (where the clouds disappear) */
    result = clamp (result+offset, 0, 1);

    /* Scale density */
    result /= (1 + offset);
    /* Modulate surface opacity by the cloud value */
    Oi = result * Os;

    /* Shade like matte, but with color scaled by cloud opacity */
    Ci = Oi * (Ka * ambient() + Kd * diffuse(faceforward(normalize(N),I)));
}
```

Note that this is the same idea that was used in `VLNoise()`, except that the distortion has greater magnitude and is at a large scale relative to the fBm.

This large-scale distortion was originally designed to provide a first approximation to the global circulation patterns in the Earth's clouds, as seen from space.

The above code produced the clouds seen in Color Plates 11.1 and 11.2. While not
a bad first approximation, it saliently lacks the eddies and swirls generated by vortices in turbulent flow.

It occurred to me that one might use an fBm-valued distortion to better emu-
late turbulence:

```
#define snoise(p) (2 * (float noise(p)) - 1)
#define vsnoise(p) (2 * (vector noise(p)) - 1)
#define filteredsnoise(p,width) (snoise(p) * (1 - smoothstep
(0.2,0.6,width)))

#define filteredvsnoise(p,width) (vsnoise(p) * (1-smoothstep
(0.2,0.6,width)))

/* A vector-valued antialiased fBm. */
vector
vfBm (point p; float filtwidth;
      uniform float maxoctaves, lacunarity, gain)
{
    uniform float i;
    uniform float amp = 1;
    varying point pp = p;
    varying vector sum = 0;
    varying float fw = filtwidth;

    for (i = 0;  i < maxoctaves && fw < 1.0;  i += 1) {
       sum += amp * filteredvsnoise (pp, fw);
       amp *= gain;  pp *= lacunarity;  fw *= lacunarity;
    }
    return sum;
}


surface
planetclouds (float Ka = 0.5, Kd = 0.75;
              float distortionscale = 1;
              float omega = 0.7;
              float lambda = 2;
              float octaves = 9;
              float offset = 0;)
{
    vector Pdistortion;        /* "distortion" vector */
    point PP;                  /* Point after distortion */
    float result;              /* Fractal sum is stored here */
    float filtwidth;

    /* Transform to texture coordinates */
    PP = transform ("shader", P);
    filtwidth = filterwidthp (PP);
```

```
    /* Add in "distortion" vector */
Pdistortion = distortionscale * VfBm (PP, filtwidth, octaves, lambda, omega);

    /* Second cirrus: replace fsnoise with vector fBm */
    PP = PP + Pdistortion;
    filtwidth = filterwidthp (PP);

    /* Compute fBm */
    result = fBm (PP, filtwidth, octaves, lambda, omega);

    /* Adjust zero crossing (where the clouds disappear) */
    result = clamp (result+offset, 0, 1);

    /* Scale density */
    result /= (1 + offset);

    /* Modulate surface opacity by the cloud value */
    Oi = result * Os;

    /* Shade like matte, but with color scaled by cloud opacity */
    Ci = Oi * (Ka * ambient() + Kd * diffuse(faceforward(normalize(N),I)));
}
```

Unfortunately, the result looks more like cotton than turbulence (see Figure 2), but it is an interesting experiment.

Once again, the essential element that our turbulence model lacks is vorticity. Large-scale vortices in the Earth's atmosphere occur in cyclonic and anticyclonic storm systems, which are clearly visible from space. The most extreme vortices in our atmosphere occur in tornadoes and hurricanes. In Figure 3 we see an onto-genetic model of a hurricane, produced by the following specification:

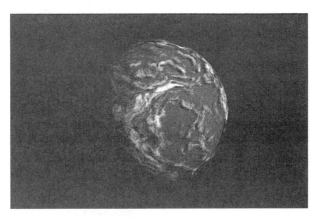

Figure 2. Clouds distorted with fBm: they look more like cotton than turbulence.
Copyright © 1994 F. Kenton Musgrave.

Figure 3. A first cut at including the vortices that comprise turbulence. Note that the smaller clouds are not distorted by the vortex-twist, only the large-scale distribution is. Copyright © 1994 F. Kenton Musgrave.

```
surface
cyclone (float Ka = 0.5, Kd = 0.75;
        float max_radius = 1;
        float twist = 0.5;
        float scale = .7, offset = .5;
        float omega = 0.675;
        float octaves = 4;)
{
    float radius, dist, angle, eye_weight, value;
    point Pt;                      /* Point in texture space */
    vector PN;                     /* Normalized vector in texture space */
    point PP;                      /* Point after distortion */
    float filtwidth, a;

    /* Transform to texture coordinates */
    Pt = transform ("shader", P);
    filtwidth = filterwidthp (Pt);

    /* Rotate hit point to "cyclone space" */
    PN = normalize (vector Pt);
    radius = sqrt (xcomp(PN)*xcomp(PN) + ycomp(PN)*ycomp(PN));
    if (radius < max_radius) {    /* inside of cyclone */
       /* invert distance from center */
       dist = pow (max_radius-radius, 3);
       angle = PI + twist * TWOPI * (max_radius-dist) / max_radius;
       PP = rotate (Pt, angle, point(0,0,0), point(0,0,1));
       /* Subtract out "eye" of storm */
```

```
        if (radius < 0.05*max_radius) {  /* if in "eye" */
            eye_weight = (.1*max_radius-radius) * 10;   /* normalize */
            /* invert and make nonlinear */
            eye_weight = pow (1 - eye_weight, 4);
        }
        else eye_weight = 1;
    }
    else {
        PP = Pt;
        eye_weight = 0;
    }

    if (eye_weight > 0) {    /* if in "storm" area */
        /* Compute VLfBm */
        a = VLfBm (PP, filtwidth, octaves, 2, omega, 1);
        value = abs (eye_weight * (offset + scale * a));
    }

    else value = 0;
    /* Thin the density of the clouds */
    Oi = value * Os;

    /* Shade like matte, but with color scaled by cloud opacity */
    Ci = Oi * (Ka * ambient() + Kd * diffuse(faceforward(normalize(N),I)));
}
```

Here we have a single vortex; to model general turbulent flow we require a fractal hierarchy of vortices. Note that I've modeled the clouds on two different scales here: a distorted large-scale distribution comprising a weighting function, which is applied to smaller-scale cloud features. This construction is based on my subjective study of clouds and storms seen from space (see (Kelley 1988) for many lovely examples of such images). The idea of undistorted small features corresponds to the phenomenon of viscosity which, as our poem indicates, damps turbulence at small scales. This may also be seen as a first step in the direction of multifractal models, as our fractal behavior is different at different scales, and therefore may require more than one value or measure to characterize the fractal behavior.

The Coriolis Effect

A salient feature of atmospheric flow on Earth, and even more so on Venus, is that it is strongly affected by the *Coriolis effect*. This is a shearing effect caused by the conservation of angular momentum as air masses move north and south. The atmosphere is moving around the planet and, like a spinning skater who spins faster as she pulls her arms and legs in closer, the air must spin around the planet faster as it moves toward the poles and more slowly as it moves toward the equator. For a given angular momentum, angular velocity (spin rate) varies as the inverse square of radius. In this respect, the following model could be thought of as a physically accurate model, but I would still call it an ontogenetic, or at best an empirical, model.

Using our modified fBm and a Coriolis distortion, we can model Venus (as imaged at ultraviolet wavelengths) quite well; see Figure 4.

```
surface
venus (float Ka = 1, Kd = 1;
       float offset = 1;
       float scale = 0.6;
       float twist = 0.22;
       float omega = 0.65;
       float octaves = 8;)
{
    point Ptexture;           /* the shade point in texture space */
    vector PtN;               /* normalized version of Ptexture */
    point PP;                 /* Point after rotation by Coriolis twist */
    float rsq;                /* Used in calculation of twist */
    float angle;              /* Twist angle */
    float value;              /* Fractal sum is stored here */
    float filtwidth;          /* Filter width for antialiasing */

    /* Transform to texture coordinates */
    Ptexture = transform ("shader", P);
    filtwidth = filterwidthp (Ptexture);

    /* Calculate Coriolis twist, yielding point PP */
    PtN = normalize (vector Ptexture);
```

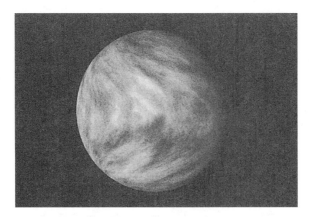

Figure 4.   A strong Coriolis twist characterizes the cloud patterns on Venus.
Copyright © 1994 F. Kenton Musgrave.

```
    rsq = xcomp(PtN)*xcomp(PtN) + ycomp(PtN)*ycomp(PtN);
    angle = twist * TWOPI * rsq;
    PP = rotate (Ptexture, angle, point(0,0,0), point(0,0,1));

    /* Compute fBm */
    value = abs (offset + scale * fBm (PP,filtwidth,octaves,2,omega));

    /* Shade like matte, but with color scaled by cloud color */
    Oi = Os;
    Ci = Oi * (value * Cs) * (Ka * ambient() +
                    Kd * diffuse(faceforward(normalize(N),I)));
}
```

Fire

Fire is yet another example of turbulent flow. I can't claim to have modeled fire particularly well, but I do have a fire texture that I can share with you. There are two peculiar features in this model. The first is the use of a "ridged" fBm, as discussed in the next chapter. The second is a distortion that varies exponentially with height, which is meant to model the upward acceleration of the hot gases of the flames.

```
surface
flame (float distortion = 0;
       float chaosscale = 1;
       float chaosoffset = 0, octaves = 7;
       float flameheight = 1;
       float flameamplitude = .5;
       )
{
    point PP, PQ;
    float chaos;
    float cmap;
    float fw;

    PQ = PP = transform ("shader", P);
    PQ *= point (1, 1, exp(-zcomp(PP)));
    fw = filterwidthp (PQ);
    chaos = VLfBm (PQ, fw, octaves, 2, 0.5, distortion);
    chaos = abs (chaosscale*chaos + chaosoffset);
    cmap =  0.85*chaos +
       0.8 * (flameamplitude - flameheight * zcomp(PP)
    Ci = color spline (cmap,
                color (0, 0, 0), color (0, 0, 0),
                color (27, 0, 0), color (54, 0, 0),
                color (81, 0, 0), color (109, 0, 0),
                color (136, 0, 0), color (166, 5, 0),
```

```
        color (189,  30,   0), color (211,  60,   0),
        color (231,  91,   0), color (238, 128,   0),
        color (244, 162,  12), color (248, 187,  58),
        color (251, 209, 115), color (254, 236, 210),
        color (255, 241, 230), color (255, 241, 230)) / 255;
}
```

While this certainly doesn't fully capture the rich structure of real flames, it's not a bad first approximation. In Color Plate 11.3 several transparent layers of this fire texture were sandwiched with some of Prusinkiewicz's early L-system tree models (Prusinkiewicz and Lindenmayer1990). Note that the colors are critical to the realism of the results. What you want is a color map that represents a range of colors and intensities of blackbody radiators, going from black to cherry red, through orange and yellow, to white.[4] Also, if you scale the flame structure down so that the high frequencies are more visible, this texture takes on a kind of astrophysical character—the ridges in the fBm form filaments and loops which, while not exactly realistic, have a distinctive character reminiscent of certain emission nebulae where stars are being born and dying. Try constructing this function without the abs(), and observe the difference (it's actually more realistic, and less surreal).

Water

To my chagrin, people have often said of my images that "the water is the best part!" Well, I'm here to tell you that it's the cheapest and easiest trick I ever did with procedural textures. Let me show you how.

Noise Ripples

I originally developed this texture in a ray tracer that didn't have the RenderMan interface. In that context, it must be implemented as a bump map. This requires that you build a vector-valued fBm function, which is no problem as it's really just three independent fBms, one for each of x, y, and z, or one fBm constructed from VecNoise3(), as we saw above in the definition of VfBm(). Since the

---

[4] Blackbody radiators are a concept from physics: they are theoretically ideal (and therefore nonexistent, in Nature) objects that are completely without color of their own, regardless of their temperature. Thus, as you raise their temperature, they glow ith a color that represents the ideal thermal (Planck) spectrum for their temperature. Real objects heated enough to glow at visible wavelengths tend to be complicated by both their underlying (i.e., cold) nonblack color and by emission lines, or certain wavelengths which have enhanced emission (or absorption) due to quantum effects. Most fires we see are made more yellow than a blackbody radiator at the same temperature, by sodium emission lines.

RenderMan language assumes the availability of displacement maps in the renderer, the implementation is simpler: It requires only a scalar-valued displacement to perturb the surface, rather than a vector-valued perturbation for the surface normal.

The water model I've always used requires only a reflective silver plane in the foreground and this simple bump or displacement map, applied to the surface:

```
displacement
ripples (float Km = 1, octaves = 2;)
{
  float offset;

  point PP;
  /* Do the calculations in shader space */
  PP = transform( "shader", P );

  /* Get fractal displacement, scale by Km */
  offset = Km * fBm( PP, 3.0, 2.0, octaves );

  /* Displace the surface point and recompute the normal */
  P += offset * normalize( N );
  N = calculatenormal( P );
}
```

We have perturbed the surface normal with a degenerate—in the mathematical sense!—fractal function of only two octaves. (Recall that we said in the previous chapter that a fractal ought to have at least three levels of self-similarity to be called a fractal; this one only has two. Of course, one may use more or less octaves, as artistry dictates.) You can stretch this function by scaling it up in one of the lateral directions, to get an impression of waves. For such a simple texture, it works surprisingly well—see Color Plates 11.9 and 11.10.

Wind-Blown Waters

In Nature, ripples on water so calm are rarely homogeneous, as they are in the above function. Usually, on the large scale, ripples are modulated by the blowing wind. Blowing wind is turbulent flow, and is therefore fractal. We can apply a large-scale (as compared to the ripples) fractal weighting function to the above ripples to generate a nice approximation of breeze-blown water:

```
displacement
windywave (float Km = 0.1;
          float txtscale = 1;
          float windfreq = 0.5;
          float windamp = 1;
          float minwind = 0.3)
```

```
{
    float offset;
    point PP;
    float wind;
    float turb;
    float filtwidth;

    PP = txtscale * windfreq * transform ("shader", P);
    filtwidth = filterwidthp (PP);            /* get fractal displacement*/

    offset = Km * fBm (PP,filtwidth,2,2,0.5);
    PP *= 8;  filtwidth *= 8;                  /* calculate wind field*/

    turb = turbulence (PP, filtwidth, 4, 2, 0.5);
    wind = minwind + windamp * turb;          /* displace the surface*/

    N = calculatenormal (P+wind * offset * normalize(N));
}
```

The weighting function we use is, as always, a variety of fBm. We use the most generic version, as there's no need for the subtleties of any of the variations. (Although, turbulence is actually multifractal, so it might be worthwhile to experiment with multifractal weighting functions.) Also, we need only a few octaves in this fBm, as we don't really want to generate fine-scale detail with the weighting function.

This effectiveness of the `Windywave()` texture is illustrated in Color Plate 11.4 and Figure 5.

Earth

Now let's look at earthly textures. Well, at least two out of three will be literally Earthly; the third will be a moon.

Sedimentary Rock Strata

Early in my career of rendering fractal landscapes, I didn't have the capacity to ray-trace terrains with very many triangles in them. Thus the "mountains" were quite chunky, and the triangles used to tessellate the surface were quite large and obviously flat, unlike any terrain *I've* ever seen. One of the early textures I devised to distract the eye's attention from this intrinsically bogus geometry was an imitation of sedimentary rock strata:

```
surface
strata (float Ka = 0.5, Kd = 1;
```

Figure 5.   The effects of breezes on the water are illustrated in "Bay Mountain."
Copyright © 1994 F. Kenton Musgrave

```
        float txtscale = 1;
        float zscale = 2;
        float turbscale = 0.1;
        float offset = 0;
        float octaves = 8;)
{
    color Ct;
    point PP;
    float cmap;
    float turb;
    PP = txtscale * transform ("shader", P);        /*turbation by fBm */

    turb = fBM (PP, filterwidthp(PP), octaves, 2, 0.5);
    /*use turb and z to index color map */
    cmap = zscale * zcomp(PP) + turbscale * turb - offset;
    Ct = color spline (mod (cmap, 1),
                color (166,131,70), color (166,131,70),
                color (204, 178, 127), color (184, 153, 97),
                color (140, 114, 51),  color (159, 123, 60),
                color (204, 178, 127), color (230, 180, 80),
                color (192, 164, 110), color (172, 139, 80),
                color (102, 76, 25),   color (166, 131, 70),
                color (201, 175, 124), color (181, 150, 94),
                color (161, 125, 64),  color (177, 145, 87),
                color (170, 136, 77),  color (197, 170, 117),
                color (180, 100, 50),  color (175, 142, 84),
                color (197, 170, 117), color (177, 145, 87),
```

```
                color (170, 136, 77),   color (186, 156, 100),
                color (166, 131, 70),   color (188, 159, 104),
                color (168, 134, 74),   color (159, 123, 60),
                color (195, 167, 114), color (175, 142, 84),
                color (161, 125, 64),   color (197, 170, 117),
                color (177, 145, 87), color (177, 145, 87)
    ) / 255;

    /* Shade like matte, but with color scaled by cloudcolor and opacity */
    Oi = Os;
    Ci = Oi * Cs * Ct * (Ka * ambient() +
                Kd * diffuse(faceforward(normalize(N),I)));
}
```

The key idea here is to index a color look-up table by altitude,[5] and to perturb that altitude-index with a little fBm. The geologic analogues to this are soft-sediment deformation, in which layers of sediment are distorted before lithification, and the distortion generated by the orogenic (mountain-buildng) forces which raised the sedimentary rock into mountains (but which are, perhaps, less likely to provide fractal features, at least on small scales).

The color look-up table is loaded with a color map that contains bands of color that you, the artist, deem appropriate for representing the different layers of rock. Both aesthetics and my observations of Nature indicate that the colors of the various layers should be quite similar and subdued, with one or two layers that "stick out" tossed in to provide visual interest. For an example of this, see the red and yellow bands in Color Plate 11.5.

Gaea: Building an Entire Planet

In fact, one can build an entire Earth-like planet with a single procedural texture. Not surprisingly, such an ambitious texture gets rather complex. And, of course, it is quite fractal. In fact, fractals are used in three ways in this texture: as a displacement map to provide continents, oceans, and a fractal coastline; as a perturbation to a climate-by-latitude color map (much like our rock strata map above) providing an interesting distribution of mountains, deserts, forests, and the like; and finally as a color perturbation, to ameliorate lack of detail in areas which would all be the same color, by virtue of their sharing the same look-up table index.

The first step in creating an earth is to create continents and oceans. This can be accomplished by quantizing an fBm texture: A parameter threshold controls

---

[5] In my original C implementation of these texture functions, the color maps are stored in 256-entry look-up tables. Larry Gritz has used RenderMan's functionality to replace those tables with splines in the code that appears in this text..

the "sea level;" any value less than threshold is considered to be below sea level, and is therefore colored blue. This gives us the effect seen in Color Plate 11.6(a). Note that in the code below, there is a Boolean-valued parameter multifractal. This gives us the option of creating heterogeneous terrain and coastlines—see how the fractal dimension of the coasts varies in Color Plate 11.2.

Next we provide a color look-up table to simulate climatic zones by latitude; see Color Plate 11.6(b). Our goal is to have white polar caps and barren, gray sub-Arctic zones blending into green, temperate zone forests, which in turn blend into buff-colored desert sands representing equatorial deserts. (Of course, you can use whatever colors you please.) The coloring is accomplished with a splined color ramp, which is indexed by the latitude of the ray/earth intersection point.

This rough coloring-by-latitude is then fractally perturbed, as in Color Plate 11.6(c). This is accomplished simply by adding fBm to the latitude value to perturb it, as with the rock strata texture. We also take into account the displacement map, so that the "altitude" of the terrain may affect the climate. Note that altitude and latitude represent two independent quantities that could be used as parameters to a two-dimensional color map; to date I have used only a one-dimensional color spline for simplicity.

Next we add an exponentiation parameter to the color spline index computed above, to allow us to "drive back the glaciers" and expand the deserts to a favorable balance, as in Color Plate 11.6(d).

We now modify the oceans, adjusting the sea level for a pleasing coastline and making the color a function of "depth" to highlight shallow waters along the coastlines. (See Color Plate 11.6(e).) Depth of the water is calculated in exactly the same way as the "altitude" of the mountains, i.e., as the magnitude of the bump vector in the direction of the surface normal. This depth value is used to darken the blue of the water almost to black in the deepest areas. It might also be desirable to modify the surface properties of the texture in the ocean areas, specifically the specular highlight, as this significantly affects the appearance of the Earth from space (again, see (Kelley 1988), though I haven't yet tried it.

Finally, we note that the "desert" areas about the equator in Color Plate 11.6(e) are quite flat and unrealistic in appearance. The Earth, by contrast, features all manners of random mottling of color. By interpreting an fBm function as a color perturbation, we can add significantly to the realism of our model—compare Color Plate 11.6(e) and 11.6(f). This added realism is of an artistic nature—the color mottling of Earth does not, in general, resemble fBm—but it is nevertheless aesthetically effective.

This code accomplishes all of the above:

```
#define N_OFFSET 0.7
#define VERY_SMALL 0.0001

surface
terran (float Ka = .5, Kd = .7;
        float spectral_exp = 0.5;
        float lacunarity = 2, octaves = 7;
        float bump_scale = 0.07;
        float multifractal = 0;
        float dist_scale = .2;
        float offset = 0;
        float sea_level = 0;
        float mtn_scale = 1;
        float lat_scale = 0.95;
        float nonlinear = 0;
        float purt_scale = .9;
        float map_exp = 0;
        float ice_caps = 0.9;
        float depth_scale = 1;
        float depth_max = .5;
        float mottle_limit = 0.75;
        float mottle_scale = 20;
        float mottle_dim = .25;
        float mottle_mag = .02;)
{
    point PP, P2;
    vector PtN;
    float chaos, latitude, purt;
    color Ct;
    point Ptexture, tp;
    uniform float i;
    float o, weight;        /* Loop variables for fBm calc */
    float bumpy;
    float filtwidth, fw;

    /* Do all shading in shader space */
    Ptexture = transform ("shader", P);
    filtwidth = filterwidthp (Ptexture);
    PtN = normalize (vector Ptexture); /* Version of Ptexture with radius 1 */
    /*******************************************************************
     * First, figure out where we are in relation to the oceans/mountains.
     * Note: this section of code must be identical to "terranbump" if you
     *       expect these two shaders to work well together.
     *******************************************************************/
    if (multifractal == 0) { /* use a "standard" fBm bump function */
       bumpy = fBm (Ptexture, filtwidth, octaves, lacunarity, spectral_exp);
    } else {                 /* use a "multifractal" fBm bump function */
       /* get "distortion" vector, as used with clouds */
       Ptexture += dist_scale * filteredvsnoise (Ptexture, filtwidth);
       /* compute bump vector using MfBm with displaced point */
       o = spectral_exp;  tp = Ptexture;
```

```
    fw = filtwidth;
    weight = abs (filteredVLNoise (tp, fw, 1.5));
    bumpy = weight * filteredsnoise (tp, fw);

    for (i = 1;  i < octaves && weight >= VERY_SMALL && fw < 1;  i += 1) {
        tp *= lacunarity;  fw *= filtwidth;
        /* get subsequent values, weighted by previous value */
        weight *= o * (N_OFFSET + snoise(tp));
        weight = clamp (abs(weight), 0, 1);
        bumpy += snoise(tp) * min (weight, spectral_exp);
        o *= spectral_exp;
    }
}
/* get the "height" of the bump, displacing by offset */
chaos = bumpy + offset;
/* set bump for land masses (i.e., areas above "sea level") */
if (chaos > sea_level) {
    chaos *= mtn_scale;
    P2 = P + (bump_scale * bumpy) * normalize(N);
} else P2 = P;
N = calculatenormal(P2);

/*****************************************************************
 * Step 2: Assign a climite type, roughly by latitude.
 *****************************************************************/

/* make climate symmetric about equator — use the "v" parameter */
latitude = abs (zcomp (PtN));
/* fractally purturb color map offset using "chaos" */
/*   "nonlinear" scales purturbation-by-z */
/*   "purt_scale" scales overall purturbation */
latitude += chaos*(nonlinear*(1-latitude) + purt_scale);
if (map_exp > 0)
    latitude = lat_scale * pow(latitude,map_exp);
else latitude *= lat_scale;

if (chaos > sea_level) {
    /* Choose color of land based on the following spline.
     * Ken originally had a huge table.  I was too lazy to type it in,
     * so I used a scanned photo of the real Earth to select some
     * suitable colors.  — lg
     */
    Ct = spline (latitude,
            color (.5,  .39,  .2),
            color (.5,  .39,  .2),
            color (.5,  .39,  .2),
            color (.2,  .3,   0),
            color (.085,  .2,  .04),
            color (.065,  .22,  .04),
            color (.5,  .42,  .28),
            color (.6,  .5,  .23),
```

```
                    color (1,1,1),
                    color (1,1,1));
        /* mottle the color some */
        if (latitude < mottle_limit) {
            PP = mottle_scale * Ptexture;
            purt = fBm (PP, mottle_scale*filtwidth, 6, 2, mottle_dim);
            Ct += (mottle_mag * purt) * (color (0.5, 0.175, 0.5));
        }
    }
    else {
        /* Oceans */
        Ct = color(.1,.2,.5);
        if (ice_caps > 0  &&  latitude > ice_caps)
            Ct = color(1,1,1);  /* Ice color */
        else {
            /* Adjust color of water to darken deeper seas */
            chaos -= sea_level;
            chaos *= depth_scale;
            chaos = max (chaos, -depth_max);
            Ct *= (1+chaos);
        }
    }
    /* Shade using matte model */
    Ci = Ct * (Ka * ambient() + Kd * diffuse(faceforward(normalize(N),I)));
    Oi = Os;   Ci *= Oi;
}
```

Selene

Now I'll show you an example of extreme hackery in pursuit of a specific visual end: my texture that can take a featureless gray sphere and turn it into an imitation of the Moon, replete with lunar highlands and maria and a single rayed crater.[6] (I reasoned that one crater, if spectacular enough, would suffice to give an overall impression of moonliness.) The highlands/maria part of the texture is just a simpler (in that it is not multifractal) variation on the continent/ocean part of the above texture. The rayed crater is the interesting part. It is a classic example of ontogenetic modeling taken to an extreme: Observing that the actual dynamics of such an impact and its consequences would be very difficult to model, physically, yet that the phenomenon was essential to the character the object being modeled (the Moon), I set out to construct a reasonable visual semblance through whatever

---

[6] If you've never seen a rayed crater before, just grab a pair of binoculars next time there's a full moon, and have a look. They're all over the place, they're not particularly subtle, and some have rays that reach more than halfway around the globe of the Moon. The rays are the result of splattering of ejecta from the impact that made the crater.

chicanery I could devise. The resulting crater has two parts, which I originally implemented as two separate C functions: the bump-mapped crater rim, and the rays, which are a color modulation of the surface (i.e., a lightening of the surface).

The crater bump map consists of a central peak (a common substrate-rebound feature seen in large impact craters); an unperturbed crater floor, which filled in with lava in the real craters; and a ring which delineates the edge of the crater. This outer ring is devised to have a steep slope on the inside and a more gradual one on the outside, again in emulation of the structure of real impact craters. Furthermore, the outside ring has a texture of random ridges, concentric with the crater. This is in emulation of compression features in the crust around the edge of the crater, formed when the shock of impact "bulldozed" the crater out from the center. We obtain this texture with radially compressed fBm. The composite result of these features is a detailed, fairly realistic model of a crater (except that I'm not yet happy with the central peak). Applied as a bump map, as I do in my ray tracers, one must be careful not to try to view it at a very low angle—then the lack of geometric detail becomes evident. A problem with bump maps is that since they do not affect geometry, (naively) bump-mapped features can never obscure one another, as the raised near rim of a real crater would obscure one's view of the far rim, at low angles of view. If your renderer supports displacement maps or QAEB primitives, this may not be a problem.

The crater ray construction is inspired by the famous Doc Edgerton photo of the splashing milk drop. (You know, the one where it looks like a crown, with all the little droplets evenly spaced around the rim of the "crater.") This high degree of regularity inspired me to build my texture in a similar way: with a number of rays, evenly spaced, but with a small random displacement in their spacing. The rays take the form of weighting functions, the width of which asymptotically approaches zero as we move out along the length of the ray. There is a discontinuity in the weighting function between rays, but this has never been visible in practice. The weighting is applied to an fBm splatter-texture, which is stretched out *away* from the crater, exactly opposite of the compression-texture outside the rim of the crater.

The above crater-ray texture looked much too regular to be realistic. This led me to experiment with random, fractal (fBm) splatter-textures; these were much too irregular. The behavior of Nature lies somewhere between the two. I eventually settled on a combination of both: I use fractal-splatter for the short-range ejecta, and the ray structure for the long-range ejecta. This combination looks reasonably good, though I think it would benefit from further, artful randomization of the ray structure. At the time this model was developed, I'd never had call to inspect the resulting moon up-close and in detail—it had always served as a backdrop for other scenes—I called it "good enough" and moved on, only slightly embarrassed to have put so much time and effort into such an entirely ad hoc construction.[7]

Below is the code for the lunar texture. Color Plate 15.2 and Figure 6 illustrate what it can look like.

```
surface
luna    (float Ka = .5, Kd = 1;
        float lacunarity = 2;
        float octaves = 8;
        float H = .3;
        color highland_color = .7;
        float maria_basecolor = .7, maria_color = .1;
        float arg22 = 1, arg23 = .3;
        float highland_threshold = -0.2;
        float highland_altitude = 0.001, maria_altitude = 0.0004;
        float peak_rad = .0075, inner_rad = .01, rim_rad = .02, outer_rad = 05;
```

**Figure 6.   The rayed crater is prominent on this procedurally textured moon.
Copyright © 1994 F. Kenton Musgrave.**

[7] Interestingly, it was good enough that Digital Domain contacted me to help model the Moon for the movie Apollo 13. Larry Gritz and I had a lot of fun for a few weeks, coming up with photorealistic models of the Moon, seen from pretty close up. The results were used in the medium-range shots of the Moon in the movie, while real images were used for both distant and close-up footage of the Moon. For reasons of Hollywood politics, Larry and I didn't get screen credit.

```
      float peak_ht = 0.005, rim_ht = 0.003;
      float numrays = 8;   /* arg10 */
      float rayfade = 1;   /* arg11 */
      )
{
    float radial_dist;
    point PP, PQ;
    float chaos;
    color Ct;
    float temp1;
    vector vv;
    float uu, ht;
    float lighten;
    normal NN;
    float pd;   /* pole distance */
    float raydist;
    float filtwidth;
    float omega;
    PQ = P;

    PP = transform ("shader", P);
    filtwidth = filterwidthp(PP);
    NN = normalize (N);

    radial_dist = sqrt (xcomp(PP)*xcomp(PP) + ycomp(PP)*ycomp(PP));
    omega = pow (lacunarity, (-.5)-H);
    chaos = fBm (PP, filtwidth, octaves, lacunarity, omega);

    Ct = Cs;
    /* Ensure that the crater is in one of the maria */
    temp1 = radial_dist * arg22;
    if (temp1 < 1)
       chaos -= arg23 * (1 - smoothstep (0, 1, temp1));
    /* determine highlands and maria */
    if (chaos > highland_threshold) {
       PQ += chaos * highland_altitude * NN;
       Ct += highland_color * chaos;
    } else {
       PQ += chaos * maria_altitude * NN;
       Ct *= maria_basecolor + maria_color * chaos;
    }
/*********************************************************************/
    /* Add crater */
    pd = 1-v;
    vv = vector (xcomp(PP)/radial_dist, 0, zcomp(PP)/radial_dist);
    lighten = 0;
    if (pd < peak_rad) {        /* central peak */
       uu = 1 - pd/peak_rad;
       ht = peak_ht * smoothstep (0, 1, uu);
    } else if (pd < inner_rad) {        /* crater floor */
       ht = 0;
```

```
    } else if (pd < rim_rad) {                /* inner rim */
      uu = (pd-inner_rad) / (rim_rad - inner_rad);
      lighten = .75*uu;
      ht = rim_ht * smoothstep (0, 1, uu);
    } else if (pd < outer_rad) {              /* outer rim */
      uu = 1 - (pd-rim_rad) / (outer_rad-rim_rad);
      lighten = .75*uu*uu;
      ht = rim_ht * smoothstep (0, 1, uu*uu);
    }
  else ht = 0;
  PQ += ht * NN;
  lighten *= 0.2;
  Ct += color(lighten,lighten,lighten);
  /* Add some noise */
  if (uu > 0) {
      if (pd < peak_rad) {         /* if on central peak */
          vv = 5*PP + 3 * vv;
          ht = fBm (vv, filterwidthp(vv), 4, 2, 0.833);
          PQ += 0.0025 * uu*ht * NN;
        } else {
          vv = 6*PP + 3 * vv;
          ht = fBm (vv, filterwidthp(vv), 4, 2, 0.833);
          if (radial_dist > rim_rad)
          uu *= uu;
          PQ += 0.0025 * (0.5*uu + 0.5*ht) * NN;
        }
  }
  /* make crater rays */
  lighten = 0;
  if (pd >= rim_rad  &&  pd < 0.4) {
      float fw = filterwidth(u);
      lighten = smoothstep (.15, .5, filteredsnoise(62*u,62*fw));
      raydist = 0.2 + 0.2 * filteredsnoise (20 * mod(u+0.022,1), 20*u);
      lighten *= (1 - smoothstep (raydist-.2, raydist, pd));
  }
  lighten = 0.2 * clamp (lighten, 0, 1);
  Ct += color (lighten, lighten, lighten);

  /* Shade like matte */
  Ci = Ct * (Ka * ambient() + Kd * diffuse(faceforward(normalize(N),I)));
  Oi = Os;  Ci *= Oi;
}
```

Random Coloring Methods

Good painters subsume worlds of color within a painting, or even in a single brush stroke. Van Gogh, who painted with a palette knife, not a brush, executed several paintings in the morning, took a long lunch, then did several more in the afternoon. Painting in a hurry, he didn't mix thoroughly before applying a thick blob to the canvas. Thus each stroke has a universe of swirling color within it. Serat's pointillism is another form of what painters call *juxtaposition,* or the use of a lot of different colors to average to another color. This is part of the visual complexity that, to me, distinguishes good paintings from most computer graphics.

Visual complexity is, more or less, the name of my game, so I've devised some methods for procedurally generating complexity in color, using the same kinds of fractal functions that we use to model natural phenomena.

Random fBm Coloring

My first attempt at random coloring was simply fBm interpreted as color. To get this, you start with a vector-valued fBm that returns three values, and interpret that 3-vector as an rgb color. This can work pretty well, as seen in Plate 11.1. Unfortunately, since our fBm has a Gaussian distribution with an expected value of zero, when one of the values (say, red) is fairly far from zero, the other two are likely to be close to zero. This yields a preponderance of red, green and blue blotches. We want more control than that.

The GIT Texturing System

My goal was to obtain a rich, fractal variation in color detail, similar to the juxtaposition in a Van Gogh stroke or a local area in a Serat. This juxtaposition should to average to a readily-determined color, even though that color may not be present anywhere in the resulting palette. I also wanted to provide easy user control of the color variation in the juxtaposition palette, as the means through which it is accomplished is too abstractly mathematical to manipulate directly via the numbers involved, i.e., the values in a transformation matrix.

Long ago I gave this idea the wonderfully unpretentious (not!) moniker generalized Impressionistic texture, or GIT for short. (We need more TLAs—three letter acronyms.) The GIT matrix generator system takes the form of a time-varying swarm of color samples in a color space (the rgb color cube). The center of the swarm is moved to the position of the desired average color in the color space. The swarm of color sample chips is then manipulated to obtain the desired variation in colors. This is accomplished by rotation and scaling of the principal axes of color variation within the color space.[8] If you think of the scattering of color samples as lying within an ellipsoid, or an elongated M&M, the principal axes

---

[8] Which color space one uses is important, as it affects the character of available color variations. To date, we've only implemented the rgb color cube. It is a little more challenging to display other color spaces as polyhedra, due to their non-rectilinear shapes. It shouldn't be hard to do, though.

correspond to the length, width and thickness of the M&M. After some manipulation, one might have a major axis of variation along, for instance, blue-to-yellow, with less significant variations along two other axes perpendicular to the major axis in the chosen color space. The idea is that you can have a lot of different colors present, with their average clearly specified and smooth interpolation between them being well-defined.[9] The major variations can be along any axis in color space, not just red, green and blue; this is the flexibility of the system.

The simplest underlying mathematical model requires that the three axes of color variation be mutually perpendicular. This model is simply that we have built a standard 4 x 4 transformation matrix, which encodes the rotations, translations, and scalings. The transformation matrix is built by the interactive controls, which let the user move the scatter plot of color samples in the three-dimensional color space. In our implementation, the scatter plot is constantly changing: It is a circular queue of vector values representing offsets from the centroid, or average color. When a sample reaches the end of the queue, it is replaced with another random sample. The random samples are gotten by evaluating vector-valued fBm at random points in its three-dimensional domain. We use about 100 samples at a time, the actual number being controlled by a slider. More samples span the range of colors more accurately, but make for slower interaction, and tend to obscure one another in three-space. My reasoning is that, by having the random samples constantly changing with time, one can get a pretty good idea of the range of colors spanned just by watching for a while.

When the desired distribution of color variations has been determined interactively, the transformation matrix that created it is dumped to a file. That file is then accessed by name by a texture routine incorporated into the renderer. (One could manually copy the transformation matrix values into a shader, if necessary.) The result is a procedural solid texture that may be applied to the surfaces of objects in the scene. The colors in the mountains in Plates 11.3, 11.4, 12.1, and 12.2 come from such "GIT" textures. I like them a lot, because they finally start to capture some of the visual complexity and subtlety of painting, in synthetic imagery.

An Impressionistic Image Processing Filter

The above scheme generates solid textures that are applied to surfaces of objects in a scene. In painting, juxtaposition is in image space (on the canvas), not world

---

[9] The average isn't quite as clear as it may seem, as the ellipsoid can violate the bounds of the color space. One can handle this by either clipping or reflection of values from the boundary back into the color space (which is the solution we use). Either solution will skew the average color away from the centroid of the ellipsoid, which marks the presumed average.

space or object space, as in texturing. Hence we (Myeong Lim, of George Washington University, and myself) sought to apply GIT texturing in image space, i.e., to preexisting digital images. In this case, the matrix is determined by performing *principal components analysis* (Gonzalez, 1992) to local areas in the image.[10] In principal components analysis, the Hotelling transform is applied to a scattering of data, yielding the *autocorrelation matrix* for the distribution. This matrix encodes some magic values known mathematically as the *eigenvectors,* which correspond to the principal axes described above, and the *eigenvalues,* which correspond to the length of those axes. More mathematical magic! The scattering of data we provide usually consists of the rgb values of the pixels in some fairly small neighborhood around the pixel in question, but it can be the whole image.

This autocorrelation matrix encodes exactly the same information as the inter-actively-derived matrix above. We will use it in a way that is similar, but a little different. The juxtaposition is now expressed in a synthetic brush stroke. This is applied as a blurring, detail-adding filter on the image; in fact, we usually expand the image by a factor of four to eight in both dimensions. Standard image processing routines are used to determine lightness gradients in the input image, and the brush strokes are applied cross-gradient (Salisbury 1994) to resemble an artists' strokes. That is, if the image faded from dark at the bottom to light at the top, the strikes would be horizontal. While blurring the image underneath along the direction of the stroke (Cabral, 1993), random detail is simultaneously added in the form of fractal color juxtaposition. Plate 11.7 shows this in practice. This application of the GIT idea is probably less successful than commercially available paint programs such as Painter. At any rate, we never spent much time on the model for the brush strokes.

The "Multicolor" Texture

I always like to automate things as much as possible, to see what the computer can be made to do on its own.[11] Being interested in the kind of painterly textures

---

[10] Explaining this is way beyond the scope of this book; see (Gonzalez 1992) for details if you're interested. But be advised, it involves some pretty heavy linear algebra and statistics.

[11] My considered view of the computer's role in generating art is that it is like an idiot savant assistant: It is extremely simple-minded, incapable of doing anything without the most exhaustively precise directions, but fantastically capable at what it does well—calculations, if you will. Its power in that area can lead to fabulous serendipity, as we will see in the final chapter, but it is never truly creative. All creativity resides in the human operator. While the computer can be made to appear fabulously creative, it is an illusion.

that the GIT ideas were designed to create, I set out to design a procedural texture that is entirely random, and appears "painterly" (see Color Plate 11.8). The result is, I think, rather striking, so I'll describe it here. It's a solution looking for a problem—I haven't found a way to include it in any images—but perhaps someday someone will find a use for it! It's also a good example of how a hacked-together texture can become brittle: Small changes in the input parameters can "break" the result (meaning that the desirable qualities are compromised).

The idea of this texture is to get a rich, painterly combination of random colors in what looks something like brush strokes, and that will average to neutral grey. (It can actually average to any color, but I like the neutrality of the 50% grey.) There are four basic elements in this texture: First, a multifractal function that modulates saturation in the random colors; second, an fBm function to provide a color vector; third, a random rotation matrix to decorrelate that vector from the rgb axes; and fourth, a fractal domain distortion (like the one seen in Figure 2, in this chapter) to give the quality of brush strokes.

We start with a neutral grey plane. We apply a modulation of saturation in the independently-derived random color with a function very similar to the one rendered as a height field in Figure 3 of Chapter 10. Where that function is zero, the grey is unchanged. Where it's positive or negative, the grey becomes colored. The color itself comes from a vector-valued fBm. As noted earlier, interpreting such an fBm vector as an rgb color doesn't give us the truly random variety of colors we want. I get such color by a cheap, random version of the GIT scheme: I simply build a random rotation matrix that corresponds to a GIT matrix, but without translations. (The translation is assumed to be inherent in the length of the fBm vector.) This may seem overly elaborate, but it has been my experience that, to lapse into the vernacular, you have to mess around with random colors a lot, to get them to be truly random and to vary in a way that it pleasing to the eye.

Here's the shader code for "multicolor." As it (and some of the other textures in this chapter) is brittle, you might also want to look at the code for original C version that appears on the CD-ROM.

```
vector vMultifractalFunc (point p; float H, lacunarity, octaves, zero_off-
set)
{
    point pos = p;
    float f = 1, i;

    vector y = 1;
    for (i = 0;  i < octaves;  i += 1) {
        y *= zero_offset + f * (2*vector noise(pos) - 1);
        f *= H;
        pos *= lacunarity;
```

```
      }
    return y;
} /* vMultifractalFunc() */

/*
 * a multifractal multicolor texture experiment
 */
surface multicolor (float arg0 = 0.7;
                    float arg1 = 2.0;
                    float arg2 = 8.0;
                    float arg3 = 0.2;
                    float arg4 = 0.5;
                    float arg5 = 8.0;
                    float arg6 = 4.0;
                    float arg7 = 5.0;
                    float arg8 = 1.0;
                    float arg9 = 1.0;
                    float arg10 = 4.0e5;
    )
{
    vector cvec, axis;
    point tx = transform ("shader", P);
    float i;

    axis  = arg6 * vfBm (tx, filterwidthp(tx), arg5, 2.0, arg4);
    cvec = tx * 0.3;
    cvec  = .5 * arg7 * vfBm (cvec, filterwidthp(tx), 7, 2.0, 0.5);
    tx += cvec;

    cvec += arg10 * vMultifractalFunc(tx, arg0, arg1, arg2, arg3);
    cvec = rotate (cvec, 3*length(axis), point(0,0,0), axis);

    Ci = .045 * arg8 * color (xcomp(cvec), ycomp(cvec), zcomp(cvec));
    Ci += Cs;
    for (i = 0;  i < 3;  i += 1) {
       float c = abs (comp(Ci,i));
       if (c > 1)
           setcomp (Ci, i, 1-c);
    }
    Oi = Os;
    Ci *= Oi;
} /* multicolor() */
```

Ultimately, I think of this texture and my genetic textures as applications of the "naturality," if you will, of the fractal functions developed earlier in this text, in pursuit of the look and feel of paintings, which I think of as being very natural. That is, they may be man-made, by they appear completely natural compared to the artificiality of digitally-synthesized images. The flow of the paint and the hand of the painter are very natural, and paintings are executed in a physical medium (rather than shuffling bits around for later output on some arbitrary device). This physicality is also completely natural, compared to the abstractions of image synthesis. So I actually think of paintings as being a part of Nature, compared to what we're doing here. At any rate, I think of painters as the masters of rendering, and I'm trying to learn from them by imitation. I find it fun and, when I get a good result, satisfying.

The "multicolor" texture provided the starting point for Dr. Mutatis, my genetic textures program described in the last chapter. It was my desire to automate the generation of textures like "multicolor" that motivated my excursion into genetic programming (brittle textures like this being a real pain to design and refine). You'll see then that some of the fundamental functionality in Dr. Mutatis derives from the ideas I've described here, about random colorations. At any rate, I think that the above constructions are mostly rather unique and non-obvious, as they involve a cross-fertilization of ideas from aesthetics and mathematics. I think that's cool! And best, of course, they can make great pictures.

Procedural Fractal Terrains 12

F. Kenton Musgrave

As I pointed out in Chapter 10, the same procedural constructions that we use as textures can also be used to create terrains. The only difference is that, instead of interpreting what the function returns as a color or other surface attribute, we interpret it as an altitude. I will now extend my discussions of terrain models, begun in Chapter 10.

Since we are designing these functions to generate terrain models external to the renderer or as QAEB primitives built into the renderer, I'm switching back from the RenderMan shading language to C code for my code examples.

Advantages of Point Evaluation

I first started working with procedural textures when I used them to color fractal terrains and to provide a sense of "environment," with clouds, water, and moons, as described above. Color Plate 11.10 is an example of this early work. The mountains I was making then were created with a version of polygon subdivision (hexagon subdivision) described by Mandelbrot in an appendix of *The Science of Fractal Images* (Peitgen and Saupe 1988). They have the jagged character of polygon-subdivision terrains, and the same-roughness-everywhere character of a homogeneous fractal dimension. Mandelbrot and I were working together at the time on including erosion features in our terrains. This led me to make some conjectures about varying the local behaviors of the terrain, which led to the two multifractal constructions I will describe next. Interestingly, I had never heard of "multifractals" when I devised these first two additive/multiplicative hybrid multifractal functions. When I showed Mandelbrot Figure 1 in 1991, he exclaimed in surprise, "A multifractal!" to which I astutely replied, "What's a multifractal?"[1]

What allowed me to intuitively "reinvent the (multifractal) wheel" was the flexibility implicit in our noise-based procedural fractals. Dietmar Saupe calls our Perlin noise-based procedural fractal construction method "rescale and add" (Saupe 1989). Its distinguishing feature, he points out, is point evaluation: the fact that each sample is evaluated at a point in space, without reference to any of its neighbors. This is quite a distinction indeed, in the context of fractal terrain generation algorithms. In polygon subdivision, a given altitude is determined by a series of interpolations between neighboring points at lower frequencies (i.e., earlier steps in the iterative construction). In Fourier synthesis, the entire terrain patch must be generated all at once; no sample can be computed in isolation. In contrast, the context-independence of our procedural method allows us to do whatever we please at any given point, without reference to its neighbors. There *is* interpolation involved, but it has been hidden inside the noise function, where it takes the form of Hermite spline interpolation of the gradient values at the integer lattice points (see Chapters 2, 3, and 6 for details on this). In practice, you could employ the same tricks described below to get multifractals from a polygon subdivision scheme, at least. It's not so obvious how one could accomplish similar effects with Fourier synthesis. The point is, I probably never would have thought of these multifractal constructions, had I not been working in the procedural idiom.

Another distinguishing feature of terrains constructed from the noise function is that they can be rounded, like foothills or ancient mountains (see Figure 2). To obtain this kind of morphology from polygon subdivision, one must resort to the

Figure 1.   A multifractal terrain patch. Note the heterogeneity: plains, foothills, and mountains, all captured in a single fractal model.
Copyright © 1994 F. Kenton Musgrave.

---

[1] His cryptic retort was "Never mind—now is not the time."

Figure 2.   "Carolina" illustrates a procedural model of ancient, heavily eroded mountains. Copyright © 1994 F. Kenton Musgrave.

complexities of schemes like Lewis' "generalized stochastic subdivision" (Lewis 1987). The rounded nature of our terrains has to do with the character of the basis function; more on that later. And, as we have already shown, another distinguishing characteristic of the procedural approach is that it naturally accommodates adaptive band-limiting of spatial frequencies in the geometry of the terrain as required for rendering with adaptive level of detail, as in QAEB rendering (described in the next chapter). Such capability makes possible exciting applications like the planetary zoom seen in Figure 3.

The Height Field

Terrain models in computer graphics generally take the form of *height fields*. A height field is a two-dimensional array of altitude values at regular intervals (or *post spacings*, as geographers call them). So it's like a piece of graph paper, with altitude values stored at every point where the lines cross.[2]

There is one, and only one, altitude value at each grid point. Thus there can be no caves or overhangs in a height field. This limitation may seem easy to overcome, but it's not. In fact, the problem is hard enough that I issued a challenge in

---

[2] This is the simplest, but not the most efficient, storage scheme for terrains. Extended areas of nearly constant slope can be represented with fewer samples, for instance. Decimation (Schroeder 1992) algorithms are one way to reduce the number of samples in a height field, and thus its storage space requirement. It may be desirable to resample such a model before rendering, however, to get back to the regular array of samples that facilitates fast rendering schemes such as grid tracing. For an animation of this zoom, see http://www.seas.gwu.edu/faculty/musgrave/animations.html.

the first edition of this book, back in 1994, offering $100 US to the first person to come up with an "elegant, general solution" to it. The reward was won at the time of this writing, in early 1998, by Manuel Gamito, who came over from Portugul to work with us in the MetaCreations Skunk Works for a year. Manuel's award-winning image, an entirely procedural model rendered in a modified version the minimal ray tracer I wrote to develop the QAEB algorithm, appears in Color Plate 13.1. Unfortunately, that image took about a day to render!

The regular (i.e., evenly spaced) samples of the height field accommodate efficient ray-tracing schemes such as *grid tracing* (Musgrave 1988) and quad tree (Kajiya 1983a) spatial subdivision. A detailed discussion of such rendering scheme is beyond the scope of this book; if you're interested in that, see (Musgrave 1993). I've always preferred to ray-trace my landscapes, but if you lack the computational horsepower for that, there are some very nice non-ray-tracing terrain renderers, such as Vistapro, available for home computers. If you'd like to try your hand at ray-tracing height fields you can buy MetaCreations' Bryce, Animatek World Builder or World Tool Set. Or you can pick up Craig Kolb's public domain Rayshade ray tracer (available on the Internet via anonymous ftp at cs.princeton.edu in directory pub/Graphics), which features a very nice implementation of hierarchical grid tracing for height fields. The hierarchical approach captures the best aspects of grid tracing (i.e., low memory overhead) and of quad-tree methods (i.e., speed). For multiple renderings of a static height field—as in fly-by animations—the PPT algorithm is the fastest rendering method. (Paglieroni, 1992)

Figure 3.

There are several common file formats for height field data. There is the DEM (digital elevation map) format of the U.S. Geological Survey height fields, which contain measured elevation data corresponding to the "quad" topographic maps available from the USGS, which cover the entire United States. The U.S. military establishment has their DTED (digital terrain elevation data) files which are similar, but are likely to include terrains outside of the United States and its territories. While one may render such data as readily as synthetic fractal terrains, as a synthesist (if you will), I consider the use of "real" data to be cheating! My goal is to synthesize a detailed and familiar-looking reality, entirely from scratch. Therefore I have rarely concerned myself with measured data sets; I have mostly worked with terrains that I have synthesized myself.

As I have usually worked alone, with no programming assistance, I generally prefer to implement things in the quickest, simplest manner I can readily devise so that I can get on to making pictures. Thus my home-grown height field file format (which is also used by Rayshade) is very simple: It is a binary file containing first a single integer (four bytes) which specifies the size of the (square) height field, followed by n^2 floats (four bytes each), where n is the value of the leading integer. I append any additional data I wish to store, such as the minimum and maximum values of the height field, and perhaps the random number generator seed used to generate it, after the elevation data. While far more compact than an ASCII format for the same data, this is still not a particularly efficient storage scheme. Matt Pharr, of Stanford University and Pixar, has implemented an improved file format, along with conversion routines from my old format to his newer one. In the new scheme, there is a 600-byte header block for comments and documentation of the height field. The elevation data is stored as shorts (two bytes), with the values normalized and quantized into integers in the range $[0, 2^{16} - 1]$. The minimum and maximum altitudes over the height field are also stored, so that the altitude values may be restored to their floating point values at rendering time, by the transformation:

$$z = \frac{a(z_{\max} - z_{\min})}{2^{16} - 1} + z_{\min}$$

where a is the quantized and scaled altitude value, z is the decoded floating point value, and $z_{\min}$ and $z_{\max}$ are the min/max values of the height field. Pharr's code also obviates the big-endian/little-endian byte-order problem that can crop up when transferring binary files between different computers, as well as automatically taking care of transfers between 32-bit and 64-bit architectures. Pharr's code is available on the Internet via anonymous ftp at cs.princeton.edu. If you intend to render many height fields, it is worth picking up, as it saves about half of the space required to store a given height field.

Homogeneous fBm Terrain Models

The origin of fractal mountains in computer graphics is this: Mandelbrot was working with fBm in one dimension (or one-point-something dimensions, if you must), like the plot we saw in Chapter 10, Figure 2. He noted that, at a fractal dimension of about 1.2 (the second trace from the top in Chapter 10, Figure 2) the trace of this function resembled the skyline of a jagged mountain range. In the true spirit of ontogenetic modeling, he reasoned that, if this function were extended to two dimensions, the resulting surface should resemble mountains. Indeed it did, and thus were born fractal mountains for computer graphics. Figure 4 is a crude example of such a simple fractal terrain model.

Again, there is no known causal relationship between the shape of real mountains and the shape of this fractal function; the function simply resembles mountains, and does so rather closely. Of course there are many features in real mountains, such as drainage networks and other erosion features, that are not present in this first model. Much of my own research has been toward including such features in synthetic terrain models, largely through procedural methods (Musgrave 1993).

Fractal Dimension

As pointed out in Chapter 10 and as illustrated by Figure 2 in Chapter 10, fractal dimension can be thought of as a measure of the *roughness* of a surface. The higher the fractal dimension, the rougher the surface. Figure 5 illustrates how the roughness of an fBm surface varies with fractal dimension: at the left edge of the patch, the fractal dimension is 2.0; on the right it is 3.0. The most interesting thing about this patch is that it is not planar (i.e., flat) on the left, nor does it fill all of space on the right. So we see that the formal definition of fractal dimension for fBm does not capture all of the useful fractal behavior available from the construction: the kind of rolling foothills that would occur off the right end of this patch are indeed self-similar, and thus fit our heuristic definition of "fractal." Yet they do not fit the formal mathematical definition of fractal dimension (at least

---

[3] It's worth noting that different methods for measuring fractal dimension may give slightly different results when applied to the same fractal. So even formal methods may not agree about the limits of fractal behavior, and the exact values of quantitative measurements of fractal behavior.

Figure 4.   A terrain patch with homogeneous fractal dimension (of ~2.2).

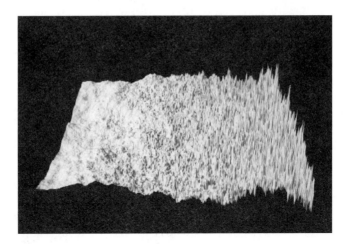

**Figure 5.   In this patch, the fractal dimension varies from 2.0 on the left to 3.0
on the right. Copyright © 1994 F. Kenton Musgrave.**

not the one for fBm)[3]. This is a good example of how fractals defy precise definition, and sometimes require that we "paint with a broad brush" so that we don't
unnecessarily exclude relevant phenomena. Many researchers in computer graphics and other fields have substituted terms such as "stochastic" and "self-similar"
for "fractal" because of this poor fit with formal definitions, but this is probably
not appropriate: There are few useful stochastic models of visual natural phe-

nomena which do not feature self-similarity, and self-similar models are best characterized as fractal, formal technicalities notwithstanding.

Visual Effects of the Basis Function

As illustrated in the previous chapter, the small spectral sums used to create random fractals for computer graphics allow the character of the basis function to show through clearly in the result. Usually the choice of basis function is implicit in the algorithm: It is a sine wave for Fourier synthesis, a sawtooth wave in polygon subdivision, and a piecewise-cubic Hermite spline in noise-based procedural fBm. You could use a Walsh transform, and get square waves as your basis. Wavelets (Ruskai 1992) promise to provide a powerful new set of finite basis functions. And again, sparse convolution (Lewis 1989) or fractal sum of pulses (Lovejoy and Mandelbrot 1985) offer perhaps the greatest flexibility in choice of basis functions. With those methods, one could even use the profile of the kitchen sink as a basis function, leading naturally to sinkholes in the terrain.

Gavin Miller (Miller 1986) showed that the creases in terrain constructed with the most common form of polygon subdivision, i.e., subdivision of an equilateral triangle, are really an artifact of the interpolation scheme implicit in the subdivision algorithm. But I think that for the most part it has simply been overlooked, that there *is* a basis function implicit in *any* fBm construction, and that the character of that basis function shows through in the result. As shown in the previous chapter, one can use this awareness to obtain certain aesthetic effects when designing both textures and terrains.

The smoothness of the Hermite spline interpolant in the noise function allows us to generate terrains that are more rounded than those commonly seen in computer graphics previously. Figure 2 and Color Plate 14.2 illustrate this well. Other examples of basis-function effects are seen in Color Plates 12.12–14, 13.1–2 and 14.4 and Figure 3–5 in Chapter 13, where the ridged basis function was used to get a terrain with razorback ridges at all scales. Note that this terrain model can only be effectively rendered with adaptive level of detail, as with QAEB and other schemes (Bouville 1985, Kajiya 1983b). Without this, in a polygonal model rendered with perspective projection, nearby ridges would take on a saw-toothed appearance, as undersampled elevation values would generally lie on alternating sides of the ridgeline, and distant areas would alias on the screen due to undersampling of the complex terrain model. A non-polygonal approach to rendering with adaptive level of detail, QAEB tracing, is described in the next chapter. It is ideal for rendering such sharp-edged terrain models.

Heterogeneous Terrain Models

It would seem that before our 1989 SIGGRAPH paper (Musgrave *et al.* 1989) it hadn't yet occurred to anyone to generate heterogeneous terrain models. Earlier published models had been monofractal, i.e., composed of some form of fBm with a uniform fractal dimension. Even Voss' heterogeneous terrains (Voss 1988) represent simple exponential vertical scalings of a surface of uniform fractal dimension.

As pointed out in Chapter 10, Nature is decidedly not so simple and well behaved. Real landscapes are quite heterogeneous, particularly over large scales, e.g., kilometers. Except perhaps on islands, mountains rise out of smoother terrains—witness the dramatic rise of the Rocky Mountains from the relatively flat plains just to their east. Tall ranges like the Rockies, Sierras, and Alps typically have rolling foothills formed largely by the massive earthmovers known as glaciers. All natural terrains, except perhaps recent volcanic ones, bear the scars of erosion. In fact, erosion and tectonics are responsible for nearly all geomorphological features on our planet, other than volcanic features, impact craters, and various features due to bioturbation (humanity's included). Some erosion features are relatively easy to model: talus slopes, for example. Others, such as drainage networks, are not so easy (Musgrave *et al.* 1989). The rest of this chapter will describe certain ontogenetic models designed to yield a first approximation of certain erosion features, without overly compromising the elegance and computational efficiency of the original fBm model. These models are, at least loosely speaking, varieties of multifractals.

Statistics by Altitude

The observation which motivated my first multifractal model is that, in real terrains, low-lying areas sometimes tend to fill up with silt and become topographically smoother, while erosive processes may tend to keep higher areas more jagged. This can be accomplished with the following variation on fBm:

```
/*
 * Heterogeneous procedural terrain function: stats by altitude method.
 * Evaluated at "point"; returns value stored in "value".
 *
 * Parameters:
 *      "H"  determines the fractal dimension of the roughest areas
 *      "lacunarity"  is the gap between successive frequencies
 *      "octaves"  is the number of frequencies in the fBm
 *      "offset"  raises the terrain from `sea level'
 */
```

```
double
Hetero_Terrain( Vector point,
          double H, double lacunarity, double octaves, double offset )
{
      double          value, increment, frequency, remainder, Noise3();
      int             i;
      static int      first = TRUE;
      static double   *exponent_array;

      /* precompute and store spectral weights, for efficiency */
      if ( first ) {
            /* seize required memory for exponent_array */
            exponent_array =
                      (double *)malloc( (octaves+1) * sizeof(double) );
            frequency = 1.0;
            for (i=0; i<=octaves; i++) {
                  /* compute weight for each frequency */
                  exponent_array[i] = pow( frequency, -H );
                  frequency *= lacunarity;
            }
            first = FALSE;
      }

      /* first unscaled octave of function; later octaves are scaled */
      value = offset + Noise3( point );
      point.x *= lacunarity;
      point.y *= lacunarity;
      point.z *= lacunarity;

      /* spectral construction inner loop, where the fractal is built */
      for (i=1; i<octaves; i++) {
            /* obtain displaced noise value */
            increment = Noise3( point ) + offset;
            /* scale amplitude appropriately for this frequency */
            increment *= exponent_array[i];
            /* scale increment by current `altitude' of function */
            increment *= value;
            /* add increment to "value"  */
            value += increment;
            /* raise spatial frequency */
            point.x *= lacunarity;
            point.y *= lacunarity;
            point.z *= lacunarity;
      } /* for */

      /* take care of remainder in "octaves"  */
      remainder = octaves - (int)octaves;
      if ( remainder ) {
            /* "i"  and spatial freq. are preset in loop above */
            /* note that the main loop code is made shorter here */
            /* you may want to that loop more like this */
```

```
                increment = (Noise3( point ) + offset) * exponent_array[i];
                value += remainder * increment * value;
        }
        return( value );

} /* Hetero_Terrain() */
```

We accomplish our end by multiplying each successive octave by the current value of the function. Thus in areas near zero elevation, or "sea level," higher frequencies will be heavily damped, and the terrain will remain smooth. Higher elevations will not be so damped, and will grow jagged as the iteration progresses. Note that we may need to clamp the highest value of the weighting variable to 1.0, to prevent the sum from diverging as we add in more values.

The behavior of this function is illustrated in the terrains seen in Figures 2 and 6, and in Color Plate 14.2.

A Hybrid Multifractal

My next observation was that valleys should have smooth bottoms at all altitudes, not just at sea level. It occurred to me that this could be accomplished by scaling higher frequencies in the summation by the local value of the previous frequency:

```
/* Hybrid additive/multiplicative multifractal terrain model. *
 * Some good parameter values to start with:
 *
 *      H:              0.25
 *      offset:         0.7
 */
double
HybridMultifractal( Vector point, double H, double lacunarity,
                    double octaves, double offset )

{
        double          frequency, result, signal, weight, remainder;
        double          Noise3();
        int             i;
        static int      first = TRUE;
        static double   *exponent_array;

        /* precompute and store spectral weights */
        if ( first ) {
                /* seize required memory for exponent_array */
                exponent_array =
                        (double *)malloc( (octaves+1) * sizeof(double) );
                frequency = 1.0;
                for (i=0; i<=octaves; i++) {
```

```
                    /* compute weight for each frequency */
                    exponent_array[i] = pow( frequency, -H);
                    frequency *= lacunarity;
            }
            first = FALSE;
    }

    /* get first octave of function */
    result = ( Noise3( point ) + offset ) * exponent_array[0];
    weight = result;
    /* increase frequency */
    point.x *= lacunarity;
    point.y *= lacunarity;
    point.z *= lacunarity;

    /* spectral construction inner loop, where the fractal is built */
    for (i=1; i<octaves; i++) {
            /* prevent divergence */
            if ( weight > 1.0 )  weight = 1.0;
            /* get next higher frequency */
            signal = ( Noise3( point ) + offset ) * exponent_array[i];
            /* add it in, weighted by previous freq's local value */
```

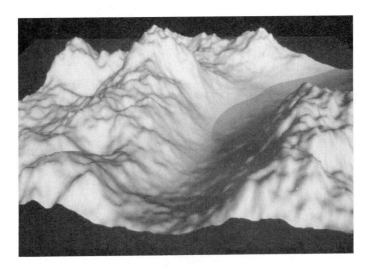

Figure 6. **This multifractal terrain patch is quite smooth at "sea level" and gets rougher as altitude increases. Copyright © 1994 F. Kenton Musgrave.**

```
        result += weight * signal;
        /* update the (monotonically decreasing) weighting value */
        /* (this is why H must specify a high fractal dimension) */
        weight *= signal;
        /* increase frequency */
        point.x *= lacunarity;
        point.y *= lacunarity;
        point.z *= lacunarity;
    } /* for */

    /* take care of remainder in "octaves"  */
    remainder = octaves - (int)octaves;
    if ( remainder )
        /* "i"  and spatial freq. are preset in loop above */
        result += remainder * Noise3( point ) * exponent_array[i];

    return( result );

} /* HybridMultifractal() */
```

Note the offset applied to the noise function to move its range from [–1, 1] to something closer to [0, 2]. (If your noise function has a different range, you'll need to adjust this.) You should experiment with the values these parameters and observe their effects.

An amusing facet of this function is that it *doesn't* do what I designed it to do: A valley above sea level in this function is defined not by the local value of the last frequency in the sum, as I have assumed, but by the local gradient of the function (i.e., the local tangent, the partial derivatives in *x* and *y*; however you care to view it). Put another way, in the above construction, we ignore the bias introduced by lower frequencies—we may be adding a "valley" onto the side of an already-steep slope, and thus we may not get a valley at all, only a depression on the side of the slope. Nevertheless, this construction has provided some very nice, heterogeneous terrain models. Figure 1 illustrates a terrain model produced from the above function. Note that it begins to capture some of the large-scale heterogeneity of real terrains: We have plains, foothills, and alpine mountains, all in one patch. Color Plate 12.1 shows a similar construction, this time using the same ridged basis function seen in Color Plate 11.4: It's like Perlin's original "turbulence" function, which used the absolute value of the noise function, only it's turned upside-down, as 1-abs(noise) so that the resulting creases stick up as ridges. The resulting multifractal terrain model is illustrated in Figure 3–5 in the next chapter. It is generated by the following code:

```
/* Ridged multifractal terrain model.
 *
```

```
 * Some good parameter values to start with:
 *
 *       H:              1.0
 *       offset:         1.0
 *       gain:           2.0
 */
double
RidgedMultifractal( Vector point, double H, double lacunarity,
                    double octaves, double offset, double gain )
{
      double          result, frequency, signal, weight, Noise3();
      int             i;
      static int      first = TRUE;
      static double   *exponent_array;

      /* precompute and store spectral weights */
      if ( first ) {
            /* seize required memory for exponent_array */
            exponent_array =
                      (double *)malloc( (octaves+1) * sizeof(double) );
            frequency = 1.0;
            for (i=0; i<=octaves; i++) {
                  /* compute weight for each frequency */
                  exponent_array[i] = pow( frequency, -H );
                  frequency *= lacunarity;
            }
            first = FALSE;
      }

      /* get first octave */
      signal = Noise3( point );
      /* get absolute value of signal (this creates the ridges) */
      if ( signal < 0.0 ) signal = -signal;
      /* invert and translate (note that "offset" should be ~= 1.0) */
      signal = offset - signal;
      /* square the signal, to increase "sharpness" of ridges */
      signal *= signal;
      /* assign initial values */
      result = signal;
      weight = 1.0;

      for( i=1; i<octaves; i++ ) {
            /* increase the frequency */
            point.x *= lacunarity;
            point.y *= lacunarity;
            point.z *= lacunarity;

            /* weight successive contributions by previous signal */
            weight = signal * gain;
            if ( weight > 1.0 ) weight = 1.0;
            if ( weight < 0.0 ) weight = 0.0;
```

```
            signal = Noise3( point );
            if ( signal < 0.0 ) signal = -signal;
            signal = offset - signal;
            signal *= signal;
            /* weight the contribution */
            signal *= weight;
            result += signal * exponent_array[i];
        }

    return( result );

} /* RidgedMultifractal() */
```

Multiplicative Multifractal Terrains

In Chapter 10 Figure 3 illustrates, as a terrain patch, the multiplicative multifractal function presented in that chapter. Qualitatively, that terrain patch appears quite similar to the statistics-by-altitude patch seen in Figure 1 in this chapter. At the time of this writing, our formal—i.e., mathematical, rather than artistic—research into the mathematics of such multifractal terrain models is quite preliminary, so I have little of use to report. The multifractal construction of Chapter 10 does appear to have some curious properties: As the value of `scale` goes from zero to infinity, the function goes from highly heterogeneous (at zero), flat (through diverging). We have not yet completed our quantitative study of the behavior, so I cannot elucidate further at this time.

For the time being, however, for the purposes of terrain synthesis it seems best to stick with the two hybrid additive multiplicative multifractal constructions presented in this chapter, rather than attempting to use the pure multifractal function presented in chapter 10. These hybrid models may be no better understood mathematically, but they *are* better behaved as functions, i.e., they don't usually need to be rescaled and are less prone to divergence.

Conclusions

I hope that in the last three chapters I have been able to illustrate the power of fractal geometry as a visual language of Nature. We have seen that fractals can readily provide nice visual models of fire, earth, air, and water. I hope that I have also helped clarify the bounds of usefulness of fractal models for computer graphics: While fractals are not the final word in describing the world we live in, they do provide an elegant source of visual complexity for synthetic imagery. The accuracy of fractal models of natural phenomena is of an ontogenetic, rather than physical, character: They reflect morphology fairly well, but this semblance does not issue from first principles of physical law, so far as we know. The world we inhabit is more visually complex than we can hope to reproduce in synthetic imagery in the near future, but the simple, inherently procedural complexity of fractals marks a first significant step toward accomplishing such reproduction. I hope that some of the constructions presented here will be useful to you, whether in your own attempts to create synthetic worlds or in more abstract artistic endeavors.

There is plenty of work left to be done in developing fractal models of natural phenomena. Turbulence has yet to be efficiently procedurally modeled to everyone's satisfaction, and multifractals need to be understood and applied in computer graphics. Trees are distinctly fractal, yet to a large extent they still defy our ability to capture their full complexity in a simple, *efficient* model; the same goes for river systems and dielectric breakdown (e.g., lightning). Reproducing other, nonfractal manifestations of heterogeneous complexity will, no doubt, keep image synthesists busy for a long time to come. I like to think that our best synthetic images reflect directly something of our depth—and lack—of understanding of the world we live in. As beautiful and convincing as some of the images may be, they are only a first approximation of the true complexity of Nature.

QAEB Rendering for Procedural Models 13

F. Kenton Musgrave

Introduction

This chapter and the next present some pretty technical discussions. In the previous three chapters, I have tried to keep the discussion at a level where the technically-minded artist might want to follow along. Now we're plunging into stuff that is probably only of interest to mathematically-minded programmers. So a word of warning: You might just want to read the introductions, which are written at a fairly conversational level, or maybe even skip Chapters 13 and 14 entirely. These chapters were written originally as technical papers, so the bulk of their verbiage is in the dry and dense idiom of scientific writing.

In the previous chapter we developed some procedural functions designed to serve as realistic terrain models. When interpreted as height fields, these terrain models are pretty good. But, as we pointed out, height fields are usually precomputed and stored at a fixed "post spacing." That is, the function is sampled at points on a regular grid, as at the points where lines intersect on graph paper. This has three undesirable side effects: First, one has to store the height field data in files that can become rather large (though this is less and less an issue as memory and disk space become ever cheaper). Second, the discrete values in the height field must be interpolated, usually linearly, leading to unnatural artifacts such as a terrain composed of triangles (try finding *that* in Nature!). Third—and the most serious problem, in my view—we have a fixed level of detail determined by the post spacing. If we get too close to our terrain model, it becomes locally flat and boring. If we view it at too great a distance, we will get aliasing, due to the triangles being smaller than the Nyquist limit.

As we have shown in the previous chapters, we can build terrain functions that are both continuous (i.e., with a well-defined value everywhere across the surface, not just at certain predetermined sample points) and band-limited, so that the features in the model can be kept at or near the Nyquist limit, whatever that limit may be locally. Thus we can generate models that have ideal appearance everywhere, even though such a model must be view-dependent. That is, the appropriate level of detail at any given point is a function of its distance from the view point, due to the perspective projection. What we require is a rendering algorithm that can take advantage of the flexibility of the procedural approach.

A few years ago I was teaching a class for which the first edition of this book was the text. To illustrate to the class just how *simply* the procedural approach can generate piles and piles of visual detail, I designed such an algorithm. Again, the goal was maximal simplicity in the algorithm, period. Accordingly, I expected it to be *really* slow. It came as a considerable surprise when is turned out to be only *very* slow, not glacial. (That is, it took on the order of a minute to create an image, when I was expecting days.) I gave this algorithm the wonderfully turgid name *quasi-analytic error-bounded ray tracing*, or *QAEB tracing* for short. To balance the scales of pretense, I pronounce the acronym QAEB whimsically "kweeb" (to rhyme with "dweeb," of course).

QAEB tracing was originally applied to height fields. A discussion with John Hart led me to the realization that, aside from the speedup scheme described below that applies only to height fields, QAEB tracing is actually a general rendering scheme for point-evaluated *implicit* models. Implicit models are isosurfaces of fields, for example, surfaces where some function F defined over 3-space is equal to zero. (We'll see examples of exactly that in our cloud models towards the end of this chapter.) So QAEB tracing is actually a pretty powerful rendering method—slow but *really* simple. I should point out that QAEB tracing is simply ray marching but with a variable step size and an implied use of band-limiting in the procedural model to provide adaptive level of detail. But the pertinent point is this: "It makes cool pictures."

Without further ado, let's launch into the pithy text of the technical paper on QAEB tracing, replete with the turgid use of the royal "we."

QAEB Tracing

We present a numerical method called *QAEB tracing* for ray tracing procedural height field functions as displacement maps. The method accommodates continuous adaptive level of detail in the height field. Spatial error in ray/surface intersections is bounded by an error specified in screen space. We describe a speedup scheme general to incremental height field ray tracing methods. Also described is a method for rendering hypertextures, for example, clouds. The QAEB algorithm is simple and surprisingly fast.

One capability distinguishing scanline rendering from ray tracing is the capability of rendering *displacement maps* (Cook 1984). We describe a method for ray tracing a subclass of displacement maps, *height fields*. Height field rendering is important for visualizing terrain data sets, as in various defense related simulation applications. Adaptive level of detail is desirable in such renderings, and this new method accommodates that simply. *Quasi-analytic error-bounded* (QAEB) ray tracing is a method for rendering general implicit functions, that is, continuous functions of n variables $F: R^n \rightarrow R$; we will show applications for height fields, where $n = 2$, and hypertextures, where $n = 3$. We call it "quasi-analytic" because it yields a numerical approximation of an analytic ray/surface intersection. This approximation is bounded by an error specified in screen space. When F is a procedural fractal function, the world space frequency content of the terrain model may be linked to its projected screen space Nyquist limit, to accommodate adaptive level of detail without aliasing. QAEB-traced images can be superior, due to their adaptive level of detail and the nonpolygonal character of the rendered height field primitive. As the QAEB algorithm is isolated in the ray/surface intersection routine, QAEB-traced objects amount to new primitives that may be added to the standard inventory of ray tracer primitives such as spheres, polygons, and so on. Development of the QAEB algorithm was originally motivated by the desire to render landscapes with adaptive level of detail. We thus describe the algorithm in the context of rendering height fields.

A striking aspect of the QAEB algorithm is its simplicity. It was expected to be slow, due to its profligate character. That is, it requires a very large number of evaluations of the implicit function. In practice it is surprisingly fast, probably due to its simplicity: The entire code can fit in cache on a contemporary microprocessor, yielding near-optimal performance. A desirable feature is that spatial precision (and error) are linked directly to the spatial sampling rate. No greater precision is calculated than is needed, potentially saving CPU cycles and time.

Problem Statement

Generally, the only moving part in a terrain animation is the view point. Freedom of movement of the view point with perspective projection requires adaptive level of detail in the terrain model. Adaptive level of detail can be readily accommodated with procedural fractal terrain models. Fractals are scaling (Mandelbrot 1982), thus detail is potentially unlimited. Procedural fractals are inherently band-limited and can have parameterized band limits, as shown in previous chapters. An argument based on similar triangles (see Figure 1) shows that, in a perspective projection, feature span (not area) in screen space varies linearly with distance. We can use this knowledge to roll off high frequencies in the model to keep them at or below Nyquist limit of the projected basis function (e.g., the Perlin noise function) in screen space. Octaves in the spectral construction of the fractal may be related to distance d as:

$$octaves = -\log_2(\tan(fov/res)) - \log_2(d) - 3.5$$

where *fov* is the lateral field of view, *res* is the number of samples across that field, and 3.5 is a constant relating our chosen Perlin noise basis function to the Nyquist frequency.

Prior Art

Procedural ray tracing of synthetic fractal terrains with adaptive level of detail has been addressed by (Kajiya 1983) and (Bouville 1985). These methods are based on polygon-subdivision fractal terrains. They require data structure overhead, for example, quad trees, to organize the numerous polygon primitives. Polygon-based methods can suffer artifacts due to discontinuities in levels of detail. This gives rise to the nontrivial problem of detecting and sealing "cracks" between polygons of different sizes, where adaptive level of detail dictates a change in local polygon size. The QAEB approach is nonpolygonal and features continuous adaptive level of detail, and thus does not suffer from this complication. Procedural fractal functions accommodating continuous frequency change for such adaptive level of detail are described in the previous chapter.

The speedup scheme for rendering height fields was originally proposed by (Anderson 1982) and (Coquillart 1984).

The QAEB Algorithm

We now describe the QAEB method in the context of the simplest case, rendering height fields.

QAEB tracing is predicated on the following assumptions:

1. A user-specified error ε in the ray/surface intersection and surface normal is acceptable.

2. The function F being rendered is a height field, that is, a continuous function $F:R^2 \rightarrow R$ with a well-defined, globally-invariant "up" direction $\vec{u}_F$.

3. F is a point-evaluated function, for example, a procedural texture, which can be efficiently evaluated at any point (x, y).

4. Near and far clipping planes are acceptable in the rendering.

The algorithm is this: Starting at the near clipping plane, we march away from the view point in error-sized increments until we either exceed the far clipping plane or cross the height field surface, in which case we return an approximate intersection point and surface normal. The marching increment, or *stride* Δ, is exactly equal to ε in the virtual screen's world-space dimensions, at the virtual screen's distance from the view point. The size of Δ varies linearly with distance, as shown in Figure 1. At each step we evaluate the height field function F and compare it against the ray's altitude relative to $\vec{u}_F$. (Note that this constitutes rendering an implicit function with the isosurface $F(x,y) = z_{ray}$) This is profligate in evaluations of F, leading to two conclusions: The algorithm is expected to be slow, and F should be as fast as possible.

C code implementing the QAEB algorithm is presented in Appendix A.

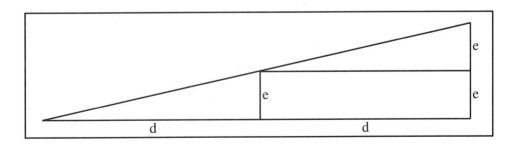

Figure 1.   **Feature span e varies linearly with distance d: at base length d, altitude is e; at base length 2d, altitude is 2e. For isosceles triangles, reflect about the base.**

Error in the Algorithm

Now we'll examine the "error" in the algorithm. This error is defined to be the difference between the analytic intersection of the ray and F, and the intersection determined by the QAEB approximation. The error ε is specified in screen space in terms of sample spacing, for example, one pixel. Both the stride and the error vary in world space proportional to εd where d is the distance from the view point. The value of ε actually specifies three somewhat independent errors along three axes: the vertical, lateral, and depth axes of the (horizontal) screen. The lateral error is exactly ε. The vertical error (the error associated with vertical perturbation of the sampling ray) is indeterminate, due to the chances of hitting or missing a ridge profile. Hitting or missing the top of a ridge can result in vastly different intersection points in world space; this problem is intractable. The depth error is more interesting. To ensure that depth error corresponds to ε, it should be proportional to the slope F' of F. For F with F' discontinuous at local maxima and maximum slope $(F_{max})'_{max}$ at such maxima, the stride Δ should vary as $1/(F_{max})'_{max}$ to ensure meeting the specified error.[1] If F yields low, smooth terrain, Δ may be increased. Note that *fractional Brownian motion* (fBm), upon which most synthetic terrain models are based, is self-affine (Voss 1988). That is, for fBm, local slope can increase as higher spatial frequencies are added. Thus the correct stride may change with the dictates of adaptive level of detail on terrain frequency content. (Note that these matters notwithstanding, we have never found it necessary to use anything other than the simple stride length εd in our applications for image synthesis of nonpathological models, in other words, anything we ever wanted to render nicely.)[2]

Near and Far Clipping Planes

Stride Δ varies linearly with distance d from the view point. It follows that at distance $d = 0$, $\Delta = 0$. Therefore ray marching must begin at a near clipping distance

---

[1] This statement is actually incorrect; the truth is more subtle. The depth error, and thus the stride, should be linked to the minimum slope occurring at local maxima of F. That is, if local maxima may be very narrow (corresponding to sharp peaks or ridges in the terrain), the stride must be small enough to capture them within the specified error. However, if maxima of F may be steep on one side only, the error corresponds to the minimum $(F_{max})'_{min}$ of the two slopes on either side of the local maximum, as $1/(F_{max})'_{min}$.

[2] Manuel Gamito has used interval arithmetic to ensure analytic ray/surface intersections in the QAEB scheme, and has used ray-domain distortion methods (Barr 1986) to render nonheight field terrains, as seen in Plate 13.1. Werner Benger (http://math1.uibk.ac.at/ ~werner/) has developed more approximate marching methods to speed up the QAEB rendering process, while sacrificing accuracy in the ray/surface intersection.

$d_0 > 0$. Features closer to the view point than d_0 will not be visible. Conversely, a greater value of d_0 implies a larger initial stride. Thus the value of d_0 can significantly impact rendering time.

A far clipping plane[3] $d_f < \infty$ is necessary to terminate computation. Beyond d_f the model is not visible. Smaller values of d_f imply a shorter ray march. Choosing the distances for the clipping planes involves the kind of tradeoff between time and realism typical in computer graphics.

Calculating the Intersection Point and Surface Normal

Ray/surface intersection is indicated when the ray altitude crosses adjacent evaluations z_{i-1} and z_i of F. As these evaluation points are exactly ε apart, either can serve as the approximate intersection point, both values being guaranteed to be within ε. Alternatively, one may use the intersection of the ray and the line between z_{i-1} and z_i. This may yield a slightly more accurate solution at a cost of a few more operations, a cost that will generally be overwhelmed by the cost of the march to the intersection.

The surface normal is constructed via the cross product of two vectors between three samples of F. The first vector $\vec{v}_d$ is from z_{i-1} to z_i. The second vector $\vec{v}_l$ is from z_{i-1} to a third sample z_l of F taken at a distance equal to the current stride Δ_i in a lateral direction (i.e., perpendicular to the plane containing the ray and $\vec{u}_F$). The normalized cross product $\left\| \vec{v}_d \times \vec{v}_l \right\|$ serves as our surface normal approximation.

C code implementing this scheme is seen in Appendix B.

Antialiasing

Antialiasing may be accomplished with ordinary supersampling methods. Supersampling implies sampling at a higher spatial frequency; this in turn implies a smaller error ε. In adaptive supersampling, this may require that the samples that indicate supersampling be recomputed with the implied smaller ε to ensure meaningful results. Uniform supersampling simply implies a smaller ε throughout, as ε should generally be equal to the screen space distance between adjacent samples.

---

[3] We refer to the near and far clipping distances as "clipping planes," though they are implemented as distances from the view point and are thus more at "clipping spheres."

To the extent that F represents an uncorrelated random function (all reasonable terrain models being in fact highly correlated), the model is self-jittering. That is, samples automatically have a stochastic character, even if equidistant in screen space. This is a property inherent in the random fractal model, not the QAEB rendering method.

A Speedup Scheme for Height Fields

Assuming (1) the scene is rendered bottom to top relative to $\bar{u}_F$, and (2) $\bar{u}_F$ coincides with the screen "up" vector $\bar{u}_s$, we may employ a simple optimization to great benefit. We keep an array A_d of depth values, of size equal to the number of lateral samples in the screen. A_d is initialized to d_0, and updated to the distance d_i from the view point of the last intersection in the corresponding column. Subsequent rays in the same column, but higher relative to $\bar{u}_F$, may begin marching at d_i rather than d_0. This speeds up rendering enormously, particularly for horizontal views of great depth. Assumption (2) may be dispensed with by indexing A_d along an axis $\bar{v}_F$ horizontal relative to $\bar{u}_F$ and in the plane of the virtual screen. The span w_A of the array indices along $\bar{v}_F$ is equal to the extent of the projection of the rotated screen onto $\bar{v}_F$ (see Figure 2). The number of buckets in A_d is $\lceil w_A / \varepsilon \rceil$. A given screen sample is projected onto $\bar{v}_F$ to determine its bucket in A_d. This bucket is within the specified error ε, laterally. The projection of a point p on the screen onto $\bar{v}_F$ is $\bar{v}_F \lceil (p - o_s) \bullet \bar{v}_F \rceil$ where o_s is the lower left corner of the screen relative to $\bar{u}_F$ and $\bar{v}_F$. This speedup scheme is complicated in cases where the screen contains the point where $\bar{u}_F$ and the view direction are parallel. Such cases may be dealt with by keeping two depth arrays, one for each of the two marching directions opposite relative to $\bar{u}_F$.

Shadows, Reflection, and Refraction

In rendering with adaptive level of detail, correct shadows depend on correct projected shadow feature size. In the QAEB scheme with a given ε, that size is equal to the stride Δ_i at the intersection point where the shadow ray is spawned. Features must retain this size in the shadow projection. For a light source at infinity, the feature size does not vary with the projection. Thus the shadow ray stride is constant and equal to Δ_i. For a light source not at infinity, for example, a point light source, feature size changes linearly with distance, as shown above. It follows that shadow rays start with stride proportional to Δ_i, and the stride goes to zero as the distance to the light source d_l goes to zero. Stride then varies with Δ_i and d_l as $\Delta_i d_l / (d_l + 1)$.

Reflection and refraction cannot be handled correctly in the QAEB scheme, as the divergence of adjacent rays is affected arbitrarily in such transport, and our assumptions about the geometric error break down. This may not be significant, as this scheme was developed to render fractal models of natural phenomena, such as landscapes and clouds, that usually feature neither type of specular transport. Experience indicates that reflective and refractive stochastic surfaces generally create visually confusing images, at any rate.

Performance

The QAEB traced terrain in Figure 3 rendered in 2 minutes, 41 seconds on a 150 MHz R4400, at 640 x 480 (NTSC video) resolution. Near and far clipping planes

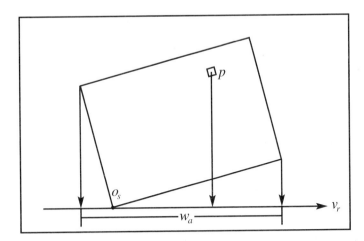

Figure 2.   Projection of rotated screen and sample onto horizontal axis.

are at 0.01 and 100.0, respectively. Figure 4 is at the same resolution, with shadows from a directional light source (i.e., a light source at infinity) at an elevation of ~ 30° above horizontal. Rendering time was 17 minutes 57 seconds. Figure 5 was rendered at a film recorder resolution of 2000 x 1333, without shadows and with atmospherics, in 62 minutes. Near and far clipping planes are at 0.4 and 100.0, respectively. All images were rendered at one ray per pixel with an ε of one pixel.

This performance is far better than was expected before testing. Expectations were low because of the profligate evaluations of the procedural height field function, which uses on the order of 10^3 floating point operations per evaluation. QAEB tracing time is dominated by evaluations of the Perlin noise function, in our implementation. Rendering time is directly impacted by the computational complexity of F, the magnitude of ε, the screen resolution, the number of screen samples, the distances to the near and far clipping planes, the angle of the view direction relative to $\vec{u}_F$, the use of shadows, and, in that case, the number of light sources and their angles to $\vec{u}_F$, and the slope considerations at local maxima described above.

Figure 3.   The very first QAEB-traced image.

Figure 4.   Shadows from a directional light source.

Figure 5.   High resolution and great depth, with atmosphere.

QAEB-Traced Hypertextures

The QAEB scheme is readily applicable, without the above speedup scheme, to volume rendering of procedural hypertextures.

Clouds

Rather than checking ray height versus F along the ray march, one can interpret values of $F > 0$ as density, with values of $F < 0$. being zero density or clear air. This corresponds to ray-marching a *hypertexture* (see Chapter 9). Accumulating the density according to Beer's Law (see Chapter 14) and computing lighting with a self-occluding, single-scattering model can yield nice results.[4] Applying a realistic high-albedo, anisotropic multiple scattering illumination model (Max 1994) yields substantially better results, as seen in Figure 6 and Plate 13.2.[5]

Our hypertexture cloud model has two parts: a procedural fractal function, usually either vanilla fBm or Perlin's "turbulence" (again, fBm constructed using the absolute value of the noise function as the basis), and a simple weighting function that modulates the fractal, making the fractal cloud a more or less distinct blob situated in clear air. The weighting function is necessary to ensure that fractal clouds do not completely permeate all of space, as the fractal functions are statistically homogeneous. This weighting function can be as simple as $F = 1.0 - d$ where d is the distance from a central point, or something more complex to shape the cloud, as seen in Plate 13.2 and Figure 6a where the cloud bottom is rather flat. (The shaping function for these clouds is included in the C code on the CD-ROM.)

In the simplest single-scattering illumination model, local illumination is attenuated by accumulating density along a shadow ray shot towards the light source. Naively, one such ray must be sent per sample, accounting for most of the cost in the rendering. In practice, the frequency of such illumination samples can be decreased, and their stride length may be increased, up to the point of objectionable artifacts. (For details on how, see the code on the CD-ROM.) Jittering (Cook 1984) samples within the interval of the stride also allows greater stride length in primary and shadow rays, with graceful degradation in image quality, as seen in

---

[4] Note that in this application, QAEB tracing is simply a slower but simpler and more accurate equivalent of the gas rendering methods in Chapter 8.

[5] Unfortunately, treatment of such physical illumination models are beyond the scope of this book. Their development is the current PhD research topic of my student Sang Yoon Lee at the time of this writing. For more on his work, see http://www.seas.gwu.edu/student/sylee.

Figure 6c. Nonjittered samples will lead to conspicuous quantization artifacts at large stride lengths, as illustrated in Figure 6b.

Simple QAEB-traced fBm clouds with single scattering illumination were used to create the Mickey Mouse and Goofy characters and a rather detailed cruise ship model in a television commercial for Disney cruise lines produced during the author's tenure at Digital Domain. Only spherical cloud primitives were used, along with animation of the hypertexture spaces and densities. These simple models yielded some striking and novel animation effects. For examples of a preliminary cloud-character animation test, see http://www.metacreations/people/musgrave/animations.html.

Billowing Clouds, Pyroclastic Flows, and Fireballs

An ontogenetic model of billowing can yield realistic dynamic models of fireballs, billowing smoke, and growing cumulus clouds. The distinctive behavior we call "billowing" results from rapid advection in a fluid medium, causing turbulent flow in three dimensions. Accurate modeling of such turbulent flow is a problem of notorious computational difficulty, which is only starting to yield to solutions practical for the field of image synthesis (Foster 1997). For entertainment applications, empirical accuracy is not the goal; visual verisimilitude is, and visual novelty might prove even more useful.

Figure 6a.   QAEB-traced cloud with multiple scattering.

Figure 6b. Quantization artifacts due to large ray-marching stride.

Figure 6c. Jittered, large strides.

The film Dante's Peak required effects simulating the fast-moving, highly destructive cloud of hot volcanic ash known as a *pyroclastic flow*. At the time, the author had already developed the realistic hypertexture cloud model just described. That model was originally designed to serve as a testbed for the diffi-cult problem of modeling the anisotropic, high-albedo multiple scattering illumi-nation required for truly realistic rendering of clouds, as seen in Plate 13.2. That cloud model can be extended to model billowing in relatively simple way.

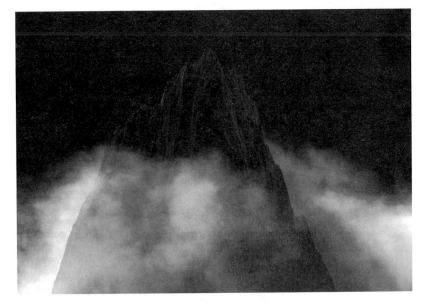

Figure 7. QAEB-traced scene with volumetric shadowing.

Our first attempt consisted of a swarm of cloudlets animated in the Alias Dynamation particle system package. This approach yielded good results when the animation consisted simply of sweeping the swarm of cloudlet-fields through a static texture space. A "popping" of high frequencies is inevitable in such a scheme, because the higher frequency details change faster than those of lower frequency, as the cloud front advances through texture space. The result was an explosive quality in the advancing cloud, which seemed appropriate. However, the director, citing footage of real volcanic clouds, requested a dynamic, billowing quality wherein the cloud appears to turn inside out as it evolves along its forward direction. This lead to the solution presented here.

A single cloudlet can be made to appear to billow by scaling the domain of the fractal function, relative to the "forward" direction of the billowing. The scaling is of the angle a given sample makes with that axis with time (see Figure 8). The result of this domain distortion is that, as the sample point is rotated toward the forward direction in magnitude proportional to the angle, cloud features appear to rotate towards a singularity opposite the "forward" direction.

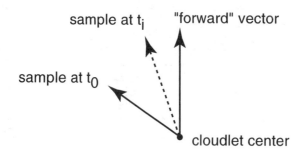

Figure 8. Rotation of samples with time in the billowing scheme.

Features get stretched longitudinally with time in this scheme. To ameliorate objectionable artifacts arising from this, the distorted, "old" texture is rolled off with time and replaced with a "young," undistorted texture that is in turn rolled off as it ages. This proceeds cyclically, yielding a cyclic model. This cyclic nature is disguised, visually, by growth in size of the cloudlet with time. For details on how this is accomplished, see the code on the CD-ROM.

Fireballs

Fireballs may be simulated by animating a color map that varies from white through yellow, orange, and red to black, as in the "flame" shader in Chapter 11. This map is indexed by radius (hotter toward the center) and time (cooling to black with age). The map color is used as the cloud texture color. Fireballs can render more efficiently than clouds, as they are self-luminous and require no illumination or shadow calculations. Preliminary models of such CG pyrotechnics were developed for a bid for certain effects scenes in the film Air Force One.[6] These early tests showed considerable promise; improved models are under development at the time of this writing.

---

[6] For examples of early animation tests, see http://www.seas.metacreations/peoplemusgrave/animations.html.

Psychedelic Clouds

As noted in Chapter 11, a vector-valued fBm can be interpreted as an rgb color vector and used to color a cloud to get a fantastical coloration, as seen in Plate 13.3. The animation "Comet Leary"[7] was accomplished with this model, by sweeping the hypertexture through five spherical weighting fields of successively decreasing density. Though not a convincing simulation of turbulent flow, it is a simple model yielding a visually appealing effect. The GIT scheme described in Chapter 11 could be used to obtain greater control over stochastic coloring.

Conclusions

We have demonstrated a numerical algorithm for ray tracing implicit procedural functions, with adaptive level of detail. It is simple, surprisingly fast, and general to all continuous functions $F:R^n{\rightarrow}R$. It features a screen space geometric error bounded by a user-specified value. The described speedup scheme, which is essential to achieving reasonable performance in rendering height fields, is general to all incremental height field ray tracing schemes. The stride we employ is the most conservative possible. It may be possible to use more sophisticated methods, such as Lipschitz conditions [(Standler 1994), (Worley 1996)] to speed rendering by extending the average stride length. The demonstrated speed of this algorithm is surprising; this speed is conjectured to be linked to the algorithm's simplicity, which allows it to reside entirely in cache memory for near-optimum microprocessor performance.

We have adapted the method to render measured height field data sets to add adaptive level of detail. For this application, one simply constrains the fractal function F by the measured data to render such data sets with added stochastic detail. The lowest frequency in the added fractal detail should be close to that of the post spacing in the measured data set.

We have also extended the method to procedural hypertextures, with a corresponding increase in rendering time. The results have been cloud models of unprecedented realism, some promising synthetic pyrotechnic effects, and some gratuitous psychedelia.

---

[7] Also available at http://www.metacreations/people/musgrave/animations.html.

Appendix A. C code implementing QAEB tracing.

```c
        /* determines 3D position along ray at distance t */
#define RAY_POS(ray,t,pos) \
            {(pos)->x = (ray)->origin.x + t*(ray)->dir.x; \
             (pos)->y = (ray)->origin.y + t*(ray)->dir.y; \
             (pos)->z = (ray)->origin.z + t*(ray)->dir.z; }

typedef struct {        /* catch-all type for 3-D vectors and positions */
        double x;
        double y;
        double z;
} Vector;


        /* returns TRUE if HF intersected, FALSE otherwise */
Boolean
Intersect_Terrain(int row, int column, double epsilon, Ray *ray, Hit *hit )
{
double  d, /* ray parameter, equal to distance travelled */
        alt,                            /* alt at current step */
        prev_d,                         /* d at last step */
        prev_alt;                       /* alt at last step */
Vector  position,                       /* current position along ray */
        prev_position;                  /* previous position along ray */

if ( row == 0 ) {       /* if at bottom of bottom-to-top rendering */
        d = near_clip_dist;             /* init march stride */
        RAY_POS( ray, d, &prev_position );      /* init previous 3-D position */
        prev_alt = Displacement( prev_position, d ); /* evaluate the HF function */
} else {        /* (this scheme is valid only for vertical columns) */
        d = prev_d = prev_dist[column]; /* start at final d of prev. ray in column */
        prev_position = prev_pos[column];
        prev_alt = prev_alts[column];
}

while ( d < far_clip_dist ) {   /* the QAEB ray march loop */
        d += d * epsilon;                       /* update the marching stride */
        RAY_POS( ray, d, &position );           /* get current 3-D position */
        alt = Displacement( position, d );      /* evaluate the HF function */
        if ( position.z < alt ) {               /* surface penetrated */
          Intersect_Surface( prev_alt, alt, d*epsilon, d,
                                position, prev_position, ray, hit );
            prev_dist[column] = prev_d;         /* update prev. distance data */
            prev_alts[column] = prev_alt;
            prev_pos[column] = prev_position;
            return( TRUE );
        }
        prev_d = d;
```

```
        prev_alt = alt;
        prev_position = position;
}

/* exceeded far clip distance; update "prev_dist" appropriately & exit. */
prev_dist[column] = d;
        return( FALSE );

} /* Intersect_Terrain() */
```

Appendix B. C code for intersection and surface normal.

```
            /* places a-b into c */
#define VEC_SUB(a,b,c)          {(c)->x = (a).x-(b).x;   \
                                 (c)->y = (a).y-(b).y;   \
                                 (c)->z = (a).z-(b).z;}

            /* places aXb into c */
#define CROSS(a,b,c)            {(c)->x = (a.y * b.z) - (a.z * b.y);    \
                                 (c)->y = (a.z * b.x) - (a.x * b.z);    \
                                 (c)->z = (a.x * b.y) - (a.y * b.x);}

        /* assigns ray/surface intersection and surface normal */
void
Intersect_Surface( double z_near, double z_far, double epsilon, double distance,
        Vector position, Vector prev_position, Ray *ray, HitData *hit )
{
        Vector  p_r,    /* point to the right, relative to ray dir and "up" */
                v_d,    /* vector from prev_position to position */
                v_l,    /* vector from prev_position to p_r */
                n;      /* surface normal */

            /* first construct three points that lie on the surface */
        prev_position.z = z_near;
        position.z = z_far;
            /* construct a point one error-width to right */
        p_r.x = prev_position.x + epsilon*camera.right_dir.x;
        p_r.y = prev_position.y + epsilon*camera.right_dir.y;
        p_r.z = prev_position.z + epsilon*camera.right_dir.z;
        p_r.z = Displacement( p_r, distance );

        /* get two vectors in the surface plane; cross for surface normal */
        VEC_SUB( position, prev_position, &v_d );
        Normalize( &v_d );
        VEC_SUB( p_r, prev_position, &v_l );
```

```
        Normalize( &v_l );
        CROSS( v_l, v_d, &n );
        Normalize( &n );

            /* assign the various hit data */
        hit->distance = distance;
        hit->intersect = prev_position;
        hit->normal = n;

} /* Intersect_Surface() */
```

Atmospheric Models 14

F. Kenton Musgrave, Larry Gritz, and Steven Worley

Introduction

Again, this chapter is highly technical and may only be of interest to mathematically minded programmers. And again, you might just want to read this introduction, which is written at a fairly conversational level. The rest of this chapter was originally written as a technical paper, so the bulk of the prose is pretty dry and terse.

Rendering realistic atmospheric effects involves three distinct elements: scattering models, geometric atmospheric density distribution (GADD) models, and numerical integration schemes for each. We present a series of simple, continuous GADD models of increasing geometric fidelity to spherical planetary atmospheres and integration schemes for each. We describe a RenderMan implementation of a planetary atmosphere and a general GADD integration scheme with bounded numerical error. We also suggest a simplified approximation of Rayleigh scattering. These models are distinctly nonphysical, ontogenetic models designed to be useful for production image synthesis rather than to provide accurate simulations. The GADDs we present and their associated integration schemes can, however, be coupled to published physical scattering models to augment the accuracy of those models.

Landscape painters have known for hundreds of years (Gedzelman 1991) that *aerial perspective*, the bluing and loss of contrast with distance, is the primary visual cue indicating large physical scale in a rendering.[1] These effects are due to atmospheric scattering of light, as described by the Rayleigh and Mie scattering models. Previous authors [(Klassen 1987), (Nishita 1993), (Tadamura 1993)] have presented physical models of such scattering. Efficiency of light scattering is modulated in part by the density of the atmosphere, which in turn varies spatially. This variation is not only with altitude: Altitude is a function of radius from the center of a planet, thus at the largest scales, the atmosphere must curve around a planet. We call a model describing the spatial distribution of atmospheric density *geometric atmospheric density distribution*, or *GADD*. In (Klassen 1987) the GADD consists of two horizontal slabs of constant density; (Nishita 1993) uses concentric shells of linearly interpolated density. We present some continuous GADDs to improve upon those models.

The global context for a landscape is the surface of a planet. In that context, all optical paths (defined as a ray's extent in a participating medium) are finite, as they either intersect a surface, are absorbed or scattered, or exit the atmosphere due to its curvature around the planet. The spatial distribution of a GADD can affect its accuracy as a function of scale: The simplest (homogeneous) GADD is accurate for small scales, an intermediate-scale model may take into account change in density with height, while a globally accurate GADD should take into account both change in density with altitude and the curvature of the atmosphere. (Modeling the true complexity of atmospheric structure remains impractical.) We will describe both locally accurate and more globally accurate GADD models, along with methods for integrating their optical density along arbitrary ray paths. The local GADD models may be integrated analytically; we will describe numerical integration schemes for the global GADD functions. We also suggest a simple, computationally minimal approximation of Rayleigh scattering, though nonphysical, produces an artistically sufficient model of aerial perspective without the unnecessary complications of physical models.

Though the models presented here are not physical models, they may in some cases represent improvements over published physical models. We claim that they are visually effective and that they are recommended by Occam's razor due to their simplicity. Most are not particularly novel, as they appear to have been repeatedly reinvented by graphics researchers. Nevertheless, they have yet to be described in the mainstream graphics literature.

---

[1] Shannon (Shannon 1995) points out that artists break aerial perspective into two components: *atmospheric perspective* and *color perspective*. The former is the change in contrast with distance, due to noncolored haze. The latter is the change in color with distance, light backdrops becoming redder and dark ones bluer, due to Rayleigh scattering. For more on this topic see http://www.seas.metacreations/people/musgrave/ 4_persp.html.

Blinn (Blinn 1982) points out that atmospherics involve two distinct types of models: scattering models and density distribution models. We assert that integration schemes for these models constitute a third essential element. Our goal is to address all three elements, to visual satisfaction, in as little computation as possible.

For our discussion, we define the *optical path* as the extent of a ray's passage through an atmosphere, *scattering* as redirection of direct illumination from a light source (implying single scattering) into the optical path and towards the view point, *out-scattering* as redirection of light out of an optical path towards the view point, and *extinction* as the cumulative effect of both out-scattering and absorption along the path.

Beer's Law and Homogeneous Fog

As a light ray traverses an optical path, some light is extinguished and some light may be added by emission and scattering. As described in (Max 1986) the sum of these effects can describe, physically, the behavior of a participating medium. (We discuss only atmospheres here, not general participating media such as glass, water, smoke, flames, and so forth.)

The effect of an atmosphere on the intensity of a light ray can be described by the differential equation $dI = \sigma(\vec{x}) + E(\vec{x})d\vec{x}$, where $\vec{x}$ is the position in three dimensions, $\sigma(\vec{x})$ describes extinction per unit length, and $E(\vec{x})$ describes emission and scattering per unit length into the optical path. When σ and E are proportional to one another and are functions solely of position x, we can define *optical depth* τ as $\tau = \int_0^{t_e} \sigma(\vec{x})dt$, the integral over the optical path of the GADD $\sigma(\vec{x})$. As in (Haines, 1989) we index the position along the ray by t, which ranges from 0 to t_e. Beer's Law gives a physical solution to this simple model and gives us the transparency T over the optical path as a function of τ: $T = e^{-\tau}$. For a homogeneous and isotropic GADD (i.e., $\sigma = c$, a constant), we have $\tau = ct_e$. Such homogeneous fog is fairly common in renderers; its effectiveness is due to its embodiment of a simple but physically accurate scattering model.

For simplicity, we consider extinction over the optical path to be 1-T. This extinguished portion of the intensity is replaced with the atmosphere color as a direct consequence of the $E(\vec{x})$ term in the differential equation above. In the models we present below, we ignore emission[2] but engineer the absorption rate σ to vary spatially. After obtaining τ by integrating σ, we may use Beer's Law to accurately compute the true effect of the atmosphere, given a scattering model. We therefore concentrate most of the rest of our presentation on nonhomogeneous density models and their integration.

Exponential Mist

A useful GADD for landscape renderings has a density distribution which varies as e^{-z} where z is altitude relative to a horizontal plane. It features local fidelity to Nature, as atmospheric optical density is known to vary exponentially with altitude (Lynch 1991). Behavior of this GADD can be parameterized as $\sigma = Ae^{-Bz}$, where A controls the overall fog density and B controls the falloff of the density with altitude. Its effectiveness in a landscape rendering is illustrated in Plate 14.2. This GADD may be integrated analytically:

$$\tau = t_e \int_{z_o}^{z_e} e^{-z} dz = \frac{At_e}{Bz_d} \left(e^{-(z_o + z_d t_e)} - e^{-z_o} \right)$$

where z_0 is the z coordinate of the ray origin and z_d is the z component of the ray's normalized direction vector. For very small z_d, corresponding to nearly horizontal rays, we substitute $\tau = At_e e^{-Bz_o}$, the asymptotic value of equation (1) as z_d goes to zero, to prevent division by zero. This GADD has unbounded optical paths for horizontal rays. The optical path of such rays is ultimately limited by the finite numerical representation of infinity in the renderer; this value can be massaged to limit integration.

A Radially-Symmetric Planetary Atmosphere

More realistic on large scales, because of the infinite optical paths cited above, is a GADD that varies exponentially with radius from a central point. For such a

---

[2] Although we do not model emission, a similar effect is nonetheless obtained. These are a nonphysical scattering models, in which conservation of energy is not maintained. Because the atmosphere color does not depend on illumination, except in our last model, energy may appear in the optical path without illumination (e.g., the white color of an atmosphere that is actually in shadow). This nonphysicality can be used to artistic advantage, as illustrated in Plate 14.1, a rendering without any light sources. The color variation in that atmosphere is attained basically by reversing the order of the rgb values for the extinction coefficients on our simplified Rayleigh scattering model from those used to get blue sky.

GADD, radius r is related to position t along the ray as $r(t) = \sqrt{\alpha^2 + 2\beta t + t^2}$ where α and β are constants determined by the ray path and the origin, or center, of the radial fog. This function forms a hyperbola. With σ given as this function of r instead of computing $\int \sigma(t)dt$, we must compute $\int \sigma\left(\sqrt{\alpha^2 + 2\beta t + t^2}\right)dt$ which can prove challenging.

A simple radial GADD is $\sigma(r) = e^{-r^2}$. This function cannot be integrated in closed form, but a numerical approximation is available in the C and FORTRAN math libraries in the *error function*: $erf(x) \approx \frac{2}{\pi}\int_0^x e^{-t^2}$. This GADD may be parameterized as $\sigma = Ae^{-Br^2}$ where A controls the overall density and B modulates falloff with radius. This GADD can provide convincing visual results (see Plate 11.2).

Consider integrating this GADD. For a ray origin $\vec{r}_o$ and unit direction $\vec{x}$, and a GADD origin $\vec{o}$, we have $r(t) = \sqrt{\alpha^2 + 2\beta t + t^2}$, where $\alpha = |\vec{r}_o - \vec{o}|$ and $\beta = \vec{r}_d \bullet (\vec{r}_o - \vec{o})$. We must compute $\tau = \int_0^{t_e} Ae^{-B\left(\alpha^2 + 2\beta t + t^2\right)}dt$. A solution to this integral is given by:

$$\tau \approx \frac{A\sqrt{\pi}e^{-B\left(\alpha^2 - \beta^2\right)}}{2\sqrt{B}}\left(erf\left(\sqrt{B}(t_e + \beta)\right) - erf\left(\beta\sqrt{B}\right)\right)$$

Unfortunately, the more physically plausible GADD $\sigma = e^{-r}$ cannot be reduced to such an expression, due to the complex dependence of r on t. Thus we may require a numerical integration method, ideally one that is tailored specifically to the hyperbolic-quadratic exponential form of the equation and specific accuracy needed for rendering. We discuss this in a later section; for now we digress to scattering.

A Minimal Rayleigh Scattering Approximation

We require at least a first approximation of Rayleigh scattering to obtain proper coloration of the atmosphere. Single Rayleigh scattering adds blue light along an illuminated optical path; this causes the sky to be blue. Rayleigh out-scattering along the optical path reddens light coming from the background causing, for instance, sunsets to be red. Similarly, direct light flux available for scattering is reddened; this effect is what often makes sunlight yellow. Though more elaborate and accurate models are available [(Klassen 1987), (Nishita 1993)] we have found the following extremely simple approximation to be sufficient for first-order visual realism. This model is responsible for all the atmospheric coloration effects seen in the color plates from Chapters 10–15.

In our discussion so far, τ has been treated as scalar value. In λ (wavelength) dependent scattering, τ is a vector over λ, each λ sample having an independent value of τ. For Rayleigh scattering, $\tau \propto \lambda^{-4}$. (Klassen 1987). Each component of the τ vector requires a separate evaluation of the $e^{-\tau_\lambda}$ expression of Beer's Law. Time complexity then varies linearly with the number of λ samples. The tristimulus nature of color vision dictates a minimum of three values for full-color images; hence the familiar triad of rgb samples. Larger numbers of samples, taken in the CIE XYZ color space may yield more accurate colors (Hall 1989).

We simply note that expanding τ to an rgb vector can give a computationally minimal and visually pleasing approximation of Rayleigh scattering (see Plate 14.3 and all color plates from Chapters 10–15). Correct discrete numerical integration of single scattering along the optical path requires ray marching with computation at each sample of the extinction of the direct illumination available for scattering. In the absence of such a correct but expensive scheme, extinction due to Rayleigh scattering along the optical path can approximated by using a yellow-brown (smog-colored) atmosphere. In Plate 14.3 the rgb color of the atmosphere is $(1.0, \ 0.65, \ 0.5)$ and $\tau = \ (3.0, \ 7.5, \ 60.0)$. Observe that the atmosphere is blue against a black background, and a white background is filtered to orange, as illustrated in Plate 14.5. Plate 14.3 illustrates that the horizon still appears white against a black background, largely due to psychoperceptual reasons—it is actually no more white than the smoggy atmosphere color. We recommend this simplest model for maximally efficient rendering.

To illustrate their simplicity, we now present pseudocode for the $\sigma = e^{-r^2}$ GADD with the Rayleigh scattering approximation.

```
/* compute distance from ray origin to closest approach */
adjacent_leg = ray.origin - fog.origin;
beta = DOT(ray.dir, adjacent_leg);
nearval = erf(sqrt(B) * beta);
farval = erf(sqrt(B) * (beta + t_e));
/* compute distance from fog origin to ray's closest approach */
r_c_squared = DOT(adjacent_leg,adjacent_leg) - beta*beta;
/* evaluate tau using constants to match Plate 15.4 */
tau.red = A/sqrt(B)*exp(-B*r_c_squared)*(farval - nearval)
tau.green = tau.red*2.25;
```

```
tau.blue = tau.red*21.0;
T = exp(-tau.red);
red = endpoint.red*T + (1.-T)*1.0; /* atm. red == 1.0 */
T = exp(-tau.green);
green = endpoint.green*T + (1.-T)*0.7; /* atm. green == 0.7 */
T = exp(-tau.blue);
blue = endpoint.blue*T + (1.-T)*0.6; /* atm. blue == 0.6 */
```

Trapezoidal Quadrature of $\sigma = e^{-r}$ GADD and RenderMan Implementation

For GADDs that are not integrable analytically, we must develop numerical quadrature (i.e., integration) schemes. The quadrature method may be arbitrarily sophisticated, according to the required accuracy. We now present an adaptive trapezoidal quadrature with sufficient accuracy for visual purposes and a RenderMan implementation of it.

Perhaps the most accurate, simple radial GADD is:

$$\sigma(r) = Ae^{-Br}$$

where A modulates density at sea level, B is the falloff coefficient, and r is the height above sea level. For exponential GADDs, the density and its rate of change are greatest close to the planet surface. This indicates quadrature with an adaptive step size. Step size should be inversely proportional to the local magnitude of σ. Thus where the density (and its rate of change) are high, the step size is small; where the density is low, the step size is relatively large. To speed up rendering, we can employ a trivial reject if the ray never comes within a minimal distance to the GADD center, returning zero when we know the integral must be very small. Also, we can integrate separately forward and backward from the point of closest approach; this may increase accuracy through preventing overly large step sizes, by basing step size on the interval end of higher density. At each step we sample both the GADD and the illumination at the sample point.

Trapezoidal integration implies an assumption that the GADD varies linearly between the samples. The optical depth of a given interval is then $\tau = \frac{\Delta}{2}\left(\sigma_i + \sigma_{i-1}\right)$ where Δ is the step size, and σ_t and σ_{t-1} are the current and previous GADD density values. Differential extinction $dO = 1 - e^{-\tau}$ and scattering $dC = I\left(1 - e^{-\tau}\right)$, where I is the direct illumintion intensity at the sample point.

These differential values are then accumulated similarly to (Drebin 1988). The RenderMan implementation operates in such a way that the atmosphere is shadowed where the light source is occluded by mountains, the planet, and so forth. If occluding features may be small, one must specify suitably low upper bounds on step sizes to prevent undersampling of shadow features.

Our implementation is as a volume shader in the RenderMan Shading Language (Upstill 1990). A simplified version of the shader is presented below. In Plate 14.6 a similarly structured light source shader causes the local illumination to undergo proper extinction. This and the full, more accurate volume shader are available on the CD-ROM.

Simplified RenderMan Atmosphere Shader

```
/* For ray index t, return the GADD (g) and illumination (li). */
#define GADD(li,g) \
        PP = origin + t * IN; \
        g = (density * exp(-falloff*(length(PP)-1))); \
        PW = transform ("shader", "current", PP); \
        li = 0; \
        illuminance (PW, point(0,0,1), PI) { li += Cl; }


volume radial_atmosphere (float density = 3, falloff = 200;
  float integstart = 0, integend = 10, rbound = 1.05;
  float minstepsize = 0.001, maxstepsize = 1, k = 35;)
{
 float t, tau, ss, dtau, last_dtau, te;
 color li, last_li, lighttau;
 point origin = transform ("shader", P+I);
 point incident = vtransform ("shader", -I);
 point IN = normalize (incident);
 point PP, PW;
 color Cv = 0, Ov = 0;   /* net color & opacity over optical path */
 color dC, dO;      /* differential color & opacity */

 /* compute optical path length */
 te = min (length (incident), integend) - 0.0001;
 /* Integrate forward from the eye point */
 t = integstart;
 GADD (li, dtau)
 ss = min (clamp (1/(k*dtau+.001), minstepsize, maxstepsize), te-t);
 t += ss;
 while (t <= te) {
        last_dtau = dtau; last_li = li;
```

```
GADD (li, dtau)
/* Our goal now is to find dC and dO, the color and opacity
 * of the portion of the interval covered by this step. */
tau = .5 * ss * (dtau + last_dtau);
lighttau = .5 * ss * (li*dtau + last_li*last_dtau);
dO = 1 - color (exp(-tau), exp(-tau*2.25), exp(-tau*21));
dC = lighttau * dO;

/* Adjust Cv and Ov to account for dC and dO */
Cv += (1-Ov)*dC;
Ov += (1-Ov)*dO;
/* Select next step size and take a step */
ss = max (min (clamp (1/(k*dtau+.001),
                instepsize, maxstepsize), te-t), 0.0005);

t += ss;
    }

/* Ci & Oi are the color and opacity of the background element.
Cv & Ov are color and
 *  opacity of the atmosphere along the viewing ray. Composite them together.
*/
 Ci = 15*Cv + (1-Ov)*Ci;
 Oi = Ov + (1-Ov)*Oi;
}
```

Numerical Quadrature with Bounded Error for General Radial GADDs

The above integration method for the e^{-r} GADD capitalizes on the smooth character of that GADD. As we may sometimes desire an error-bounded integration scheme suitable for more general radial GADDs, we now present such a scheme.

As τ may be evaluated for every ray in a rendering, we require efficiency in its computation. Our knowledge of the integrand may be used to derive a suitable algorithm. Consider the general radial GADD $\sigma(r(t))$ where

$$r(t) = \sqrt{\alpha^2 + 2\beta t + t^2}\,.$$

We can simplify by completing the square: $r(t) = \sqrt{(t - t_c)^2 + r_c^2}$ where r_c is the value of r at the closest point on the line containing the ray to the center $\vec{o}$ of the radial GADD and t corresponds to the t_c index at this closest approach. (This t_c might lie beyond the ray's extent on that line.) We can then make the substitution $s = t - t_c$ and rewrite the integral:

$$\tau = \int_0^{t_e} \sigma\left(\sqrt{\alpha^2 + 2\beta t + t^2}\right)dt = \int_{t_e}^{t_e - t_c} \sigma\left(\sqrt{s^2 + r_c^2}\right)ds$$

The integrand is symmetric about $s = 0$. If the limits of integration straddle 0, this symmetry can reduce the work of the numerical integrator by up to half. We can also specify a bounding radius for the atmosphere, that is, where the integral of an infinite optical path ultimately maps to a luminance value of zero. Let us specify this radius as r_{max}. Since $r = \sqrt{s^2 + r_c^2}$, the bound is $s = \pm\sqrt{r_{max}^2 - r_c^2}$. We can also trivially set $\tau = 0$ if $r_c > r_{max}$.

We are ultimately computing a transparency value that is in turn used to compute a quantized luminance sample. For 8-bit quantization, an error in $e^{-\tau}$ of less than $\varepsilon = \pm\frac{1}{512}$ is insignificant. The symmetric integrand and high error tolerance allow for a specialized adaptive integration routine. An outline of a simple algorithm of this type is given below; it returns a guaranteed bounded estimate for any radial GADD that decreases monotonically with radius.

1. Compute distance of closest approach r_c and ray index t_c at r_c.

2. If $r_c > r_{max}$ return 0. Let radial cutoff bound $s_m = \sqrt{r_{max}^2 - r_c^2}$. If $s_m > t_c$, return 0. Compute intgration bounds a and b: Set

    $$a = -\min(t_c, s_m). \text{ Set } b = -\min(t_e - t_c, s_m); \text{ if } b < -s_m, \text{return } 0.$$

3. If $a < 0$ and $b > 0$, define two "regions" $R^{[1,2]}$. Region $R^{[1]}$ has left bound $R_l^{[1]} = 0$, right bound $R_r^{[1]} = \min(-a, b)$, and a weight R_w of 2.0; region $R^{[2]}$ has right and left bounds $R_l^{[2]} = \min(-a, b)$ and $R_r^{[2]} = \max(-a, b)$, and a weight $R_w = 1.0$. Otherwise, make a single region with $R_l = a$ and $R_r = b$, with $R_w = 1.0$.

4. Compute the values of σ at left and right region bounds; label them $R_{\sigma l}$ and $R_{\sigma r}$. The maximum error $R_{\delta \tau}$ for the region, assuming Euler integration (i.e., the worst case), is $\left| R_{\sigma r} - R_{\sigma l} \right| \left(R_r - R_l \right) R_w$. The (trapezoidal) estimate for the region's integral R_τ is

$$\tfrac{1}{2} \left(R_{\sigma l} + R_{\sigma r} \right) \left(R_r - R_l \right)_.$$

5. The total error $\delta \tau = \sum_R R_{\delta \tau}$. The total integral estimate $\tau = \sum_R R_\tau$. If $\left(e^{\delta \tau - \tau} - e^{-\tau} \right) \leq \varepsilon$, return τ.

6. Find the region with the highest error estimate. Bisect that region; one evaluation of σ is required. Compute integral and error estimates for both new regions. Go to step 5.

Potential modifications to this algorithm include splitting several regions at a time to allow less frequent checks of the error criterion and using Simpson's Rule for integration.

Conclusions

We have presented a series of GADD models of increasing fidelity to the geometry of a planetary atmosphere. We have suggested a Rayleigh scattering model at level of fidelity comparable to the ambient/diffuse/specular surface illumination model (i.e., highly nonphysical but simple, intuitive, and useful). We have illustrated the successful use of these models in image synthesis. Occam's razor may recommend these models due to their simplicity; indeed some are simple enough to be candidates for hardware implementation in real-time graphics systems. RenderMan implementations of these models are available on the CD-ROM accompanying this book.

Genetic Textures | 5

F. Kenton Musgrave

Introduction: The Problem of Parameter Proliferation

As we saw in Chapter 11, one problem confronting us in the construction of procedural textures or shaders is that of *parameter proliferation*. The "terran" texture has 22 user-definable parameters, plus some 51 hard-coded constants hidden in the shader code. The resluts of changes to these parameters are often far from obvious and sometimes downright bizarre. For use in a production environment by artists who didn't write the shader, this kind of situation is simply absurd. Most users of shaders—digital artists—don't know about, or want to be confronted with, the rich logical complexity and odd machinations of the shader's operation. They generally have another job to get done: making certain images, within rigid constraints on time and quality. It is unfair and counterproductive to require them to learn about the methodology of shaders. And yet the gaea shader illustrates how, in fact, shaders are built and operate.

On the other side, neither is it all that easy for the programmer or shader writer to define and implement all those parameters. It's tedious, arduous, and generally time-consuming to write and refine such complex texture code. The ultimate product that the programmer should ideally deliver is a simple, intuitive user interface to the elaborate shader that's easy for an artist, with no programming or math background, to understand and use. Unfortunately, if effective shader-writing is a black art, then devising such interfaces is a black hole.[1]

A Useful Model: Aesthetic N-Spaces

Here is one way of thinking about the textures and their controls that I find useful: They represent an *aesthetic n-space*. The "aesthetic" part simply means that changing values of the parameters affects the aesthetics of the result. The "n-space" part is more subtle. The "n" in "n-space" is simply some whole, positive number, from zero to infinity. Each separate one of those n numbers represents a *degree of freedom*. Think of a degree of freedom as a new direction in which we can move. For $n = 1$ we have a line and exactly one axis along which we may move in two directions, call them left and right, for convenience. For $n = 2$ we have a plane, wherein we may move left and right and, say, forward and backward. For $n = 3$, we have the familiar 3-space in which we live, wherein we may move left and right, forward and backward, and up and down. When n equals 4 or higher, we move into the higher dimensions for which human intuition fails us but into which mathematicians never hesitate to go.

In this model, the "terran" texture presented in Chapter 12 represents a 73-dimensional aesthetic space! No wonder you wouldn't want to hand that shader over to the hapless digital artist as written. Believe me, it took more than a few hours to define and determine values for those 73 parameters, too. How can we deal with these two problems, the overwhelmed user and the overworked programmer? *Genetic programming* can provide a fascinating solution to both. But before I describe exactly what genetic programming is, let me first describe some motivating concepts behind our process.

---

[1] I hate to sound cynical here, but ever since Gavin Miller first pointed out this problem to me in 1988, when he was working at what is now Alias/Wavefront, I have been bemused by this problem. I have not met anyone who has an effective, general strategy for reducing a huge number of parameters to a few intuitively obvious sliders that maintain the power of the underlying functionality. I obtained direct experience in managing this problem when producing the Disney Cruise Lines commercial, where Mickey and Goofy are made out of clouds, at Digital Domain in the spring of 1997. In that case, we—the art director and myself—simply revealed parameters to the artists one at a time, as we perceived that they needed them or that the look would benefit from their knowing about them. The vast majority of parameter values were preset by myself, the programmer. Unfortunately, this requires that the programmer also be something of an artist, something that is not always possible to achieve in a production context.

The process of defining the n parameters in a procedural texture corresponds to the *creation* or *specification* of the n-space. The process of determining good values for the parameters may be thought of as *searching the n-space for local maxima of an aesthetic gradient function*.[2] This is an abstraction of which I am particularly fond: As we change the values of the parameters, we move about in the n-space, in a manner exactly analogous to the low-dimensional spaces described above. As we move about, the aesthetics change. How they change is determined by an entirely subjective aesthetic judgment on the part of the user. But clearly some sets of values will provide images that are "better" and other images that are "worse." The aesthetic gradient function is then the user's subjective evaluation of how the "goodness" of the result changes with changes in the parameter values, the gradient being between "better" and "worse." A local maximum represents a set of parameter values where, if any one is changed a little, the image gets worse. Thus we're in a position analogous to being on a local hilltop or local aesthetic maximum. Small movements in all directions in n-space correspond to moving downhill in terms of our aesthetics. Yet this hilltop is only local—there is no guarantee that, if we move far enough away from our current point, we'll cross the equivalent of some "aesthetic valley" and be able to climb up a higher hill to a better local aesthetic value. Such is life; I suppose it's better than poor Sisyphus's lot at any rate. The nice thing about this model of the creation and search of n-space, is that it is independent of the value of n and therefore of the complexity of the texture or shader.

Control Versus Automaticity

An inevitable outcome of the growth of complexity (e.g., the number of parameters) is that there arises an eternal tension, which is general to models for image synthesis: control versus clarity and ease of use. If you make things clear, simple, and easy for the user, you necessarily have to compromise control, because that control lies in the complexity of the procedures. If you give the user full control, the interface becomes overwhelming in its baroque complexity. Anyone who's used 3D modeling and/or rendering software, from low-end consumer to the top-of-the-line professional packages, has confronted this problem.

As we've tried to make clear through much of this book, the whole paradigm of proceduralism is intimately caught up with this idea of *amplification*, which I

---

[2] This model is based on what are called hill-climbing optimization methods, such as simulated annealing (Press 1986).

described in Chapter 10, whereby lots of visual expression issues from a relatively small number of controls, or parameters. Unfortunately, the flip side of this wonderful power is that automaticity implies lack of control. Just as in any human project large enough to require delegation of subtasks to colleagues, one abdicates full control over the results. Thus we may construct the beautiful planet Gaea, imbued with the capacity to be imaged at any range and/or field of view and resolution (see Figure 12.3 and Plate 12.2), from a very small amount of computer code, but we cannot, without compromising elegance, *control* any of the specific features found there. We only have global, qualitative controls.

Nevertheless, we can obtain some striking and useful[3] results. But what if we take this amplification/automaticity to its logical extreme and let the computer do *everything*? Then the user would simply sit back and pick and choose from various offerings, like some fickle child. In this paradigm, the computer simultaneously *specifies* and *searches* the aesthetic n-space. The method is spectacularly fecund in its creativity, wonderfully automatic (once a lot of programming has been done) but hard to direct to a desired end, for example, a wood grain texture. From a practical point of view, this last point may be a fatal flaw. Yet I'll describe the genetic programming paradigm here, because it illustrates the functional nature of procedural textures, clarifies through extreme abstraction how such textures are built, and simply because genetic programs are the most fun software systems I've ever played with. I'll describe the paradigm at a high level here. Details of implementation are tedious, while the concepts driving them are quite clear. Since I am, at the time of this writing, developing a genetic texture program commercially, and the company probably wouldn't be too happy with me if I gave the store away, we'll stick to the concepts. But rest assured that there are no magic secrets I'll keep from you.

A Model from Biology: Genetics and Evolution

Genetic programming starts with a model borrowed from biology and proceeds to use it by analogy. The idea was introduced to the computer graphics community by Karl Sims in his classic 1991 SIGGRAPH paper (Sims 1991). Sims in turn got the idea from Richard Dawkins' book *The Blind Watchmaker* (Dawkins 1987) and

---

[3] The bubbles spiraling off the propellers of the *Titanic* in the only all-CG scene in the movie—the underwater scene right after they decide to throttle up and use all the boilers in an attempt to set a speed record for an Atlantic crossing—were modeled by applying a multifractal RenderMan shader I wrote, applied to the surfaces of spheres, the dynamics of which were modeled using a particle system. The funny part about this project was that James Cameron, the movie's director, simply gave us footage of prop cavitation-bubbles from about eight different movies, telling us, "I hate these!" This defined what artists would call a *negative space* around the solution: what not to do, where not to go. We all have our strange terminologies when it comes to space!

the simple computer graphics program called "BioMorph" Dawkins uses to illustrate the power of the theory of evolution in explaining the origins and complexity of life on Earth. Unlike Dawkins, I assure you that I have no metaphysical ax to grind vis-á-vis the origins of life or competing religious and scientific models thereof. I simply have found genetic programming to be the coolest thing one can do with procedural textures and computer art!

We start with a few definitions that should be familiar from your high school biology classes. Recall that the *genotype* is the genetic description for a given organism. The genotype is encoded in a fantastically long molecule of *deoxyribonucleic acid*, or *DNA*. The genotype is a specific instance from a *genome*, as in the Human Genome Project, a major scientific initiative to map the general layout of all human genes. That is, the genome is general to a species and has variations among individuals, while the genotype is specific to a single organism. A *gene* is a specific part of the genome that encodes a certain function, generally instructions for building a certain biologically active protein.

The *phenotype* is the physical manifestation of the instructions encoded in the genotype: It is a specific organism, such as you or I. Your genotype is similar to mine, but they are not identical, so while we are both human beings, we are not identical twins or clones (I hope!). Different instances of a given genotype will, given similar environments during development, reliably give rise to a certain, well-defined phenotype, as with identical twins (who are, in fact, clones).

Charles Darwin's famous and controversial theory of evolution posits that life has literally risen from the primordial ooze through *evolution*—the refinement of genomes through what he called *natural selection*: the preferred survival and propagation of individuals whose genotype has given rise to a "more fit" phenotype.[4]

Natural selection acts on phenotypes. No progress would occur if the phenotypes didn't change over generations. In Nature they do, by two mechanisms: *mutation* and *sexual reproduction*. Mutation occurs through errors introduced in the DNA replication process and by direct alterations to DNA molecules by external mechanisms such as ionizing radiation (for example, ultraviolet light and radioactive decay byproducts). Sexual reproduction is presumed, in biology, to be a clever adaptation by higher organisms. In sexual reproduction, genes from two parents are mixed and matched to "reshuffle the deck," providing random combinations of proven genes. This is a safer strategy for productive change than the purely random variations provided by mutation, most of which presumably would not produce viable phenotypes.

---

[4] Note that Darwin's theory of evolution preceded the discovery of DNA by about a century. The theory of evolution is predicated only on the idea of *inheritance*, whereby offspring acquire the genetic information of their ancestors. It is in no way dependent on the mechanism for encoding or passing on that information. This independence helps bolster the analogy we're making here.

Evolution is the accumulation of "improvements" in the phenotypes through these changes, as culled by natural selection, in inheritable genomes. It can be convincingly argued to account for all the glorious complexity and variation in life on Earth, as Dawkins's series of books on the topic attempt to do.

I have come to think of DNA as being like the operating system, or *O/S*, of an organism, while the cells of which the organism is composed are like the computer on which the O/S runs. (Fortunately, the human O/S is generally more reliable than those we've devised for our computers.) The coding of both DNA and an O/S is very abstract: The program code that comprises a computer O/S bears little resemblance to the user interface it presents to us, just as the DNA molecule little resembles a hamster, a redwood tree, or you. Also similarly, both are highly nonportable: The encoding is practically worthless without the platform on which it is designed to execute. Hence you can't just install and run DOS on a Mac, nor can you put human DNA into a starfish cell nucleus and expect to grow a nice, healthy, clone human baby. This is a little unfortunate for our application here, as we'd like to have a universal computer-genome that would could be run on any computer, so that we could develop a kind of universal artificial life, or "A-life" as it's called.

The Analogy: Genetic Programming

What we're interested in here is procedural textures and how to create beautiful ones efficiently. Enter our analogy: We will regard the code that specifies a texture to be its genotype and an image of the resulting texture to be the corresponding phenotype. Evolution is directed by what I call *unnatural selection*:[5] God-like intervention by the user, deciding which phenotypes, and thus their underlying genotypes, survive and propagate. Change in the genome is accomplished by methods analogous to mutation and sexual reproduction: We design the program to introduce random variations in genotypes and to be able to share "genes" in an analogy to sexual reproduction.

What then, is a gene in a genetic texture program? As with DNA, it is a unit of genetic "code" specifying some functionality within the resulting texture, for example, an fBm procedure. DNA is composed of the four nucleic acids cytosine, guanine, adenosine, and thymine, commonly referred to by their initials C, G, A, and T. The DNA molecule is a long sequence of these *bases*, as they are called,

---

[5] I like this tongue-in-cheek term "unnatural selection" because it points out the artificial separation of humankind from Nature. In my view, humans and their actions are natural phenomena. If you disagree, I suggest you try separating humans entirely from Nature and see where that gets you!

paired across from one another in the famous double-helix. A certain functional sequence of bases can comprise a gene.

Our encoding scheme is a little different. Our bases are all complete functions, analogous in DNA more to genes than to bases. A combination of our bases can, however, function as a gene. The difference between genes and bases is that bases are *atomic*: Bases cannot be subdivided into smaller parts.

The encoding scheme for our genetic information is, rather than a linear sequence as in DNA, an *expression tree*, which is analogous to a genealogical family tree. (See Figure 1.) A tree is a special kind of graph. The graph is composed of *nodes*. There are two relevant kinds of relationships between nodes: *parent* and *child*, the meaning of which is obvious. There are three types of nodes: the *root* node at the top of the tree (though it might seem that it should be called the bottom), which has no parent and usually has children; *interior* nodes, which have both parents and children; and *leaf* nodes, which have parents but no children. The root node has to return three values to create an rgb value to display as the phenotype.

The expression tree operates via *functional composition*, described in Chapters 2 and 11 as "perturbation." The idea of functional composition is simply that a function takes as its input parameters, the output of another function or functions. We saw the effects of simple functional composition in those earlier chapters; now we take the idea to an extreme. In the expression tree, only leaf nodes provide values that are not determined by functions. (In fact, the leaf nodes are usually simple linear functions of x, y, or z; that is, they are simply the x, y, or z value of the point where the texture is being evaluated. The rest are simply random numbers.)

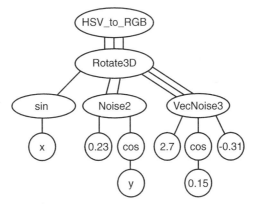

Figure 1.   An expression tree. The circles are nodes; the lines between them are *links* **representing relationships.**

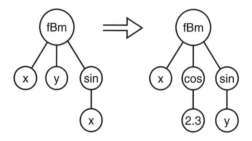

Figure 2.   Mutation in an expression tree.

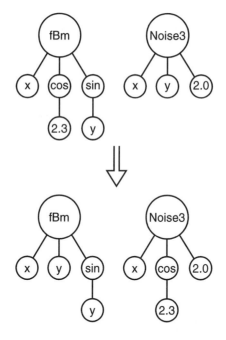

Figure 3.   Sexual reproduction between two expression trees.

Implementation

The expression tree is perhaps most easily implemented in a high-level, functional language such as Lisp, as in Sims's original genetic texture program. Unfortunately, Lisp is slow, unless you happen to have something like a

Connection Machine 2. Indeed, my first experience with this paradigm was running Karl's code on a CM-2 using 16,000 processors. However, pedestrian users like you and I generally require a more efficient implementation for our paltry little processors. In fact, I'm now developing my genetic texture code primarily on a laptop! Steven Rooke has informed me that ditching Lisp in favor of C or C++ can immediately give a speedup by a factor of up to 100.

It turns out that genetic programming is a perfect application for C++. The data structures required for the various types of nodes, their relationships, and the operations defined upon them, are succinctly described in C++ classes. The devil is in the details, mostly in memory management. For efficiency, I have each evaluation of a function in the tree process and entire scanline's worth of data. (This saves a whole lot of tree traversals that would be necessary if you evaluate the tree pixel by pixel.) For large trees, this can get into a lot of memory. Again for efficiency, I do all my own memory management in the program, because the C and C++ memory allocation routines "malloc" and "new" are relatively slow. So I end up with piles of pointers and memory pools—and lots of room for bugs. But that's just standard programming and thus outside the scope of this book.

There are two interesting issues in programming genetic textures that I'd like to point out: the meaning of the root node, in terms of color, and the effect that a given library of genetic bases has on the kinds of images produced.

Interpretation of the Root Node

Ultimately, we want to make color images. Thus each pixel will require a separate value for red, green, and blue. A solution that immediately pops into mind is that we simply have the root node consist of three separate subtrees, one each for red, green, and blue. In practice, though, this is usually unsatisfactory: You tend to end up with unrelated, overlaid images in red, green, and blue. You can interpret the values as lying in another color space, such as HLS (hue/luminosity/saturation), but similar problems remain. The usual solution is to have the root function return a single value that serves as an index into a color lookup table. This brings up the separate and unrelated problem of generation of, and making changes to, that lookup table. It is easy enough to automatically generate random color maps (Musgrave 1991), but the obvious solutions are a little inelegant compared to the rest of our fully procedural paradigm.

The solution I'm currently using is based on the ideas behind the random-color textures presented in Chapter 11. The root node comprises a three-vector valued function, which has been passed through a random rotation matrix to correlate, in the final rgb color space, the influence of the three components of the vector. Mathematically, we'd say that the three vector components are then *linear combinations* of the *basis vectors* that correspond to red, green, and blue. That is, rather than having each component of the 3-vector mapping to only red, green, or blue, each component contributes to all of red, green, and blue, albeit indirectly through a final HLS to rgb transform (see the expression tree in Figure 1). From a mathematical perspective this insight is obvious; my apologies if it's not exactly clear when translated into English prose. Such is the divergence of the two modes of thinking and communication. But it's cool to see again, as in the GIT schemes described in Chapter 11, that a mathematical perspective can provide useful aesthetic insights.

This approach is not without its own problems. First, constructing a random rotation matrix requires at least six input values: two—altitude and azimuth—to specify the random rotation axis, one to specify the angle of rotation, and three to specify the vector being transformed by the resulting matrix. This implies a bushy tree at the root, which in turn implies increased evaluation time. It also implies a rather large amount of storage in the vector class—a maximum of six double-precision floating-point numbers,[6] which adds up when you need to store a lot of vectors. This approach also tends to consistently produce rainbows, due to the final HLS to rgb transform. These rainbows become boring to annoying but can be excised through the process of unnatural selection. The advantage of the approach, as I see it, is that it nicely preserves the pure functional paradigm.

The Library of Genetic Bases

An important aspect of any genetic image-generation program is its library of bases, the functions out of which the expression trees are formed. This library literally provides the expressive vocabulary of the system. Thus different genetic texture programs have different "looks." Karl Sims's system has a library of primitive mathematical functions such as sine, log, arc tangent, and so on, as well as iterated function systems (Sims 1991) that give rise to characteristic fractal patterns. Steven Rooke's system (http://www.concentric.net/~Srooke/) is heavy on deterministic fractal functions that are generally iterations on the complex plane, including a genetic generalization of the kinds of functions people experiment with in the well-known Fractint freeware program. My own system

---

[6] My experience indicates that single-precision floating point does not provide sufficient accuracy for the kind of multiple functional composition involved in genetic textures.

(http://www.metacreations/people/musgrave/mutatis.html) is based primarily on the kind of random fractal functions described in Chapters 10 and 12. Thus each system tends to create images with a certain, fairly consistent character. Certainly each produces images that the others are not capable of generating, due to the expressive limitations of their respective libraries of bases.

My own peculiar base functions tend to be very natural looking, as they were originally honed for the modeling of natural phenomena such as mountains, clouds, and water. They thus tend to generate images that look like they were executed in a natural medium, such as oil paint. In fact, one of my main motivations in going into this area was to automate the generation of painterly textures such as that seen in Plate 11.8. If I succeed in creating a system that can create what Mandelbrot would call "forgeries" of abstract impressionist paintings, I'll be very happy indeed. (Examples of my system's output are seen in Plates 15.1 and 15.2.)

Note that the longer you work with a genetic program, the more "evolved" the results become. That is because as you accumulate a library of "fit" individuals, they can trade genetic information via sexual reproduction. Indeed, one feature of my program is being able to have individuals breed with the entire population of saved genomes, in a sort of orgiastic exchange of genetic information. An effect of this continued evolution is that subtrees become genes in their own right, being swapped in whole in the breeding process. Thus the "library" of genes can grow both in size and complexity as evolution proceeds. (We are now referring to a single function—what computer scientists would call a "primitive" or "atomic" function—as a base, and a tree of any size as a gene.)

Other Examples of Genetic Programming and Genetic Art

Karl Sims has taken this paradigm of genetic programming and genetic art farther than the rest of us. For example, he evolves the behaviors of three-dimensional textures (Sims 1991) and virtual creatures (Sims 1994) (see http://www.biota.org/ conf97/ksims.html). William Latham (Todd and Latham 1992) has done some remarkable work in a system designed to generate 3D sculptures that can bear uncanny resemblances to creatures from the Cambrian epoch of life on Earth (http://www.artworks.co.uk/). Roman Verostko—http://www.mcad.edu/home/ faculty/verostko/ EPIGENET.html—employs the related concept of *epigenesis*, or the unfolding of form in the phenotype in the process of growth, in his plotter-generated artworks.

This is by no means an exhaustive listing of artists and scientists working in this exciting area. A search on the World Wide Web will turn up a plethora of related sites. (A good general site is Linda Moss's at http://www.marlboro.edu/~lmoss/planhome.) For more on the concepts of genetic programming, see Koza's exhaustive treatment (Koza, 1992).

A Final Distinction: Genetic Programming Versus Genetic Algorithms

In the literature, you'll read of genetic programming and genetic algorithms. The former is what I've described here, wherein the very code of the program that generates the phenotype is itself transforming over time. The former is a little different: It assumes a fixed value on n for the n-space it explores and is thus perhaps more closely related to optimization strategies than to free-form artificial evolution. That is, it only searches the n-space for local aesthetic maxima, while genetic programs simultaneously define and search their n-space, with the value of n constantly changing. Thus they tend to be simultaneously more chaotic, hard to control, and creative—a familiar set of characteristics among creative people! At any rate, it may be helpful to be aware of the difference, so I'm pointing it out here.

Conclusions

In conclusion, I hope I've been able to demonstrate that genetic programming is one cool paradigm. It is amazingly automatic, has the world's best user interface—simply point and click on what you like—and it takes proceduralism to its logical end. While it may not be terribly *useful*, because it's so hard to control and direct, it certainly is fun to play with, and it does create some striking images at turns. It also gives the computer the greatest role in the creation of digital art of any paradigm I know. This is exciting in itself, as the computer can be a very capable, if simple-minded and cranky, artistic assistant.

With my own program, Dr. Mutatis,[7] I hope to bring "genetic programming to the people." The fun thing about that is that people could start trading genomes on the Internet, thus accelerating evolution by cross-breeding between populations that spend most of their time in isolation on a given user's machine. This is analogous in Nature to the evolutionary divergence of populations isolated on

---

[7] The lawyers require me to insert this disclaimer: Dr. Mutatis represents pure research being pursued in the MetaCreations Skunk Works; it will not necessarily become a product.

islands, which are occasionally intermingled by migration, chance travel, or formation of a land bridge.

Such universal exchange of genetic information will require standard encoding and interpretation machinery, just as DNA from some extraterrestrial organism would have zero chance of intermingling with that of life on Earth. Again, the genotype is like the operating system, and the cell is like the computer it runs on. Genotypes and O/S's are not highly portable. I foresee that, should I succeed in bringing genetic art to the people, we will all suffer for some time to come for my lack of foresight in the design of a robust and flexible system. Ah, well such is life; better to try and be stoned for your efforts than never to try at all. (Famous last words—we shall see!)

Bibliography

(Abhyankar and Bajaj 1987a) Abhyankar and C. Bajaj. Automatic parametrization of rational curves and surfaces I: Conics and conicoids. *Computer News*, 1:19, 1987.

(Abhyankar and Bajaj 1987b) S. Abhyankar and C. Bajaj. Automatic parametrization of rational curves and surfaces II: Conics and conicoids. *Computer News*, 3:25, 1987.

(Ahlberg *et al.* 1967) J. Ahlberg, E. Nilson, and J. Walsh. *The theory of splines and their applications.* Boston: Academic Press, 1967.

(Amanatides 1984) John Amanatides. Ray tracing with cones. In H. Christiansen, ed., *Computer Graphics (SIGGRAPH '84 Proceedings)*, 18:129–135, July 1984.

(Anderson 1992) D. Anderson. Hidden line elimination in projected grid surfaces. *ACM Trans. on Graphics,* 1(4):274–288, 1992.

(ANSI 1986) American National Standard Institute, 1986. *Nomenclature and Definitions for Illumination Engineering, ANSI/IES*, RP-16-1986.

(Arvo and Kirk 1989) J. Arvo and D. Kirk. A survey of ray tracing acceleration techniques. In Andrew Glassner, ed., *An introduction to ray tracing*, 201–262. Boston: Academic Press, 1989.

(Badler *et al.* 1980) N. I. Badler, J. O'Rourke, and B. Kaufman. Special problems in human movement simulation. *SIGGRAPH '80 Proceedings*, 189–197, July 1980.

(Bagby 1984) D. Bagby. *Parameterization of elliptical elements, letter to ANSI X3H3 Committee (August 16, 1984)*, 17, 1984.

(Barr 1986) A. H. Barr. Ray tracing deformed surfaces. In *Computer Graphics, (SIGGRAPH 86 Proceedings)*, 20:287–296, 1986.

(Barr 1991) A. H. Barr. Teleological modeling. In N. I. Badler, B. A. Barsky, and D. Zeltzer, eds., *Making them move: Mechanics, control, and animation of articulated figures*, 315–321. San Mateo, CA: Morgan Kaufmann, 1991.

(Bian 1990) B. Bian. *Accurate simulation of scene luminances.* Worcester, MA: Worcester Polytechnic Institute, 1990.

(Birkhoff and MacLane 1965) G. Birkhoff and S. MacLane. *A survey of modern algebra, 3rd edition*. Exercise 15, Section IX-3, 240; *also corollary*, Section IX-14, 277–278. New York: MacMillan, 1965.

(Blinn 1977) J. F. Blinn. Models of light reflection for computer synthesized pictures. In *Computer Graphics (SIGGRAPH '77 Proceedings)*, 11:192–198, July 1977.

(Blinn 1978) J. F. Blinn. Simulation of wrinkled surfaces. In James George, ed. *Computer Graphics (SIGGRAPH '78 Proceedings)*, 12:286–292, August 1978.

(Blinn 1982a) J. F. Blinn. Light reflection functions for simulation of clouds and dusty surfaces. In *Computer Graphics (SIGGRAPH '82 Proceedings)*, 16(3):21–29, July 1982.

(Blinn 1982b) J. F. Blinn. A generalization of algebraic surface drawing. *ACM Transactions on Graphics*, 1(3):235–256, July 1982.

(Bloomenthal 1985) J. Bloomenthal. Modeling the mighty maple. In *Computer Graphics (SIGGRAPH '85 Proceedings)*, 19(3): 305–311, July 1985.

(Bloomenthal *et al.* 1997) J. Bloomenthal, C. Bajaj, J. Blinn, M. P. Cani-Gascuel, A. Rockwood, B. Wyvill, and G. Wyvill. *Introduction to implicit surfaces*. Morgan Kaufman Publishers, Inc., 1997.

(Bouville 1985) C. Bouville. Bounding ellipsoids for ray fractal intersection. In *Computer Graphics (SIGGRAPH '85 Proceedings)*, 19(3): 45–52, July 1985.

(Bracewell 1986) R. N. Bracewell. *The fourier transform and its applications*. New York: McGraw Hill, 1986.

(Brigham 1988) E.O. Brigham. *The fast fourier transform and its applications*. Englewood Cliffs, NJ: Prentice Hall, 1988.

(Brown 1983) L. M. Brown. *Most of the good stuff*. New York: American Institute of Physics, 1983.

(Brown and Rigden 1993) L. M. Brown and J. Rigden, eds. *Most of the good stuff*. New York: American Institute of Physics, 1993.

(Cabral and Leedom 1993) B. Cabral and L. Leedom. Imaging vector fields using line integral convolution. *Computer Graphics Proceedings, Annual Conference Series,* 263–270, 1993.

(Cabral *et al.* 1987) B. Cabral, N. Max, and R. Springmeyer. Bidirectional reflection functions from surface bump maps. In M. C. Stone, ed., *Computer Graphics (SIGGRAPH '87 Proceedings)*, 21:273–281, July 1987.

(Calvert *et al.* 1980) T. W. Calvert, J. Chapman, and A. Patla.The integration of subjective and objective data in the animation of human movement. In *Computer Graphics (SIGGRAPH '80 Proceedings)*, 14:198–203, July 1980.

(Carpenter 1984) L. Carpenter. The A-buffer, an antialiased hidden surface method. In H. Christiansen, ed., *Computer Graphics (SIGGRAPH '84 Proceedings)*, 18:103–108, July 1984.

(Catmull 1974) E. E. Catmull. *A subdivision algorithm for computer display of curved surfaces*. PhD thesis, Department of Computer Science, University of Utah, December 1974.

(Chen *et al.* 1985) L. Chen, G. T. Herman, R. A. Reynolds, and J. K. Udupa. Surface shading in the cuberille environment. *IEEE Computer Graphics and Applications*, 5(12):33–43, December 1985.

(Cline *et al.* 1988) H. E. Cline, W. E. Lorensen, and S. Ludke. Two algorithms for the three dimensional reconstruction of tomograms. *Medical Physics*, 15(3):320–327, May 1988.

(Cook 1984) R. L. Cook. Shade trees. In H. Christiansen, ed., *Computer Graphics (SIGGRAPH '84 Proceedings)*, 18(3):223–231, July 1984.

(Cook 1986) R. L. Cook. Stochastic sampling in computer graphics. *ACM Transactions on Graphics*, 5(1):51–72, January 1986.

(Cook *et al.* 1984) R. L. Cook, T. Porter, and L. Carpenter. Distributed ray tracing. In H. Christiansen, ed., *Computer Graphics (SIGGRAPH '84 Proceedings)*, 18(3):137–145, July 1984.

(Cook *et al.* 1987) R. L. Cook, L. Carpenter, and E. Catmull. The Reyes image rendering architecture. In M. C. Stone, ed., *Computer Graphics (SIGGRAPH '87 Proceedings)*, 95–102, July 1987.

(Cook and Torrance 1981) R. L. Cook and K. E. Torrance. A reflectance model for computer graphics. In *Computer Graphics (SIGGRAPH '81 Proceedings)*, 15:307–316, August 1981.

(Crow 1984) F. C. Crow. Summed-area tables for texture mapping. In H. Christiansen, ed., *Computer Graphics (SIGGRAPH '84 Proceedings)*, 18:207–212, July 1984.

(Cychosz 1986) J. M. Cychosz. *Vectorized ray tracing of polygonal models.* Unpublished results, 1986.

(Dawkins 1987) R. Dawkins. *The blind watchmaker.* New York: W. W. Norton & Co., 1987.

(Dippé and Wold 1985) M. A. Z. Dippé and E. H. Wold. Antialiasing through stochastic sampling. In B. A. Barsky, ed., *Computer Graphics (SIGGRAPH '85 Proceedings)*, 19:69–78, July 1985.

(Drebin *et al.*1988) R. Drebin, L. Carpenter, and P. Hanrahan. Volume rendering. In *Computer Graphics (SIGGRAPH '88 Proceedings)*, 22(4):65–74, 1988.

(Duff 1985) T. Duff. Compositing 3-D rendered images. In B. A. Barsky, ed., *Computer Graphics (SIGGRAPH '85 Proceedings),*19:41–44, July 1985.

(Dungan, Jr. 1979) W. Dungan, Jr. A terrain and cloud computer image generation model. In *Computer Graphics (SIGGRAPH '79 Proceedings)*, 13:143–150, August 1979.

(Ebert 1991) D. S. Ebert. *Solid spaces: A unified approach to describing object attributes*. PhD thesis, The Ohio State University, 1991.

(Ebert 1997) D. S. Ebert. Volumetric modeling with implicit functions: A cloud is born. In David Ebert, ed., *SIGGRAPH 97 Visual Proceedings, (SIGGRAPH 97, 03-08 August 1997, Los Angeles, California),* 147, ACM SIGGRAPH, August 1997.

(Ebert and Parent 1990) D. S. Ebert and R. E. Parent. Rendering and animation of gaseous phenomena by combining fast volume and scanline A-buffer techniques. In Forest Baskett, ed., *Computer Graphics (SIGGRAPH '90 Proceedings)*, 24:357–366, August 1990.

(Ebert *et al.* 1989) D. Ebert, K. Boyer, and D. Roble. Once a Pawn a Foggy Knight ... [videotape]. In *SIGGRAPH Video Review, 54.* ACM SIGGRAPH, New York, November 1989. Segment 3.

(Ebert *et al.* 1990) D. Ebert, J. Ebert, and K. Boyer. Getting Into Art [videotape]. Department of Computer and Information Science, The Ohio State University, May 1990.

(Ebert *et al.* 1994a) D. Ebert, W. Carlson, and R. Parent. Solid spaces and inverse particle systems for controlling the animation of gases and fluids. *The Visual Computer*, 10(4):179–190, 1994.

(Ebert *et al.* 1994b) D. Ebert, F. K. Musgrave, D. Peachey, K. Perlin, and S. Worley. *Texturing and modeling: A procedural approach*. Cambridge, MA: Academic Press, October 1994.

(Ebert *et al.* 1997) D. Ebert, J. Kukla, T. Bedwell, and S. Wrights. (A Cloud is Born). In *ACM SIGGRAPH Video Review (SIGGRAPH 97 Electronic Theatre Program, 03-08 August 1997, Los Angeles, California)*. ACM SIGGRAPH, August 1997.

(Evertsz and Mandelbrot 1992) C. J. G. Evertsz and B. B. Mandelbrot. Multifractal measures. In Peitgen, Jurgens, and Saupe, eds., *Chaos and fractals,* Appendix B, 921–953. New York: Springer-Verlag, 1992.

(Feibush *et al.*1980) E. A. Feibush, M. Levoy, and R. L . Cook. Synthetic texturing using digital filters. In *Computer Graphics (SIGGRAPH '80 Proceedings)*, 14:294–301, July 1980.

(Foster and Metaxis 1997) N. Foster and D. Metaxas. Modeling the motion of a hot, turbulent gases. In Turner Whitted, ed., *SIGGRAPH 97 Conference Proceedings*, *Annual Conference Series,* 181–187. ACM SIGGRAPH, Addison Wesley, August 1997.

(Fournier *et al.* 1982) A. Fournier, D. Fussell, and L. Carpenter. Computer rendering of stochastic models. *Communications of the ACM*, 25(6):371–384, June 1982.

(Fu and Lu 1978) K. S. Fu and S. Y. Lu. Computer generation of texture using a syntatic approach. In *Computer Graphics (SIGGRAPH '78 Proceedings)*, 12:147–152, August 1978.

(Fuchs *et al.* 1977) H. Fuchs, Z. M. Kedem, and S. P. Uselton. Optimal surface reconstruction of from planar contours. In *Communications of the ACM*, 20(10):693–702, October 1977.

(Fusco and Tice 1993) M. J. Fusco and S. Tice. Character motion systems course notes. In *SIGGRAPH '93 Course Notes 01*, 9–22. ACM SIGGRAPH, August 1993.

(Gagalowicz and Ma 1985) A. Gagalowicz and S. D. Ma. Sequential synthesis of natural textures. In *Computer Graphics, Vision and Image Processing,* 30:289–315, 1985.

(Gallagher and Nagtegaal 1989) R. S. Gallagher and J. C. Nagtegaal. An efficient 3D visualization technique for finite element models and other course volumes. In J. Lane, ed., *Computer Graphics (SIGGRAPH '89 Proceedings)*, 23:185–194, July 1989.

(Garber 1981) D. D. Garber, *Computational models for texture analysis and texture synthesis.* PhD thesis, University of Southern California, May 1981.

(Gardner 1984) G. Gardner. Simulation of natural scenes using textured quadric surfaces. In H. Christiansen, ed., *Computer Graphics (SIGGRAPH '84 Proceedings)*, 18:11–20, July 1984.

(Gardner 1985) G. Gardner. Visual simulation of clouds. In B. A. Barsky, ed., *Computer Graphics (SIGGRAPH '84 Proceedings)*, 19(3):297–304, July 1985.

(Gardner 1990) G. Gardner. Forest fire simulation. In Forest Baskett, ed., *Computer Graphics (SIGGRAPH '90 Proceedings)*, 24:430, August 1990.

(Gedzelman 1991) S. D. Gedzelman. Atmospheric optics in art. In *Applied Optics*, 30(24):3514–3522, August 20, 1991.

(Ghezzi and Jazayeri 1982) C. Ghezzi and M. Jazayeri. *Programming language concepts.* Wiley, New York, 1982.

(Girard and Maciejewski 1985) M. Girard and A. A. Maciejewski. Computational modeling for the computer animation of legged figures. In B. A. Barsky, ed., *Computer Graphics (SIGGRAPH '85 Proceedings)*, 19:263–270, July 1985.

(Gonzalez and Woods 1992) R. C. Gonzalez and R. E. Woods. *Digital image processing.* Reading, Massachusetts: Addison Wesley, 1992.

(Gordon and Reynolds 1985) D. Gordon and R. A. Reynolds. Image space shading and 3-dimensional objects. *Computer Vision, Graphics, and Image Processing*, 29:361–376, 1985.

(Greene 1986) N. Greene. Applications of world projections. In M. Green, ed., *Proceedings of Graphics Interface '86,* 108–114, May 1986.

(Grossman and Morlet 1984) A. Grossmann and J. Morlet. Decomposition of hardy functions into square integrable wavelets of constant shape. *SIAM Journal of Mathematics*, 15:723–736, 1984.

(Haines 1989) E. Haines. Essential ray tracing algorithms. In A. Glassner, ed., *An Introduction to Ray Tracing*, Boston: Academic Press, 1989.

(Haines and Worley 1993) E. Haines and S. Worley. Point-in-polygon testing. In *Ray Tracing News*, 2:1, 1993. E-mail available under anonymous ftp from weedeater.math.yale.edu.

(Hall 1989) R. A. Hall. *Illumination and color in computer generated imagery*. New York: Springer-Verlag, 1989.

(Hanrahan 1990) P. Hanrahan. Volume rendering, SIGGRAPH 90: *Course Notes on Volume Visualization,* August 1990.

(Hanrahan and Lawson 1990) P. Hanrahan and J. Lawson. A language for shading and lighting calculations. In F. Baskett, ed., *Computer Graphics (SIGGRAPH '90 Proceedings),* 24:289–298, August 1990.

(Haruyama and Barsky 1984) S. Haruyama and B. A. Barsky. Using stochastic modeling for texture generation. *IEEE Computer Graphics and Applications*, 4(3):7–19, March 1984.

(He *et al.* 1991) X. D. He, K. E. Torrance, F. X. Sillion, and D. P. Greenberg. A comprehensive physical model for light reflection. In T. W. Sederberg, ed., *Computer Graphics (SIGGRAPH '91 Proceedings),* 25:175–186, July 1991.

(Hearn and Baker 1986) D. Hearn and M. P. Baker. *Computer graphics*. Englewood Cliffs, NJ: Prentice-Hall, 1986.

(Heckbert 1986a) P. S. Heckbert. Filtering by repeated integration. In D. C. Evans and R. J. Athay, eds., *Computer Graphics (SIGGRAPH '96 Proceedings)*, 20:315–321, August 1986.

(Heckbert 1986b) P. S. Heckbert. Survey of texture mapping. *IEEE Computer Graphics and Applications,* 6(11):56–67, November 1986.

(Hoehne *et al.* 1990) K. H. Hoehne, M. Bomans, A. Pommert, and U. Tiede. Voxel based volume visualization techniques. In *SIGGRAPH 90: Course Notes on Volume Visualization*. ACM SIGGRAPH, August 1990.

(Inakage 1991) M. Inakage. Modeling laminar flames. In *SIGGRAPH '91: Course Notes, 27*. ACM SIGGRAPH, July 1991.

(Kajiya 1983) J. T. Kajiya. New techniques for ray tracing procedurally defined objects. In *ACM Transactions on Graphics*, 2(3): 161–181, July 1983.

(Kajiya 1983) J. T. Kajiya. New techniques for ray tracing procedurally defined objects. In *Computer Graphics (SIGGRAPH '83 Proceedings)*, 17(3): 91–99, July 1983.

(Kajiya 1985) J. T. Kajiya. Anisotropic reflection models. In B. A. Barsky, ed., *Computer Graphics (SIGGRAPH '85 Proceedings)*, 19:15–21, July 1985.

(Kajiya 1986) J. T. Kajiya. The rendering equation. In David C. Evans and Russell J. Athay, eds., *Computer Graphics (SIGGRAPH '86 Proceedings)*, 20:143–150, August 1986.

(Kajiya and Kay 1989) J. T. Kajiya and T. L. Kay. Rendering fur with three dimensional textures. In Jeffrey Lane, ed., *Computer Graphics (SIGGRAPH '89 Proceedings)*, 23:271–280, July 1989.

(Kajiya and Von Herzen 1984) J. T. Kajiya and B. P. Von Herzen. Ray tracing volume densities. In H. Christiansen, ed., *Computer Graphics (SIGGRAPH '84 Proceedings)*, 18:165–174, July 1984.

(Kay and Kajiya 1986) T. Kay and J. Kajiya. Ray tracing complex scenes. *Computer Graphics*, 20(4):269–278, 1986.

(Kelley 1988) K. W. Kelley. *The home planet*. New York: Addison Wesley, 1988.

(Keppel 1975) E. Keppel. Approximating complex surfaces by triangulation of contour lines. In *IBM Journal of Research and Development*, 19(1):2–11, January 1975.

(Kirk and Arvo 1991) D. Kirk and J. Arvo. Unbiased sampling techniques for image synthesis. *Computer Graphics*, 25(4):153–156, 1991.

(Klassen 1987) R. V. Klassen. Modeling the effect of the atmosphere on light. *ACM Transactions on Graphics*, 6(3):215–237, 1987.

(Knuth 1973) D. Knuth. *The Art of Computer programming: Sorting and searching, 2nd printing*. Reading, MA: Addison-Wesley, 1973.

(Koza 1992) J. R. Koza. *Genetic Programming*. Cambridge, MA: MIT Press, 1992.

(Lee *et al.* 1985) M. E. Lee, R. A. Redner, and S. P. Uselton. Statisically optimized sampling for distributed ray tracing. In B. A. Barsky, ed., *Computer Graphics (SIGGRAPH '85 Proceedings)*, 19:61–67, July 1985.

(Levoy 1988) M. Levoy. Display of surfaces from volume data. *IEEE Computer Graphics and Applications*, 8(3):29–37, May 1988.

(Levoy 1990a) M. Levoy. Efficient ray tracing of volume data. *ACM Transactions on Graphics*, 9(3):245–261, July 1990.

(Levoy 1990b) M. Levoy. A hybrid ray tracer for rendering polygon and volume data. *IEEE Computer Graphics and Applications*. 10(2):33–40, March 1990.

(Levoy 1990c) M. Levoy. Volume rendering by adaptive refinement. *The Visual Computer*, 6(1):2–7, February 1990.

(Lewis 1984) J. P. Lewis. Texture synthesis for digital painting. In H. Christiansen, ed., *Computer Graphics (SIGGRAPH '84 Proceedings)*, 18:245–252, July 1984.

(Lewis 1986) J. P. Lewis. Methods for stochastic spectral synthesis. In M. Green, ed., *Proceedings of Graphics Interface '86*, 173–179, May 1986.

(Lewis 1987) J. P. Lewis. Generalized stochastic subdivision. *ACM Transactions on Graphics*, 6(3):167–190, July 1987.

(Lewis 1989) J. P. Lewis. Algorithms for solid noise synthesis. In J. Lane, ed., *Computer Graphics (SIGGRAPH '89 Proceedings)*, 23(3):263–270, July 1989.

(Lorensen and Cline 1987) W. E. Lorensen and H. E. Cline. Marching cubes: A high resolution 3D surface construction algorithm. In M. C. Stone, ed., *Computer Graphics (SIGGRAPH '87 Proceedings)*, 21:163–169, July 1987.

(Lorensen and Cline 1990) W. E. Lorensen and H. E. Cline. *Volume Modeling*. First Conference on Visualization on Biomedical Computing, April 1990.

(Lovejoy and Mandelbrot 1985) S. Lovejoy and B. B. Mandelbrot. Fractal properties of rain and a fractal model. *Tellus*, 37A: 209–232, 1985.

(Mallat 1989a) S. G. Mallat. Multifrequency channel decompositions of images and wavelet modeling. *IEEE Transactions on Acoustic Speech and Signal Processing*, 37(12):2091–2110, December 1989.

(Mallat 1989b) S. G. Mallat. A theory for multiresolution signal decomposition: The wavelet representation. *IEEE Transactions on Pattern Analysis and Machine Intelligence*, 11:674–693, July 1989.

(Mandelbrot 1982) B. B. Mandelbrot. *The fractal geometry of nature*. New York: W.H. Freeman and Co., 1982.

(Max 1986) N. L. Max. Light diffusion through clouds and haze. In *Computer Vision, Graphics and Image Processing*, 33(3):280–292, March 1986.

(Max 1994) N. L. Max. Efficient light propagation for multiple anisotropic volume scattering. In *Fifth Eurographics Workshop on Rendering*, 87–104, Darmstadt: Germany, June 1994.

(McCool and Fiume 1992) M. McCool and Eugene Fiume. Heirarchical poisson disk sampling distributions. In *Proceedings of Graphics Interface '92*, 94–105, 1992.

(Miller 1986) G. S. P. Miller. The definition and rendering of terrain maps. In D. C. Evans and R. J. Athay, eds., *Computer Graphics (SIGGRAPH '86 Proceedings)*, 20(4):39–48, 1986.

(Miller 1988a) G. S. P. Miller. From wire-frames to furry animals. In *Proceedings of Graphics Interface '88*, 135–145, 1988.

(Miller 1988b) G. S. P. Miller. The motion dynamics of snakes and worms. In J. Dill, ed., *Computer Graphics (SIGGRAPH '88 Proceedings)*, 22:169–178, August 1988.

(Mitchell 1987) D. Mitchell. Generating antialiased images at low sampling densities. In *Computer Graphics*, 21(4):65–72, 1987.

(Mitchell 1991) D. Mitchell. Spectrally optimal sampling for distribution ray tracing. In *Computer Graphics*, 25(4):157–164, 1991.

(Mitchell and Netravali 1988) D. P. Mitchell and A. N. Netravali. Reconstruction filters in computer graphics. In J. Dill, ed., *Computer Graphics (SIGGRAPH '88 Proceedings)*, 22:221–228, August 1988.

(Musgrave 1988) F. K. Musgrave. Grid tracing: Fast ray tracing for height fields. Research Report, YALEU/DCS/RR 639. New Haven, CT: Yale University Dept. of Computer Science, July 1988.

(Musgrave *et al.* 1989) F. K. Musgrave, C. E. Kolb, and R. S. Mace. The synthesis and rendering of eroded fractal terrains. In J. Lane, ed., *Computer Graphics (SIGGRAPH '89 Proceedings)*, 23(3):41–50, July 1989.

(Musgrave 1990) F. K. Musgrave. A note on ray tracing mirages. In *IEEE Computer Graphics and Applications*, 10(6):10–12, November 1990.

(Musgrave 1991) F. K. Musgrave. A random colormap animation algorith. In *Graphics Gems II*, J Arvo, ed., Boston: Academic Press, 1991.

(Musgrave 1993) F. K. Musgrave. *Methods for realistic landscape imaging*. New Haven, CT, Yale University, May 1993.

(Musgrave 1994) F. K. Musgrave. *Methods for realistic landscape imaging*. PhD Thesis, Ann Arbor, Michigan: UMI Dissertation Services (Order Number 9415872), 1994.

(Musgrave and Mandelbrot 1989) F. K. Musgrave and B. B. Mandelbrot. Natura ex machina. *IEEE Computer Graphics and Applications*, 9(1):4–7, January 1989.

(Neyret 1997) F. Neyret. Qualitative simulation of convective cloud formation and evolution. In *Eighth International Workshop on Computer Animation and Simulation*. Eurographics, September 1997.

(Nielson 1991) G. M. Nielson. Visualization in scientific and engineering computation. In *IEEE Computer*, 24(9):58–66, September 1991.

(Norton *et al.* 1982) A. Norton, A. P. Rockwood, and P. T. Skolmoski. Clamping: a method of antialiasing textured surfaces by bandwidth limiting in object space. In *Computer Graphics (SIGGRAPH '82 Proceedings)*, 16:1–8, July 1982.

(Nishimura *et al.* 1985) H. Nishimura, A. Hirai, T. Kawai, T. Kawata, I. Shira kawa, and K. Omura. Object modelling by distribution function and a method of image generation. In *Journal of papers given at the Electronics Communication Conference '85*, J68-D(4), 1985. In Japanese.

(Nishimura *et al.* 1987) T. Nishita, Y. Miyawaki, and E. Nakamae. A shading model for atmospheric scattering considering luminous intensity distribution of light sources. In M. C. Stone, ed., *Computer Graphics (SIGGRAPH '87 Proceedings)*, 21:303–310, July 1987.

(Nishimura *et al.* 1996) T. Nishita, E. Nakamae, and Y. Dobashi. Display of clouds and snow taking into account multiple anisotropic scattering and sky light. In H. Rushmeier, ed., *SIGGRAPH 96 Conference Proceedings, Annual Conference Series*, 379–386. ACM SIGGRAPH, Addison Wesley, August 1996. held in New Orleans, Louisiana, 04-09 August 1996.

(Nishita *et al.* 1993) T. Nishita *et al.*. Display of the earth taking into account atmospheric scattering. In *Computer Graphics*, Annual Conference Series, 175–182, August 1993.

(Oppenheim and Schafer 1989) A. V. Oppenheim and R. W. Schafer. *Discrete-time signal processing*. Englewood Cliffs, NJ: Prentice Hall, 1989.

(Peachey 1985) D. R. Peachey. Solid texturing of complex surfaces. In B. A. Barsky, ed., *Computer Graphics (SIGGRAPH '85 Proceedings)*, 19:279–286, July 1985.

(Peitgen and Saupe 1988) H. O. Peitgen and D. Saupe, eds. *The science of fractal images*. New York: Springer-Verlag, 1988.

(Peitgen *et al.* 1992) H. O. Peitgen, H. JŸrgens, and D. Saupe. *Chaos and fractals: New frontiers of science*. New York: Springer-Verlag, 1992.

(Perlin 1985) K. Perlin. An image synthesizer. In B. A. Barsky, ed., *Computer Graphics (SIGGRAPH '85 Proceedings)*, 19(3): 287–296, July 1985.

(Perlin 1992) K. Perlin. A hypertexture tutorial. In *SIGGRAPH'92: Course Notes, 23*. ACM SIGGRAPH, July 1992.

(Perlin and Hoffert 1989) K. Perlin and E. M. Hoffert. Hypertexture. In Jeffrey Lane, ed., *Computer Graphics (SIGGRAPH '89 Proceedings)*, 23:253–262, July 1989.

(Phong 1975) B. Phong. Illumination for computer generated pictures. *Communications of the ACM*, 18(6):311–317, June 1975.

(Pixar 1989) Pixar, *The RenderMan Interface: Version 3.1*. Pixar, San Rafael, California, 1989.

(Porter and Duff 1984) T. Porter and T. Duff. Compositing digital images. In H. Christiansen, ed., *Computer Graphics (SIGGRAPH '84 Proceedings)*, 18:253–259, July 1984.

(Poulin and Fournier 1990) P. Poulin and A. Fournier. A model for anisotropic reflection. In F. Baskett, ed., *Computer Graphics (SIGGRAPH '90 Proceedings)*, 24:273–282, August 1990.

(Press *et al.* 1986) W. H. Press *et al.. Numerical recipies*. New York: University of Cambridge, 1986.

(Prusinkiewicz and Lindenmayer 1990) P. Prusinkiewicz and A. Lindenmayer. *The algorithmic beauty of plants*. New York: Springer-Verlag, 1990.

(Reeves 1983) W. T. Reeves. Particle systemsÑa technique for modeling a class of fuzzy objects. *ACM Trans. Graphics*, 2:91–108, April 1983.

(Reeves *et al.* 1987) W. T. Reeves, D. H. Salesin, and R. L. Cook. Rendering antialiased shadows with depth maps. In M. C. Stone, ed., *Computer Graphics (SIGGRAPH '87 Proceedings)*, 21:283-291, July 1987.

(Rich 1983) E. Rich. *Artificial intelligence*. New York: McGraw Hill, 1983.

(Rushmeier and Torrance 1987) H. E. Rushmeier and K. E. Torrance. The zonal method for calculating light intensities in the presence of a participating medium. In M. C. Stone, ed., *Computer Graphics (SIGGRAPH '87 Proceedings)*, 21:293–302, July 1987.

(Ruskai 1992) M. B. Ruskai, ed.. *Wavelets and their applications*, Boston: Jones and Bartlett, 1992.

(Sabella 1988) P. Sabella. A rendering algorithm for visualizing 3D scalar fields. In J. Dill, *Computer Graphics (SIGGRAPH '88 Proceedings)*, 22:51–58, August 1988.

(Sakas 1993) G. Sakas. Modeling and animating turbulent gaseous phenomena using spectral synthesis. *The Visual Computer*, 9(4):200–212, January 1993.

(Salisbury *et al.* 1994) M. B. Salisbury *et al.*. Interactive pen-and-ink illustration. Computer Graphics Proceedings, Annual Conference Series, 101–108, 1994.

(Saupe 1988) D. Saupe. Algorithms for random fractals. In H. O. Peitgen and D. Saupe, eds., *The science of fractal images*, 71–136. New York: Springer-Verlag, 1988.

(Saupe 1989) D. Saupe. Point evaluation of multi variable random fractals. In H. Juergen and D. Saupe, eds., *Visualisierung in Mathematik und Naturissenschaft–Bremer Computergraphik Tage 1988*, Heidelberg: Springer-Verlag, 1989.

(Saupe 1989) D. Saupe. Point evaluation of multi-variable random fractals. In H. Jurgens and D. Saupe, eds., *Visualisierung in Mathematik und Naturwissenschaften,* 114–126. Springer-Verlag, 1989.

(Saupe 1992) D. Saupe. Random fractals in image synthesis. In P. Prusinkiewicz, ed., *Fractals: From Folk Art to Hyperreality (Siggraph '92 Course 12 notes)*, 10-1–10-29, 1992.

(Sayre 1992) R. Sayre. Antialiasing techniques. In A. Apodaca and D. Peachey, eds., *Writing RenderMan Shaders (Siggraph '92 Course 21 notes)*, 109–141, 1992.

(Schacter 1980) B. J. Schacter. Long-crested wave models. *Computer Graphics and Image Processing*, 12:187–201, 1980.

(Schacter and Ahuja 1979) B. J. Schacter and N. Ahuja. Random pattern generation processes. *Computer Graphics and Image Processing*, 10:95–114, 1979.

(Schlick 1994) C. Schlick. Fast alternatives to Perlin's bias and gain functions. In Paul S. Heckbert, ed., *Graphics Gems IV,* volume IV, 401–403, Cambridge, MA, 1994. AP PROFESSIONAL.

(Schroeder *et al.* 1992) W. J. Schroeder, J. A. Zarge, and W. E. Lorensen. Decimation of triangle meshes. In E. E. Catmull, ed., *Computer Graphics (SIGGRAPH '92 Proceedings)*, 26(2):65–70, July 1992.

(Shannon 1995) S. Shannon. *The Chrome Age: Dawn of Virtual Reality.* Leonardo, 28(5):369–380, 1995.

(Shirley 1993) P. Shirley. Monte carlo simulation, 1993. Global Illumination course notes, ACM SIGGRAPH '92, Course #18, July 1992.

(Shoemake 1991) K. Shoemake. Interval Sampling, In James Arvo, ed., *Graphics Gems II*, 394–395. Academic Press, Boston,1991.

(Sims 1990) K. Sims. Particle animation and rendering using data parallel computation. In Forest Baskett, ed., *Computer Graphics (SIGGRAPH '90 Proceedings)*, 24:405–413, August 1990.

(Sims 1991) K. Sims. Artificial evolution for computer graphics. In T. W. Sederberg, ed., *Computer Graphics (SIGGRAPH '91 Proceedings)*, 25(4):319–328, July 1991.

(Sims 1991) K. Sims. Interactive evolution of dynamical systems. In *Proceedings of the european conference on artificial life*. Paris: MIT Press, December, 1991.

(Sims 1994) K. Sims. Evolving virtual creatures. In *Computer Graphics, (SIGGRAPH 94 Proceddings)*, 15–22, 1994.

(Smith 1984) A. R. Smith. Plants, fractals and formal languages. In H. Christiansen, ed., *Computer Graphics (SIGGRAPH '84 Proceedings)*, 18:1–10, July 1984.

(Stam 1995) J. Stam. Multiple scattering as a diffusion process. In *Eurographics Rendering Workshop 1995*. Eurographics, June 1995.

(Stam and Fiume 1991) J. Stam and E. Fiume. A multiple-scale stochastic modelling primitive. In *Proceedings of Graphics Interface '91*, 24–31, June 1991.

(Stam and Fiume 1993) J. Stam and E. Fiume. Turbulent wind fields for gaseous phenomena. In J. T. Kajiya, ed., *Computer Graphics (SIGGRAPH '93 Proceedings)*, 27:369–376, August 1993.

(Stam and Fiume 1995) J. Stam and E. Fiume. Depicting fire and other gaseous phenomena using diffusion processes. In Robert Cook, ed., *SIGGRAPH 95 Conference Proceedings*, Annual Conference Series, 129–136. ACM SIGGRAPH, Addison Wesley, August 1995.

(Standler and Hart 1994) B. Standler and J. Hart. A lipschitz method for accelerated volume rendering. In *1994 Symposium on Volume Visualization*, 1994.

(Stephenson 1992) N. Stephenson. *Snow crash*. New York: Bantam Doubleday, 1992.

(Tadamura *et al.* 1993) K. Tadamura *et al.* Modeling and skylight and rendering of outdoor scenes. In *Eurographics '93*, 12(3):189–200, 1993.

(Todd and Latham 1993) S. Todd and W. Latham. *Evolutionary art and computers*. Boston, MA: Academic Press, 1993.

(Turk 1991) G. Turk. Reaction diffusion textures. In *Computer Graphics*, 25(4):289–298, 1991.

(Turk 1991) G. Turk. Generating texures for arbitrary surfaces using reaction-diffusion. In T. W. Sederberg, ed., *Computer Graphics (SIGGRAPH '91 Proceedings)*, 25:289–298, July 1991.

(Upstill 1990) S. Upstill, *The renderman companion*. Reading, MA: Addison Wesley, 1990.

(van Wijk 1991) J. J. van Wijk. Spot noise-texture synthesis for data visualization. In T. W. Sederberg, ed., *Computer Graphics (SIGGRAPH '91 Proceedings)*, 25:309–318, July 1991.

(Voorhies 1991) D. Voorhies. Space filling curves and a measure of coherence. In James Arvo, ed., *Graphics Gems II*, 26–30. Academic Press, Boston, 1991.

(Voss 1983) R. Voss. Fourier Synthesis of Gaussian Fractals: $1/f$ noises, landscapes, and flakes. In *SIGGRAPH 83: Tutorial on State of the Art Image Synthesis*, 10. ACM SIGGRAPH, 1983.

(Voss 1988) R. F. Voss. Fractals in nature: From characterization to simulation, In H. O. Peitgen and D. Saupe, eds., *The science of fractaliImages*, 21–70. New York: Springer-Verlag, 1988.

(Ward 1991) G. Ward. A recursive implementation of the Perlin noise function. In James Arvo, ed., *Graphics Gems II,* 396–401, 1991. AP PROFESSIONAL, 1991.

(Waters 1987) K. Waters. A muscle model for animating three-dimensional facial expression. In M. C. Stone, ed., *Computer Graphics (SIGGRAPH '87 Proceedings)*, 21:17–24, July 1987.

(Westover 1990) L. Westover. Footprint evaluation for volume rendering. In F. Baskett, ed., *Computer Graphics (SIGGRAPH '90 Proceedings)*, 24:367–376, August 1990.

(Williams 1990) L. Williams. Pyramidal parametrics. In *Computer Graphics*, 17(3): 1–11, July 1983.

(Willis 1987) P. J. Willis. Visual simulation of atmospheric haze. *Computer Graphics Forum*, 6(1):35–42, January 1987.

(Winston and Horn 1984) P. H. Winston and B. K. P. Horn. *LISP, 2nd edition.* Reading, MA: Addison Wesley, 1984.

(Witkin and Kass 1991) A. Witkin and M. Kass. Reaction-diffusion textures. In T. W. Sederberg, ed., *Computer Graphics (SIGGRAPH '91 Proceedings)*, 25:299–308, July 1991.

(Worley 1993) S. Worley. Practical texture implementation. *Procedural Modeling and Rendering Techniques course notes, ACM SIGGRAPH '93, Vol. 12*, August 1993.

(Worley and Hart 1996) S. Worley and J. Hart. Hyper-rendering of hyper-textured surfaces. In *Implicit Surfaces '96*, 1996.

(Wyvill and Bloomenthal 1990) B. Wyvill and J. Bloomenthal. Modeling and animating with implicit surfaces. *SIGGRAPH 90: Course Notes, 23,* , ACM SIGGRAPH, August 1990.

(Wyvill *et al.* 1986a) B. Wyvill, C. McPheeters, and G. Wyvill. Data structure for soft objects. *The Visual Computer*, 2(4):227–234, January 1986.

(Wywill *et al.* 1986b) G. Wywill and G. McPheeters and B. Wywill. Data structure for soft objects. In *The Visual Computer*, 2:227–234, January 1986.

(Yang 1988) X. D. Yang. Fuzzy disk modeling and rendering of textured complex 3D surfaces of real objects. Technical Report, TR-88-414. New York: New York University, November 1988.

Index

abs function, 26
abstraction, 2
A-buffer algorithm, 251
actor/script-based systems, 257
adaptive band-limiting, 284
adaptive level of detail, 327–29, 343
additive cascade, 286
aerial perspective, 361
aesthetic gradient function, 375
aesthetic N-spaces, 374–75
affect, 256
Alias Dynamation particle system package, 354
alias, 48–51
aliasing, 50–53
    prevention, 48–49
    procedural textures, 53–55
alpha blending technique, 17
alpha channel, 22
ambient function, 18
amplification, 281–82, 375–76
amplitude, 278
animation
    expressions and mood, 269–72
    facial movement, 260–69
    gas, 176–84
    linear speed, 170
    paths, 169–70
    sneeze definition, 269
anisotrophic shading models, 8
ANSI C, 29–30, 115
antialiased shadows, 9
antialiasing, 4, 135–48, 347–48
    See also, Clamping, Edge events, Index
        aliasing.
    alternative methods, 63–64, 148
    analytic, 48–53, 58–59
    automatic, 52
    brick texture, 61–63
    clamping, 53–55, 57–58
    optimization and verification, 146–48
    shadows, 9, 348–49
    spot sizes, 136–40
    supersampling, 51, 64, 135–36, 140 2D, 148
Apollo 13, 315
application languages
    See also, C++, LISP.
    definition of, 23
architexture, 230–33
artifacts
    lattice, 66–68, 86
    micropolygon grid, 93–94
    stairstepping, 23–27, 135

Arvo, Jim, 98
AT&T Pixel Machine, 221, 237
atmospheric models, 361–71
attractor, 188–89
    extensions, 189–90

band-limited, 279
Barr, Al, 289
basis function, 34–35, 278
Beer's Law, 363
beveling, 102–03
bias, 34–35, 210–11, 262, 270
bifurcation, 241, 246
bioturbation, 333
black box texture, 121, 1432
blackbody radiators, 305
Blind Watchmaker, The (book), 376
blobby texture, 110
Bloomenthal image, 295
Blue Moon Rendering Tools (BMRT), 293
bombing, 88–91
boxstep, 62
brick texture, 35–43, 61–63, 87–88
B-splines, 69
bump mapping, 9, 19, 38–43, 101–05
bump-mapped brick, 38–43
bump-mapped features, 314

C coding, 113–15, 297–98, 322–23
C language, 30–31, 293
C++, 297–98, 381
C-2 and C-3 continuity, 296
caching, 114
Calvert, 257
Catmull-Rom filters, 59–60, 77splines, 30, 69, 73–74
catstep filters step function, 60
ceiling function, 30, 115
chaos function, 278, 283
characteristic function, 210
checkerboard pattern, 35–37
CIE XYZ color space, 366
clamp function, 25
clamping, 57–58
clip animation, 256, 346–47
clouds, 294–303

animation, 206–08
cirrus cloud texture, 203–05, 298–303
creatures, 205
cumulus, 201–03
global circulation, 298–303
macrostructure, 199
microstructure, 199
puffy cloud texture, 294–95
stratus, 203–05
volumetric models, 201–06
color look-up table, 32
color mapping methods, 32, 99–101
color table equalization, 107–109
composition, 21–23, 379
Computer Graphics & Principles and Practice, 104
computer-aided drawing (CAD), 230
cone tracing, 251
Coriolis effect, 303
crater bump map, 314
craters, 314–18
creation of N–space, 375
Crouch, Steve, 289
cylindrical projections, 95–96

Dante's Peak (film), 353–54
Darwin, Charles, 377
database amplification, 2
Dawkins, Richard, 376
decimation algorithms, 328
degree of freedom, 374
deoxyribonucleic acid (DNA), 377–79, 385
diffuse model, 8
diffuse reflection color, 101
diffuse shading, 8, 18
Digital Domain, 315, 353
digital terrain elevation data (DTED), 328
dilation symmetry, 278
displacement
    bound, 41
    mapping, 9, 41, 343
    value, 172
distribution estimation, 144–45
DTED. See, Digital terrain elevation data (DTED).

earth planet texture, 308–10
Ebert, David S., 1–5, 117, 169–208
edge events, 241
Edgerton, Doc, 314
efficiency, 340
eggs, hypertexture life forms, 226–29
eigenvectors, 320
electron density clouds, 3
elongated texture direction, 138
emittance, surface texture, 117
environmental mapping. See, Reflection mapping.
equal-angular mapping, 119
essence, 2
evolution, 376–78
exact self-similarity, 281
explicit noise algorithms, 80
exponent arrays, 284
expression tree, 379
extinction, 363

fabs() function, 240
facial action coding system (FACS), 261
fast Fourier transform (FFT) algorithm, 46, 80–81
See also, Stochastic subdivision.
fat ray (cone), 251
fBm. See, Fractional Brownian motion (fBm).
feature space, 21
Feynman, Richard, 289
filters
    Catmull-Rom, 59–60, 77
    high contrast, 51, 55–56, 58, 63, 65
    impressionistic image processing filter, 320–21
    low-pass, 244–46
    percentage closer, 9
    position, 93–94
Fiume, Eugene, 199
flame texture, 305–06, 353–57
floor macro, 115
floor() function. See, Functions, floor.
flow field functions, combining, 192
flow into an opening, 194
fog animation, 176
Foley, J.D., 104

4D quadratic B-spline value noise, 82
Fourier
    analysis, 46–47, 50, 80–81
    spectral synthesis, 10, 13, 80–81, 326, 332
Fournier, Alan, 290
fractal dimension, 330
fractal fBm splatter textures, 315
fractal sum of pulses, 295
fractals, 278–91
    amplitude, 278
    band limits, 279
    crossover scale, 279
    definition, 276–77
    dimension, 277–78, 291
    Euclidean dimension, 277–78
    fractalsum, 84–86
fractional Brownian motion (fBm), 279, 284–88, 295, 299, 303, 307, 309, 320, 333, 346
    synthesis methods, 329–32
frequency domain, 57
functional composition, 22, 298, 379
functional flow field tables, 186–87
functional programming, 23
functions
    abs, 26
    bias, 34–35
    boxstep, 58–59
    calculate normal, 40–41
    ceiling, 30, 115
    clamp, 23–27
    cos, 27–30
    floor, 28–30, 115
    fractalsum, 84
    gain, 34–35
    gammacorrect, 33–35
    max, 25–26
    min, 25–26
    mod, 28–30
    noise, 68–82
    pattern, 140–41
    pulse, 28–30
    sawtooth, 28
    sin, 27–30
    smoothstep, 26–27, 42, 54–55, 59
    spline, 30–32

step, 23–27
texture, 92–94
3–D scalar, 105
fuzzy objects, 3
fuzzy region, 210

Gaea texture, 310–14
gain, 34–35, 210–12, 262, 270
Gamito, Manuel, 328, 346
gamma correction function, 33–34
gamma correction texture, 118
Gardner, Geoffrey Y., 117, 176, 197
gas animation, 176–79
Gaussian distribution, 318
Gaussian kernel, 212
generalized stochastic subdivision, 327
genetic bases library, 382–83
genetic programming, 276
genetic programming, 374–84
    versus genetic algorithms, 384
Genetic Sand Painting, 276
genotype, 377
geometic modeling, 2–3
geometric atmospheric density distribution
  (GADD), 361–71
geometry, 275, 277, 279
    See also, Fractional Brownian motion
      (fBm).
    heterogeneous, 286
    increment, 278
    lacunarity, 87, 278, 291
    multifractal, 284–88
    octaves, 278, 283–84
    offset argument, 287
    ontogenetic models, 288–90
    perturb, 118
    polygon subdivision, 344
    self-similarity, 281
    solid textures, 293–323
    spatial frequency, 278
    sum of pulses, 295
    turbulence, 199, 240–41, 281, 291,
      301–03
George Washington University, Washington
  D.C., 320
gesture, 257–73

GIT texturing systems. See, Global illumination techniques (GIT),
global illumination techniques (GIT), 8,
  319–22, 357, 382
globe wrap. See, Spherical image map.
goal determination module (GDM), 259–60
gradient noise, 69–73, 80
graftals, 3
grammar-based models, 3
graphical user interface (GUI), 105–10, 205
    color table equalization, 107–10
    parameter ranges, 106
Graphics Gems III series, 98
grid tracing, 328
Gritz, Larry, 293, 315
GUI. See, graphical user interface (GUI).

height field, 327–29, 343
    definition, 327
    DTED, 328
    grid tracing, 328
helical paths, 177–79
Hermite
    blending functions, 63–64, 103–04
    interpolation, 73, 326, 332
    splines, 326
heterogeneous terrain models, 332–38
heterogenous fractals, 286
hexagon mesh, 102
high contrast filter, 244–46
hill-climbing optimization methods, 375
Himalayas, 279
HLS color space, 381
homogeneous fog, 363–64
homogenous, definition, 284
homogeous fBm terrain models, 329–32
Horner's rule, 26
Hotelling transform, 321
HSV, 118, 379
hue/luminosity/saturation color properties. See,
  HLS color space.
Human Genome Project, 377
hybrid multifractal, 335–36
hypertexture, 209–10, 224–26
    animation, 194–95
    caching, 248–49

explosions, 224–25
interaction, 222–23
life forms, 226–29
marble animation, 194–95
surflets, 248–55
woven cloth, 229–30

IBM, 282
illumination, 8, 319–22, 357, 382
image clipping (CLIP), 223
image synthesis theory, 255
image texture. See, Texture.
implicit functions, 199–200
impressionistic image processing filter, 320–21
index aliasing, 140–46
inherently high frequencies, 242
integer lattice, 66–69
integral function, 60–61
interior nodes, 379
Internet, The, 328, 383
isosurface, 3
isotropic, 284, 286 definition, 65 spot size, 138–39

jaggies, 48–49
Java applet, 263
JFK airport, 279

Kajiya, James T., 197, 344
Kalra's formalism, 261
KISS principle, 289
Knickknack (film), 91
knot values, 30
Kolb, Craig, 328

Labanotation, 257
lacunarity, 278, 284, 290
    definition, 87
Lambertian model, 8
landscape photography, 289
Latham, William, 121, 383
lattice noises, 66–68, 86
layering, 21–23
leaf nodes, 379
LED texture, 123–27
lerping. See, Linear interpolation.

Levoy, 255
Lewis, John Peter, 77, 80, 327
Lim, Myeong, 320
linear interpolation, 22
Lipschitz conditions, 357
LISP, 11, 23, 121, 298
list processor (LISP) programming language.
    See, LISP.
local models, 8
look-up table, color, 309
Lovejoy, S., 295
lower crossover scale, 279
low-pass filtering, 51, 55–56, 58, 63, 65
L-Systems, 3

Mandelbrot set, 112, 118
Mandelbrot, Benoit, 277, 279, 281–82, 286,
    289, 295, 325–26, 329–30, 344
        See also, Fractal, geometry
marble animation, 84–87, 172–75
marble_forming procedure, 172–75
marble_forming2 procedure, 173
Mercator mapping, 119
Meta Creations, 328, 384
metaballs, 3
metallic reflection map shader, 32–33
micropolygon, 93–94
        definition of, 136
        tiling direction, 94–95
Mie scattering model, 362
Miller, Gavin, 257, 332, 374
monofractal, 291
Monte Carlo method, 140
moon, 314–16
movement model, 262–64
movement vocabulary, 266–73
moving_marble procedure, 174–75, 178
multicolor texture, 321–24
multifractal, 284–88, 291, 310
        definition, 286
        hybrid, 335–38
        multiplicative cascade, 286, 339
        ridged, 102–03
        terrain patch, 288, 326
        turbulence, 199, 240–41, 281, 291,
            301–03

multiplicative cascades, 286
multiplicative multifractal terrains, 338
Musgrave, F. Kenton, 275–340
mutation, 377
Mutatis, Dr., 323, 384

natural selection, 377–78
nature objects. See, Fuzzy objects.
Navier-Stokes equations, 281
Negative lobes, 59
New York University torch logo, 234
Neyret, 198
Nobel Prize for Physics, 289
nodes, 379
noise value normalization curve, 109
noise, 11, 61, 64–66, 98–99, 212–14,
    4D, 82
    algorithms, 80
    B-spline, 69
    caching, 114, 248–49
    convolution, 74–79
    Ebert's implementation, 117, 169–208
    facial expressions, 260–73
    Fourier, 80–81
    gestures, 258
    gradient, 69–73, 80
    lattice, 66–68, 76, 82
    pink, 65
    ripples, 307–08
    slices of, 75
    value, 67–69, 108–09
    value–gradient, 73–74
    white, 64
nonelongated texture direction, 138
N-space specification, 375
null bump mapping, 95
Nyquist frequency, 50–52, 66
Nyquist sampling limit, 280, 284

Occam's Razor, 280–81, 289–90, 371
octaves, 278definition, 283–84
ontogenetic modeling, 288–90, 303, 314
    definition, 289
optical path, 363
optimization in smoke, 237–40
orders of magnitude, 115

orogenic (mountain–building) forces, 309
out-scattering, 363
oversampling, 51

parameter control, 2
parameter domain, 110–11
parameter processing, 113
parameter proliferation, 373–74
particle systems, 3
pattern functions, 18–20
Peachey, Darwyn R., 7–96, 136
penumbra, 253–54
percentage closer filtering, 9
periodic functions, 27–29
Perlin, Ken, 66, 73, 111–12
    fractal noise, 98, 112, 143, 283, 326
    marble function, 171
    turbulence function, 337
perturbation of surface color, 87–91, 118, 379
Pharr, Matt, 329
phenotype, 377
Photorealistic RenderMan (prman), 15, 52, 54,
    91–92, 293
pink noise, 65
pips, 127
Pixar, 1, 91, 293, 329
Planck spectrum, 305
planetary rings texture, 131–34
plastic wood effect, 10
plateau width, 103
pointillism, 318
Poisson process, 77
polygon subdivision,344
pops, in texture, 57
post spacing, 327
PPT algorithm, 328
procedural fBm, 282–84
procedural texture, 10–12
    advantage, 2, 13–14, 325–27
    antialiased rendering, 241–47
    disadvantages, 14
    fractal, 98–99
    heightfields, 327–29
    implicit and explicit models, 12–13
    multifractal, 326–40
    terrain models, 325–40

proceduralism, 281–84
    definition of, 1–2
fractals, 281–82
Prusinkiewicz's L-system tree models, 306
pseudorandom knots, 212
pseudorandom number (PRN), 65, 67–68, 71, 82
pseudorandom wavelet, 213
pyroclastic flow, 353–54

quad-tree methods, 328
qualitative dynamics, 208
Quasi-analytic error-bounded (QAEB) algo-
    rithm, 283–84, 294, 314, 325, 328, 344–45
        error, 346
        tracing, 342–43, 350

radially-symmetric planetary atmosphere,
    364–65
Rajkumar, Ajay, 234
random coloring methods, 318
random fBm coloring, 319
random placement patterns, 88–89
random rotation matrices, 99
ray marching, 219–22, 251
ray tracing, 328
rayed craters, 314–18
Rayleigh scattering model, 362, 365–67, 371
Rayshade ray tracer, 328
Rayshade, 328–29
reconstruction 49–50, 245–46
reflection mapping, 9
rendering, 327, 332
RenderMan Esoterica, 16, 24, 91–96
RenderMan shaders, 15, 18–20, 368–69
        atmosphere, 368–69
        cloudplane, 46–48
        star, 44–45
RenderMan, 17, 309
        Du, 55–56
        Dv, 55–56
        implementation, 367–68
        micropolygon, 136
        noise function, 81–82
        PhotoRealistic,15, 52, 54, 92
        shading language, 1, 14–16, 23, 30–35,

53, 55, 293, 297–98, 306
RGB colors, 7, 17, 117–18, 318, 379, 382
RiCoordinateSystem call, 21
Ridge algorithm, 105
ridged fBm, 304
ridges, 102–03
ripples texture, 306–07
robots, 261
Rocky Mountains, 333
Rooke, Steven, 382
root-finding, 381–82
rotation, 379, 381

sampling, 49–53
        interval, 55–56
        rate, 54–56
Saupe, Dietmar, 326
sawtooth wave, 295
scalar value, 259
scattering, 363
scene description modules (SDMs), 258–60
Science of Fractal Images, The, 277, 279, 284, 325
sea level terrain modeling, 334–35
sedimentary rock strata, 308–09
Selene texture, 314–19
self-similarity, 281
semblance, 289
serendipity, 14
Seurat, Georges, 319
sexual reproduction, 377, 380
shade trees, 11
shading model, 8, 15–17, 356
Shoemaker, Ken, 98
SIGGRAPH. See, Special Interest Group on
    Computer Graphics (SIGGRAPH).
signal processing, 49–53
Sims, Karl, 121, 191, 276, 298, 376, 382–83
simulated talking, 269
sin and cos functions, 27–28
sin, 379
single-instruction-multiple-data (SIMD),
    242–43, 246
sinusoid, 9
skeletal elements, 3
Smith, Alvy Ray, 282

smoke
  optimization, 237–40
  rings, 236
  rising column of, 81–84, 234
smooth step function, 26–27, 47–48, 72
soft objects, 3
solid space animation, 9, 169–95, 209–10
  of transparency, 175–76
sparse convolution, 77, 295
spatial frequency, 278
Special Interest Group on Computer Graphics
  (SIGGRAPH), 120, 332, 376
spectral synthesis, 46–48
  using noise, 82–87
specular reflection, 16
specular shading, 48
spherical coordinates, 119
spherical image map, 119
spline function, 32
spot noise, 77, 148
squiggliness, 106
Stam, Jos, 198–99
star pattern, 43–45, 90–91
statistical self–similarity, 281
steam_moving procedure, 180–81, 192–93
step function, 23–24, 62
stippling or stairstepping artifact, 135
stochastic control of gesture, 257–58
stochastic sampling, 9, 52–53, 65
stochastic subdivision, 11
strata texture, 308–09
sum tables, 145
summed-area table, 60–61
surface color, 117
surface intersection, 347
  four-octave spectral synthesis, 84
surface models, 3
surface refinement, 251–52
surflets, 248–55
synthetic texture, 12

teleological modeling, 289
teleological models, 289
terrain models altitude, 333–35
heterogeneous, 332–40
homogeneous fBm, 329–32

textual limb animation, 256–60
textural gesture, definition of, 257
texture algorithms, 114
texture
  artificial evolution, 121
  billowing clouds, 353
  cirrus clouds, 203–05, 298–303
  clouds, 47, 294–303, 352–53
  Coriolis, 303–05
  Earth planet, 308–10
  fBm, 284–88, 295, 299, 303, 307
  fireballs, 353
  flame, 304–06
  fog, 363–65
  Gaea, 309–10
  hybrid multifractal, 321–23
  impressive, 101
  layering technique, 21–23
  LED, 123–27
  marble, 84–87, 172–74, 194–95
  moon, 314–16
  multicolor, 321–24
  planetary rings, 131–34
  puffy clouds, 294–95
  ripples, 306–07
  Selene, 314–18
  spaces, 20–21
  spot size scaling, 148
  strata, 308–09
  Venus, 304
  water, 306–18
  windy, 307–08
  wood, 376
three letter acronyms (TLAs), 319
three-dimensional tables, 184–86
  access formula, 186
threshold parameter, 310
Titanic, 376
tomographic X-ray scanners, 13
trapezoidal quadrature, 367–68
turbulence, 199, 240–41, 281, 291, 301–03
  function, 83–84
  Perlin's function, 83, 337
  simulation of air currents, 179
Turk, Greg, 120
2D maps, 18, 119–20, 127–30

2D special cases, 116

upper crossover scale, 279

Van Gogh, Vincent, 318–19
Variable lacunarity noise (VLNoise), 296–99
VecNoise, 296, 379
vector
    definition of, 284
    noise, 70–72
vector-valued perturbation, 307
Venus texture, 303–04
Verostko, roman, 383
virtual procedural actors, 4
Vistapro, 328
volume, rendering, 117
volume_fog_animation procedure, 179–81

vortices, 301 spiral, 190–92
W
Walsh transform, 331
Ward, Greg, 73
water texture, 306–18
water, 306–07
wavelets, 212–16, 295
white noise, 64
wind effects, 192–93, 307–08
wood-grain solid texture, 10, 376
Worley, Steven, 97–148

Z
Z-buffer algorithm, 251
zero crossings, 280